AF270345

COVERAGE DENIED

In the aftermath of the assassination of UnitedHealthcare CEO Brian Thompson in December 2024, everyday Americans took to social media to share stories of the challenges they'd faced trying to navigate the American health insurance system. Why did this event strike such a nerve with the American public?

For a topic as central to the lives of Americans as health care, there is no book that examines the impact of coverage denial, whereby health insurers decide whether to cover health services that appear to be within the scope of a plan's benefits – not until now. In *Coverage Denied*, health policy professor Miranda Yaver offers a sobering account of the ways in which coverage denials damage patient health and exacerbate inequalities along income, education, and racial lines. Combining rich interview material with original survey data, Yaver draws critical attention to the tens of millions of medical claims denied by health insurers every year, shining a necessary light on our inequitable health care system.

Miranda Yaver is an assistant professor of Health Policy and Management at the University of Pittsburgh. She was the 2025 Author-in-Residence at the Roosevelt Institute. Her research has been published in several journals, including *American Journal of Political Science* and *Journal of Health Politics, Policy, and Law*. Her op-eds and other health care commentary have appeared in *The New York Times*, *The Guardian*, *Washington Post*'s Monkey Cage Blog, *STATNews*, and *The Hill*.

Miranda Yaver

How Health Insurers Drive Inequality in the United States

Shaftesbury Road, Cambridge CB2 8EA, United Kingdom

One Liberty Plaza, 20th Floor, New York, NY 10006, USA

477 Williamstown Road, Port Melbourne, VIC 3207, Australia

314–321, 3rd Floor, Plot 3, Splendor Forum, Jasola District Centre,
New Delhi – 110025, India

103 Penang Road, #05–06/07, Visioncrest Commercial, Singapore 238467

Cambridge University Press is part of Cambridge University Press & Assessment,
a department of the University of Cambridge.

We share the University's mission to contribute to society through the pursuit of
education, learning and research at the highest international levels of excellence.

www.cambridge.org
Information on this title: www.cambridge.org/9781009649810

DOI: 10.1017/9781009649803

When citing this work, please include a reference to the
DOI 10.1017/9781009649803

First published 2026

A catalogue record for this publication is available from the British Library

A Cataloging-in-Publication data record for this book is available from the Library of Congress

ISBN 978-1-009-64981-0 Hardback

For my husband,
and for the patients who shared their stories

Contents

Preface

On December 4, 2024, Americans across the nation awoke to the stunning news that the CEO of UnitedHealthcare, Brian Thompson, had been assassinated outside his midtown Manhattan hotel early that morning, by a man later identified as Luigi Mangioni. Not only did this occur in one of the busiest parts of New York City, but it was soon found to be a targeted attack, with the shell casings bearing the words "deny," "defend," and "depose," an apparent reference to Jay Feinman's book on private insurance practices, *Delay, Deny, Defend: Why Insurance Companies Don't Pay Claims and What You Can Do about It.*

While many expressed shock and horror, the events also prompted nationwide discourse on the everyday challenges that Americans face in navigating the American health insurance system (especially the 65 percent of Americans in private insurance plans[1] such as through UnitedHealthcare, Cigna, Elevance (formerly Anthem), or CVS (Aetna)).

People posted on social media platforms tales of being denied coverage by private insurers and having their conditions worsen as a result.

Of facing delays through tools such as prior authorization, or required insurance pre-approvals for prescribed health care, ranging from prescription drugs to MRIs to cancer treatment.

Of anger at the use of artificial intelligence (AI) tools through which private insurers process prior authorizations and claims in bulk.

Of frustration at the inequitable and expensive nature of the American health care system, which for all its cost does not generally produce impressive population-level health outcomes.

Of confusion navigating the health care system's complexities, and the government's seeming inability to address the challenges associated with placing health care decisions in the hands of for-profit institutions that have fiduciary duties not to patients but to shareholders.

Alongside these expressions of patient anger and consternation – notably from across the political spectrum – were questions as to whether these surreal events might prompt not just social media posts and op-eds, but legislative change. The answer is unclear, though the results of the 2024 elections do not suggest a likely departure from the managed care setting in which these denials and delays are most prominent. Employer-based private insurance, where denials are particularly common, is locked in. If anything, the second Trump Administration is likely to accelerate America's already growing reliance on privatized Medicare and Medicaid, both of which have heavy reliance on prior authorization and consequently issue coverage denials at higher rates than does original Medicare.[2]

While such questions of health reform are hotly partisan, events surrounding UnitedHealthcare have laid bare how profoundly widespread and *American* the experience of health insurance barriers is. In fact, these challenges are so pronounced that 21 percent of those in employer-sponsored insurance experience coverage denials in a given year,[3] and extrapolation from a survey of 516 acute care hospitals across the United States suggests that an astonishing 3 billion claims are denied each year.[4] And even though a little over half of such denials are overturned upon appeal, appeals are highly burdensome, inequitable, and rare.

The burden of this coverage denial regime is something that I knew all too well even before writing this book. When I decided to retrain in health policy at the University of California at Los Angeles's Fielding School of Public Health, I had a few research ideas in mind but was still getting acquainted with the state of the field, and the most fruitful avenues to pursue. But while I was poring through academic journals, I was forced to multitask in an unforeseen way: As I was working to get established with new physicians in Los Angeles, get new prescriptions, and undergo a couple of fairly inexpensive tests, I was running into coverage denials and prior authorization-induced delays in health care.

At first, I thought it *had* to be in error. Perhaps a code had been entered incorrectly by the medical practice. Surely, this would be simple to rectify.

It turned out that the challenges were not billing code errors. In some cases, the prior authorization simply dragged on over weeks. In other cases, there were determinations of medical necessity or, as the case may be, lack thereof.

In retrospect, one of the denials of prior authorization was unsurprising, as it was for Botox injections for the treatment of migraines. Though highly effective, this is an expensive course of treatment, and thus ripe for utilization management. But one of these delays was for a forty-eight-hour cardiac holter monitor for diagnosis of syncope, a one-time test that costs in the neighborhood of $600, and for which prior authorization is not always required depending on the insurer.

I was no stranger to health insurance barriers, even outright denials, having navigated many of these challenges over the preceding ten years, across different insurers who I eventually learned would expedite claim processing once getting tagged on social media.

. I spent extensive time on the phone, getting rerouted from staffer to staffer, seeking clarity on the reasons for the delays I was experiencing. I felt overwhelmed, and thought to myself, "*I'm supposed to be doing full-time research and instead I'm spending time in the middle of my work day talking with my insurance company! I can't afford to be doing this!*"

And then something clicked. The metaphorical light bulb went off.

I'm from the United States and a native English speaker. I have a doctorate degree from Columbia University. I knew the American health care system well (the mixed blessing of having chronic medical problems). I was working in a premier school of public health. I had a flexible job that allowed me to spend time in the middle of the day sorting out these challenges. I had all of the advantages, and it was still a struggle. *If I couldn't remedy these delays, what on Earth would happen to my neighbor?* It was a dimension of American exceptionalism that was discussed among patients and physicians, but not nearly as much among academics.

I then zeroed in on two core themes, which form the basis of this book: administrative burden and equity. I was familiar with University of Michigan Ford School of Public Policy scholars Pamela Herd and Donald Moynihan's *Administrative Burden: Policymaking by Other Means*, which, in contrast to my own political science research on administrative agency implementation (namely, by the Environmental Protection

Agency), focused on the everyday hassles of encounters with agencies and the imposition of administrative burdens impeding access to government programs. And not only were the themes of this work resonant, highlighting both the scope and the inequitable nature of these burdens (with more marginalized populations less able to weather these storms), but it struck me that that framework could easily be applied throughout the American health insurance system, including the private insurance on which the majority of Americans rely.

And so, this book was born. It has been a labor of love, and I hope that you find it enlightening, whether you are thinking about academic research, policy interventions, or navigating the health care system for you or your loved ones.

Every day as American patients from all walks of life work to access their health care – perhaps going to the pharmacy to pick up their prescription drugs or waiting to schedule their prescribed scan – they are confronted with prior authorizations. These pre-approvals are a significant, though not exclusive mechanism for coverage denials that disrupt the health and finances of far too many Americans every year. One reason for insurers' reliance on this tool is the concern about the notably high amount of overtreatment in the United States, which contributes toward the nation's high health costs. While prior authorization can constitute a guardrail on overprescribing – that is, the prescribing of care that is of low or questionable value – it can also induce delays and denials of care for patients, even in realms of medicine where there is not a notable pattern of overprescription. It is thus perhaps unsurprising that prior authorization has not been without its share of controversies, some of which have led to policy changes within select health insurers or segments of the American health insurance setting – and, as discussed above, it has occupied considerable national attention in light of Thompson's assassination.

For example, on August 1, 2023, UnitedHealthcare announced that it would scale back its reliance on prior authorizations in its commercial, Medicare, Medicaid, and community plans, such that there would be a 20 percent reduction in its overall prior authorization volume effective November 1, 2023.[5] Among the health care services for which prior authorization would no longer be required are genetic testing and cardiac stress tests, the latter of which accounts for approximately 316,000 prior authorization requests per year.[6] This move aligned almost exactly with Cigna's August 2023 announcement that it would remove prior authorization requirements for 25 percent of medical services.[7] Aetna has made more modest reductions in reliance on prior authorizations, eliminating such requirements for cataract surgeries in July 2022 and for physical therapy in January 2023. What's more, UnitedHealthcare implemented in 2024 a national Gold Card program for provider groups that meet certain eligibility requirements – that is, reducing the prior authorization burden for those who consistently adhere to what they deem to be evidence-based guidelines in prescribing.

Such moves were on the one hand surprising, given the persistence of these practices over recent decades amid the growth of managed care, though on the other hand they do align with significant pushback from patients, physicians, and physician organizations, including the American Medical Association. Indeed, one Humana medical reviewer turned whistleblower observed of this practice, "They take in premiums and don't pay claims. That's how they make money."[8]

Interestingly, UnitedHealthcare's decision to reduce its reliance on prior authorization followed a May 2023 decision to *increase* its reliance on prior authorization within the sphere of diagnostic colonoscopies and other endoscopic procedures aimed at diagnosing diseases in the esophagus, stomach, or colon.[9] The stated goal of this policy shift was to ensure that the procedures were safe, affordable, and effective for their intended use by their customers. Patients and physicians alike protested that it would lead to troubling delays in care. Amid significant pushback, the day that this new policy was to take effect, UnitedHealthcare reversed course, announcing that they would require only "advance notification." Physicians would simply submit patient data to UnitedHealthcare online or by phone prior to performing the relevant procedures.[10] UnitedHealthcare similarly opted in August 2024 to *increase* prior authorization in Medicare Advantage plans within the realm of outpatient physical therapy and chiropractic services, a move that is particularly ironic given that prior authorization requests for MRIs are often denied before patients have undergone a course of physical therapy. And this ubiquity is not lost on patients, who have been vocal on social media platforms and elsewhere about the ensuing frustrations.

Though by no means the *exclusive* explanation for the prevalence of health insurance coverage denials in the United States – for example, the Office of US Senator Claire McCaskill found that Anthem denied 12,200 emergency department claims in Missouri, Kentucky, and Georgia between July and December 2017 (a denial rate of 5.8 percent)[11] – prior authorization has proven to be a significant vehicle for denials, with Optum finding in 2024 that 42 percent of claim denials in the most recent plan year were "front end," for example, through prior authorization.[12] And one specific type of prior authorization, step therapy ("fail first"), causes patients and their physicians headaches and more as they are tasked with first trying a series of less expensive (potentially even off-label) prescription drugs before the preferred drug will be approved as medically necessary.

Delays and denials of care to patients across the country are a deeply problematic, if not devastating outcome of insurance practices ostensibly aimed at cost containment and reducing health care overutilization, but they are not the only challenges stemming from prior authorization and other barriers to accessing prescribed treatments. Prior authorization can lead to the imposition of significant administrative burdens for both patients and their physicians to navigate to secure access to care. The administration of prior authorization is costly for physicians tasked with coordinating with insurers or hiring adequate support staff to do so. It can also be costly *for the insurers themselves*, which must process high volumes of prior authorization requests, not all of which are electronic, and risk having patients whose health is declining and necessitating more extensive medical intervention due to delayed care – though the costs to insurers are admittedly declining as they adopt artificial intelligence (AI) tools with which to process prior authorizations and claims in bulk, albeit with variable accuracy. Indeed, while AI can promote tremendous efficiency in the setting of a high volume of processing, when errors arise, they can be quite dangerous. In training, the California Assembly Committee on Privacy and Consumer Protection reported in 2024 that one California hospital's most accurate AI model wrongly recommended outpatient treatment for asthmatics with pneumonia due to a statistical correlation: that subset of patients has lower mortality, but it is precisely *because* they have been escalated to higher-level care given the risk factor.[13] When these tools are deployed by health insurers, they can lead to highly disruptive delays, denials, and medical bills that can be rectified only upon appeals, which require time, knowledge, and effort, often in the setting of a health challenge. Thus, it may come as little surprise that the burdens of coverage denials pose unique challenges to patients from marginalized groups who lack the health literacy that is often necessary to successfully navigate the complexities of America's health insurance bureaucracy.

In the pages that follow, I work to explore not only vulnerabilities to coverage denials, but also the impact that this practice has on patients and their physicians. While patients denied coverage through prior authorization can experience delays in care ranging from days to weeks or months, those who were denied through other means (that is, post-treatment) can face devastating and destabilizing financial circumstances due to unexpectedly being left to pay out-of-pocket for prescribed care that they believed to be within the scope of their insurance benefits. Thus, these guardrails on high costs (and, relatedly, prescription of low-value care) have profound accompanying adverse impacts on patients and their trusted physicians, disrupting current *and future* health care utilization.

Discussions about the utility and impact of prior authorization are ongoing within insurers, among physicians, and within Congress, though for the most part these practices persist in the nation's largest private health insurers and beyond. However, reform has proven challenging, with stalled congressional legislation, a fragmented health care system that constrains state efforts to regulate these practices, and insurers guarding against declining profit margins in the event of more extensive health care utilization. With monetary costs at stake for both patients and insurers, there are no easy solutions to this health policy problem affecting millions of Americans. This book hopes to shed light on the human impact on patients as well as physicians, and thus the stakes in proposed policy interventions in this space.

While more has been written to date on the challenges that physicians face in navigating bureaucratic insurance practices, less has been written from the patient perspective, a deficit that this book hopes to remedy.

Yet these patient stories not only illustrate the adverse impact of coverage denials on patients' ability to heal and thrive, but also speak to what journalist Annie Lowrey characterizes in *The Atlantic* as a "time tax" as individuals struggle to navigate bureaucracies that too often spur administrative burdens.[14] That is, accessing program benefits and complying with bureaucratic requirements can constitute "paperwork, aggravation, and mental work imposed on citizens" to a degree that "this time tax is a public policy cancer."

This framework was adopted in the Biden Administration's Burden Reduction Initiative, which sought to address not only the "time tax," but also the stress and stigma that can accompany the navigation of bureaucratic public programs and, worse, contribute to individuals opting out of participation due to the administrative burden. And while Lowrey and the Biden Administration's 2024 OIRA report "Tackling the Time Tax" characterize the government as rationing public services through bureaucratic barriers, in the pages that follow I extend this analysis to examine the time tax in the context of health insurance coverage denials, especially through prior authorization, and the rationing of care not just by public entities, but also by private insurers, aimed not only at cost containment, but also at profit maximization.

These burdens on American patients are neither accidents nor inevitabilities, and I explore in Chapter 9 some ways to reform the American health insurance system to mitigate the resulting inequities and inefficiencies, though political realities and the fragmentation of the American health care system pose important challenges to these efforts. However, the stories and data that lie ahead offer insights into the rationing of health care through accumulated bureaucratic inconveniences on patients and their physicians and offer motivation to challenge the status quo.

CHAPTER 1

The Political Origins of Coverage Denials

I cannot keep sitting here for another night watching for my child to stop breathing.

Carol

FOR CAROL AND JASON, parents of four children in Arizona, the emergency department visit for their four-year-old daughter felt overwhelming. They were scared about their daughter Emma's worsened ability to breathe. And they were scared about the medical costs that would ensue, given their limited economic means. Their UnitedHealthcare plan was provided through Jason's employer, an airline.

One day, Emma developed a sore throat, and because of her thinness, they could see her tonsils protruding out of her neck. Their doctor informed them that because of the significant enlargement of her tonsils, she would require a tonsillectomy, and they were referred to a specialist. In fact, one of her tonsils was so abnormally large that it was closing in on her windpipe and there was even concern that it was cancerous. However, they would have to wait a week for the operation.

"It was scary, and being just four years old, it was hard for her to communicate to us what was happening as she gasped for air," Carol recounted of the wait for surgery. "I was watching her in the dark and she stopped breathing several times. Then, she would wake up crying and upset."

For two consecutive nights, Carol stayed awake watching Emma try to sleep. But, fearful of yet another night when Emma would stop breathing, especially as it seemed to be getting worse, Carol broke down in tears and took Emma to the local emergency department. The doctors administered steroids which shrank her tonsils a bit, and when Emma was able to relax, there was enough of an airway that she could breathe again. Two days later, the surgery was performed, and the biopsies were negative.

The problem was that when she and Jason went to the emergency department's intake, Emma's condition was classified as a "sore throat," and not a breathing difficulty amid severe tonsillitis. Consequently, approximately five weeks later, they received a bill for $8,800 for the emergency department visit because UnitedHealthcare did not deem treatment of a sore throat to be medically necessary, nor did it seemingly fall within the scope of the "prudent layperson standard" in coverage of emergency care.

Jason was sure it *had* to be a mistake. "The frustrating thing was they kept saying it was non-emergent and I kept trying to figure out, *How is our daughter not being able to breathe not a medical emergency?* We would have been absolutely devastated financially if we had to pay in full. We don't have anywhere near the access to that kind of money. We don't have savings. We could have lost our house."

"To me, that was sad because I wouldn't take my daughter to the ER for a sore throat," Carol reflected of this. "It's so expensive that we don't even take them to urgent care for anything. Most of the time, we just hope for the best."

This was neither the first nor the last time that Carol and Jason struggled to pay for their children's needs, whether clothes or health care. Insurance challenges made it difficult for them to take their children to their annual wellness visits, lest their providers perform tests that their insurance would decline to cover. "Four kids times a $25 copay is $100 just to see the doctor. One time we got another bill for $8.36 per kid because UnitedHealthcare denied payment for the eye exam even though they just stood in the hallway, looked at a chart at the end of the hallway, and read off the chart. They charged for that, and the insurance company wouldn't pay for it. We don't have an extra $32. The nickel and diming is too much."

Appealing UnitedHealthcare's denial was far from easy when raising four children, taking time and energy that they did not have. "You can't run around copying and faxing things when you're looking after kids." Enraged by the denial, Jason took to Twitter initially just to vent, but the tweet went viral, at which point Jason became hopeful that UnitedHealthcare would respond and be shamed into assisting him with this predicament.

That's exactly what happened. After a reply to Jason's tweet, UnitedHealthcare contacted Carol and Jason. Ultimately, the hospital resubmitted the billing under different codes, and after a few weeks, they were left only with the cost of the emergency department copayment.

Carol observed that it felt like the insurer "hoped that people won't complain. They'll just go, 'This is terrible, but I have to pay it.' But as a low-income family, there's *no chance in the world* that we would have been able to pay that. But we know health is important, and we made the choice to protect our kids insurance-wise. After all of that, getting that $8,800 bill was heart-wrenching on top of the other stress."

The effects of this denial would extend well beyond the month that it took to rectify it. There would be dozens of times that they waited in pain to go to the emergency department because of money and wondered, "Is this worthy of going to the emergency room? Will we get another huge bill? Sometimes we just deal with it and hope for the best."

"I really think they make it so difficult that people just give up. And I find myself giving up too when they tell me these things aren't medically necessary," Emily reflected of her experience with coverage denials and subsequent efforts at appealing.

Emily, a forty-nine-year-old disabled woman in Palm Beach County, Florida, formerly did correspondence work for the governor, in addition to working as a therapist and a health care case manager. Given her background, Emily thought that it would be relatively easy to navigate the health care system to support her needs through her privatized Medicaid plan through Humana. Nothing could be farther from the truth.

"I think it makes it *that much worse* to be honest," Emily reflected of this irony. "I know what their job is, and I know when they're lying to me, and half the time, they're making stuff up as they go along. It's so infuriating."

No stranger to the American health insurance system, Emily has epilepsy, takes antidepressants, and has a foot deformity that precludes her from walking with any semblance of ease. She can sometimes use a walker, though it strains her greatly. Like most Medicaid enrollees in most states, Emily is covered by a private managed care insurer, despite being in a public health insurance program. Her plan will not cover the cost of a wheelchair. If she attempts to wear shoes, she develops cuts and sores on her feet, which sometimes get infected and necessitate intravenous antibiotics in the emergency department. After seeing multiple podiatrists, she pursued a referral to a foot surgeon who could correct the condition without resorting to amputation.

Despite numerous complications from the deformity, the surgery to correct her condition was denied because it was deemed cosmetic "as though I just want my toes to look pretty," and thus outside the scope of her plan benefits.

"I'm not walking again. My feet drag and get bruised," she emphasized. While a rehabilitation center helped her to regain some function, her insurer suddenly withdrew from Palm Beach County, leaving her without anyone to cover her ongoing medical needs. She would be out of options.

"It makes you feel completely impotent and ineffective and it's dehumanizing …. We're talking about four years where I can't walk. Four years between forty-four and forty-nine. Those are prime years, and I'll never get that time back. I'll never recover what it did to my life. And it's emotionally devastating to constantly get these letters of denial, saying you're not worth it."

Looking ahead to a possible diagnosis of oral cancer, Emily has already elected not to pursue chemotherapy. "If the fight to get coverage for diagnostics is this hard, can you imagine how hard I'm going to have to fight to get coverage for treatment? That's not how I want to spend my final days."

The reality is that few, if any, are immune to these challenges.

When Mark and his wife Annie enrolled in her employer's health insurance plan with Blue Cross Blue Shield of Georgia (Anthem), they were relieved to learn that their plan would cover infertility testing and treatment, which would otherwise cost tens of thousands of dollars. Before pursuing intrauterine insemination (IUI) cycle treatments and invitro fertilization (IVF) treatments, the couple consulted with Emory Healthcare's financial counseling office, which confirmed after communicating with Anthem that the pursued treatment was within their plan benefits and thus would be covered in-network. They could not foresee the insurance challenges that they would face over the course of these treatments.

Healthy thirty-four-year-old attorneys, they were both highly educated and financially comfortable. They had consulted with their insurer and the hospital. They knew the system as well as patients might be expected to.

Yet after covering the IUI procedure without incident, Anthem declined to cover the egg retrieval on the ground that Annie's plan did not cover this care, leaving them with a $13,213 bill.

What would next unfold would be a bureaucratic nightmare made more complicated by the timing of their IVF procedures such that simply postponing care until the issue was resolved would be infeasible. There would be several more appointments over the course of which the eggs would be fertilized, grow into embryos, and be transferred into the uterus. Because of Anthem's denial, Mark and Annie could not proceed with the scheduled treatment dates (including the embryo transfer) until Anthem paid the claim or until Mark and Annie supplied on a self-paid basis the $4,341 cost of the embryo transfer.

Supplying a large sum of money is no easy task for most Americans, who cannot afford an unexpected $1,000 bill,[1] and Mark and Annie were fortunate in this respect. Though confident that Anthem would reprocess the claims, they had to pay the hospital $4,341 with the promise of reimbursement from Emory Healthcare upon Anthem's claim payment. So would begin Mark and Annie's navigation of not one, but *two* health care bureaucracies: the insurer and the hospital. Mark spoke with a customer service representative who could find no basis for the IVF coverage denial, and Anthem reversed its denial about two weeks later, but not without costs: they had charged the payment for the egg retrieval, incurring credit card interest while they awaited claim resolution and later, delays in hospital reimbursement.

Carol and Jason's, Emily's, and Mark and Annie's are but three of the stories that, along with the data that I describe below, shape my analysis of health insurance coverage denials and how this insurer practice deepens health and economic inequality by imposing unevenly distributed administrative burdens (or the costs of navigating programs, the benefits of which may be kept of reach). The diversity of these stories highlights not only the profound disruptions that coverage denials can have on patients' health and economic lives, but also the broadly *American* experience of these everyday insurance barriers.

That is, the average American sees a physician four times annually. These visits might lead to the ordering of a scan or procedure, or the prescribing of a new medication, which might be among the 10 percent of prescriptions dispensed that are brand-name (and therefore more expensive than generic alternatives).[2] Each interaction with the American health care system presents opportunities to experience barriers not only to care (e.g., due to physician shortages in one's community), but also to coverage *even if one is enrolled in an insurance plan*. Though the notorious fragmentation of the American health insurance system makes it challenging to know exactly how many denials occur, one estimate in the *Wall Street Journal* put the total at a whopping 850 million claims per year.[3] And while no patients are immune from experiencing denials, I argue over the pages that follow that their effects are more pronounced for patients from marginalized groups. And these burdens don't only keep care of out of reach for many Americans: they also weaken patients' sense of trust in the health care system on which they rely.

This chapter highlights the scope of this policy problem of a less discussed dimension of underinsurance – health insurance coverage denials – and the political context that contributes toward this practice, which over the course of this book I argue undercuts patients' (especially marginalized patients') health and economic security. Before evaluating the health and economic impact of this insurer practice, it is helpful first to consider what coverage denials are, and the political context fueling privatization, from which this insurance practice emerges and comes to impact American patients.

UNDERSTANDING DENIALS IN THE AMERICAN HEALTH CARE SYSTEM

A notorious irony of the American health care system is that despite an ostensible goal of cost containment, it often drastically overspends. The

United States spent 17.7 percent, or nearly a fifth, of its gross domestic product (GDP) on health care in 2024 (projected to grow to 19.7 percent in 2032), with total health care spending reaching $4.9 trillion in 2023.[4] Yet, for all these rising health care costs, not only is there significant wasteful spending (whether on administrative costs or the prescribing of medical care that is of low or questionable value), but also there are overall poor population-level health outcomes when looking at such subjects as life expectancy, infant and maternal mortality, chronic disease, and avoidable deaths.[5]

Moreover, in addition to an estimated 25.4 million non-elderly adults being uninsured in 2024,[6] the *underinsured* rate was 23 percent in 2024.[7] For these 23 percent of Americans, the health insurance plan in which they are enrolled is inadequate, whether due to high health plan deductibles or other high out-of-pocket medical expenses (excluding premiums). Thus, these individuals are still exposed to substantial financial risk if medical needs arise. This can lead patients to forego care or else struggle to pay their medical bills if they do utilize their health plans in the most expensive health care system in the world.[8] Indeed, The Commonwealth Fund finds that the highest rates of medical bill problems and medical debt were reported among adults who were underinsured or who lacked continuous health insurance coverage, and 57 percent of the underinsured reported that they avoided getting needed medical care due to cost.[9] It is in this context of high costs and inadequate coverage that health care expert Shannon Brownlee observes, "It's not as if we haven't tried to fix the system .... Instead, we've decided to put up with an unfair, dysfunctional, and spectacularly expensive system."[10]

We often hear talk of Americans being uninsured or underinsured, which makes it challenging for them to access health care when they need it. This book looks at a more specific barrier: that of health insurers deciding whether to cover prescribed medical care (whether a prescription drug, surgery, a scan, an emergency department visit, or other care). This is a story of coverage denials, which contribute to underinsurance in a way that has historically been overlooked. This dimension of underinsurance is the inability to access care within one's plan benefits not because of cost per se, but because of insurer decisions not to supply the needed coverage, whether because it is "not medically necessary," is "experimental or investigational" for the patient's condition and thus outside the scope of health plan benefits, "lacking in the required prior authorization" (also known as pre-certification, or pre-approval for coverage of health services), or for other reasons on which I elaborate in Chapter 2. These determinations are made even more complicated by the opacity of medical necessity definitions, which in turn create uncertainties for patients and physicians alike.

It is this medical necessity on which political scientist Daniel Skinner focuses his superb scholarly attention, observing the intensely political context in which medical necessity is defined to the consternation of professional associations, which have tended to resist oversight of physicians' assessments of their patients due to concerns about autonomy. Ongoing medical necessity debates can "collectively amount[] to a persistent uncertainty about the basic mechanisms and aims of medical decisionmaking,"[11] which is no longer solely between patients and their physicians, but rather with the insurer ultimately determining courses of treatment. In this context, Skinner observes persistent uncertainty about the fundamental aims of medical decisionmaking, the repercussions of which are at the heart of my analysis because patients can and often do get caught in the middle between their physicians and insurers (and are themselves typically poor judges of medical necessity).

The story of shifting risk from corporations (in this case, health insurers) to the public is a familiar one, confronted notably by political scientist Jacob Hacker, who observes in the context of economic insecurity that "a myriad of risks that were once managed and pooled by government and private corporations have been shifted onto workers and their families ... creat[ing] both real hardship for millions and growing anxiety for millions more."[12] This disrupts individuals' economic (and in this case, health) security in ways that are reinforced by the politics of health care reform over the decades. In this setting, health insurers are mindful not only of cost containment, but also of their profit maximization, shifting risk to American patients who are faced with insecurity about whether they can access prescribed care that may be prohibitively expensive absent insurance approval. Thus, the lack of health security is felt even among those with comprehensive benefit plans because this system allows insurers to overrule physician determinations, keeping care out of reach.

These coverage denials can come pre- or post-treatment, with pre-treatment denials constituting prior authorization denials and post-treatment denials including such care as emergency department care or other claims reviewed and later deemed to be not medically necessary. Prior authorization is a common vehicle for coverage denials outside of traditional, or original Medicare, which relies on this tool very sparingly and consequently issues few denials. And as I argue throughout the book, the type of denial one experiences can have an immense impact on the patient's resulting health versus financial fragility. Because coverage denials are driven in part by insurers' economic concerns, it is instructive first to consider America's largely for-profit health care system in which these delays and denials – and their associated, inequitable administrative burdens – arise.

PRIVATIZATION OF AMERICAN HEALTH INSURANCE

Political scientist E. E. Schattschneider famously declared that "a new policy creates new politics."[13] That is, policy can be both an *outcome* (e.g., resulting from bipartisan cooperation to adopt legislation) as well as a *cause*, reshaping the subsequent political environment. This observation of policy feedback rings true in the context of health insurance, where one can observe a new politics of insurance evolving and becoming increasingly entrenched, especially as new constituencies form in defense of health insurance programs. This observation is consistent with Theda Skocpol's assessment that "policies, once enacted, restructure subsequent political processes" – that is, there is *path dependence*.[14]

Much of traditionally government-run health insurance is now in private hands, such that, according to the United States Census, just over 65 percent of Americans had private health insurance in 2023.[15] This privatization fits squarely within the framework of the social policies explored by political scientist Suzanne Mettler in her analysis of the "submerged state."[16] That is, rather than federal policymakers directly disbursing benefits, they increasingly turn to less visible private entities that can obscure the role of government and create critical gaps in knowledge of individuals navigating entities such as health insurance companies. Such policies thus, through reliance on private actors, lie "beneath the surface of U.S. market institutions and within the federal tax system."[17]

Americans can enroll in one of any number of types of health insurance – whether Medicare (typically for the elderly, and much of which is privatized through Medicare Advantage), Medicaid (typically for the low-income, and often administered through private insurers such as Centene or Elevance (formerly Anthem)), a private plan through the Affordable Care Act marketplace exchange, or (most commonly) a private plan through one's employer. In fact, employer-sponsored insurance (ESI) through insurers such as UnitedHealthcare and Elevance is the primary source of health insurance in the United States, covering 63 percent of working-age adults[18] and nearly half of children.[19]

Though this particular constellation of options has been a familiar arrangement since the Affordable Care Act's implementation in January 2014, the prevalence of private health insurance was not always the case. It is thus instructive to consider the cost containment goals that emanated from the adoption of public insurance and subsequent concerns about runaway spending by these health programs.

For decades, America had contemplated the prospects of national health insurance, but to no avail amid concerns from the American Medical Association and others about the dangers of "socialized medicine."[20] While President Franklin Delano Roosevelt spoke clearly in 1934 about the importance of providing for unemployment insurance amid the Great Depression,[21] he was more cautious when speaking of national health insurance, offering instead, "Whether we come to this form of insurance soon or later on I am confident that we can devise a system which will enhance and not hinder the remarkable progress which has been made and is being made in the practice of the professions of medicine and surgery in the United States."[22]

Though the Committee on Economic Security had recommended tying Social Security to a national health care program, it was ultimately removed from the legislation, with the Social Security Act signed into law in 1935 focused more squarely on the provision of pensions, unemployment insurance, and assistance for dependent mothers and children. Much of this shift in policy has been attributed to the ardent opposition of the American Medical Association's decrying of the prospects of "socialized medicine," though it was ultimately likely that, even with Roosevelt's popularity, pursuing both Social Security and national health insurance would have met with more expansive opposition that would have imperiled the passage of both programs.[23]

Instead, amid World War II, America witnessed the proliferation of employer-sponsored insurance, offering new protection for those in the workforce, but leaving many behind. The explanation for these developments was simple: amid wartime, America faced a critical labor shortage alongside inflation that led to the freezing of wages, so employers turned to offering health insurance as an alternative means to remain competitive. It is for this reason that employer-sponsored insurance – the dominant model in the United States today – has been characterized by some as an "accident of history,"[24] though in 1943 the Internal Revenue Service acted to accelerate this trend by exempting employer-based health insurance from taxation. By 1945, 32 million people had employer-sponsored health benefits,[25] offering new access to care though at the risk of perpetuating job lock, or the reluctance to leave a place of employment due to dependence on the health benefits. What's more, the share of Americans reliant on employer-sponsored insurance would be quick to balloon to 142 million just five years later amid the post-war economic boom.[26]

While Social Security would prove to be unparalleled in impact, national health insurance would have to wait until President Roosevelt's successor, Harry S. Truman, took up the mantle.

President Truman did not waste time upon assuming office. In fact, in a Special Message to Congress on November 19, 1945, he called attention to the inequities of the American health care system, in which "the benefits of modern medical science have not been enjoyed by our citizens with any degree of equality," and laid out his preferred plan for a compulsory health insurance system to be financed through a new tax that all Americans would pay.[27] Though adamant that "[t]his is not socialized medicine," and emphasizing in a May 19, 1947 Special Message to Congress that the program protecting against the "economic threat of sickness" is "crucial to our national welfare,"[28] the American Medical Association again decried this government intervention into health insurance delivery. Indeed, in 1950, the American Medical Association spent $1.1 million on advertising in 11,000 newspapers, 30 national magazines, and 1,000 radio stations, with an additional $2 million in tie-in advertising to help kill the proposal.[29]

President Truman would admit defeat toward the end of his presidency, after years of advocacy, and his successor, President Dwight D. Eisenhower, fueled the national opposition to "socialized medicine," though he did not undo the progress of the New Deal. However, what this era marked was on the one hand an acknowledgment that "too many of our people find the cost of adequate medical care too heavy," while also arguing in the 1954 State of the Union Address that access to hospital and medical services would best be assured not through government intervention, but through the initiative of private and non-profit insurance plans.[30] It is hardly surprising, then, that it was during this time that America continued to cement its reliance on employer-sponsored insurance, made even more convenient by the Internal Revenue's 1954 decision to treat these premiums as tax deductible.[31]

On January 31, 1955, President Eisenhower offered a Special Message to Congress, in which he recommended the establishment of a federal health reinsurance service to encourage private health insurance plans to offer broader benefits to American individuals and families.[32] Thus, America would see the proliferation of privatization in the health care sector, though the seeds for Medicare would soon be planted by President John F. Kennedy, who as part of his "New Frontier" program called for the expansion of Social Security to provide for medical care for the elderly.

President Kennedy's preferred Medical Care Bill failed by just two votes in the Senate in 1962, on the one hand constituting what he called "a most serious defeat for every American family, for the 17 million Americans who are over 65," and on the other also indicating that the need for health insurance expansion was not lost on many within Congress and the public. President Kennedy added, "I hope that we will return in November a Congress that will support a program like.Medical Care for the Aged, a program which has been fought by the American Medical Association and successfully defeated."[33] He would not live to see health insurance reform come to fruition, but he successfully laid the groundwork for what would become Medicare.

Taking up this cause under the umbrella of the expansive Great Society reforms, President Lyndon B. Johnson assured the nation that health insurance expansion was a "logical extension of our proven social security system" and "will supply the prudent, feasible and dignified way to free the aged from the fear of financial hardship in the event of illness."[34]

Eventually signed into law together on July 30, 1965 by President Lyndon B. Johnson and through extensive compromise with influential House Ways and Means Committee Chairman Wilbur Mills, Medicare and Medicaid were designed as amendments to the Social Security Act and offered a vast expansion of health care options for the elderly and the poor respectively. This legislation was what Mills had termed a "three layer cake": first the Johnson Administration's proposed Medicare program (what would come to be known as Medicare Part A's hospital insurance), then the voluntary coverage for the elderly's physician costs (what would come to be known as Medicare Part B's medical insurance), then finally the expansion of federal funds to states to offer health insurance for the indigent (Medicaid). As a nod to the hard-fought efforts toward this end by his predecessors, upon signing the bill into law, President Johnson spoke in Independence, Missouri alongside President Truman, saying, "No longer will older Americans be denied the healing miracle of modern medicine. No longer will illness crush and destroy the savings that they have so carefully put away over a lifetime so that they might enjoy dignity in their later years."[35]

President Johnson would find in his successor, President Richard Nixon, an unlikely advocate for health insurance expansion, who offered in 1971 the Family Health Insurance Plan (FHIP), a health insurance proposal that would have mandated employer health coverage, federalized government-supported health insurance for the poor, and offered sliding scale subsidies to assist with the purchase of health insurance – a model not unlike that of the Affordable Care Act.[36] However, this proposal was ultimately abandoned.

Though the sole purpose of Medicare was to expand health insurance for the elderly, cost was still a concern. It was estimated that Medicare would come with a $2.2 billion price tag, but by 1969, the initial price had doubled. It was in this setting of concern about runaway costs from government health insurance that, in 1970, pediatrician Paul Ellwood put forward the idea of health maintenance organizations (HMOs), which were perceived as incentivizing the provision of better care at a lower cost than the traditional fee-for-service model in which the plan pays the provider a specific fee for each service provided to the insured.[37]

President Nixon then signed into law the Health Maintenance Organization and Resources Development Act of 1973, seen as an opportunity to develop a private sector-based alternative to the national health care proposals that had been offered from the left. The legislation likewise accelerated America's reliance on employer-sponsored insurance, not only encouraging private investment in HMOs, but requiring employers with twenty-five or more employees to offer these plans.

This would not be the last of President Nixon's health reform efforts, though it would be his only success in this space. On February 6, 1974, President Nixon would again deliver a special message to Congress, offering a Comprehensive Health Insurance Plan (CHIP) because "gaps in health protection can have tragic consequences." This plan was centered largely around the employer-sponsored health insurance that was housed in the private sector and relied on "maintaining a private enterprise approach" seen by President Nixon as more effective at the plan's cost containment objectives.[38] The Watergate scandal would ultimately undercut the proposal's success and lead to his resignation later that year, on August 8, 1974, so as to avoid inevitable impeachment and removal from office.

While President Nixon was ultimately unable to achieve most of his goals of reforming America's health insurance system, the spirit of his proposals has influenced subsequent efforts to privatize American health insurance, whether by expanding reliance on employer-sponsored insurance or by privatizing the traditionally public realms of insurance.[39] Indeed, even as HMOs fell out of favor due to their narrow provider networks, they paved the way toward Medicare Advantage.

Thus, with the creation of Medicare and Medicaid, America saw a vast expansion in insurance coverage, including for marginalized populations,[40] though reliance on private insurance within these spheres would soon continue to proliferate and, beginning in 1982, states began to get Section 1115 waivers from the federal government to experiment with managed care programs consistent with promoting the Medicaid program's objectives.

These decades of efforts toward health care reform in the United States have been thorny to put it mildly, rife with competing stakeholders, and with emerging political compromises typically operating within the constraints of a for-profit health care system dominated by entities such as private health insurance companies, the pharmaceutical industry, and pharmacy benefit managers (the latter of which I discuss in greater detail in Chapter 4). That is, while the United States witnessed great progress in the number of insured individuals, the politics typically drove policy adoption toward privatization in health insurance delivery – a series of choices that would contribute not only to job lock for the large swath of the public enrolled in employer-sponsored insurance, but also to growing exposure to coverage denials as private insurers' cost containment tools of prior authorization proliferated.

The growth of managed care over the course of the 1980s and 1990s was quite dramatic, with the US Bureau of Labor Statistics reporting just 1 percent of employer plan enrollment in managed care in 1980, compared with 81 percent by 1997, when Congress further accelerated privatization through the creation of Medicare Advantage (also known as Medicare Part C). Though these managed care arrangements were seen as advantageous from a cost containment perspective, their business model was also seen as running counter to patients' interest in quality health care as well as disrupting doctor–patient relationships.[41]

It was alongside this growth of managed care that state legislatures, in response to stories of denials of coverage, began to pass laws aiming to protect health care consumers, though with mixed success in view of the health care advocacy organization Families USA.[42] What's more, state efforts toward reform were stymied in the context of employer-sponsored insurance, much of which is governed by the Employee Retirement Income Security Act (ERISA) of 1974, which preempts state laws that "relate to" self-insured (or self-funded) health plans, according to which the employer (typically, a larger employer) collects premiums from employees and directly pays for medical claims, often relying on a third-party administrator (typically a private insurer). Not only does ERISA's preemption provision run counter to the notions of federalism embedded in many domestic policies, but also, given that the KFF 2023 Employer Health Benefits Survey finds that 65 percent of covered workers are in self-insured health plans, the limitations of state efforts to more tightly regulate health insurance practices are all too clear.

Thus, while managed care backlash manifested itself amid concerns about health care access and quality, political scientist Mark Peterson observed that the "backlash ... has not ... engendered a true counter-revolution," rather leaving the status quo "deeply imbued" with managed care features.[43] The failures at efforts toward comprehensive health reform in the 1990s offer insights into the persistence of the cost containment-minded practices fueling coverage denials.

HEALTH REFORMS THAT WEREN'T. Even the most ambitious efforts at health coverage expansion have operated within the confines of the private health insurance model. The notoriously failed efforts at expansive health care reform through the Health Security Act under President Clinton were, though critical of shortcomings to health care access, deeply rooted in the belief that health insurance could be achieved through the private sector such as through a mandate to hold insurance (whether public or private), with subsidies for those in need. Despite the absence of proposed radical transformation of the American health insurance framework, in September 1994, Senator George Mitchell (Democrat, ME) declared the bill DOA, leading health policy scholar Paul Starr to characterize this as "one of the great lost political opportunities in American history."[44]

After the failures of the Health Security Act, Congress and the Clinton Administration pursued some health reforms to expand protections on the margins, though they did not confront the broader philosophical arrangement of privatization of health insurance. In 1996, Congress passed and President Clinton signed into law the Health Insurance Portability and Accountability Act to safeguard sensitive patient health information from disclosure without the patient's consent. Just one year later, amid increased media portrayal of patients being injured by their private health plans' decisions, Representative John Dingell (Democrat, MI) and Senator Ted Kennedy (Democrat, MA) pursued the passage of a Patient's Bill of Rights that would, among other things, provide legal remedies for those who were denied coverage by the increasingly prevalent ERISA-governed self-insured employer-provided plans.

The absence of legal remedies was seen as a core impediment to health insurer accountability, leading Senator Kennedy to observe in a 1998 Senate HELP Committee hearing on ERISA remedies that this statutory feature was "an incentive for unscrupulous plans to deny payment for costly services, knowing they can't be held liable for the serious injuries that result." However, there were concerns about cost containment in the event of added insurer liability, as well as concerns about the exacerbation of frivolous lawsuits, and as Republicans turned their eye toward President Clinton's sex scandal and the looming impeachment process, the Patients' Bill of Rights was abandoned.[45]

MEDICARE AND MEDICAID GET PRIVATIZED. It was around this time that Congress advanced legislation that set ostensibly public health insurance programs down on the path of privatization. Though private plans have been an option within Medicare since the 1970s, with sixty-five HMOs contracting with Medicare in 1979,[46] it was in the Balanced Budget Act of 1997 (PL 105-33) that Congress created Medicare Part C (then called Medicare + Choice, now known as Medicare Advantage). The dual aims were to offer enrollees a greater choice of health insurance plans beyond traditional Medicare and to bring to the Medicare program the private sector's motives of efficiency and cost savings,[47] in addition to some other covered services (e.g., vision and dental care, both largely excluded from traditional Medicare). Political scientist Jonathan Oberlander observes that in expanding private insurance options for Medicare, the Balanced Budget Act was able to "fundamentally alter Medicare's character as a public, federally operated insurance program," such that many Medicare beneficiaries were expected to leave traditional Medicare in favor of enrollment in managed care organizations.[48]

In the early years of Medicare Part C, payments to plans were initially set at 95 percent of the average per-beneficiary costs in traditional Medicare. This was based on the principle that these private plans could provide care that was of both higher quality and lower cost than would be possible in traditional fee-for-service Medicare.[49] Though private plan enrollment within Medicare had increased from 1.3 million in 1985 to 6.9 million in 2000, the Balanced Budget Act of 1997 limited annual payment increases in Medicare private plan capitation rates, or the fixed payments to health care providers for patients under their care, in addition to changing health insurer risk adjustment methods. Following the introduction of these changes, Medicare private plan enrollment declined to 5.8 million by 2005.[50]

In light of this declining enrollment, Congress sought to find new ways to promote health insurer participation and beneficiary enrollment in private plans, and the Medicare Prescription Drug, Improvement, and Modernization Act (MMA) of 2003 did just that. The MMA not only increased Medicare Advantage plan payment rates in an effort to reverse the downward trend in enrollment, but also saw the establishment of Medicare Part D Prescription Drug Plans, creating new private plan options such that by 2006 all Medicare beneficiaries had access to at least one private plan.

Not surprisingly, given these boosted rates and enhanced benefits, America soon witnessed a skyrocketing of Medicare Advantage enrollment, with 24 percent of all beneficiaries being enrolled in Medicare Advantage plans by 2010. And with the MMA's increase of Medicare payments to Medicare Advantage, such plans were paid more for their enrollees than would be expected under traditional Medicare.[51] It is this heavy reliance on private insurance in the business of Medicare benefit delivery that leads political scientists Kimberly Morgan and Andrea Campbell to characterize the MMA as a "paradigmatic example of marketized, delegated governance."[52] By 2024, 54 percent of Medicare beneficiaries were enrolled in a Medicare Advantage plan, with the share projected to continue to increase.[53]

Medicare is not the only ostensibly public insurance program that has been increasingly privatized, with the 1990s also seeing a growing reliance on Managed Medicaid. In fact, according to the Medicaid and CHIP Payment Access Commission (MACPAC), 15 percent of Medicaid beneficiaries were enrolled in comprehensive risk-based managed care plans in 1995,[54] and the share increased to 75 percent by 2022.[55] This growth is no accident, but reflects political choices by state and federal governments such that, by 1997, the federal government had approved fourteen Medicaid waivers, enrolling 8 million individuals in managed care.[56]

The legislation further permitted states to impose deductibles, copayments, and other cost-sharing mechanisms on Medicaid beneficiaries who were enrolled in managed care organizations (MCOs).[57] This cost-sharing primarily seeks to deter overuse of health care services, a goal underlying the utilization management practices (e.g., prior authorization) on which this book focuses. Moreover, in the Balanced Budget Act of 1997 through which America saw the emergence of Medicare Advantage, Congress also allowed states to *compel* Medicaid beneficiaries to enroll in managed Medicaid plans without obtaining a waiver. This privatization only increased in the 2000s with Congress's passage of the Deficit Reduction Act of 2005, which promoted state flexibility in requiring cost-sharing for Medicaid enrollees despite the (by definition) low-income nature of this patient population.

Not only are the vast majority of Medicaid beneficiaries now enrolled in a managed care plan, but nearly 52 percent of federal and state Medicaid spending in fiscal year 2023 (nearly $457 billion) was on managed care.[58] With approval from the Centers for Medicare and Medicaid Services (CMS), states are empowered to *require* that beneficiaries enroll in a managed care plan to obtain some or all Medicaid benefits. The MCOs with which many states have these contractual arrangements are prominent figures in the private health care setting, with UnitedHealth Group, Centene, Elevance (formerly Anthem), Molina, and CVS (Aetna) comprising half of all Medicaid MCO enrollment as of 2020.[59]

The shift from traditional Medicaid to managed Medicaid can be attributed to a couple of central goals (however unrealized) on the part of states: to increase the predictability of health care spending and to facilitate better coordination of care. That private insurers would come to occupy such a large space in health care provision even within ostensibly public programs reflects the divided welfare state characterized by Jacob Hacker,[60] which would in turn inform and constrain future health reform efforts to promote access to care. But while the extent of managed care was only growing, absent even a floor vote on the Patient's Bill of Rights, attention shifted back from coverage denials within the insured population to expanding the number of covered persons.

MAJOR, BUT NOT RADICAL. The 2010 enactment of the Patient Protection and Affordable Care Act (ACA) (PL 111-148) expanded coverage to millions of Americans – the largest health care expansion since 1965's creation of Medicare and Medicaid – while preserving the core private health insurance infrastructure that would now provide more expansive coverage to more Americans through the newly created marketplace exchanges and compelling the purchase of health insurance.

Indeed, on March 22, 2010, the day after the ACA's historic vote in Congress, President Barack Obama assured the American public that, quite apart from moving away from a private insurance model to something akin to "socialized medicine" as some conservatives denigrated the Act, the ACA had instead drawn inspiration from former Republican Governor Mitt Romney of Massachusetts and operated within the constraints of the private insurance system while "reining in the worst excesses and abuses of the insurance industry" – that is, fixing what was wrong rather than targeting its elimination. President Obama continued that "long after the debate fades away ... what will remain standing is not the government-run system some feared ... or the status quo that serves the interests of the insurance industry, but a health care system that incorporates ideas from both parties .... [T]his isn't radical reform. But it is major reform."[61] This pattern of reliance on private insurance – not to mention the complicated role of the American Medical Association amid proposed and enacted health reforms over the decades – is consistent with health policy scholar Paul Starr's observation that the unique complexity of the American health care system has led liberal reformers to avoid interest group resistance associated with upending its public–private fragmentation, by instead seeking to build upon existing law and institutions.[62]

Of course, this fragmentation – or the multitude of administrative actors with which individuals (e.g., patients) interact to access their benefits (e.g., health care) – comes at a price. As public policy scholar Pamela Herd and her coauthors keenly observe, fragmentation not only emerges amid preferences for market-based delivery of public services, but in the process imposes added administrative costs to those navigating the system at hand (in this case, the American health care system) because "[a] person walking between organizations can get lost,"[63] potentially losing out on benefits.

Though the ACA sought to constrain payments to Medicare Advantage plans so that they would be on par with traditional Medicare, the existing structure of Medicare Advantage was left undisturbed, with incentives for Medicare Advantage plans to improve quality and patients' experiences. The result has been that the share of Medicare beneficiaries enrolled in Medicare Advantage plans has continued to climb, with the Congressional Budget Office projecting that 61 percent of Medicare beneficiaries will be enrolled in such plans by 2032. This growing reliance on Medicare Advantage is notable because, in stark contrast with traditional Medicare, 99 percent of Medicare Advantage enrollees have prior authorization requirements in their plans, and there were over 49.8 million prior authorization requests in Medicare Advantage plans in 2024.[64] Barriers for the Medicare Advantage population can be particularly consequential because this population may at the same time have more pressing health needs but lack the cognitive capacity to successfully challenge health insurers' decisions. What's more, though the ACA's passage saw the encouragement of Medicaid expansion to those with incomes up to 138 percent of the federal poverty level,[65] it did not disrupt Medicaid's overarching managed care arrangements, which for some can come at the price of experiencing barriers to care.

THE PRICE OF PRIVATIZATION. This privatization comes at a price for American patients. In the United States, business interests (including health insurers) are well-resourced "repeat players" in pursuit over policy control.[66] According to law professor Marc Galanter in his seminal analysis of inequitable features of the American legal system, "one-shotter" plaintiffs who only infrequently navigate the legal system are disadvantaged in facing "repeat players," or those entities (e.g., employers, insurers) who know the system well through repeated litigation. In the business setting, insurers (the "haves") are advantaged over "one-shotter" patients who are less familiar with the ins and outs of the complex American health care system.[67] Ultimately, for insurers, "the critical prize is the ability to shape the terms, distribution, and boundaries of economic governance, and the contest for this prize is waged over an extended period and on multiple fronts."[68] The nature of this American political economy story is such that these political and economic systems are linked, shaping the policy that emerges.

What these pages have sought to illuminate so far is that insurer discretion over health coverage determinations has been facilitated by decades of intentional political choices that have facilitated the growth of privatized health coverage even in the traditionally public spheres of Medicare and Medicaid. Indeed, for all the exorbitant spending that the United States contributes toward health care, Jacob Hacker aptly notes that what sets the American welfare state apart from other nations is not its *level* of spending, but rather the *source* of that investment, with many duties otherwise carried out by the government instead placed in the hands of private actors such as employers.[69] This public–private framework characterizes the American health care system, in which entities making decisions about health coverage often have fiduciary obligations to shareholders, which can in turn inform how much they want to cover. In this divided welfare state, while we see the expansion of the private sector's ability to administer and finance benefits, this system "substitutes in whole or in part for the emergence of comparable state capacity, reinforcing reliance on alternative policy instruments such as tax subsidies and regulation."[70]

Cumulatively, this points to entrenchment and seeming path dependence of health insurance privatization consistent with political scientist Margaret Levi's assertion that "once a country or region has started down a track, the costs of reversal are very high."[71] And it is with this privatization of the American welfare state that we see starkly the motivation and persistence of coverage denials (including, but extending beyond, prior authorization) largely by for-profit payers.

Unsurprisingly, this privatization has been fueled not only by the preferences of those holding political office, but also by the powerful organized interests influencing them.

THE ROLE OF THE AMERICAN MEDICAL ASSOCIATION

While the American Medical Association (AMA) historically opposed the enactment of national health insurance, instead advancing a politics that pushed America toward health insurance privatization, it is now among the leading champions of reforming managed care practices (including coverage denials) that are harmful to physicians and their patients – namely, prior authorization. So, how did we get here?

As Jacob Hacker observes, the battle over health care has historically been as much about politics as it is about policy.[72] Reform efforts can easily be stymied because, while organized interests such as health insurers have become increasingly entrenched amid America's growing reliance on managed care, the patients harmed by this system are far more diffuse.

Many physicians have expressed consternation about the intrusion on their autonomy that prior authorization can constitute,[73] with ophthalmologist and comedian "Dr. Glaucomflecken" repeatedly characterizing this practice as "practicing medicine without a medical license."[74] However, physician organizations have historically characterized reform efforts toward national health insurance as "socialized medicine" or, as with the Health Security Act, otherwise leveled critiques over potential impacts on doctors' practice of medicine. The devil is in the details of health reform, to paraphrase the leaders of the AMA in their 1993 op-ed in the *Journal of the American Medical Association*, in which they argued that managed competition demands a "new public–private partnership" among the government, employers, insurers, and the medical profession.[75]

That is, while the AMA and other physician associations have ardently opposed the utilization management system currently in practice, rife as it is with coverage denials and administrative burdens for physicians and their patients, decades of political choices concerning advocacy efforts have contributed to the current extent of reliance on managed health care. Health policy scholar Paul Starr observes that the interest group power of physicians helped tip the balance against health insurance under the Franklin D. Roosevelt Administration, such that it was extracted from Social Security legislation.[76] The AMA likewise decried as "socialized medicine" President Harry Truman's efforts to adopt a unified national health insurance system, instead seeking to preserve the "American way,"[77] despite that American way involving high uninsured rates. And the AMA additionally famously decried Medicare as "the beginning of socialized medicine" that would be characterized by bureaucratic incompetence, though they did support the extension of health insurance to low-income individuals through the creation of Medicaid. Thus, at every available turn in early-to-mid-twentieth-century health insurance reform moments, the AMA opposed universal public insurance, instead seeing privatization as a superior alternative.

Of course, the AMA's fears about Medicare proved not to be realized: doctors and hospitals cooperated with Medicare implementation, America would not see the long waiting lines feared by some, and interest group opposition to the program disappeared as the policy became entrenched in American political life.[78] Here, we see policy feedback in action, with the Medicare program's adoption creating a new politics surrounding its defense, including the investment of the American Association of Retired Persons (AARP) in Medicare's preservation, and leading to large majorities of both political parties supporting Medicare today.[79]

The AMA's role in health care reform in recent years has been conciliatory, though it has shied away from endorsing a more radical transformation of the American health insurance system that would reduce reliance on private insurance. Though ultimately endorsing the passage of the ACA in 2010, at its 2019 House of Delegates meeting, it voted narrowly to maintain its opposition to a single-payer system, even as a growing majority of physicians come to support the policy.

It is hardly unusual to see evolving political stances, especially in a complex and fluid policy domain such as health insurance reform. But, as this section highlights, it is ironic that the organization leading the call to "#FixPriorAuth" has typically, *even recently*, opposed the reform efforts that would scale back this health policy problem faced by physicians and their patients. Health insurance coverage denials have been empowered by decades of political choices by politicians and powerful organized interests safeguarding a substantial private sector role in America's health care delivery. This is all to say that the story of health insurance coverage denials in this largely managed care setting is also one of "political–economic outcomes [being] forged within … coalitional politics" because "building and transforming large-scale policies requires sustained efforts by well-organized and highly motivated organized actors, operating in interaction (and often in partnership) with other similarly institutionalized actors."[80]

Having elaborated on the coalitional politics that led to this current state in managed care-dominated American health policy, I turn now to examine the types of health insurance coverage barriers to which American patients are vulnerable, focusing in particular on the role of prior authorization in the American health care system.

TYPES OF COVERAGE DENIALS

Every time American patients utilize their health plans, they run the risk of an insurance barrier in one form or another as health insurers seek to impose guardrails on prescribing behaviors and the resulting costs of care. To understand the potential impact of managed care practices on patients, one must know not only *whether* one was denied coverage, but also *when* and *why*.

There are four types of denials that one might experience when utilizing one's health benefits: prior authorization, concurrent, retrospective, and retroactive. Their respective processes and impacts on patients are summarized in Table 1.1.

When a prior authorization denial arises, the physician has prescribed a medical service (e.g., prescription drug, scan, procedure) that requires insurer pre-approval, or pre-certification, but which the insurer determined does not constitute a covered service, is experimental or investigational for the patient's condition, or is not medically necessary according to the guidelines on which they rely, often developed by the medical benefits management company EviCore, which is owned by Cigna. Even though, in the notoriously expensive American health care system, prior authorization-induced denials do not leave American patients saddled with medical debt, this is a setting in which prescribed medical care is kept out of reach, at least pending appeal, thus raising the possibility that the patient's condition could worsen. This is a significant, though by no means exclusive, mechanism through which denials are issued.

Table 1.1 Types of health insurance coverage denials

Type of denial	Process of denial	Implications
Prior authorization	Insurer denies request for pre-approval of prescribed medical care	Delay or denial of initiation of medical treatment, risk of exacerbation
Concurrent	During a course of medical treatment, insurer denies coverage for further care	Disruption and potentially premature discontinuation of ongoing medical treatment
Retrospective	Insurer denies payment for medical care already rendered	Risk of medical debt
Retroactive	Insurer retracts payment for a service previously approved	Risk of medical debt

Some patients may also experience coverage denials through concurrent review processes, according to which the insurer reviews and makes judgments about the necessity of continued treatment, whether inpatient or outpatient. Adverse decisions might be rendered for any number of reasons, including the medical necessity of the treatment as well as its apparent efficacy for the patient at hand. In some cases, the insurer may decide that a lower level of care is more appropriate moving forward. When denials arise in this setting, decisions must be made as to whether to discontinue the current treatment or continue to appeal the denial, which can typically be handled by the insurer on an expedited basis if the patient is currently in the hospital.

When a patient experiences a retrospective review, they have already received their prescribed care, but the health insurer has determined that it does not meet coverage guidelines and thus they deny the claim. As with the other forms of denial, this may be because it is not a covered service, because it is deemed experimental or investigational for the patient's condition, or because it is not medically necessary, though some denials are also elicited due to billing code errors. While the patient in this case need not worry as much about their health status – they have not been denied care – they may receive unexpected medical bills for potentially large amounts. Thus, they might find themselves among the 20 million American adults who have medical debt, with an astonishing 41 percent of patients having a broader definition of medical debt that includes debt owed on credit cards as well as debt owed to family members.[81] While some of this debt is certainly attributable to high deductibles and other high out-of-pocket medical costs, some is undoubtedly attributable to insurer denials of payment.

Lastly, patients may experience retroactive denials, in which case the insurer, upon review, retracts its coverage for services previously approved or for which it has rendered payment, leaving the patient responsible for the amount. The result is that, as with retrospective denials, the patient may be asked to assume new medical debts, which can have a broader economic destabilizing effect (e.g., affecting credit).

On the basis of analysis of 124 million claims, Optum (affiliated with UnitedHealthcare) identified that nearly half (44 percent) of denials are "front-end," such as through prior authorization.[82] Given the significance of this as a vehicle for coverage denials, an in-depth analysis of this subject is critical to understanding American patients' barriers to health care and coverage, and the ways that these processes can be especially harmful to those from marginalized groups.

IMPLEMENTATION AND ORIGINS OF PRIOR AUTHORIZATION

Though I examine the practice of medical coverage denials across *all* rationales – whether prior to or following a patient's receipt of medical care – it is instructive to understand the origins of one of the most widely used utilization management controls: prior authorization. Prior authorization's implementation has been to the chagrin of many, with physician researcher Andrew Miller and his coauthors characterizing the challenges of prior authorization as "among the biggest pain points for health care professionals" across America.[83]

CURRENT IMPLEMENTATION OF PRIOR AUTHORIZATION. According to current procedures, the prior authorization process operates in several steps. First, the provider is notified whether prior authorization is required, in order to provide the test or treatment at hand. If it is required, they submit the prior authorization request, which is then received by the health plan. The provider may then be asked to submit additional documentation to demonstrate medical necessity, which is then received by the health plan, which then adjudicates and replies to the provider, who will then be notified of the decision whether to approve or deny the health care service in question. If the care is approved, the patient can schedule the treatment or pick up their prescription, as the case may be. And about 10 percent of the time, it will be denied, in which case there is an appeal process, rife though it can be with burden to patients and their physicians.

A prominent justification for the imposition of this practice is the avoidance of unnecessary medical care – especially that which can pose risk to the patient. After all, Dr. Mario Molina, former CEO of Molina Healthcare, emphasized, "Even things like CT scans, which seem fairly benign, expose someone to something like 40 times the radiation of a chest x-ray. So do you *really* need that? There are some more invasive procedures, where people are sticking catheters in you, sticking needles in you, doing biopsies. Those kinds of invasive procedures often require prior authorization as well."[84] While the Peter G. Peterson Foundation finds that as much as 25 percent of health care prescribed in the United States is "wasteful,"[85] contributing to the country's notably high health costs, the question remains how best to identify which care meets this definition, and whether prior authorization is the best tool to eliminate it. Related to the health policy problem of overutilization is the effort to guard against excess health costs, and Dr. Molina noted that it is for this reason that higher-cost procedures often require prior authorization, which was put in place broadly to guard against fraud, waste, and abuse.

Despite physician consternation with insurer overreach into clinical decisionmaking, a 2019 survey by America's Health Insurance Plans (AHIP), the national association of health insurers, found that the primary perceived objectives of prior authorization were "improve quality/promote evidence-based care" (98 percent), "protect patient safety" (91 percent), "address areas prone to misuse" (84 percent), and "reduce unnecessary spending" (79 percent), with the lion's share of respondents perceiving positive impacts on patient care (91 percent), affordability (91 percent), and safety (84 percent),[86] a stark contrast with physician perspectives on prior authorization reflected in American Medical Association surveys.

This, however, raises the question of how evidence bases for prescribed care are assessed. In keeping with Daniel Skinner's observation about the discretion-laden nature of medical necessity, 70 percent of

AHIP respondents indicated that they relied on "vendor-provided proprietary evidence-based resources." The vendor on which insurers typically rely is EviCore by Evernorth, a medical benefits management company owned by Cigna, which scrutinizes prior authorization requests for approximately 100 million patients nationwide and "highlight[s] areas of over-utilization and unnecessary spending, and pinpoints areas of the greatest opportunity to improve care and increase savings."[87] These prior authorizations are reviewed by the hundreds of physicians, therapists, and nurses employed by EviCore to ensure that prescribed care is safe, necessary, and cost-effective.

While EviCore states that its assessment of medical necessity and appropriateness is based on large-scale statistical studies, *ProPublica* and Capitol Forum analysis found that EviCore's AI-backed algorithm can yield inappropriate denials, which can in turn reap a profit for the large health insurers with which it contracts with a promise of a three-to-one return on investment.[88]

To be sure, prior authorizations do not necessarily result in denials. However, the American Hospital Association reported in 2020 that 89 percent of hospitals and health systems have seen an increase – often a *significant* increase – in denials in the last three years,[89] with many of those denials occurring through prior authorization. In fact, despite prior authorization being aimed in no small part at imposing guardrails amid overprescribing, they observe that prior authorization was being applied to wide-ranging services "including those for which the treatment protocol has remained the same for decades and there is no evidence of abuse."[90] This perceived rise in prior authorization is supported by a Medical Group Management Association survey from September 17, 2019, which reflected a widespread perception (90 percent) among health care leaders that prior authorization requirements were on the rise compared with the previous year.[91]

One speculated reason for the growth in reliance on prior authorization is the increasing consolidation of managed care,[92] which imposes on insurers financial pressures in reporting quarterly profits that may benefit from utilization management if it reduces the number of medical services paid for. In fact, as of 2022 and in the aftermath of a series of mergers and acquisitions over the course of the 2000s and 2010s, at the national level the top five health insurers control 54 percent of the commercial health insurance market share and 69 percent of the Medicare Advantage market share, an increase from two years previously.[93]

Insurers have three main tools with which to remain competitive amid consolidation: they can increase premiums, which is not feasible in the long run, given consumers' finite resources; they can lower costs by fixing how much will be paid for a service (which raises political barriers with physician associations); or they can impose administrative hurdles through utilization management to reduce prescribing, especially amid consolidation-related financial pressures. Former Aetna Chief Medical Director Dr. Troyen Brennan noted, "I think anybody in the insurance industry is not going to be telling the truth if they say that anything but cost is driving prior authorization."[94]

Increased reliance on prior authorization may also reflect an unintended consequence of the implementation of the Affordable Care Act. Though constituting a once-in-a-generation expansion of health coverage, compelling health insurers to cover patients with previously declinable preexisting medical conditions imposed new cost pressures for which utilization management proved a potent tool in reducing services covered by private insurers. As former Vice President of Cigna Wendell Potter reflected, "When you're putting new requirements and new restrictions on these companies to have them operate more fairly, they are still under the same pressure from investors and Wall Street analysts to meet profit expectations. What's left to them is the tools of managed care, which have long been available to them, which they can ratchet up. This is one of the reasons we're seeing increases in prior authorization. It's a means to avoid paying claims they would have paid back in the old days."[95]

Hospital and physician impressions of increasing reliance on prior authorization are borne out by the data within the realm of prescription drugs. I analyzed the 2016 through 2022 formularies of Cigna, a major health insurer whose formularies are made public online over several years.[96] Identifying the total number of formulary drugs and the total with prior authorization requirements for each year, I find that the share of prescription drugs in the formularies requiring prior authorization has increased from 18 percent in 2016, to 23 percent in 2019, to

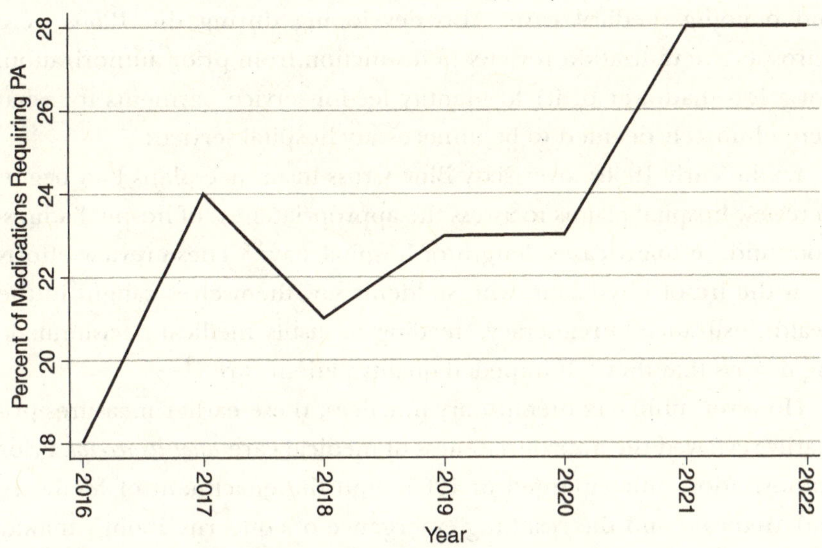

1.1 Cigna prescriptions requiring prior authorization, 2016–2022.
Source: Hand-coding of Cigna formularies, 2016–2022.

28 percent in 2022, a marked (albeit nonlinear) increase in just six years (see Figure 1.1). This coding accounts specifically for prior authorization, and not the broader constellation of barriers that patients might face in filling their prescriptions (e.g., quantity limits on prescribing), but offers a glimpse at the increasing opportunities for patients to experience coverage denials that necessitate either delays in care (or delays in *optimal* care) or out-of-pocket medical expenditures.

Having considered the overarching role that prior authorization plays in American health insurance, I now turn to discuss the political conditions from which prior authorization originated.

THE EARLY YEARS OF UTILIZATION MANAGEMENT. Between 1920 and 1965, as more Americans gained access to health care through their employers' insurance plans, health insurers' main tools with which to contain the costs of health care involved management of who could enroll (the risk pool), what plan benefits could be offered, and controls on payments to providers.[97] With advancements in medical technology and more modernized techniques came increased treatments and longer survival times with illnesses, potentially necessitating more costly and ongoing medical care. Also developing during the 1950s were retrospective utilization reviews (a distinction from prior authorization, but a foreshadower of it) to identify fee-for-service payments for what were ultimately deemed to be unnecessary hospital services.

By the early 1960s, over sixty Blue Cross insurance plans had begun to review hospital claims to assess the appropriateness of hospital admissions and, in many cases, length of hospital stay.[98] These review efforts drew the ire of physicians, who suddenly saw themselves caught in the health insurance bureaucracy, needing to justify medical decisionmaking in ways that they felt impeded quality patient care.[99]

However, unlike contemporary practices, these earlier measures primarily reviewed the appropriateness of medical care *after its receipt.* Prior authorization only emerged in 1965 amid the enactment of Medicare and Medicaid and the resulting emergence of concerns about runaway costs and how to curb them.[100]

The goals in adopting these utilization controls were simple: to avoid the possibility of paying for unnecessary use of medical services and to encourage reasonable, less expensive health care treatments when available. To participate in Medicare, hospitals and extended-care facilities were required to operate utilization review committees that would assess both quality of care and medical necessity.[101] This utilization review was typically administered by registered nurses (RNs) in acute hospital settings. But even as health plans began to review the medical necessity of hospital admissions and subsequent admission days, this was a far narrower sphere of health care than that in which such reviews would ultimately become adopted throughout the health care system.

The 1970s saw further developments in utilization review amid the development of managed care, with the primary goal of guarding against costly and unnecessary treatments. In the Social Security Act Amendments of 1972 (PL 92-603), Congress established a peer review system, in which physicians would review through physician-controlled community organizations (PSCOs) the health care services provided under the Medicare and Medicaid programs. In the mid 1970s, furthermore, Congress gained interest in surgical second-opinion programs to guard against performance of unnecessary surgeries.

PRIOR AUTHORIZATION IN THE 1980S AND 1990S. In the Tax Equity and Fiscal Responsibility Act of 1982 (PL 97-248), Congress instituted utilization and quality control peer review organizations (PROs) comprised of physicians tasked with ensuring "efficient and effective administration" by performing reviews of the patterns of quality of care measured against "objective criteria which define acceptable and adequate practice." Specifically, they would review whether specific health care services or items were "reasonable and medically necessary or otherwise allowable," and whether the service quality met professionally recognized standards of health care. In the event of a denial, there would be an opportunity for review of the decision.

During this time, America saw substantial growth in the number and types of organizations that integrated cost containment efforts into their business model. The number of health maintenance organizations (HMOs) in the United States grew from 175 in 1976 to over 600 in 1988,[102] with 25.2 percent growth between 1985 and 1986 alone.[103] In backlash against managed care plans' narrowing of networks, preferred provider organizations (PPOs) were developed, beginning in 1983.[104] The irony was that this meant losing another mechanism for cost control, thus creating another incentive to use greater utilization management. This time also witnessed a proliferation of managed care organization (MCO) approaches to states' Medicaid implementation, with the share of Medicaid enrollees in managed care more than tripling between 1987 and 1995.[105]

While prior authorization programs still focused on hospital admissions and high-cost procedures, with more widespread prescription drug coverage as well as pharmaceutical spending, both public and private insurers began to extend utilization management to include medication prior authorization, quantity and dosage limits, and step therapy (or "fail first") requirements.[106] The result has been the rapid spread of prior authorization requirements pertaining to prescription drugs, sometimes even for generic drugs that lack a lower-cost substitute. This thus represents a departure from earlier prior authorization efforts more squarely aimed at reducing lower-value, costly tests and hospitalizations.

By the late 1990s, dissatisfaction with managed health care fostered the emergence of a "patient rights movement" aimed at curbing managed health care plans' ability to limit patients' access to certain kinds of hospital and physician care.[107] In fact, over thirty states passed legislation aimed at guaranteeing access to certain forms of health care absent interference from managed care plans upon coverage denial.[108] However, because states are unable to regulate traditional Medicare or self-insured employer-provided plans governed by ERISA, the scope of possible intervention by means of such state legislation is limited.

All this while per capita health spending was on the rise, from $353 in 1970 to $4,845 in 2000, to eventually $12,531 in 2020.[109]

Unlike the private insurance setting, traditional Medicare plans require prior authorization only under a limited number of conditions (e.g., for durable medical equipment or prostheses). But, with the adoption of Medicare Advantage in the Balanced Budget Act of 1997, beneficiaries gained access to health insurance plans beyond the traditional Medicare program, and, in this setting, prior authorization became a staple of plan terms.

PRIOR AUTHORIZATION SINCE THE AFFORDABLE CARE ACT. With the enactment of the Affordable Care Act (ACA) in 2010, Congress left intact much of private health insurers' ability to use prior authorization, though it was prohibited as applied to emergency department visits at out-of-network hospitals, and non-grandfathered health plans (that is, plans not yet in effect as of March 23, 2010) were prohibited from requiring prior authorization to see an obstetrician/gynecologist (OB-GYN), pediatrician, or primary care provider. While preserving much of prior authorization's role within the affected plans, the ACA also provided for both internal (within the health plan) and external (with an independent reviewer apart from the insurer) appeal processes upon denial of prior authorization, denial of other claims, or rescission of coverage. Thus, while the implementation of the ACA imposed only modest restrictions on prior authorization within a subset of health plans, it provided recourse for those who faced denials and sought to secure eventual coverage.

While it is difficult to gauge precisely what percentage of treatments are subject to prior authorization, a 2021 study of Medicare Part B (which is not subject to prior authorization requirements) by physician and health services researcher Aaron Schwartz and his colleagues found that 41 percent of beneficiaries received at least one service that would have been subject to prior authorization under a different form of health insurance.[110] This highlights not only the profound differences between Medicare Part B (traditional Medicare) and other forms of health insurance, but also the broad scope of services potentially subject to prior authorization requirements, including even less costly care.

Having evaluated the conditions accounting for the proliferation of prior authorization, it is helpful to understand the factors affecting whether health insurers choose to approve or deny coverage of prescribed care within this setting.

HEALTH INSURERS' DECISIONMAKING PROCESS

There are multiple steps to evaluating whether coverage will be approved for prescribed care. First, insurers review for evidence of coverage, which is a legal document that describes what the health plan contractually covers. Next, the insurer determines whether the test or treatment requires a prior authorization, which is especially likely if the prescribed care is expensive. Then, the insurer determines whether the required prior authorization was in fact obtained. If it was not obtained, the health insurer may deny coverage *even if it was medically necessary* because the proper procedure was not followed.

Related to the prior authorization review is the determination of medical necessity because of patient safety concerns. Assessing whether prescribed care is medically necessary and non-experimental is meant to police physicians' prescribing behavior on the outer bounds amid the overtreatment that Shannon Brownlee discusses in her seminal analysis of the subject, in settings in which patients seek potentially "too much" medicine. Health policy consultant Linda Bergthold observes that the medical necessity criterion has become a tool to control the use of scarce health care resources and not only is subjective, but is even more important amid the growth of managed care just described.[111] Thus, a challenge is that the term "medical necessity" is flexible, promoting discretion on the part of the insurers empowered in this health care system as they seek to contain rising health care costs.[112] In fact, political scientist Daniel Skinner opines that "[t]he problem is not the politicization of medical care, but the depoliticizing tendency to treat medical necessity decision making as a matter of facts to be found rather than sets of values to be defended."[113]

In general terms, Cigna defines "medically necessary" according to several criteria: the service must be (1) for the purpose of evaluating, diagnosing, or treating an illness, injury, disease, or its symptoms; (2) in accordance with generally accepted standards of practice, (3) clinically appropriate and considered to be effective for the patient's illness, injury, or disease; (4) not primarily for the convenience of the patient, health care provider, or other physicians or health care providers; and (5) not more costly than an alternative service at least as likely to produce equivalent results. Of course, there are ambiguities in many of these assessments, including distinguishing the "necessary" from the "appropriate," especially given that medicine is a balance of art and science.

Those reviewing claims in the public–private health care state function as "street-level bureaucrats" (to borrow the language of political scientist Michael Lipsky) upon whom the American health care system has conferred substantial powers in defining access to prescribed care or payment for services rendered to America's insured population. These street-level bureaucrats, applying insurers' rules for coverage provision, balance "aspirations for the work and the coping requirements of the job,"[114] ever mindful of pressures toward profitability as they engage in policy delivery.

I have described the political conditions giving rise to managed care and prior authorization mechanisms, and how insurers render coverage decisions in this setting. Considering the cost containment arguments in favor of prior authorization implementation, it is instructive next to explore the monetary cost associated with their administration.

PRIOR AUTHORIZATION'S COSTS TO THE HEALTH CARE SYSTEM

Though prior authorization aims at cost containment amid America's rising health care costs, little work has examined how effectively this policy accomplishes its monetary goal. After all, there is the risk that

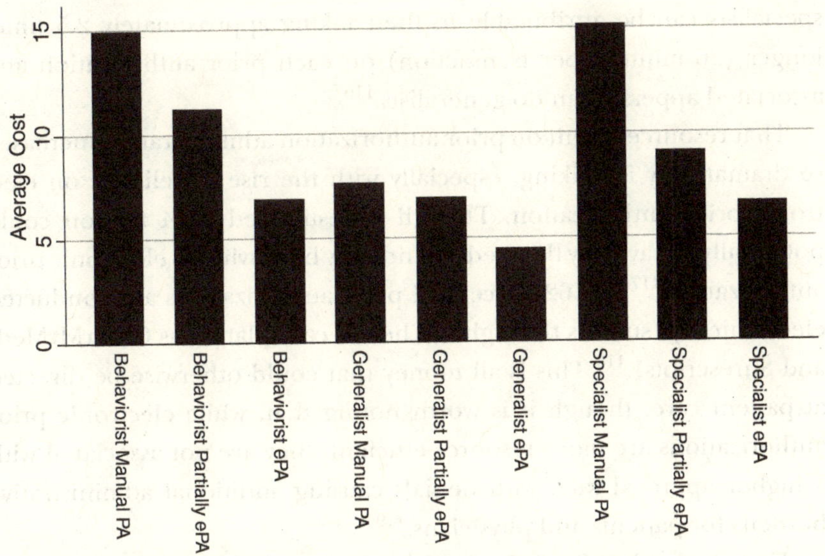

1.2 Average cost of prior authorization transactions across specialties.
Source: Council for Affordable Quality Healthcare (CAQH) (2023).

coverage denials can necessitate more expensive treatment (e.g., in the emergency department) as patients' health conditions decline. Here, I discuss the administrative costs associated with prior authorization implementation.

The 2023 annual administrative burden report by the Council for Affordable Quality Healthcare (CAQH), a non-profit organization comprised of health insurers, characterized prior authorization as "continu[ing] to be one of the most burdensome administrative tasks for providers," with the overall volume of prior authorizations growing 23 percent in 2022 after having experienced a brief downturn amid the COVID-19 pandemic.[115] What's more, the total prior authorization price tag for the medical industry came in at a whopping $1.3 billion, a 30 percent increase from the previous year.

The CAQH index identifies the electronic and manual prior authorization costs to providers across specialties, with the greatest burdens shouldered by specialists and behaviorists as opposed to generalists ($15.12 and $14.92 per manual transaction, compared with $7.60 respectively), and with considerable cost savings associated with electronic prior authorization (see Figure 1.2). The greater financial burden for specialists can be attributable to their taking approximately 2.5 times longer (26 minutes per transaction) on each prior authorization and associated appeals than do generalists.[116]

That resources spent on prior authorization administration increased so dramatically is striking, especially with the rise in reliance on electronic prior authorization. Though an estimated $494 million could potentially be saved by the medical industry by moving to electronic prior authorization,[117] just 62 percent of prior authorizations are conducted electronically (such as through the health care platforms CoverMyMeds and Surescripts).[118] This is all money that could otherwise be directed at patient care, though it is worth noting that, while electronic prior authorizations are more resource-efficient, they are not associated with a higher approval rate, with denials causing additional administrative burdens for patients and physicians.[119]

That electronic prior authorization would not be universally adopted by plans is perhaps surprising, because physicians are not the only ones who shoulder an administrative cost associated with prior authorization: the 2023 CAQH Index estimates that manual prior authorizations cost plans $3.52 per transaction, with an estimated 87 million manual prior authorizations in 2022, accumulating to $306.2 million. CAQH observes that industry adoption of electronic prior authorization has faced the barriers of provider awareness, vendor support, "inconsistent use of data content allowed in the standard, state laws mandating manual processes, and lack of an attachment standard to support exchange of medical documentation."[120]

Controlling these extensive administrative costs is important not only because it can reduce overall health care spending, but also because it can direct more resources toward patient care. In fact, researchers at *Health Affairs* estimated in 2022 that anywhere from 15 percent to 30 percent of health costs are directed to administrative spending, including but extending beyond prior authorization management.

That prior authorization might undercut cost containment objectives is a puzzle that some health services researchers have probed within segments of American health care delivery. Victoria Lee and her coauthors find when looking at prior authorization denials (6.1 percent) and reversals of denials (nearly 40 percent) that prior authorization is not a cost-effective means to manage the utilization of outpatient superficial venous procedures when the surgeon practices are already aligned with insurance guidelines.[121] Though their analysis is restricted to a narrow set of medical procedures, it highlights the limitations of this insurance practice's achievement of cost containment objectives. These findings suggest that prior authorization creates significant financial and bureaucratic burdens on patients, physicians, and even the insurers themselves.

This raises the question of what accounts for the durability of this policy inefficiency. Political scientists have characterized policy as following a pattern of path dependence, according to which choices made amid policy formation constrain future policy decisionmaking. That is, while "critical junctures" can open up the possibilities for policy reform at key moments, policies can often become self-reinforcing over time.

Prior authorization amid growing reliance on managed care has reshaped subsequent health politics and imposed new constraints on future policymaking, a policy feedback dynamic examined by political scientists Daniel Beland and Jacob Hacker, who observe that private health insurance "created deep ideological and political obstacles to the emergence of national health insurance" and argue that "institutional constraints are necessary but not sufficient to explain the path-dependent journey of U.S. social policy."[122] Rather, attention must also be paid to private social policies and agenda-setting processes. What we have ultimately observed in the context of prior authorization is bias toward a status quo policy that has demonstrable shortcomings, but which is reinforced because, while the interests it ostensibly benefits are increasingly entrenched, the patients harmed by this practice are diffuse. Indeed, even if prior authorization were cost containing (which is unclear), this system imposes unevenly distributed burdens that deepen health (and consequently, economic) inequities across the nation. Thus, as much as containing costs, the practice appears to *shift* costs to patients and their physicians.

I turn now to discuss briefly the current scale of the health policy problem of the coverage denials that can emerge from this process.

FREQUENCY OF COVERAGE DENIALS

The fragmentation of American health insurance makes difficult a comprehensive assessment of the scope of coverage denials, though evidence of denials – whether through prior authorization or following treatment – can be found across large swaths of the insurance market. For example, in September 2020, the California Department of Managed Care fined Aetna $500,000 for "failure to follow California law for reimbursing emergency room claims" after the Department's analysis of a sample of emergency department claims found that a whopping 93 percent had been wrongly denied by the insurer.[123] Aetna is not an anomaly, and *Los Angeles Times* journalist Michael Hiltzik even characterizes Anthem Blue Cross as being a "pioneer" in the practice of imposing bureaucratic hoops to secure medical claim acceptance. This 2020 finding raises a host of questions at the heart of this book.

Despite the common American experience of health insurance barriers causing delays and denials, scant systematic attention has been paid to their scope and impact. One notable exception is the KFF reporting on the rate of claim denials in plans purchased through ACA marketplace exchanges. Claim denials are distinct from prior authorization denials, because claims refer to medical services that have already been rendered, so this is just one subset of denials that occur. However, KFF researchers find, on the basis of 2023 plan year data released by the Centers for Medicare and Medicaid Services, that 19 percent (or 73 million) of marketplace claims were denied, with merely 0.05 percent of denied claims (or 376,527) appealed to the marketplace insurer, even though, in 2023, 46 percent of denials were reversed upon appeal to the insurer.[124] These findings are in line with the previous several plan years, also documented by KFF, though the aggregate number of denials reported in 2023 was higher due to growth in ACA plan enrollment.

These denials are not isolated to marketplace plans. Physician and health services researcher Aaron Schwartz and his colleagues find in the context of Medicare Advantage plans that beneficiaries experience 0.81 denials per year.[125] Also examining Medicare Advantage, researchers at KFF find not only that nearly 50 million prior authorization requests were submitted to Medicare Advantage plans in 2023 (an increase from 42 million in 2022), but also that 3.2 million of those prior authorization requests were fully or partially denied.[126] This raises important questions about the extent to which these denials constitute impediments to medically necessary, and not just low-value, care.[127]

What's more, by polling 516 acute care hospitals about their 2022 claims, the company Premier found that 15.7 percent of Medicare Advantage and 15.1 percent of managed Medicaid claims were denied, while 13.9 percent of commercial claims were denied. While fee-for-service (FFS) Medicaid claims were found to be denied the most frequently (16.7 percent), traditional Medicare was found to have the lowest denial rate (8.4 percent), which is unsurprising, given the infrequency with which it relies on prior authorization, a significant vehicle for denials. From the 15 percent overall denial rate, Premier extrapolates that a whopping 3 billion claims are denied nationwide each year,[128] though this estimate is quite a bit higher than the still-high 850 million denials estimated by the *Wall Street Journal*. Even though over half of these denials were overturned, as this book illustrates, those appeals are highly burdensome – imposing learning, compliance, and psychological costs – and induce further inequities in the health care system because not everyone has health literacy or other resources with which to be successful in this endeavor.

The UnitedHealthcare-affiliated organization Optum's 2024 analysis of 124 million claim remits from over 1,400 hospitals finds that 12 percent of claims (or 14.9 million) were denied nationally in 2023 – holding steady from 2022, but up from 9 percent in 2016.[129] Figure 1.3 plots the national trend from 2016 to 2023 (data were missing for 2017 and 2018). Forty-four percent of denials were issued prior to the receipt of treatment, such that care was kept out of reach. The analysis characterizes 32 percent of such denials as "unequivocally avoidable" and another 52 percent of denials as "situationally avoidable," and attributes the increase in denials across the nation to staffing issues and inadequate training amid complex cases, lack of denial prevention strategies earlier in the claim processing cycle, and inadequate technological investment. Thus, not only is there a relatively high number of denials, many of them through the vehicle of prior authorization, but also the frequency appears to have been increasing in recent years. Indeed, since the start of the COVID-19 pandemic, denials rose 11 percent nationally (from 10 percent in the first quarter of 2020 to 11.1 percent in the third quarter of 2020), with

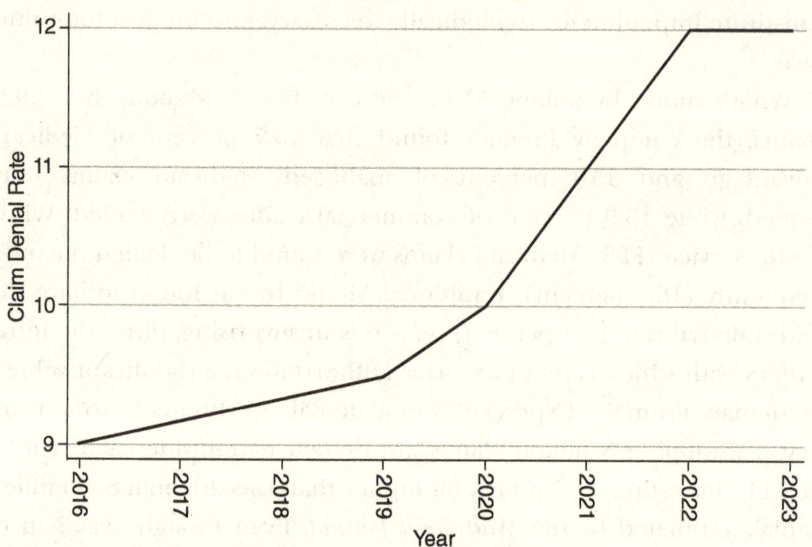

1.3 Optum analysis of claim denial rate, 2016–2023.
Source: Optum Revenue Cycle Denial Indexes, 2016–2023.

the highest denial rates found in the regions with the highest initial wave of COVID-19 outbreaks: the Pacific Coast and the Northeast.[130]

Health economist Joshua Gottlieb and his coauthors examine this policy problem from a different angle, that of billing complexity and resulting denials. Observing 44.5 million claims submitted in 2015, they find both managed and fee-for-service Medicaid to have the highest billing complexity and a higher proportion of claims challenged.[131] In fact, FFS Medicaid's claim denial rate is 17.8 percentage points higher than that of traditional Medicare, which they attribute in large part to billing complexity. Overall, private insurers were slightly (1.3 percentage points) more likely to deny a claim than were public insurers. While their data have the advantage of relying on individual claims, this book offers, through more contemporary survey and interview data, a unique window into patients' and physicians' experiences with denials and the varied ways that these insurer decisions impact health and economic security.

Coverage denials are inconvenient, but what if they are simply imposing valuable guardrails on the prescription of low-value medical care that drives up America's health care costs? At least in some cases, audits suggest a pattern of not just denials, but *wrongful* denials. Of the 140 Medicare Advantage Organization contracts that CMS audited between 2012 and 2016, 56 percent were cited for inappropriately denying requests for coverage.[132] This raises concerns about not only the extent to which people are wrongly experiencing coverage denials, but also the degree to which they experience subsequent administrative burdens in accessing this care that is being kept out of reach.

DENIALS AS INEQUALITY-INDUCING ADMINISTRATIVE BURDENS

Prior analyses of denials and appeals demonstrate the need for a comprehensive investigation into how public and private insurers' decisions to deny health coverage (whether through prior authorization or otherwise) deepen health and economic inequality in the United States. This book aims to complete such an investigation, by way of shedding light on the sorts of patients and health care services most vulnerable to experiencing both coverage denials and the administrative burden of appealing them, who opts in versus out of appealing to access prescribed care, and how this insurance practice can disrupt patients' health and economic security. It also seeks to investigate the administrative burden impact of these practices on physicians, who are tasked with leading the charge in communicating with insurers following the issuance of denials. In this context of burden (or individuals' cumbersome experiences of policy implementation), risk is shifted from payers to the patients themselves, as well as their physicians, breeding a new economic insecurity among those seeking health care.

That administrative bureaucracy could keep coverage out of reach for many Americans is a familiar insight, and the resulting inequities are consistent with political scientists Jacob Hacker, Suzanne Mettler, and Diane Pinderhughes's observation that inequality is particularly pronounced in the United States "in part because U.S. public policy is less focused on trying to ensure equality."[133] In light of this, it is perhaps unsurprising that the Commonwealth Fund published in 2024 a report on "the failing U.S. health system" and identified pronounced shortcomings in equity of health care access.[134]

Discussion of the impact of administrative burden on social policy has typically been isolated to access to government programs such as Medicaid, the Supplemental Nutrition Assistance Program (SNAP), and Supplemental Security Income. For example, political scientist Jamila Michener observes in the context of Medicaid that "beneficiaries must confront a program that is extraordinarily complex .... The prevalence of red tape and administrative burden means that there are many possible points of contention and correspondingly, many choices about whether and how to resist adverse bureaucratic decisions."[135] And public policy scholars Pamela Herd and Donald Moynihan characterize Medicare administrative burden as arising from the complexity of shared reliance on the public traditional Medicare as well as the array of third-party actors increasingly operating in that space, while observing that SNAP administrative burden is more complex, "oscillating between periods of bipartisan support for accessibility and high take-up of benefits, followed by greater polarization and new efforts to impose burdens."[136]

Outside the scope of US public policy, public administration scholars Ayesha Masood and Muhammad Azfar Nisar characterize individuals as accumulating "administrative capital" in response to public policies that demand high levels of knowledge of bureaucratic rules, processes, and behaviors.[137] However, even though citizens can find ways to reduce burden, it is nevertheless onerous and has an accompanying learning curve, with administrative capital increasing through repeated bureaucratic interactions and, unsurprisingly, not being uniformly distributed.

These burdens can come with a heavy price. Pamela Herd and Donald Moynihan note in their seminal analysis of administrative burdens that such burdens "affect whether people can access benefits that can improve quality of life, such as health insurance," in addition to which they can "alter the effectiveness of public programs."[138] After all, they write, this is "consequential in terms of the burdens citizens bear" and they "make a difference in our lives."[139] These administrative burdens can be understood as a combination of learning, psychological, and compliance costs that citizens must bear in their potentially onerous interactions with the state[140] – or, in this case, the health insurance system. These burdens not only reflect political choices in policy design and implementation, but also are distributive, harming some groups more than others, because people from marginalized groups are less able to weather the storm amid red tape.[141]

But, while their analyses focus on the challenges associated with enrolling and staying enrolled in public programs, this book addresses how administrative burdens and the "time tax" of program navigation can undercut, even outright deny, benefits for those who are ostensibly enrolled and covered by a set of health plan benefits, whether public *or private*. While this burden does not always come directly from the state, it emanates from political calculations about policy design, and the patient experience when confronted with barriers is strikingly similar. The complexity of navigating the American health insurance system is a setting ripe for administrative burden analysis because patients (especially those from marginalized groups) are confronted with the learning costs of identifying what falls within their benefits and how to access them, the compliance costs of navigating prior authorization and appeal processes (both internal within the insurer and potentially external, through an independent medical review), and, of course, the psychological costs associated with fighting in this complex system to access care, especially when already facing health challenges. Here, I examine both public and private health care delivery and the barriers that arise for those who are prescribed – or are prescribing – care.

There are two stories of coverage denials that are important to illuminate from the patient's perspective. One is the extent to which this insurance practice deepens health and economic inequality in the United States, with denials and their impact (whether keeping care out of patients' reach or deepening patients' financial fragility) potentially being more concentrated among historically marginalized populations. The other is that of the burdens that lead some patients to have health coverage on paper but not meaningfully in practice due to a rationing of medical care.

While physician and health services researcher Benjamin Sommers and his colleagues examine the bureaucratic burdens leading some patients to lose their Medicaid coverage amid onerous work requirements *despite working the required number of hours*,[142] and Pamela Herd and Donald Moynihan examine administrative burdens across a range of social policies including but not exclusive to health care,[143] extant studies have not emphasized from the patient perspective the burdens associated with utilization of health plan benefits. And, in a vast health insurance bureaucracy, there are important unanswered questions as to which populations will more effectively cut through the red tape associated with accessing not just health coverage, but health care. The fact that these dynamics can be seen across insurers reflects an unanticipated consequence of the "delegated welfare state": entangling public programs (e.g., Medicare) with the private health care market (e.g., Medicare Advantage) can lead to reduced accountability in the delivery of plan benefits as insurers take advantage of program complexity and the limitations of programs' target populations.[144] And amid this public–private entanglement (e.g., with the growing privatization of Medicare and Medicaid) comes extra administrative burden because the presence of additional actors in benefits delivery brings in additional veto players as well as discretion to impose burdens.[145]

While the original and public data highlighted in this book demonstrate a highly pervasive practice of coverage denials in the American health insurance system, they also highlight a high rate of *reversal* of the initial determinations (albeit after burdens have been incurred for patients, for their physicians, *and by insurers as well*). If coverage denials result in frequent care *deferral* as opposed to final *denial*, this calls into question the extent to which this insurance practice is effective in reducing costs to the American health care system. However, even if it is cost-containing (and that is an untested assumption), this system leaves behind patients, especially those from marginalized groups, who struggle to access and afford their prescribed care as a direct result of political choices empowering payer goals of cost containment and profit maximization.

And, although quantifying the administrative burden emanating from this insurance practice is beyond the scope of this study, organizational theorist Jeffrey Pfeffer and his coauthors analyze administrative burdens of employees dealing with health insurance administration (both in terms of time and in terms of lost work and burnout) and suggest that the "sludge" of accessing benefits in the American health care system induces not just headaches, but also a hefty monetary price tag.[146]

There is also an important story of coverage denials from the physician perspective. While administrative burdens have been examined in the context of those enrolling in public programs, what has been substantially less studied is the burdens on those prescribing services. Yet, through interviews and survey evidence, one finds that these barriers elicit not only frustrations and impediments that can lead to abandonment of patients' treatment, but also physician burnout. What's more, we can find inequities not only among patients, but also among medical practices, some of which are better resourced than others to process potentially large volumes of prior authorizations.

Here, I have worked to illustrate the significant, and *growing*, policy problem of insurers' denials of coverage, often through the increasingly common mechanism of requiring prior authorization. Through this vehicle, many patients learn that their prescribed care is not, in fact, deemed medically necessary, or is experimental, leaving both patients and their physicians forced to reconsider treatment options, potentially foregoing treatment or opting for suboptimal care. Such practices reflect in part the financial considerations of the health insurance entities in which the American political system has housed coverage determinations even within the ostensibly public programs of Medicare and Medicaid.

To be sure, it is hardly inappropriate to exercise caution, even concern, about overtesting and overtreatment in the American health care system – and its associated costs – given medical practice entrenchment and anxiety about medical malpractice litigation. What's more, some patients conflate more care and better care, when that might not be the case. But, as I argue in the pages that follow, while prior authorization is aimed in part at guarding against this overprescribing, these onerous requirements can actually overcorrect, not only contributing to patient and physician administrative burden, but even leading to *underprescribing* by those seeking to avoid prior authorization-related hassles.

PLAN OF THE BOOK

Chapter 2 introduces my nationwide survey of 1,340 US adults on the subject of coverage denials and discusses the overall patterns and persistence of this health insurance practice. Chapter 3 examines the demographic and other factors associated with coverage denials. Chapter 4 conducts an in-depth analysis of the particular challenges that patients face in securing coverage for prescription drugs, on which nearly two-thirds of Americans rely. Chapter 5 examines the patterns of (reduced) health care utilization and purchasing postponement following denied health coverage, and delayed care's possible exacerbation of the costs of medical care. Thus, here I highlight how coverage denials might not actually contain costs, but rather *shift* costs from payers to patients. Chapter 6 discusses physicians' administrative burdens associated with managing prior authorization administration, including associated staffing (and, in turn, financial) pressures. Chapter 7 examines the administrative burdens associated with appealing coverage denials and draws on survey and interview evidence to assess who appeals and who does so successfully. I additionally examine here the comparative administrative burdens of conducting additional appeals external to the health insurer, drawing on state-level public data. Chapter 8 considers the impact of coverage denials within the realm of mental health, and the apparent shortcomings of mental health parity legislation, drawing both on my survey and interview findings as well as on publicly available data and enforcement actions identified by ParityTrack. Chapter 9 offers conclusions about the scope and impact of this insurer practice on patients and providers and considers possible policy reforms to address the problems that this book illuminates.

Throughout the chapters, I will introduce (and reintroduce) the patients, physicians, and others with whom I spoke over the course of writing this book. All patient names have been anonymized for the purpose of this work, but their stories are real, and their struggles are reflective of a large patient population dependent on their insurance to access needed care within the private welfare state. They are the stories behind my data.

A NOTE ON METHODOLOGY

To study this underexamined problem of coverage denials in the American health care system from the patient perspective, I first conducted in April 2020 a pilot survey of 2,183 US adults with participation recruitment through Amazon's Mechanical Turk ("MTurk"), a popular survey recruitment method in social science studies.[147]

Though MTurk does not constitute a random sample, political scientists Connor Huff and Dustin Tingley[148] and others have found that the MTurk respondents are highly similar to those on other survey platforms, such that meaningful inferences can be gleaned from such studies.[149] I then conducted in May 2022 an original survey using the platform of SurveyMonkey, a leading non-traditional survey recruitment method.[150] Survey responses were gathered within the United States, across all ages, genders, races, and income levels. The price per response was $5.50, with a total of 1,340 respondents. Data were collected over the course of one week.

Researcher Frank Bentley and his coauthors find a survey error of 3.6 percent in SurveyMonkey surveys, compared with 8 percent in MTurk,[151] such that both methods compare favorably with survey methods that are slower and more costly to implement. They likewise find that both survey platforms provide diversity of ages, education, and income level, but tend to overrepresent college graduates, a fact that is likely attributable to the online nature of these surveys.

I combine the original survey data with analysis of state-level publicly available external appeal data and additional prior authorization data from state Medicaid programs, as well as 111 in-depth semi-structured interviews with patients, health care providers, patient advocates, health insurance lawyers, and people within (or formerly within) the insurance industry to assess the scope and impact of this insurance practice.[152] The snowball sample of 111 interviews was drawn from across the country (representing 28 states and the District of Columbia), with variation in age, race, socioeconomic background, gender identity, health insurance provider, and health status, reflecting the many facets of health insurance utilization in the United States (see the Appendix to Chapter 1 for additional discussion of interview methodology). When available, accompanying medical and insurance records were examined.

Interviewees were recruited through social media as well as word of mouth. While there are limitations of such an interview recruitment method, I do *not* claim that the interviewees constitute a representative sample of patients and health care providers, but rather the interviews offer important new insights into the human patient and physician experiences reflected in the survey of 1,340 individuals. Thus, while this analysis of coverage denials is not comprehensive, it offers a unique treatment of patients' and physicians' experiences navigating the challenges of coverage denials and the health care bureaucracy subsequently thrust upon them.

This mixed-methods approach – combining survey and administrative data along with thick description to highlight the challenges of navigating the American health insurance system – helps me to identify broader patterns of coverage denials and their impacts, as well as to bring to light the many and varied stories within the qualitative data, such as the following: the insurance salesperson who was unable to get approval for on-label use of a needed subcutaneous immunoglobulin (SCIg) for a rare immunodeficiency condition and needed to enlist the support of her US Senator; the mother of two who was unable to get approval for her son's enteral food despite his failure to respond to other food options, and who gave up trying to get coverage after multiple failed appeals; the mother who tried repeatedly to secure a communication device for her son with Down Syndrome; the disabled woman at high risk for breast cancer whose magnetic resonance imaging (MRI) was denied as being on an "experimental schedule" despite a prior approval, and who subsequently delayed seeking medical treatment; the multiple sclerosis patient who was bed-bound because of her insurer's refusal to cover longer-term physical therapy; the patient prescribed a wrist MRI with contrast only to learn that, while the contrast was covered, the scan was not.

And there are many more. Some interviews shed light on the trials of accessing care for the interviewees' conditions, and the discouragement of facing uphill battles in health care bureaucracy. Other interviewees shed light on the triumphs of overcoming red tape to access the care they sought.

CONCLUSION

This chapter has offered an orientation into the American exceptionalism of reliance not only on private insurance, but also on accompanying utilization controls such as prior authorization to curb America's propensity to spend and overtreat. These tools are no accident, but emerge from accumulated political choices to on the one hand expand access to health coverage, while on the other hand continuing to house substantial and even increasing authority in private insurers with fiduciary responsibilities to shareholders.

And, while misperceptions about appropriate care abound among patients, thus creating pressures for physicians in a litigious medical malpractice environment that can yield defensive medicine, additional challenges stem from the discretion-laden nature of definitions of medical necessity. This discretion then breeds uncertainty for patients and their physicians, who can be left to navigate an administratively burdensome health care bureaucracy in order to access what they believe to be appropriate medical care.

The product of this political environment is hundreds of millions of denials each year across medical, behavioral, and pharmaceutical benefits. In the chapter that follows, I turn more specifically to the types of denied care that survey and interview respondents experienced, and the ways that these insurer determinations disrupted the patients' care and broader lives.

CHAPTER 2

Causes and Types of Coverage Denials

We literally click and submit. It takes all of 10 seconds to do 50 at a time.

Cigna-employed doctor interviewed by ProPublica

"**M**Y HEALTH INSURANCE COMPANY AND I, we have a love–hate relationship, and we know each other pretty well," Jessica said. Working in insurance sales, Jessica marveled at the struggles she still faced in navigating the red tape of her employer-provided Blue Cross Blue Shield plan in Louisiana.

Jessica, a twenty-eight-year-old woman in New Orleans, Louisiana, was not a stranger to experiencing coverage denials, having been denied coverage for an X-ray because the insurer had not realized that her plan did not have a single in-network radiologist in the region. But her challenges became considerably more pronounced when she was diagnosed in 2019 with immunodeficiency, which precludes her from producing normal antibodies to bacteria. She is one of the 2.7 percent of Americans who currently experience immunosuppression.[1] The treatment is a subcutaneous form of immunoglobulin replacement therapy (SCIg), an infusion medication that replaces one's antibodies and that can bill for tens of thousands of dollars annually.[2] In light of its high price tag, it requires prior authorization.

"I got a denial right away when I was diagnosed and prescribed this medication," which was puzzling in itself and because Blue Cross Blue Shield even denied her physician the opportunity for a peer-to-peer review of the prescription (that is, a conversation between the prescribing physician and a physician employed by the insurer), which struck her as legally dubious. She was pursuing treatment in-network for what the Food and Drug Administration had approved as on-label use. From everything she could glean about her health insurance plan, which she read carefully, the treatment should have been covered. However, Blue Cross Blue Shield informed Jessica that she must experience a "life-threatening infection" before they would cover the drug.

It struck her as odd that her insurer would demand that such a dangerous event occur before she could be treated. *Did they also wait for diabetics to go into diabetic ketoacidosis before approving treatments?* she pondered.

Jessica's story would not end there: "I got two more denials of it before I was eventually able to get the treatment. And I had the assistance of my physician's office the entire time, as well as the specialty pharmacy. All of us were working on this together, going back and forth on group emails with updates on next steps and what was being sent. They were cc'ing me on PDF copies of their appeal letters." These denials went on for several months, requiring significant efforts to navigate the American health insurance system, and even reaching out to her US Senator for assistance.

Though Jessica's condition is rare, her story is not, and it highlights not only the adverse impact of insurance denials, but also the tremendous amount of knowledge, resources, and determination needed to sustain a successful challenge.

The KFF analysis of data reported by Centers for Medicare and Medicaid Services found that nearly one in five marketplace claims are denied each year by insurers, with that 19 percent representing an astonishing 73 million denied claims in the 2023 plan year alone.[3] And that just scratches the surface of the health insurance market, in which just 10.2 percent are enrolled in direct-purchase coverage, while 53.7 percent are enrolled in employer-provided coverage, 18.8 percent in Medicare, and 18.9 percent in Medicaid.[4]

Jessica's story and the broader findings on denied claims call attention to the importance of understanding the barriers that insured patients face in accessing prescribed care, which patients are most vulnerable to the practice of health coverage denials, and the extent to which this insurer practice varies across sources of health insurance. Having discussed in the previous chapter the political context in which this insurance practice arose, here I address this problem by drawing on my original nationwide survey evidence, supplementary data, and semi-structured interviews. Understanding vulnerabilities to, and the impact of, coverage denial through the lenses of administrative burdens and resulting inequities demands analysis from the patient perspective, which is lacking in academic analyses to date. To do this, I surveyed in May 2022 a sample of 1,340 US adults through the common non-traditional survey platform of SurveyMonkey.[5]

Survey research has both advantages and limitations in assessing this health policy problem. On the one hand, it allows for a unique evaluation of not only the prevalence of barriers to care, but also their inequitable effects, given the collection of wide-ranging demographic data. On the other hand, it is subject to some challenges, namely that it relies on patient recall about complex health insurance processes (processes that affected respondents in profound and personal ways, but complex nonetheless) and does not allow for an assessment of the overall volume of denials and appeals. That is, while it offers new insights into *who* is centrally bearing the costs of this health insurance privatization, it offers less in the way of system-wide analysis of the scale of the health policy problem.

What's more, SurveyMonkey's selection of survey respondents is not a random sample of the US population, thus demanding that the results be interpreted with caution, though it has been found to perform well compared with similar platforms such as Amazon's Mechanical Turk, "MTurk,"[6] and yielded findings nearly identical to my pilot survey from 2020. Given these constraints, I approach this health policy problem from multiple angles – survey data, administrative data, and interviews – which collectively paint a clear picture of substantial barriers that American patients, especially those from marginalized groups, face every day when trying to access care.

I begin by describing the survey itself and proceed to discuss more specifically the findings it produced.

THE SURVEY

In addition to collecting demographic information, respondents were asked about their health care utilization and self-reported health status;

Table 2.1 Summary statistics

Characteristic	Sample mean	National mean
Age	45	38
Female	57%	51%
White	63%	76%
Black	11%	13%
Hispanic	11%	19%
Asian	12%	7%
College-educated	51%	38%
Income	$70,000	$80,610
LGBTQ	17%	7%
English first language	90%	78%
Fair or poor health status	32%	19%
Insurance: marketplace	7%	6%
Insurance: Medicaid	9%	21%
Insurance: Medicare	18%	15%
Insurance: employer	50%	49%

whether they were denied medical coverage and, if so, for what service(s) and with what denial rationale; whether they appealed the coverage denial and, if so, whether they were successful; and to what extent, if at all, the coverage denial impacted their subsequent purchasing, health care utilization, and health status. The survey contained a total of fifty questions, most of which were multiple-choice (though not all respondents were directed to answer all questions). If respondents had *never* been denied coverage, they were not directed to answer questions beyond demographics, health status, and perceptions of the health insurance system. If respondents had been denied coverage, they were asked about whether they appealed (and, if so, the outcome), and the extent of health care and non-medical purchasing postponement. If they did not appeal, they were directed to answer a different set of questions about their rationale for not appealing. Respondents spent an average of seven minutes completing the survey.

Table 2.1 reports summary statistics of my sample, compared with the national figures as estimated by the United States Census, the Centers for Disease Control and Prevention, and KFF.

SURVEY RESPONDENT DEMOGRAPHICS. The average survey respondent age was forty-five years old, and respondents were broadly distributed from ages eighteen to over sixty-five. The sample skewed female (57 percent) and educated (51 percent college-educated),[7] but was largely nationally representative with respect to income (median household income of approximately $70,000) and relatively representative with respect to race (63 percent White alone, 11 percent Black, 11 percent Hispanic, and 12 percent Asian).

Thirty-two percent of survey respondents self-identified as being in fair or poor health, a higher rate than that estimated by the 2023 CDC Behavioral Risk Factor Surveillance System. Thirty-five percent reported as being under the care of a health care provider in the last twelve months for a physical health condition, and 24 percent reported as being under the care of a health care provider in the last twelve months for a mental health condition. This finding is consistent with an estimate that, in 2021, 22.8 percent of the population experienced mental illness.[8]

Survey respondents were close to nationally representative with respect to the main source of their health insurance,[9] with half of respondents indicating that they obtain their insurance through their or their partner's employer. Over half of respondents (54 percent) reported struggling to afford out-of-pocket medical costs either "most of the time" or "some of the time," a finding that is consistent with a December 2021 poll by KFF finding that 46 percent of insured Americans struggle to afford their out-of-pocket medical costs.[10]

Collectively, and in combination with the parallels to my pilot survey and my additional quantitative and qualitative data, this gives me confidence that I can obtain meaningful inferences from this sample of participants.

I turn now to discuss the survey's central substantive findings on the scope and rationale of coverage denials.

PREVALENCE OF COVERAGE DENIALS

It is perhaps unsurprising to see a high rate at which patients experience denials, given the complexity of medical decisionmaking. This vulnerability to denials may be exacerbated by evolving knowledge of treatments and their efficacy compared with their risk of harm, which can at times lead to dissensus as to necessary and appropriate courses of treatment. Thus, disagreements between medical professionals and insurers

Table 2.2 Coverage denials among MTurk and SurveyMonkey survey participants

	MTurk	SurveyMonkey
Denied coverage	34%	36%
Multiple denials for those denied coverage	62%	59%

regarding medical necessity may be inevitable, though this book focuses on the significant harm that these resulting denials have wrought for patients and physicians across the country because they lead to not only delays in care, but also administrative burdens of appeal.

After being surveyed on their demographics, health status, and overall level of health care utilization (as measured by whether they received a diagnosis in the last year and the annual frequency with which they see a physician), all respondents were asked whether they have ever been denied coverage for prescribed care. Thirty-six percent responded that they had experienced a denial, and of those respondents, 59 percent reported experiencing not one, but *multiple* coverage denials. I provide in Table 2.2 a side-by-side comparison of findings from the two surveys, illustrating a high degree of similarity across the two samples, bolstering my confidence in the findings.

While this is not a random sample of the US population, the findings through surveys using two widely used survey platforms support the assertion that the experience of coverage denials is highly pervasive – an observation in line with claim-level estimates about the large scale of this problem. In fact, taking into account these survey results as well as data from KFF and Optum, coverage denials directly affect over 100 million Americans across the nation every year – and that doesn't even account for the broader ways that families might be disrupted if – as was the case for Carol and Jason's daughter in Chapter 1 – one person among them is having medical care kept out of reach (if it is a prior authorization denial) or is facing unexpected accumulations of medical bills (if it is a claim denial). Sixty-seven percent of respondents were denied health coverage by their current health insurer (and for some, another insurer as well).

Blue Cross Blue Shield was by far the most common insurer in which respondents were enrolled (24.5 percent), while 12.3 percent were enrolled

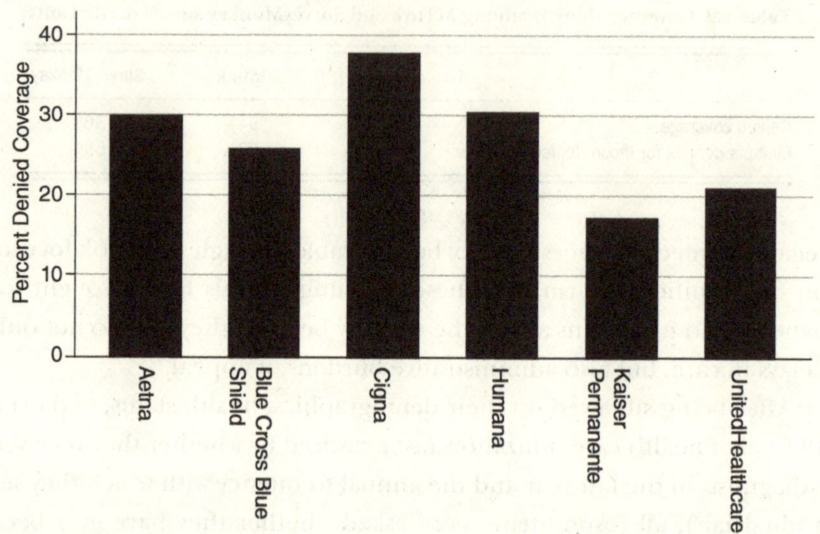

2.1 Denials by private insurer.
Source: Survey of the 482 respondents within the 1,340-person survey who experienced a coverage denial.

in UnitedHealthcare, 8.0 percent were enrolled in Aetna, 4.3 percent were enrolled in Cigna, 4.1 percent were enrolled in Kaiser Permanente, and 2.4 percent were enrolled in Humana. Figure 2.1 plots the proportion of coverage denials by each of the six most common private insurers in which survey respondents were enrolled. ValuePenguin released a report in 2024 finding that UnitedHealthcare denies at the highest rate – a whopping 33 percent of claims[11] – while Kaiser Permanente denies the least (6 percent)[12] – and, while I do not find that the UnitedHealthcare-enrolled survey respondents experience denials at the highest rates, I do find few denials among respondents enrolled in Kaiser insurance. What's more, ValuePenguin's assessment relies on a very different unit of analysis: while ValuePenguin evaluated the proportion of claims processed and denied, I evaluate only the proportion of survey respondents within those insurers' schemes who experienced one or more denials.

Figure 2.2 plots the proportion of respondents experiencing coverage denials, by whether they were enrolled in Medicare, Medicaid, or commercial insurance. The horizontal dashed line indicates the sample-wide average rate at which people experience coverage denials (36 percent). While there are not dramatically different rates at which respondents

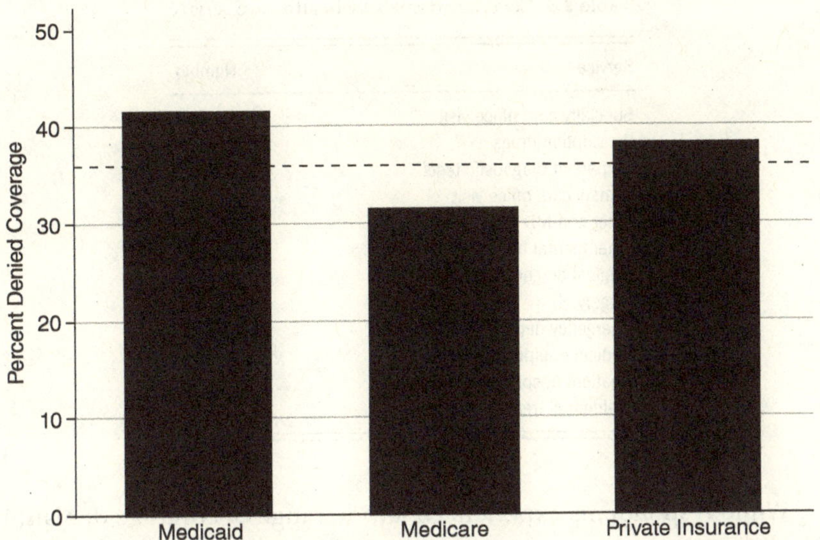

2.2 Percentage denied by insurance type.
Source: Survey of the 482 respondents within the 1,340-person survey who experienced a coverage denial.

experienced denials across insurance types, one can observe that Medicaid and commercial insurance appear to engage in this more frequently than Medicare, which is perhaps unsurprising given Medicare's very limited use of prior authorization, a prominent vehicle for denials. Further, it is consistent with other findings of traditional Medicare denying claims significantly less frequently (8.4 percent claim denial rate) than do other insurers (nearly 15 percent overall).[13] Of course, these are still quite different levels of analysis – that is, the patient level in this survey as opposed to the claim level more commonly analyzed, which point toward different types of insights about this health policy problem. However, what is clear is that this insurer practice is far from isolated to one subset of the American health insurance system.

All respondents who expressed that they had experienced coverage denials were asked about the medical services that were denied coverage by their insurer. They were permitted to select as many of the options as they had experienced, which was important because most of these individuals had experienced not just one, but *multiple* coverage denials. Table 2.3 reports the prevalence of coverage denials by health care service.

Table 2.3 Coverage denials by health care service

Service	Number
Specialty care office visit	83
Prescription drugs	69
Outpatient diagnostic tests	61
Primary care office visit	46
Other non-MD health care	46
Other mental health care	39
Surgical diagnostic tests	35
Surgery	33
Emergency department	31
Medical equipment	26
Inpatient hospitalization	21
Residential treatment	13

While respondents experienced a wide range of coverage denials, by far the most common health care services denied coverage were specialist office visits and prescription drugs. That prescription drugs would rank high on this metric is hardly surprising. After all, over 131 million (or 66 percent of Americans) use at least one prescription drug.[14] Thus, prescription drug users are a large population potentially vulnerable to this sort of denial. Not only are most Americans on a prescription drug, but also the Department of Health and Human Services Office of Science and Data Policy finds that approximately 20 percent of prescription drugs dispensed are for costlier brand drugs, which account for 80 percent of spending[15] and are more vulnerable to utilization management practices such as prior authorization and its subtype, step therapy (or "fail first"), which I discuss in greater detail in Chapter 4.

These prescriptions come with a hefty price tag: a September 2019 Gallup survey identified that 58 million Americans cannot afford their prescription drugs,[16] and a January–February 2024 KFF tracking poll found that 55 percent of Americans are "very worried" or "somewhat worried" about their ability to afford their prescription drugs.[17] Of course, this cannot disentangle whether people are struggling to afford their prescriptions because of high out-of-pocket costs (e.g., for brand drugs), or whether these difficulties stem from insurer decisions not to cover the prescribed treatments at all (whether for higher- or lower-cost drugs).

The broad sweep of these coverage barriers is not only apparent but reinforces inequities in the American health care system. While a January 2020 poll on income inequality released by NPR, the Robert Wood Johnson Foundation, and the Harvard T. H. Chan School of Public Health revealed that over a third of adults across all income groups say that, in the past year, they or a household member were told their health insurance plan would not cover a prescription drug,[18] KFF found in its January–February 2024 tracking poll that higher proportions of Black and Hispanic patients (compared with white patients) are worried about the cost of their prescriptions, and that substantially higher proportions of lower- and middle-income Americans struggle with prescription drug costs (as compared with those earning $90,000 or more annually).[19] Thus, while these difficulties affording care – potentially though not exclusively due to denials – are pervasive, this phenomenon also reinforces health and economic inequities.

While adjudicating between necessary and lower-value care is beyond the scope of this study, as Harvard T. H. Chan School of Public Health Professor Robert Blendon observed, "What you see is insurers are not paying for some drugs that physicians are recommending and that patients think they need."[20] And, as I demonstrate in the chapters that follow, these denials not only keep care and financial security out of reach for many (especially those who are lower income), but also result in patients and their physicians getting ensnared in the health insurance bureaucracy through which appeals are processed. They may even have work productivity and earnings disrupted due to time spent navigating this administrative complexity in the manner described by organizational behavior scholar Jeffrey Pfeffer and his colleagues, who characterize the "sludge" associated with accessing benefits.[21] While the survey data presented here provide only a limited picture of the extent of care denied by patients' insurers, they offer new insights into the breadth of services vulnerable to coverage denial by public and private insurers.[22]

Indeed, when asked to describe in their own words the health services denied, survey responses varied widely, including "childbirth costs," "a lung scan to rule out pulmonary embolism," "mental health meds," "vaccinations," "colonoscopy," "pain blocking injection," "pre-surgery testing," "routine blood work," and "ultrasound after placement of IUD."

Jackie knows all too well the frustration of being denied coverage for something as clearly medically indicated as vaccines. When taking her two-month-old son to the doctor for his scheduled vaccinations, she found that his vaccinations were denied by UnitedHealthcare despite being a covered benefit. Months of frustration would ensue for Jackie and her husband, who was a poorly paid doctoral student. They did not have the money to accommodate mounting medical bills. And, taking care of her infant son, she resented how many insurance staffers with whom she spoke acknowledged an administrative error but would not resolve her claim. While UnitedHealthcare eventually resolved most of the complaints, it would not be in time for all the damage to be rectified: she was on the hook for $500 for her son's vaccinations because the appeal had taken more than a year.

Jackie is not alone in this: in their analysis of claim denials in ACA marketplace plans in the 2023 plan year, researchers at KFF found that 18 percent of denials were for "administrative reasons" and 6 percent required resubmission, such as due to a billing code error. For some, these errors may not be resolved before payment is demanded.

Having examined the distribution of survey respondents' denials, I now turn to discuss in depth a select number of impactful domains in which survey and interview respondents experienced coverage denials. This will highlight the diversity of patient experiences with denials, which later chapters will show can affect some patients in particularly acute ways.

EMERGENCIES. Carol and Jason (from Chapter 1) were not alone in being denied coverage for emergency department care. Six percent of survey respondents were denied coverage for emergency department care.

What sets emergency department care apart from that in other settings is that insurers are meant to apply a "prudent layperson standard," according to which care will be covered if a "prudent layperson" would have had cause to believe that the condition required emergency attention. Thus, coverage is determined on the basis of the initial presentation of symptoms (e.g., chest discomfort) and not the final diagnosis (e.g., an anxiety attack or heartburn).

Applying the prudent layperson standard has not always been supported by health insurers. In a 2021 bulletin, UnitedHealthcare announced that it would begin to review emergency department claims for its 70 million policy holders on the basis of several factors, including the patient's presenting problem, the intensity of the diagnostic services that were performed, and complicating factors, with the ultimate assertion that "[c]laims determined to be non-emergent will be subject to no coverage or limited coverage in accordance with the member's Certificate of Coverage."[23] This proposed policy was estimated to yield a $32 billion savings opportunity per year, but led to considerable backlash,[24] with the American College of Emergency Physicians emphasizing that "[p]atients who fear having a true emergency should not be deterred from going to the emergency department." In fact, one estimate found that as many as one in ten emergency department claims might be denied under this policy, despite the Centers for Disease Control and Prevention finding that only 3 percent of emergency department visits are non-urgent.[25]

President and CEO of the American Hospital Association Richard J. Pollock offered a public denunciation of UnitedHealthcare's proposed policy, noting that it would have a "chilling effect on seeking emergency care" and that "[d]eferred and delayed care during the pandemic has already contributed to adverse health conditions and increased acuity," necessitating that the insurer instead adhere to the "prudent layperson standard."[26] Thus, it was asserted that this policy would not only inconvenience those who might otherwise seek emergency care, but also worsen health outcomes.

UnitedHealthcare was not the first to propose this policy. In May 2017, Anthem Blue Cross Blue Shield notified its Missouri policyholders that it would deny emergency department claims for services ultimately determined to be non-emergent, having already implemented similar policies in Kentucky in August 2015 and in Georgia in July 2017.[27] Under this policy, between July and December 2017, Anthem denied 6 percent of emergency department claims (12,000) as not medically unnecessary, a sharp increase from the previous half of the year. What's more, Anthem reversed the vast majority (73 percent) of Missouri emergency claim denials that were appealed, with similar findings in Kentucky and Georgia, which raised concerns about an "overly restrictive initial approach to reviewing ER claims."[28] This led several hospital groups, including the American Hospital Association, America's Essential Hospitals, the Federation of American Hospitals, and the Association of American Medical Colleges to express concern about Anthem's departure from the prudent layperson standard to wrongly deny claims.[29]

Even the "prudent layperson standard" would not have saved Jim from the debt he accrued by following his physician's advice to go to the local emergency department. A sixty-year-old high school math teacher in south Texas, Jim had been healthy until he developed a hernia that his surgeon had decided to monitor cautiously over the course of about a year. He hoped to schedule the procedure during winter break so that he would not need to take time off away from his teaching responsibilities.

However, after months of conservative monitoring, the hernia became incarcerated (or unable to be reduced), causing Jim "horrific" pain that he rated at an eight on a scale of one to ten. Jim called his surgeon, who advised that he go to the emergency department where he had admitting privileges, and where he would call ahead to have Jim admitted for surgery the next morning. Jim promptly followed his surgeon's advice but, before Jim arrived, there was a shift change and not all the pertinent information about his case was properly conveyed to the new team of doctors. Rather than admitting him, the doctors treated the hernia non-surgically with massage, ordered a CT scan to rule out a bowel obstruction, and sent him home. On Monday, Jim called his surgeon (who was understandably puzzled by Jim's discharge) and arranged for the surgery to be scheduled shortly thereafter, bringing Jim the needed relief.

But then Jim received a $2,900 hospital bill despite his insurance plan providing that emergency department visits would require only a $500 copayment. Blue Cross Blue Shield of Texas informed him that, on the basis of the coding submitted from the emergency department, he ought not to have gone to the emergency department in the first place. He thought, *Of course I was supposed to go there. My doctor told me to go.*

"No, it wasn't an emergency," they insisted.

From Jim's vantage point, he had done all the right things. He pursued a conservative, non-surgical course of action for months, he called his surgeon's office once he was in tremendous pain, and he followed his surgeon's directions to go to that emergency department.

Jim went back and forth over the phone between the hospital and the insurance company ("I felt like a ping pong ball") and submitted formal letters to his insurance company, along with a letter from the surgeon certifying that he had advised Jim to go to the emergency department for admission for surgery. These efforts proved fruitless: the insurer would not cover the emergency department charge. "I felt like I got blamed for going to the emergency room because I was in tremendous pain," an emotional strain that typifies the psychological costs of administrative burden.

Jim made a payment to forestall collections, paying the rest in installments rather than in a lump sum, but, with each payment, he received warnings about being reported to the credit bureau, only amplifying his growing anxieties within the American health insurance system.

SCANS. Thirteen percent of my survey respondents who experienced denials were denied coverage for outpatient diagnostic tests such as diagnostic scans. It is little wonder that prior authorization is utilized so heavily within the realm of high-tech imaging, given that not only are scans expensive (a lumbar spine MRI costs over $1,000 on average), but also several studies have suggested that as many as 20 percent to 50 percent of high-tech imaging procedures (e.g., CT scans, MRIs, PET scans) "fail to provide information that improves patient welfare," raising questions about the scope of unnecessary or low-value imaging services.[30] Prescribing low-value care can contribute to America's sky-high health care spending, such that there is an estimated $75.7 billion to $101.2 billion in wasted spending on overtreatment or low-value care.[31]

MRIs are a notorious realm of health care in which overprescribing is observed,[32] both driving up health care costs and straining health care systems such that there are longer waiting times for necessary MRIs.[33] But while scans *overall* may run the risk of being of low value, the extent of unnecessary MRI imaging appears to vary markedly depending on the underlying condition. Prior authorization has been found to contribute to slowed growth in the use of advanced imaging for Medicare beneficiaries between 2006 and 2009, though it is unclear whether this is attributable to less unnecessary prescribing or to treatment abandonment following denial.[34]

The question then becomes, *which* of the ordered scans fall under the umbrella of low-value care, and which ones are medically necessary and thus worthy of insurance coverage approval?

In some cases, denials can be in error, though such denials are no less disruptive to the patient experience of insurance bureaucracy. For Amir, a fifty-six-year-old man working in medical device sales in Maryland, Cigna's restriction on scans was not only deeply problematic, but also did not align with the facts of his case. Amir was diagnosed with two separate benign tumors – one on his brain, and the other around his masseter muscle (along the jawline) – with treatment by an ear, nose, and throat specialist (ENT) as well as a head and neck surgeon. The agreed-upon regimen on his previous health insurance plan was to monitor the tumor growth with MRIs every six months, a conservative "wait and see" approach. When switching to Cigna, the MRI prior authorization was denied on the bizarre, unfounded grounds that he had already had surgery to remove the tumor, and thus no longer required the scan. The problem was that the denial was for the scan of the tumor that had *not* been recently removed surgically. The insurer had mixed up which tumor was still present and thus required monitoring.

Sean's case was likewise frustrating, though the issue was attributable not to insurer error, but rather to the lack of a holistic review of his medical history. Sean, a supply chain executive in his early forties in the Chicago metropolitan area, has had three bouts of an aggressive form of stage IV synovial sarcoma, a soft tissue cancer that usually forms in one's extremities, but which in Sean's case is quite diffuse throughout his body. When Sean's company switched to Cigna, his PET scan to check for recurrence was denied.

While PET scans are not always prescribed with as much regularity as in Sean's case, he experienced cancer recurrence when on an every-six-months schedule, following which he had surgery and monitoring was switched to a schedule of PET scans every three months. After the prior authorization was declined, Sean called Cigna, which informed him that an internal medicine physician had reviewed his case and determined that the PET scan was not medically necessary. "The letter was very generic. 'Your cancer shouldn't need this PET scan because it is found in these parts of the body.' They had no knowledge of my medical history.

It didn't sit well with me," Sean reflected, fearful of another recurrence amid the insurance battle for otherwise prohibitively expensive care. He did not want to wait in the dark in anticipation of his next cancer recurrence.

"I had been worried that it wouldn't get approved because of the bureaucracy. I think the fact that I've had cancer three times and am a multiple time transplant recipient helped me get approval. But it shouldn't come to that."

DURABLE MEDICAL EQUIPMENT (DME). Just over 5 percent of the denials in my survey were for durable medical equipment (e.g., a wheelchair, CPAP devices, insulin pumps), and this is one of the few areas of medicine in which prior authorization is applied in traditional Medicare as well as other insurances. CMS holds that prior authorization within their realm of the health care industry "helps to protect the Medicare Trust Fund from improper payments while ensuring that beneficiaries can receive the DMEPOS [Durable Medical Equipment, Prosthetics, Orthotics, and Supplies] items they need in a timely manner." CMS lays out a master list of hundreds of such devices that may be covered by insurance but are subject to prior authorization.[35] Within the realm of durable medical equipment, survey respondents indicated that they were denied for leg braces, a knee brace, a boot in the aftermath of foot surgery, a powered wheelchair, a CPAP machine, and CPAP supplies.

Having established that over a third of the survey respondents experienced health insurance coverage denials, with denials spanning a broad range of prescribed health services, I now examine *why* patients were told that their prescribed care will not be covered, drawing on both survey and interview findings on these denials and their disruption of care.

RATIONALES FOR COVERAGE DENIALS

I asked each of the 482 respondents denied medical coverage what the health insurer had stated to specify why they issued the denial. Respondents were given the option of "Lack of medical necessity," "Services not covered," "Billing code error," "Lack of prior authorization,"

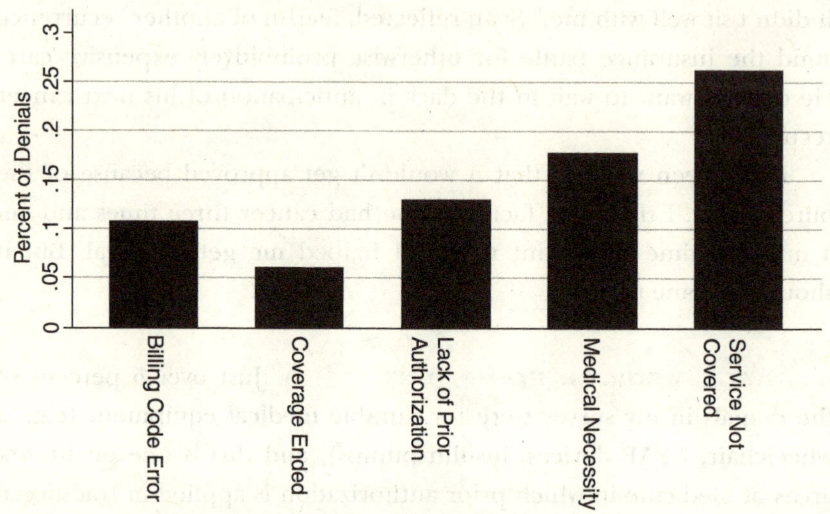

2.3 Distribution of rationales for coverage denial.
Source: Survey of the 482 respondents within the 1,340-person survey who experienced a coverage denial.

"Coverage had ended," or "Unable to recall." Of the 482 respondents, 158, or 33 percent, were unable to recall the rationale for their coverage denial(s), which is understandable in light of the complexity of health insurance decisionmaking and the generally low health literacy of the American public.

Figure 2.3 plots the distribution of responses of the remaining 324 survey respondents who could recall why they were denied coverage.

MEDICAL NECESSITY. Seventeen percent of respondents reported that they were denied coverage because their prescribed care was deemed to be not medically necessary. Services denied for lack of medical necessity ranged from scans to rule out a pulmonary embolism, to hospitalization following an emergency department visit, to prescription medication, to specialist appointments. Thirteen percent of the services denied for lack of medical necessity were for emergency department visits, and 27 percent were for prescription medications.

For Emily, the forty-nine-year-old disabled woman in Palm Beach County, Florida introduced in Chapter 1, the medical necessity denials felt deeply personal and insurmountable. Because she was suffering also from severe back spasms, Emily's doctor prescribed the muscle relaxant Tizanidine. Her insurer denied the medical necessity of the prescription on the grounds that she had not yet pursued physical therapy, which her insurer believed would be helpful for her condition. She was subsequently denied coverage for physical therapy on the grounds that she could instead be treated with Tizanidine, *the drug they had just refused to cover.* "What's the point of these processes? It was infuriating."

PRIOR AUTHORIZATION. Slightly less prevalent an explanation for denied care (13 percent) was that of a lack of prior authorization, though, to be sure, a subset of denials in other categories (e.g., medical necessity) were through the prior authorization process – that is, these categories overlap to some degree. Twenty-nine percent of the prior authorization denials in my survey sample were for outpatient diagnostic tests (e.g., CT or MRI scans), and 19 percent were for prescription drugs (though my survey does not differentiate between higher- and lower-cost prescriptions).

Prior authorization aims to not only confirm medical necessity and guard against unnecessary risk to the patient, but also (relatedly) protect against runaway health costs. Despite these rationales, the American Medical Association has referred to prior authorization as "overused, costly, inefficient, opaque and responsible for patient care delays" and calls for its reliance to be "greatly reduced." Moreover, an April 2022 Department of Health and Human Services Office of the Inspector General report found that 13 percent of Medicare Advantage's denied prior-authorization requests met the clinical coverage rules of traditional Medicare, and thus were not only denied, but *wrongly* denied[36] – a dynamic that later chapters will show can fundamentally disrupt patients' health and economic lives.

These prior authorizations are destabilizing for both patients and physicians. The opacity of the process is exacerbated by the inconsistency across insurance plans, such that "it's essentially a black box. It's learning by doing," reflected Montana family medicine physician Dr. Gabe Charbonneau.[37] And this uncertainty can produce denials that then take time and administrative burden to rectify.

For Emily, receiving prior authorization was not the end of her insurance battles. Knowing the health care system well, she went through the proper channels to see a neurosurgeon to receive spinal fusion, laminectomy, and removal of osteophytes to treat her paralysis after several emergency department visits and hospital admissions, and she received the prior authorization after five months of procedural delays. Approximately three months after the procedure was performed, the insurer retroactively deemed it "experimental," despite its initial prior authorization. "What was the point of getting the prior authorization if they're going to turn back around and refuse payment?"

EXCLUSIONS: "EXPERIMENTAL OR INVESTIGATIONAL." The most common explanation (26 percent) for denial of coverage that was offered by health insurers was simply that the services sought were not covered in their plan benefits, such as because the prescribed care was determined to be experimental or investigational for the patient's condition. This designation is given when there is insufficient evidence that prescribed care is safe and effective for its intended use, even if it has been approved for other uses. For example, there may be sufficient evidence to support a particular form of radiation treatment for cancer A, but it may be deemed experimental or investigational treatment of cancer B.

But what did "services not covered" include, among the survey respondents? A visit to the neurologist. Surgery to remove a tumor. An MRI. Mental health visits. Surgery for back pain. A prescription for migraines. Thus, the services denied under this rationale appear to extend beyond those that might be more obviously experimental. One challenge is that treatments are routinely prescribed for off-label use – that is, prescribing where there is evidence of benefits, but in the absence of Food and Drug Administration approval for this use. Though off-label prescribing is accepted medical practice, these treatments can be more vulnerable to an "experimental" designation and thus denied, a dynamic I explore in greater depth within the realm of prescription drugs in Chapter 4.

Nancy, a writer and journalist in her fifties, reflected on her unsuccessful battle to secure coverage for new-onset hearing loss following COVID-19 infection, "Winning an Emmy Award was easier than getting my insurance company to pay for my care."

She banged things on the kitchen counter, in anticipation of their familiar sounds, but she characterized her sensation as, "You know how when you get on a plane, and you can't pop your ears? That's what I've been living with for months. Everything feels underwater." This was not only frightening, but isolating for Nancy, a previously hearing person. This health-related anxiety and social isolation combined to lead Nancy to experience depression and suicidal ideation amid diminished ability to communicate.

After consulting with an ENT specialist, Nancy and her physician came to the mutual conclusion that, because neither steroids nor relieving the pressure on her eardrums had restored her hearing meaningfully, the appropriate path forward was a procedure called eustachian tube balloon dilation surgery, which involved putting a balloon in the eustachian tubes to open them up. The procedure first came into practice in 2010 and has been shown to be beneficial with respect to symptom relief as well as patient safety.[38] They scheduled the procedure for the following week, and the hospital pursued the prior authorization from UnitedHealthcare, which did not respond with a decision.

On the day of the procedure, she frantically contacted UnitedHealthcare as well as her doctor and the hospital, which assured her that her procedure could be performed.

Nancy was in her hospital gown in the operating room, connected to an IV drip. Within ten minutes of the scheduled time of the procedure, her surgeon looked at her, aghast. The surgery had just been denied, and UnitedHealthcare would not permit an emergency peer-to-peer review to explain the case over the phone to a physician employed by the insurer.

The doctor and nurses said they had never seen it come down to the wire like this before as they removed Nancy's IV, leaving her to cry on her way home, a medical bracelet still on her wrist but no surgery to show for it. *I can't believe I have to live with this deafness.*

The procedure was experimental and thus outside of the scope of her health plan benefits, despite the procedure being in practice for over ten years. When her ENT specialist pursued a peer-to-peer conversation with UnitedHealthcare, he found himself discussing Nancy's case with not a fellow ENT specialist, but a gynecologist who was unfamiliar with the treatment being pursued, and who again determined that coverage was inappropriate for this procedure. Nancy would suffer for several more weeks while a second-level appeal played out.

Whether health insurers are adhering to the scope of plan benefits is beyond the reach of this study, as denied services cannot be compared against survey respondents' and interviewees' individual insurance plan benefits and coverage guidelines. But the survey and interview findings raise questions about the ease with which patients can navigate obtaining health care within their *understanding* of their health insurance plans, especially in the context of discretion-laded determinations of medical necessity.

EXCLUSIONS: "COSMETIC" PROCEDURES. Emily was not the only one to have a medical condition seemingly erroneously designated by the insurer as "cosmetic." For some of the other patients whom I interviewed, surgeries to correct painful conditions were designated as "cosmetic" and thus not within the scope of their plan benefits. For Catherine, it involved the correction of a several-year-long jaw pain that impeded her ability to sleep well, remain physically active, and feel like herself again.

Catherine is a thirty-five-year-old attorney specializing in insurance defense and workers' compensation defense law and obtains health insurance coverage through her husband's employer. She has mandibular hypoplasia, which indicates that the jaw is underdeveloped and small, potentially impairing both eating and speech development. What's more, she described, "The bones were grinding on each other and wearing down, and it was causing these really excruciating headaches."

Catherine's first attempted treatment was braces in adolescence, and she obtained a set of retainers from an orthodontist, who did a set of X-rays and asked Catherine whether she experienced problems in the back of her jaw. Catherine said that she had, but for so many years, she didn't know why.

The recommendation was combined comprehensive orthodontics and orthognathic surgery (that is, corrective jaw surgery), with an estimated treatment length of eighteen months. She felt relieved when the prior authorization sailed through with Blue Cross in a matter of days.

But, months before the surgery was scheduled to occur, her husband took a new job, which offered health plans through UnitedHealthcare.

When the surgeon submitted the new prior authorization to UnitedHealthcare, after much delay, she finally got a letter saying it was denied, citing the Exclusions and Limitations section of her plan documents, which specified that among excluded services were jaw surgeries of a cosmetic nature.

Catherine's surgeon resubmitted the prior authorization along with documentation to support the necessity of this care to treat Catherine's symptoms, with her oral surgeon attesting to her chewing, speech, and breathing symptoms affecting her daily life, such that Catherine needed the treatment. What's more, he specified that it was a congenital anomaly and thus, "Due to the maxillomandibular dysfunction from this congenital anomaly, this surgery would be medically necessary."

Two months later, the appeal was denied again on the grounds that cosmetic procedures were excluded from plan benefits.

At first, she was unsure of what recourse she had. The second-level appeal was taking "forever" to get a determination, despite her placing countless phone calls to UnitedHealthcare to follow up regarding her case, only to get the runaround from entry-level employees. This was even more exasperating because Blue Cross Blue Shield *had approved the surgery as medically necessary.* "It furthered my belief that UnitedHealthcare's denial was not in good faith and that they were being intentionally obstructive."

Despite her own training as a lawyer, Catherine still felt frustrated and daunted by the cumbersome bureaucracy, with each UnitedHealthcare response adamant that coverage was inappropriate because it was cosmetic.

Yet, absent treatment, Catherine experienced debilitating headaches. "There were days that I would only be able to work a couple of hours before I would have to stop. It was so bad that I couldn't concentrate on anything. On a lot of days, I couldn't eat much because it was too painful to chew. I was constantly taking Tylenol or Aleve for the headaches, which is not good for your liver or your stomach."

Catherine broke down in tears out of frustration. "I'm not really a crier, but it was so emotionally overwhelming. I couldn't keep living like this." Ultimately, the second-level appeal was likewise denied, leading her to reach out to the Department of Insurance, where a staffer informed her, "They deny everything without reviewing it. Don't waste your time." Instead, she pursued an independent medical review, for which she obtained additional letters from dentists who had treated her dating back to her childhood, and who attested to her having had that condition for as long as they had treated her and that it had posed problems: "She has had occlusal and muscular problems for all of the [twenty years]. Now, as an adult, she has difficulty incising and chewing food. She also has pain and soreness associated with chewing and this malocclusion has had negative effects on her speech and breathing. These problems affect her daily life and are not limited to any one area …. It is my belief that she does need treatment for this problem based on her symptoms."

About a month later, the letter from the independent medical review surgeon stated that the surgery was medically necessary and thus should be covered: "The prime surgical indication is to restore normal physiologic function … as well as to relieve the other functional impairments …. There is no primary cosmetic indication involved." Nine months after the initial prior authorization was denied, Catherine was finally able to schedule her jaw surgery.

But the eventual approval did not entirely assuage Catherine's broader anxieties about her health insurance. "If they're going to deny this, what's going to be the next thing that I need treatment for that they're going to deny?" Catherine had lost something greater than confidence in her insurance plan's willingness to treat her long-time ailment. What she had lost was trust in the system itself.

That burdens in navigating access to health care could diminish this trust was contemplated in the Biden Administration's 2024 Burden Reduction Report, "Tackling the Time Tax: Making Important Government Benefits and Programs Easier to Access," which reflected on the impact of adverse interactions experienced by people seeking to access government programs, and policy interventions to mitigate this burden. Indeed, the analysis by the Office of Management and Budget observed that "[a]dministrative burdens do not just keep eligible individuals from accessing programs: they also sap Americans' trust in the ability of government to meet their basic needs or operate efficiently or fairly."[39] Burdens within the private insurance setting put this analysis more squarely within political scientist Suzanne Mettler's "submerged state" analysis of public policy, potentially making it more likely that denied patients would extend their frustrations and diminished trust to disengagement from civic life. However, patient stories of repeated adverse interactions with health insurers make clear the ways that these negative experiences could color one's perception of the fairness of the system through which one seeks to access health care.

Catherine's story of wrongful denial on these grounds is not anomalous. The *New York Times* profiled patients whose reconstructive surgeries were deemed cosmetic and thus outside of the scope of their health plan benefits.[40] Misconceptions about that which constitutes purely cosmetic medical care leave some patients to, as Catherine and her providers did, rely on a high degree of health literacy to navigate a complex health insurance bureaucracy to access care.

These were not the only reasons why survey respondents indicated that they were denied coverage. Eleven percent were denied coverage due to a billing code error. To be sure, this type of denial is generally distinct from those grounded in medical necessity or prior authorization, in which there is an insurer challenge to a physician determination of appropriate medical care. But, as I discuss in future chapters, it nevertheless brings patients into the very same sphere of denial appeals and care postponement, navigating a complex health insurance system that many patients said required of them a Herculean effort when they were at their worst.

An additional 6 percent of respondents were denied coverage because their insurer determined that their coverage had terminated – that is, they had been disenrolled. Tens of thousands of Americans each year are dropped from their health plans over payment issues,[41] and others are dropped through administrative error. The risk of being erroneously dropped from coverage is noteworthy in the case of Ohio's Medicaid program, which in 2022 was given a shortened time frame for determining the eligibility of its 3.1 million enrollees, leading to the possibility that "[e]rrors could cause many eligible enrollees to lose their Medicaid coverage."[42] And physician and health services researcher Benjamin Sommers and his coauthors show that the administrative burdens of demonstrating compliance with state-imposed Medicaid work require-ments can result in coverage losses *despite compliance with the program requirements.*[43]

These coverage denials – with some rationales clearer and more expli-cable in the eyes of patients than others – come with psychological costs, which I now discuss.

THE PSYCHOLOGICAL TOLL

Public policy scholars Pamela Herd and Donald Moynihan character-ize psychological costs (a component of administrative burden) as com-prising the stigma of participation in public programs, as well as the sense of a loss of autonomy in interactions with these programs, and the associated stresses and frustrations.[44] These costs are no less apparent when the analysis is expanded to private insurance, and my survey and interview evidence consistently highlighted the emotional toll that each denial wrought as patients grappled with how to access what they per-ceived to be needed care.

Each of the 482 survey respondents denied coverage was asked, "Please describe in your own words how you felt after your coverage was denied." Respondents offered such answers as "a prisoner," "frus-trated, hopeless, fearful," "defeated," "crushed," "left without options," "confused. I feel like I have no real understanding of how 'medically necessary' is determined," "felt like I was being farmed for money," and "sad and stressed, I cried a lot, I felt taken advantage of." Still others expressed fear that they would be unable to get specific treatments for conditions such as a pulmonary embolus or a heart problem requiring surgery. Yet another expressed their efforts to be as health literate as possible, to no avail when seeking to utilize their insurance: "I do get mad and frustrated because I try to be careful and read the schedule of benefits to understand the things that are covered."

"There's a feeling of helplessness," one respondent wrote, echoing the sense of overwhelm expressed by many others such as the interviewee Isabelle, who was not well-acquainted with insurance denials when her twelve-year-old daughter began to have a twenty-minute-long episode of supraventricular tachycardia (SVT). SVT is a type of cardiac arrhythmia that causes a very fast or erratic heartbeat (usually between 150 and 220 beats per minute), and, while it is not usually life-threatening absent other cardiac conditions, if severe, it has the potential to lead to cardiac arrest.[45]

At the cardiologist's recommendation, Isabelle took her daughter to the emergency department at Connecticut Children's Medical Center in Hartford. There, the doctors unsuccessfully attempted vagal maneuvers, then sent her to the cardiac intensive care unit (CICU) for overnight observation, where it was recommended that she get an eventual cardiac ablation (a minimally invasive procedure designed to restore a normal heartbeat) in the event of SVT recurrence. This seemingly life-threatening situation was "intense and traumatic" enough, but then, shortly after the hospital visit, she received a letter stating that the CICU observation was not medically necessary.

"I hadn't even recovered from the sleep deprivation. And there was this upsetting dissonance, having the most major health crisis that my child had had, that seemed in the moment to be life-threatening, and then getting this letter saying that they didn't need to keep her in the hospital. It was scary in the sense that I might get this big bill, and it was incredibly angering because it was going to take me so much time to sort out and I'm going to have to fight this, and it's going to be a pain in the ass. They're telling me that this horrible experience doesn't count as serious," Isabelle recounted.

These anxieties are not isolated to the initial denial. There would continue to be weeks of anxiously waiting for another shoe to drop as they pursued the cardiac care her daughter now required.

I sought through my survey to understand the extent to which respondents' anxieties about coverage denials were isolated to that which they experienced, or whether it reshaped their perspective on their insurance and the extent to which it will cover their future care. Each survey respondent who had experienced at least one denial was also asked, "How concerned are you that you will experience more denials in the future?"

Just 23 percent of survey respondents indicated that they were "somewhat unconcerned" or "very unconcerned" about experiencing subsequent coverage denials. Thus, patients appear to experience not only anxieties surrounding the initial denial, but also uncertainty about how their health plan benefits will be reviewed in incidents to come, and are fearful of what the future may hold for them. These anxieties are even more pronounced among those who were denied coverage for more costly treatment: while 49 percent of those denied coverage feared facing more denials, 78 percent of those survey respondents denied for care exceeding $5,000 expressed this anxiety. Indeed, the survey and interview evidence combine to show that experience of denials disrupted patients' broader trust in the American health care system.

Isabelle is not the only patient I interviewed who expressed the psychologically taxing nature of fighting denials that were not only expensive, but also implicated their child's health. For Carol and Jason (from Chapter 1), the psychological cost manifested itself not only in fear for their daughter's health and their financial security, but also in shame. Not only did they feel ashamed and embarrassed at their inability to pay for their children's vision exams (let alone urgent care) if their insurer again challenged its coverage as it had in the past, but also, having had this experience of a denial, Carol delayed treatment for conditions ranging from a gallbladder problem to a kidney stone so as to avoid accruing any additional medical debt and its accompanying stressors. "It's all just so heart-wrenching. *This is my life.* It's such a demeaning process, jumping through these hoops, especially when we already pay this much every month for our insurance."

These stresses can be particularly pronounced for those not naturally adept at navigating bureaucracies, as Angela reflected on when unsuccessfully appealing to obtain coverage for her son's enteral formula: "I'm not naturally well-organized. I have ADHD and to devote this persistent time and energy to this, it takes a lot. And I don't like confronting people. I like to be pleasant," and she would be simultaneously consumed with stress and guilt as she repeatedly hounded her family's insurer.

Having elaborated on the rationales for coverage denial in my nationwide survey and interview evidence, as well as the psychological havoc it can wreak for American patients, I turn to analyze the extent of denials within two states, Louisiana and Iowa, across emergent, non-emergent, and pharmaceutical treatment.

DENIALS IN THE STATES

In addition to the survey and interviews in which I analyze health insurers' denial of coverage for prescribed care, I draw on administrative data from the states of Louisiana and Iowa, both of which have publicly available data for multiple years on the rate at which claims are denied by managed Medicaid organizations. One of the challenges of utilizing government data within states is that only eleven states publicly report information on denials and appeals, and just nine of those states report on the outcomes of those appeals, making difficult a comprehensive analysis.[46]

Within Louisiana, one can see in Figure 2.4 a relatively high rate (as high as 24 percent) at which Medicaid managed care entities denied medical claims in non-emergency contexts between 2016 and 2021, with (not surprisingly) quite sparing emergency department denials, likely attributable to prior authorization not being applied in emergency conditions.

In addition to the overarching observation that approximately one in five claims in Louisiana is denied by managed Medicaid entities, the Louisiana Department of Public Health finds that these entities are more likely to spend more time reviewing claims if they are going to accept

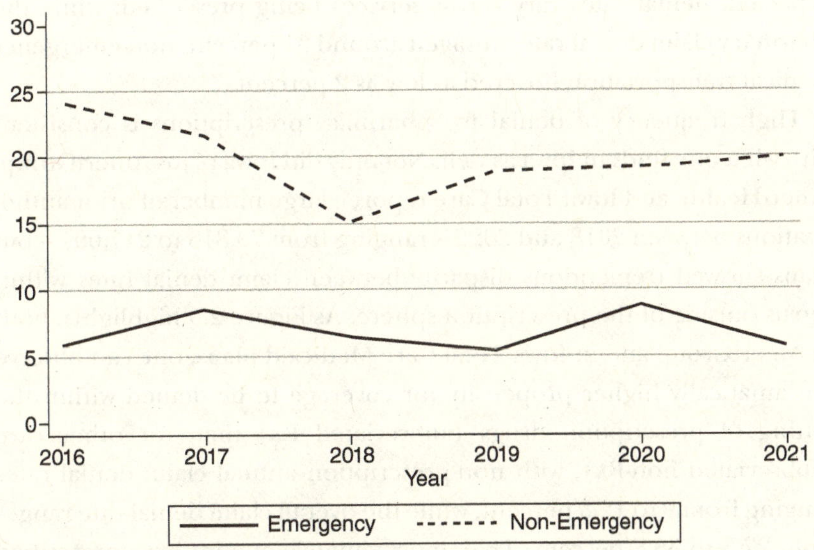

2.4 Claim denial rate in Louisiana, 2016–2021.
Source: Louisiana managed Medicaid data, 2016–2021.

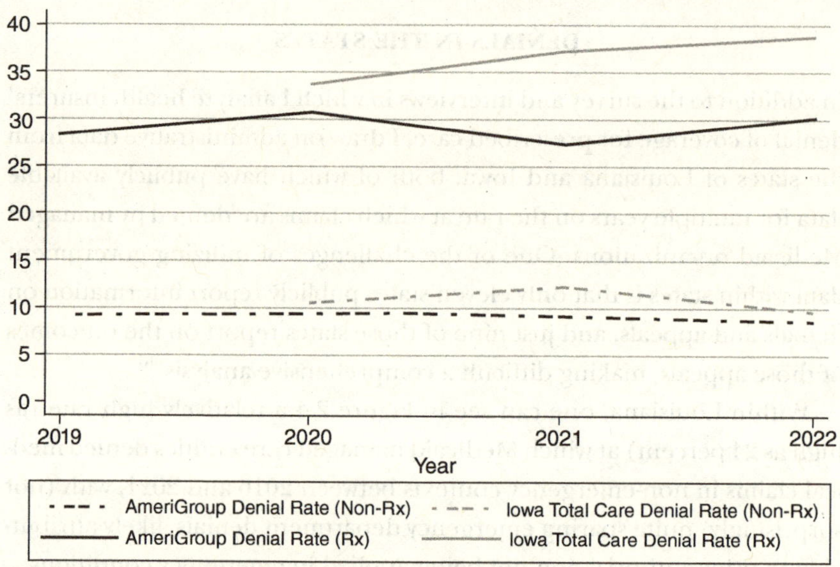

2.5 Iowa denials in Rx and non-Rx settings, 2019–2022.
Source: Iowa managed Medicaid data, 2019–2022.

them than if they are going to deny them: in 2021 and 2022, managed Medicaid entities took an average of 5.9 days to deny a claim, compared with 7.8 days spent reviewing a claim that would be accepted.[47] And, as expected, denial rates vary across services being prescribed: while the pharmacy claim denial rate averaged around 31 percent, non-emergency medical transportation hovered as low as 2 percent.

High frequency of denial for pharmacy prescriptions is consistent with what one finds in Iowa as well. Not only did Iowa plans AmeriGroup, AmeriHealth, and Iowa Total Care report a large number of prior authorizations between 2018 and 2022 – ranging from 78,818 to 217,007 – but plans showed tremendous disparity between claim denial rates within versus outside of the prescription sphere. As Figure 2.5 highlights, both in AmeriGroup and in Iowa Total Care Medicaid plans, one can observe a dramatically higher propensity for coverage to be denied within the setting of prescription drugs (abbreviated Rx) than for other care (abbreviated non-Rx), with non-prescription annual claim denial rates ranging from 9 to 12.3 percent, while the overall claim denial rate ranges from 27.3 to 38.8 percent. That approximately one in three prescribed services gets denied by managed Medicaid plans in Iowa lays bare the reality of Medicaid recipients' experience of barriers to health coverage and, in turn, care.

What's more, a federal audit revealed that not all these denials in Iowa were indeed appropriate: the Office of the Inspector General found, for a sample of 100 prior authorization denials and appeals for requested medical services between 2018 and 2019, that 20 were inappropriate.[48] Of these twenty inappropriate denials, nineteen involved AmeriGroup not complying with federal and state requirements that enrollees be provided with correct or any information regarding their rights of appeal, and one involved AmeriGroup's inability to provide documentation to support the denial. The provision of this information is essential when taking into consideration the simultaneous complexity of the American health insurance system and the generally low health literacy of the American public, factors that combine to make it difficult to understand what is covered, why something was denied, and what avenues of recourse are available.

This federal audit highlights the problematic reality that some patients are denied the information to make informed decisions about whether to appeal denials of coverage for their prescribed care, which may be why appeal rates are quite low despite – as the Office of the Inspector General found in the context of AmeriGroup – 62 percent of appeals in this segment of the Iowa Medicaid market being successful.[49] These government failures to provide appropriate information about available options can not only damage patients seeking to access prescribed care that they understand themselves to need, but also undercut patients' trust in the insurance system on which they rely.

I have now established that a large number of claims and prior authorizations are denied throughout the managed care system, and that this can be disruptive to patients' physical and psychological state. It is helpful now to consider these findings in light of the overarching concerns about overtreatment and health care cost containment.

OVERTREATMENT AND CONTROLLING HEALTH CARE COSTS

That her health insurer was second-guessing her physician's clinical judgment frustrated Sarah, a medical doctor-turned-venture capitalist in

Berkeley, CA. But she also suspected that the procedure prescribed in her case was not medically necessary.

Sarah tried with her husband for a year to get pregnant, and, after she had a positive home pregnancy test, she was eager to get established with prenatal care. At her OB-GYN appointment around her eighth week of pregnancy, her physician's office did a urine dip pregnancy test, confirming her pregnancy. The doctor then told her that they would perform a transvaginal ultrasound scan. This puzzled Sarah, given how early in the pregnancy she was,[50] and she asked to confirm that the procedure was covered by her insurance, after which she consented.

Soon thereafter, she received a $500 bill for the ultrasound scan, which was deemed to be not medically necessary on the grounds that she was not pregnant, despite the pregnancy having been confirmed during that visit. Sarah suspected that the ultrasound scan was not actually necessary so early in her pregnancy, but she also felt her insurer was wrong to deny the prenatal care upon which her doctor insisted. It was an administrative error that would take months to correct, requiring a payment to avoid an adverse effect on her credit report.

But this raises the question of whether coverage denials constitute *wrongful* second-guessing of valid physician judgments, as opposed to reasonable efforts by health insurers to guard against rising health care costs associated with overtesting and overtreatment.

According to health policy researcher Shannon Brownlee, the path to overutilization of health care has been complex, a product of Americans' simultaneous belief that medicine has become all powerful and distrust toward doctors disinclined to do more prescribing even when that prescribing is not evidence-based.[51] That is, there is a perception, sometimes a misperception, among patients that more care equals better care. And, as Ezekiel Emanuel and Victor Fuchs (physician and economist respectively) observe in the *Journal of the American Medical Association*, distrust in the health care system is reciprocated, with physicians fearful of medical malpractice litigation or complaints about failure to treat.[52]

Thus, legal liability is no small piece of this puzzle. In her seminal analysis of the "big business" of the American health care system in *American Sickness*, Elizabeth Rosenthal observes that part of the explanation for overprescribing in the United States is that "American patients desire this kind of high-priced exploration and treatment; they want their illnesses fixed on the spot. Doctors worry about missing something and getting sued. Runaway testing and ancillary treatment are not only culturally desirable and, perhaps, legally prudent but also lucrative."[53] Physician researcher Leonard Berlin likewise observes parallels between malpractice lawsuits and the practice of defensive medicine, which can lead to overdiagnosis,[54] though economists Frank Sloan and John Shadle find minimal effect of malpractice reform on prescribing when examining Medicare data from 1985 to 2000.[55]

This finding notwithstanding, health law professor David Studdert and his coauthors find, through surveying physicians in high-liability medical specialties, that the vast majority practiced defensive medicine that fell under the umbrella of "assurance behavior," such as ordering additional tests and diagnostic procedures, or referring patients for consultation to specialists, and that these practices in medicine were correlated with anxieties about medical malpractice insurance.[56] Thus, while the findings of malpractice liability's effects on physician prescribing are not consistent, there is suggestive evidence that it can reshape the practice of medicine – and, in turn, insurers' utilization review.

Elizabeth Rosenthal further confronts how the American health care system creates perverse incentives that can drive overutilization. Within the context of orthopedic devices, she observes that "the most effective way to make sure that the newest, most expensive products end up in the highest number of patients was in forming tight, codependent relationships with orthopedic surgeons," with manufacturers marketing heavily to doctors, leading many to take "a bite of the apple," given the ability to reap profit.[57] Extending her analysis to the context of MRI prescribing, Rosenthal notes one radiology resident observing that they were being asked to order more MRIs at great cost to patients, despite the patients not presenting features that textbooks and lectures had defined as requiring medically necessary follow-up. What's more, reliance on such radiology services conveniently declined after Medicare and other insurers reduced payments.

Thus, while multiple factors contribute toward the physician's decision to prescribe their patient a given test, including their judgment of medical necessity, "the doctors (perhaps) and the hospitals (definitely) directly profited from the ordering of more MRIs,"[58] a trend that insurers have since resisted, albeit in ways that leave patients in precarious positions. This overutilization is disproportionately aimed at well-insured Americans – leading policy analyst Judith Garber to raise the question, "Do rich patients get better care, or just more care?"[59] – while poorer individuals are less likely to obtain recommended screenings.[60]

Physicians are aware of the pervasiveness of overtreatment in the United States. Physician and health services researcher Heather Lyu and her coauthors surveyed 2,106 physicians about health care overutilization and its implications for health care in the United States, with overtreatment constituting preventable harms for patients as well as waste in the health care system. They find that 21 percent of medical care was judged unnecessary, including 22 percent of prescription medications, 25 percent of tests, and 11 percent of procedures, with an overall perception that at least 15–30 percent of medical care is unnecessary.[61] In fact, one estimate finds that unnecessary scans alone come with a hefty price tag of potentially $35 billion wasted each year,[62] in a health care system that is an outlier in its high spending.

Political scientists Eric Patashnik, Alan Gerber, and Conor Dowling likewise find that many common medical treatments are not based on sound science, and have the potential to cause patient harms, such that "[o]nce doctors decide that a particular treatment 'works,' it can become 'locked in,'" despite ongoing scientific developments that might suggest changing course.[63] That is, medical practices can become entrenched, failing to be updated when new information about their efficacy comes to light. They note further that reducing sixty-five-year-old and older patients' overuse of low-value treatments could help to control the growth of Medicare spending.

A notorious example of this overprescribing dynamic that they explore is arthroscopic knee surgery to treat osteoarthritis, a procedure that at one point was the preferred treatment, but which was found to perform no better than sham surgery (a fake operation), a finding that did not result in the discontinuation of this procedure.[64] In fact, 750,000 such procedures are performed annually in the United States, at a cost of $4 billion.[65] This failure to respond adequately to new clinical findings is attributable in part to the "unhealthy politics" surrounding efforts to address reliance on medical evidence, with federal politicians taking only modest actions toward the identification and elimination of wasteful and unnecessary services between the 1970s and the late 2000s.

While the Patient-Centered Outcomes Research Institute (PCORI) was established through the Affordable Care Act in an effort to promote research on comparative effectiveness in prescribing, with the goal of reducing wasteful spending in the American health care system, Patashnik observes that PCORI has been "comparatively ineffective," failing to drive significant change in clinician decisionmaking.[66] He attributes this shortcoming to the significant political, financial, and cultural impediments to incorporating new medical evidence in the American health care system. Despite this perpetuation of non-evidence-based medicine, there remains high public confidence in doctors, and the support of physician organizations is critical to the success of efforts toward comparative effectiveness research.[67]

Overtreatment in American medicine can have sweeping effects, with Patashnik, Gerber, and Dowling observing that the medical evidence problem harms not just marginalized groups, but rather all Americans, even those covered by generous health insurance plans and whose physicians do not follow best practices.[68] The challenge becomes determining the best way to mitigate these harms to the American health care system and the patients within it.

Imposing prior authorization requirements can, at least on the face of it, appear to be an effective way to impose guardrails on physicians' prescribing habits, helping to ensure the appropriateness of prescribed care. However, Wendell Potter, former Vice President of Corporate Communications for Cigna, expressed skepticism, noting, "It's the narrative everyone has bought into. Of course, there is no doubt that there are doctors who overtreat. And a lot of doctors, when a patient insists on a given treatment or medication, have some concerns about being sued for malpractice. But what has happened is prior authorization has become very big business, and insurance companies have figured out how to profit on prior authorization," beyond focusing on the patient care elements of the health care problem.[69] That is, while there is general agreement on the problem, the question is whether prior authorization constitutes an appropriate – and appropriately tailored – solution.

While prior authorization implementation may constrain costs by reducing this overprescribing, there has been limited analysis of cost savings to insurers. Potter continued, "They've bought into the narrative that the way we're doing things is necessary, without stepping back and analyzing whether there's a better way to make sure that people are getting the right care that they need and not being undertreated or overtreated."

In fact, according to Potter, the insurers' incentive to deny can extend beyond the immediate concerns of fraud, abuse, and overtreatment, to address not simply cost containment but rather profit maximization. In addition to the subjectivity of claim review based on potentially unclear medical necessity guidelines, there can be internal pressures to deny coverage despite the absence of explicit instructions to do so. "You need to do your part to make sure that the company is meeting profit expectations. It's making sure that shareholders are happy and that the company can achieve profitable growth – not just growth, but *profitable* growth – and that the people doing medical management are making sure that unnecessary care is not covered. If you become an outlier in the company, that will get noticed. You always want to be seen as a team player. Otherwise, it could be detrimental to your career." This observation is consistent with *ProPublica* findings on the speed with which Cigna doctors were pressured to process claims sufficiently efficiently: "Deny, deny, deny. That's how you hit your numbers."

Thus, while there are real reasons to guard against prescribing – especially that which has a limited evidence basis – not only do some of the patient narratives presented thus far highlight that destabilizing errors can arise in the setting of insurer discretion, but also there is limited internal accounting of the profitability of implementing this utilization management. I turn now to evaluate an unintended consequence that can arise for patients and their insurers: that overly rigid insurance guidelines can compromise cost containment objectives.

THE UNINTENDED CONSEQUENCES OF REDUCING OVERUTILIZATION. Ironically, denials often do not always track with cost control: when Raul's wife needed shots of Heparin, a common blood thinner, to address an uncommon, miscarriage-causing clotting disorder, the Heparin was denied, while the hematologist's alternate prescription of the *more* expensive Lovenox was approved.

There is the additional possibility that delays in care resulting from prior authorization could be associated with more expensive treatment at a later point, a concern echoed by gastroenterologist and Governor of the American College of Gastroenterology Dr. Tauseef Ali: "In chronic illness, there are the conditions where you can't put 'life-threatening' as a way to expedite authorization, but we all understand the critical nature of the timing of a prescription. If you don't treat promptly, they could end up in urgent care or the emergency room …. Patients will have more disease progression, getting admitted to the hospital."[70]

Even when there are not *complications* per se, more expensive tests may become necessary, further increasing America's (and Americans') health care costs. For example, when Veronica was unable to obtain coverage for a minimally invasive $250 "experimental" stool test to assess a Crohn's flare-up, despite efforts to appeal the denial, she instead was directed to obtain a colonoscopy (the cost of which was about $2,500). And, in the context of prescription drugs, physician researcher Jeffrey Kotzan and his coauthors lament that "[t]he long-term impact of PA programs has not been documented. If the drug programs are devised solely based on economic consideration without regard for medical consequences, then it is likely that more expensive services will replace those expensive drugs removed from the formulary."[71] Thus, utilization management controls can incur both health and monetary costs.

The relationship between cost containment and prior authorization can be strained in part due to the American health care system's fragmentation. With authority divided between medical benefits and pharmacy benefit managers (not to mention carve-outs between physical and behavioral health benefits), the insurance entity aiming at cost savings on a drug might not assess the risk of losing money on a hospitalization resulting from denied or suboptimal treatment. Thus, even when relying on utilization management, health care fragmentation can not only confuse and frustrate patients, but also work against insurers' potential cost savings.

Patient churn throughout health insurers further contributes to this problem. A 2016 Finn Partners nationwide survey of 1,000 patients found that half of respondents had changed health insurers within the prior three years.[72] Some patients might find a better deal on the Affordable Care Act marketplace; they might change employers; their employer might change the insurers with which they contract; or the patient might age into Medicare (that is, turn sixty-five). In this setting of frequent churn (or coverage instability), insurers may not take ownership of the patient's preventive health. In this setting, up-front investments to lower hemoglobin A1C (e.g., paying for a continuous glucose monitor) may not be viewed as an efficient use of resources because complications arising from poorly managed diabetes may not arise until the patient is on another insurance plan.[73] Thus, churn can not only undercut efforts to provide effective health care[74] for a patient pool that is typically a significant utilizer of health care services,[75] but also fuel myopic decisionmaking on the part of insurers aimed at maximizing quarterly profits at the price of not covering preventive care that has a good longer-term return on investment.

A challenge with efforts at curbing "unnecessary" treatment is the aforementioned discretion in medical necessity judgments as well as the reality that the practice of medicine is both art and science. What's more, returning to Elizabeth Rosenthal's point, patients themselves are not easily able to assess what constitutes a "medically necessary" test versus one that can be avoided or postponed with more conservative treatment in the interim – an issue at the heart of patient pressures for physicians to *do something*. Patients rely on their trusted physicians to make that medical assessment and find themselves frustrated if not overwhelmed at having to jump through administrative hoops to secure their prescribed care. In a setting of overprescribing, the result can be that patients are caught in the middle between their physicians and a risk-averse health insurer seeking to guard against what it perceives (correctly or not) to be wasteful spending, even if that view has sometimes arisen from looking only at an incomplete picture of the patient's medical history.

This book does not attempt to adjudicate between patients' "necessary" and "unnecessary" pursuits of medical treatment, nor should it. What it *does* attempt to do is highlight the human impact of resulting coverage denials on patients and their physicians. The tensions between physicians' clinical judgments and insurers' assessments of medical necessity may help to reduce waste in the system, but they also impose new burdens on patients and physicians alike. I explore these burdens in Chapters 5 and 6.

CONCLUSION

Though prior studies examined the prevalence of coverage denials within smaller segments of the health insurance system, extant studies had not compared this practice across public and private insurance, across health care services rendered, and across denial rationales. Moreover, while prior studies examined the practice of denials at the claim level, scholars had not examined these experiences at the patient level. Doing so is important because it highlights not just the overall prevalence of this patient experience, with over a third of survey respondents experiencing at least one denial (and often more), but also the physical and psychological toll it takes to subsequently navigate the American health insurance system.

The pervasiveness of coverage denials – affecting 36 percent of the survey respondents – is no accident. Rather, it is a product of political choices to house American health insurance largely within the private sector, bringing America to the status quo in which two-thirds of Americans are enrolled in some form of private insurance, embedded within which is fiduciary duty to shareholders. The irony is that not only does the practice of denials leave many patients behind, but also it operates quite poorly as a cost control mechanism when patients become sicker and require higher-level care.

For some patients, denials take the form of a requirement that they engage in "step therapy," or a mandate that they try other less-expensive (though potentially suboptimal) treatments prior to pursuing a particular type of prescription drug. For Jessica, the requirement that she first experience a "life-threatening event" barred her from accessing needed care and necessitated over a dozen courses of antibiotics while she pursued the appeal, all the while making her body vulnerable to more threatening and antibiotic-resistant infections, including during the COVID-19 pandemic. For still others, the denial appeared to emanate from inadequate review of unique aspects of the patient's medical history – whether the painful nature of a jaw condition, or the aggressiveness of a cancer that recurred with a vengeance when on a more spaced-out schedule of PET scans. There remain open questions regarding whether coverage denials actually deliver on the promise of cost containment and protecting patients from unnecessary, potentially even harmful, tests and treatments and whether this practice can be justified in light of the health equity concerns that I discuss in the pages that follow.

This chapter has highlighted through a combination of original survey and interview data, along with administrative data from two states' managed Medicaid programs, the broad scope and destabilizing impact of health insurance coverage denials, whether through prior authorization (causing delays in care) or following receipt of treatment (causing financial constraints, such as making the difficult decision to pay for the treatment so as to forestall collections and avoid a bad credit rating). I now turn my attention to the factors that make certain patients at greater risk of experiencing denials, including repeated denials.

Whose Coverage Is Denied?

You trust [your insurer] until you don't, because it becomes clear that "no" is their automatic response to everything.

Patient

66 **I**'M READY TO DIE. I cannot live anymore in this pain," Daniel recounted of his years of trials seeking to identify the cause of and treatment for his pain.

Daniel, a financial analyst in the northwest Chicago suburbs, was happily married with four children. He felt fortunate. Life had treated him well. But then, on April 22, 2014, everything changed.

A week before he turned thirty-six, he woke up on a Sunday experiencing significant pain in his feet and he decided that, if it continued for another couple of weeks, he would go to a podiatrist to identify the cause. With the pain only escalating, he saw a podiatrist, who was unable to diagnose the cause of his discomfort, though Daniel felt fortunate that, after exhausting his "bag of tricks," he received a referral to a rheumatologist. While continuing to pursue the underlying cause of his pain, the rheumatologist started Daniel on opioids and eventually connected Daniel with a pain clinic. Daniel would get temporary relief from the opioids for "an hour or so," but then the pain would resume. This was the life he now led.

Over the next six months, Daniel began to lose weight. Previously around 175 or 180 pounds, he had dropped to a mere 130 pounds because of the debilitating pain. He looked and felt unhealthy.

Daniel and his rheumatologist tried multiple avenues of treatment and symptom relief, including five different biologics (an expensive form of prescription drug), MRI and CT scans. Typically, his employer-provided

Cigna plan would deny coverage initially, and then his doctor would conduct a peer-to-peer conversation with the insurance company's physician, resulting in eventual approval. "Anything more than just an antibiotic would initially just be denied."

And all this time, while battling for coverage of tests and treatments, Daniel was in a tremendous amount of pain. He was on one opioid that he would take in pill form throughout the day, and he was additionally prescribed the opioid patch Butrans to give him a steady stream of pain management, which *also* began to get denied. Given its prohibitive cost, Daniel would then go without the medication, and he suffered, lying on the floor moaning and crying.

Daniel didn't fancy himself as a natural fighter. "I'm very Midwestern. We usually just keep our heads down and stand in the right line. We're rule followers. I figured if they tell you 'No,' it's probably for a good reason." But when he began getting denied, "there didn't seem to be a reason." The first couple of denials were an annoyance, but a year and a half into receiving multiple denials, he felt hopeless.

Yet, through all this agony, Daniel reflected, "I'm dumb lucky. I'm a white guy who gets paid well and has a wife and family around and *every* benefit. We have education. So, I kept my head down, thinking, 'What I have must not be that bad.' You trust them until you don't, because it becomes clear that 'no' is their automatic response to everything. Then you start thinking more strategically."

An eventual trip to the Mayo Clinic in Rochester, Minnesota resulted in an MRI that revealed an abnormality that turned out to explain his pain. By this point, Daniel's pain had been continuing over the course of about three years. Three years of pain; of weight loss; of difficulty managing his work.

The new neurologist met with Daniel for about two hours and, after reviewing his history, informed him that he had a cyst, or syrinx, in the middle of his spinal cord.

Daniel's condition is called syringomyelia, in which a fluid-filled cyst forms in the spinal cord. The cyst, when growing, can damage the spinal cord and compress and injure the nerve fibers. This condition affects approximately 8 out of every 100,000.[1] This disease, of which he had never heard before, was why he had been in pain for years.

The diagnosis was only part of what needed to happen. *Now he needed to secure treatment for it.*

What Daniel needed to manage this condition was a spinal cord stimulator, which costs tens of thousands of dollars. He submitted the prior authorization at the end of 2016, and it was denied as "experimental" for his condition. "Again, I'm a Midwestern guy and I keep my head down when they tell me 'No' and I keep plodding along. But at the same time, I'm going, 'I've got to keep this job. I've got this family. I've got to provide. I've got to keep taking the medicine and keep going and we'll figure something out.'"

Every three months, his pain doctor would propose resubmitting the prior authorization request for the spinal cord stimulator. And every time, it would be denied. They would appeal via peer-to-peer review by the insurer's physician, and the appeal would get denied despite the consensus among his pain doctors that the spinal cord stimulator was the best course of action, especially when compared with long-term reliance on opioids.

By 2019, Daniel couldn't take it anymore. "I'm in this god-awful pain every day. I'm barely hanging on at my job, and only because the guys I worked with were taking care of me and helping me hang on. Other people would have become bankrupt or divorced by this point." Through a Facebook group, Daniel learned of a clinic in Barcelona dedicated to syringomyelia and scoliosis. The clinic proposed that Daniel undergo a minimally invasive procedure, filum terminale sectioning, that could give him some relief from the pain, though he would have to pay out-of-pocket for international medical care.

After the surgery in April 2019, Daniel could hardly believe how much better he felt. He got off the opioids that summer, after being dependent on them for pain management since 2014. He returned to the pain doctor, who was pleased with Daniel's progress, and they agreed to apply *yet again* for the spinal cord stimulator. And this time, "out of the opioid fog zombie mode," Daniel was ready to fight for it.

The prior authorization was, predictably, denied. "Now I'm having normal human emotions again, so I call up the insurance company, I had my case manager call in, and I was getting as many people as possible from Cigna on the call. At one point I had six different people because I'm like, 'You're not hanging up. I'm not taking "no" today. I'm ready to kill myself over this. I can't live this way. I need to know why I don't have this even though I had been told by seven different doctors that I should have this.'"

By the end, they agreed to a peer-to-peer conversation, which finally resulted in approval.

When Daniel got the permanent spinal cord stimulator, he woke up in the recovery room and chatted happily with the nurses because it was the first time in six years that he wasn't in pain. People looked at him and said, "You just had *spinal surgery*," to which he replied, "Yeah, and it's nothing compared to the pain I was in for six years of my life."

It infuriated Daniel to know that someone who had his advantages got to this point. "I can only imagine if this were one of my brothers who has a physical job. And if I was single or if I didn't have kids, I wouldn't still be here. That was the only way I was getting through this."

Daniel's constant pain and serious medical needs had two core effects on him: Worsened health status necessitated additional medical work-ups that produced coverage denials (the subject of this chapter), and it made it more onerous to navigate the American health care system upon denial (drawing on the themes of chapters that follow).

Daniel is one of the many patients with whom I spoke who was denied medical coverage, highlighting both health-related and demographic vulnerabilities to coverage denial, which I explore below. I turn now to lay out the core theories that I explore related to who is most likely to experience denials.

HYPOTHESES ABOUT COVERAGE DENIALS

Drawing on survey and interview evidence, I test the theory that several demographic and health-related characteristics – namely, gender, health literacy, health care utilization, and sexual orientation – will shape patients' experience navigating the American health insurance system, influencing the likelihood with which they might be denied.

GENDER HYPOTHESIS. Despite the protections of the Affordable Care Act, which moved America beyond a state in which women paid higher insurance premiums and were more likely to be denied coverage altogether,[2] many women still face challenges accessing health care for reasons that include but extend beyond insurers' coverage exclusions. That women might experience more denials than their male counterparts would come as little surprise to Ariana, who faced numerous barriers accessing health coverage for treatment of a high-risk pregnancy, which affects 6–8 percent of pregnant women.[3]

She was a thirty-two-year-old doctoral student at Georgetown University, and her pregnancy came as a complete surprise. After all, she was on birth control and thought that she was protected. In fact, she was so sure that she was safe that for weeks, she thought she was ill, and she went to the doctor for tests, though she was not tested for pregnancy. She was placed on various medications including antibiotics to treat her symptoms, but the cause of her illness was, for the time, a mystery. It wasn't until she reached the end of the three-month cycle with her birth control but didn't get her period that she took a pregnancy test, which was positive.

What's more, she was now twelve weeks into her unplanned pregnancy. Not only did her insurance plan not cover abortion services at all (which would have left her to pay the total cost of around $500), but also there were uncertainties as to the health and even viability of this pregnancy, given the sickness she had experienced, as well as the medication trials she had undergone. In addition to being shocked, she was frightened.

While Ariana's insurance plan typically covered just one ultrasound scan over the course of an entire pregnancy (including the ultrasound scan that confirmed the pregnancy at the end of her first trimester), her OB-GYN believed that, given her first-trimester complications, combined with her chronic medical conditions, her pregnancy needed to be monitored extra closely with additional tests (e.g., to assess for fetal viability and abnormalities) for which her insurance denied coverage because they were deemed "not medically necessary."

Ariana was outraged and went through multiple rounds of appeal of the denials, trying to enlist her doctor's office to make calls on her behalf.

The appeals ultimately led to the insurer reimbursing some of the medical expenses, but, while these battles had persisted, she had had to put thousands of dollars on her credit card to continue to access the care that her OB-GYN knew was necessary for her high-risk pregnancy, and she is still paying off this credit card debt eleven years after delivering her healthy baby girl.

Ariana reflected on this time, "It's not just that the system was failing me. It's that every stage of that failure was also mocking me … . It was clear that people who know how the system works can function within that system, but if you don't, you don't have a prayer."

Ariana is not alone, and her experience highlights the difficulty that women can face when experiencing high-risk pregnancies that necessitate more ongoing testing and treatment than is typical for pregnancy care, but which health insurers' inadequate or lacking individualized review might miss. What's more, health policy researchers Dania Palanker and Karen Davenport find that insurers continue to exclude coverage of conditions and procedures from which women disproportionately would reap benefits (e.g., genetic testing, fetal reduction surgery, treatment of self-inflicted conditions),[4] and others find persistent barriers to coverage and access for women despite the implementation of the Affordable Care Act such that "serious threats to women's health still exist."[5] What's more, health services researcher Jusung Lee and his coauthors additionally observe in their study of insurance coverage of pregnancy and postpartum care that not only did 21.5 percent of study participants experience unaccepted insurance for pregnancy and postpartum care, but, furthermore, these coverage denials are associated with significant delays in care – for as high a proportion as 72.7 percent of women during pregnancy[6] – in a country with a shockingly high maternal mortality when compared with other Organisation for Economic Co-operation and Development (OECD) countries.[7]

In light of the interview-based and systematic evidence, I expect that insurance coverage denials will be more prevalent among female patients.

HEALTH LITERACY HYPOTHESIS. Navigating the American health care system is no easy feat even when one knows well its complexities, but it may feel like an impossible task to ensure that care will be covered if America's fragmented insurance system is unfamiliar. Many of the patients with whom I spoke experienced difficulty not only learning the ins and outs of the prior authorization process, but even learning what care would or would not be covered and why. In fact, Ohio patient advocate Julie Neff spoke to the lack of clarity with which many patients seeking her assistance understood their health plans and what should properly be covered.

To be sure, there are many reasons why coverage might be denied – and I examine additional factors in the pages that follow, including health status and utilization – but I expect that greater ability to navigate the bureaucracy of the American health care system will elicit fewer denials of medical coverage. I categorize this broadly as falling under the umbrella of health literacy, which the United States Department of Health and Human Services defines as "the degree to which individuals have the capacity to obtain, process, and understand basic health information needed to make appropriate health decisions."[8] This health information might relate to access of health care – that is, understanding one's condition and the appropriate course of treatment – or how to obtain insurance coverage for it.

One's degree of health literacy can be affected by several factors, including poverty, education level, race and ethnicity, age, and disability.[9] Evaluating health literacy among patients at two public hospitals, physician and researcher Mark Williams and his coauthors find that "[m]any patients could not read and understand basic medical directions containing numerical information," in addition to which "[p]atients also did poorly on the reading comprehension passages."[10] In fact, the Department of Health and Human Services estimates that 35 percent of American adults have only basic or below basic health literacy, while nearly half (49 percent) of adults who did not graduate from high school rank low in health literacy.[11] Understanding health literacy is important because lower levels are associated with greater difficulty accessing care.[12]

The astonishingly low rate of health literacy in the United States raises serious concerns as to many patients' ability to navigate health care and coverage – whether ensuring proper documentation for insurers, complying with deadlines to submit materials related to prior authorizations, or understanding what constitutes covered services. Thus, while low health literacy might not be associated with more *wrongful* coverage denials, it may elicit more denials that then cause more administrative burdens for the patient, who might be left to learn how to appeal (but be particularly ill-equipped to do so successfully), pay for the prescribed care (potentially going into debt for uncovered services), or alter or abandon altogether the course of treatment.

Health literacy divides can be seen not only across education levels, but across racial and ethnic categories as well. Indeed, the 2003 National Assessment of Adult Literacy found that 58 percent of African Americans and 66 percent of Hispanics had basic or below basic health literacy, compared with 28 percent among white respondents. These disparities extend to language minority status: physician and researcher Jane Brice and her coauthors find that while 74 percent of Spanish-speaking patients had inadequate health literacy, only 7 percent of English-speaking patients did.[13] This finding is consistent with the observation that not speaking English indicates a risk for decreased access to health care.[14]

Given the complexity of the American health insurance system, it should come as little surprise that health literacy disparities based on language minority status are not isolated to the Spanish-speaking population. When Ellen's three-week-old son spiked a fever and needed emergency department treatment that was denied by their insurer, she and her husband Hans panicked. Her husband was from Germany and was familiar with neither the American health care system nor the medical terminology with which they were being confronted. While Ellen did not believe that they would necessarily be on the hook for the full amount, she was unsure of how long it would take to resolve, and consequently to what extent this ordeal would adversely affect her credit report. Educated but less fluent in the American medical and insurance vocabulary, Hans delegated to Ellen the task of appealing the denial and felt grateful that she was equipped to take on this task.

Of course, the testing of this theory is complicated by the reality that higher income and educational attainment may also be more associated with a propensity to file a medical malpractice suit, in turn eliciting from physicians the practice of defensive medicine. Such a finding would be consistent with Shannon Brownlee's observation that well-insured

Americans are getting more care, even if that care is potentially of lower value and thus subject to not only prior authorization, but potentially outright denial.

HEALTH CARE UTILIZATION HYPOTHESIS. Some patients whom I interviewed were denied coverage for one of the few visits in which they sought care. But, as can be seen plainly in Daniel's many trials to obtain scans, drugs, and ultimately the spinal cord stimulator, being a heavier utilizer of the American health care system (e.g., due to chronic illness) can make one more vulnerable to experiencing coverage denials, even repeated denials. Thus, I expect that those who more frequently seek medical attention will be more likely to experience denials, as they will be submitting more medical claims to be reviewed by their insurer, thus creating more opportunities to be denied.

Similarly, I expect those who are in worse self-reported health to rely on more care that is vulnerable to coverage denial, whether requiring more ongoing health care utilization or requiring more costly medical intervention involving prior authorization. Denials of coverage for this population can be particularly costly because, when compared with coverage decisions related to healthier patients, they may be more likely to lead to exacerbations of the patient's condition.

LGBTQ HEALTH HYPOTHESIS. In response to the 2020 Supreme Court decision of *Bostock v. Clayton County*,[15] the Department of Health and Human Services Office for Civil Rights promulgated a rule in 2021 to prohibit discrimination in health against the LGBTQ community in the processing of insurance coverage and the exclusion of certain health care procedures.

However, given documented disparities in access to care within the LGBTQ community,[16] resulting in worse health outcomes,[17] especially in the transgender community,[18] I expect that identification as LGBTQ will be associated with more denials of insurance coverage. Indeed, while predating the HHS rule, health policy researchers William Padula and Kellan Baker note that "[a]lthough medical experts recognize the importance of this care, some insurers deny coverage for expensive reconstructive surgical procedures. Insurers that do not cover gender-affirming care frequently cite financial concerns."[19] Public health researchers Alex Dubov and Liana Fraenkel likewise observe a lack of access to coverage for gender-affirming surgery, with gender reassignment surgery typically being accessible but facial feminization surgery sometimes excluded under insurers' medical necessity guidelines, even though it "is in direct opposition to the scientific community's understanding of gender dysphoria and professional guidelines for transgender health."[20] That is, while research supports gender-affirming care as a means to address gender dysphoria, it can be vulnerable to treatment as "cosmetic" and thus outside the scope of plan benefits.

In addition to coverage exclusions, many LGBTQ health services are subject to prior authorization requirements and thus are vulnerable to delay and denial. Beyond the realm of gender-affirming surgery, Jamie, a twenty-six-year-old non-binary individual in the greater Seattle metropolitan area, experienced a prior authorization requirement for their testosterone, which resulted in them being told that they should try and fail injectable hormones before having access to the topical gel. "It's very difficult being told, 'No, you can't rub a gel on yourself. You need to be able to stab yourself once a week.' Not everyone can do that. Not everyone is comfortable with needles." The previous time they went through the prior authorization process for their testosterone, they had to pay out-of-pocket with the assistance of a discount card because it was such a protracted delay: "There was indignation but also resignation."

Further, HIV prevention services and treatments often require prior authorization. With 35 percent of gay and bisexual men at risk of HIV using PrEP,[21] which typically requires prior authorization, PrEP users and those receiving HIV treatment account for a large share of the community who may be vulnerable to experiencing coverage denials. What's more, people within the LGBTQ community express mental health concerns – whether depression, anxiety, or suicidal thoughts or behaviors – at higher rates than do their cisgender heterosexual counterparts. Concerns do not always translate into seeking and accessing care, though scholars have found that 55 percent of LGBT people in need of mental health treatment sought and received it.[22] And, as Chapter 8 illuminates, a substantial proportion of mental health care – from higher-cost prescription drugs to higher levels of treatment (e.g., intensive outpatient or residential care) – likewise requires prior authorization, through which many denials occur. In fact, antidepressants are among the five most common classes of drugs assigned prior authorization requirements by insurers.[23] This likewise amplifies the coverage barriers that female patients face, as women experience depression at relatively high rates.

Collectively, I have painted a picture of the myriad factors that might make one more vulnerable to experiencing a health insurance coverage denial – from gender and sexual orientation, to health status and health care utilization, to broader issues of health literacy, which aligns with demographic factors such as race and socioeconomic status (with the caveat of potentially eliciting more treatment of questionable value) – and, relatedly, how coverage denials might not only be disruptive overall, but also deepen inequities.

I turn now to the survey data to highlight the patterns and to what extent the findings align with these expectations. First, I will describe the variables that I measure.

COVARIATES

I asked each survey respondent several demographic questions with which to test my core theories. To examine the *gender hypothesis*, I measure whether each respondent identifies as *female*, which takes the value of 1 if they do so, and 0 otherwise. To examine the *health literacy hypothesis*, I asked each respondent to specify their highest level of education completed and from that I created the variable *college graduate*, which is coded as 1 if they completed a college education or higher, and 0 otherwise, with the expectation that college graduates will have more health literacy. What's more, those who identify as *Black or Hispanic* are coded as 1, and those who identify as some other race are coded 0 for this variable. Each respondent was also asked whether *English is their first language*, giving a variable which takes the value of 1 if English is the respondent's native language, and 0 otherwise. I also identify whether each respondent has an annual *household income under $50,000* – that is, constituting lower or lower-middle income – and they are coded as 1 if so, and 0 if their annual household income exceeds $50,000.

To examine the *health care utilization hypothesis,* respondents were coded as 1 if they identified as being in fair or poor health, and 0 if they identified as being in good, very good, or excellent health. Further, I asked respondents how often they typically see a physician, and coded respondents as 1 if they reported seeing a physician four times annually or more and 0 otherwise. Fifteen percent of respondents see their physicians this often.

Lastly, to examine the *LGBTQ health hypothesis,* each respondent was asked whether they identify as *LGBTQ,* and respondents were coded as 1 if they did, and 0 otherwise.

I account for other factors as well: I asked respondents whether they *struggle to pay out-of-pocket costs* (coded as 1 if yes), and I account for whether the respondent obtains their insurance through the ACA marketplace, Medicare, Medicaid, their or their partner's employer, or another source.

Having now discussed the coding of key independent variables of interest, I turn to the dependent variable and its prevalence across these categories.

DESCRIPTIVE FINDINGS ON COVERAGE DENIALS

The dependent variable, *denied coverage,* takes the value of 1 if the respondent indicated that they had ever experienced a coverage denial, and 0 otherwise. Figure 3.1 is a bar chart of the percentage of respondents across categories that experienced a coverage denial, with the dashed horizontal line indicating the sample-wide average share of denials, 36 percent. Thus, those variables whose bars are above the dashed line have a higher share of respondents experiencing coverage denial.

To begin with, there appears to be some evidence in support of the *gender hypothesis:* that is, women are 5 percentage points more likely than their male counterparts to report having experienced a coverage denial. While the effect is relatively modest, it is in the expected direction and performance of a difference-in-means test indicates that it is statistically significant ($p = 0.04$). This raises important questions as to whether this is driven by the denial of services from which women disproportionately

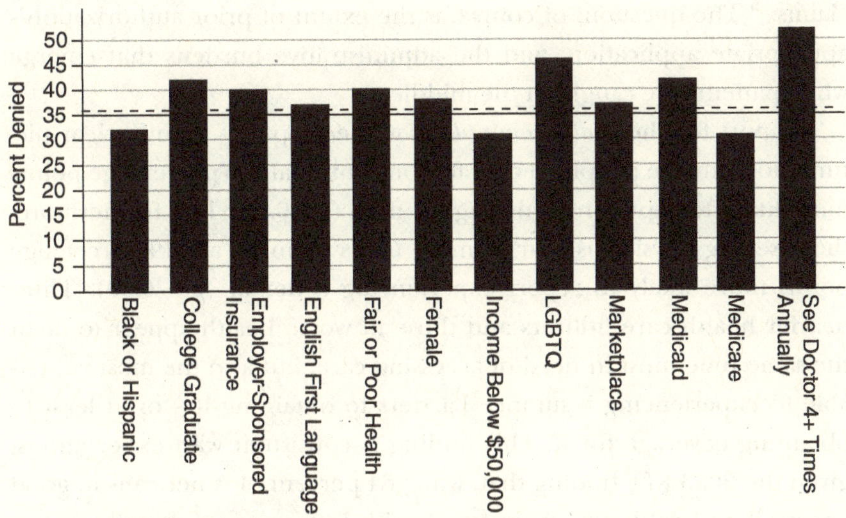

3.1 Characteristics associated with coverage denials.
Source: Survey of 1,340 US adults.

benefit, or whether there are shortcomings in the enforcement of Affordable Care Act protections.

There does not appear to be support for the *health literacy hypothesis*. In fact, many of the results go in the direction opposite to that which I expected, with less affluent respondents 8 percentage points *less* likely to experience a denial ($p = 0.01$), though many of these findings (for *Black or Hispanic, college graduate, English first language*) do not reach conventional levels of statistical significance. That less affluent people would be denied less may reflect the dynamic relationship between economic status and health care utilization, because this may be a population that forgoes care to a greater degree, leaving them with fewer interactions with health insurers. However, middle- and upper-income respondents were not significantly more likely to report seeing a physician four times annually or more. Alternatively, this may reflect health policy scholars Sungchul Park and Rishi Wadhera's finding that more affluent non-elderly patients may be more likely to be prescribed not only high-value care, but also some lower-value care, for which prior authorization may impose an appropriate guardrail.[24] The added prescription of lower-value care may be attributable to less affluent patients being significantly less likely than their counterparts to file medical malpractice claims.[25] The question, of course, is the extent of prior authorization's appropriate application, and the administrative burdens that emerge when patients are caught in the middle.

Support for the *health care utilization* theory paints a quite clear picture: not only are people in only fair or poor health 6 percentage points more likely to experience coverage denials ($p = 0.03$), but, furthermore, those seeing physicians four or more times annually are 19 percentage points more likely to report experiencing a denial ($p = 0.00$). Thus, heavier health care utilizers and those in worse health appear to be at the same time most in need of accessing care, but also the most vulnerable to experiencing insurance barriers to obtaining it – or at least to obtaining coverage for it. This finding is consistent with expectations, given the 2023 KFF finding that, while 84 percent of Americans in good or excellent health give their own health insurance an overall positive rating, 68 percent of those in fair or poor health do, suggesting that this population experiences more challenges accessing coverage for prescribed care.[26]

This survey evidence is consistent with interview findings: while some interviewees were denied for "one-off" necessitations of medical tests or treatments, it appears that (as was the case with Daniel) coverage denials most squarely affect those who struggle with more significant health conditions. Notably, I find that people with a behavioral health diagnosis are 28 percentage points more likely than their counterparts to experience denials ($p = 0.00$) and, given the emotionally taxing nature of navigating complex health insurance processes and facing either delays in care or medical bills, this suggests that there may be especially pronounced psychological costs associated with this health insurance practice.

There is likewise strong support for the *LGBTQ hypothesis*: those respondents identifying themselves as such are 12 percentage points more likely to report having experienced a coverage denial ($p = 0.00$). What's more, those in employer-sponsored health insurance – all of which is private – are significantly more likely than their counterparts to experience denials, which contributes to the broader expectation that denials are more heavily associated with private health insurance and its associated cost containment and profit maximization concerns discussed in Chapter 1.

Overall, apart from gender and LGBTQ status, health status and utilization (both of which correlate significantly with gender and LGBTQ status) appear to have stronger effects on patient experience of health insurance coverage denials than do other demographic characteristics related to race, language, and socioeconomic status.

Consistent with the difference-in-means tests, in the Appendix I include multivariate logistic regression model specifications that demonstrate that either being female or being in fair or poor health is associated with a 6-percentage point increase in propensity to experience a coverage denial, holding other factors constant. What's more, those who identify as *LGBTQ* are 13 percentage points more likely than their counterparts to experience coverage denial.

Thus, there appears to be both interview and survey (bivariate and multivariate) support for the hypothesis that women are more vulnerable to coverage denials, as well as support for the hypothesis that sicker patients are more vulnerable to coverage denials, and that those identifying as LGBTQ are more likely to be denied. However, health literacy as proxied by language minority status, lower education, race, and lower income does not appear to be associated with higher rates of coverage denials.

Not surprisingly, the majority of those who are denied experience not one, but *multiple* coverage denials. I turn now to examine the factors that predict multiple denials.

REPEATED DENIALS

When Sharon, a forty-seven-year-old elementary school teacher in Worcester, Massachusetts, switched from the Tufts Health Plan to her husband's employer-sponsored insurance plan through Cigna, she had no idea of the struggles that lay ahead.

Diagnosed in 2020 with non-Hodgkin's lymphoma, Sharon is now in remission after a stem cell transplant in January 2021, but remains on a tight regimen of infusions, shots, and prescription medications, both to help her body to "accept" the transplant and to help prevent illnesses to which she is more vulnerable having had the transplant. Sharon was given a two-year course of treatment for her disease, and she had been one year into this regimen when switching insurers. For Sharon, Cigna's pushback was frustrating because she had an existing treatment plan that was working for her with minimal side effects, and now her insurer was imposing barriers.

Every three weeks, Sharon receives an immunotherapy infusion to keep herself in remission, and, after the infusion, she receives five days of Neupogen injections to raise her white blood cell count to help prevent her from getting sick. In addition to the infusion and shots, she has seven prescriptions that she fills, some at CVS, and others at the hospital pharmacy. The four-hour Rituximab infusion that Sharon takes to stay in remission costs thousands of dollars. The series of five shots that she receives cost $1,400. Paying out-of-pocket is *not* an option.

Under the Tufts Health Plan, the five Neupogen injections would be approved together at once. After taking a class to learn how to self-administer injections, she was permitted to self-administer them at home rather than going to the doctor's office to receive them. Because she was busy as a schoolteacher and a mother of two, this system worked well for her. After she had switched to Cigna, not only did they require separate approvals for each injection on each day, but also they denied her the ability to self-administer, requiring that she leave work early enough to get to the medical office, pay for parking, pay a copayment for each office visit at which she received the injection, and pay for extra childcare.

And then, one Wednesday, they simply declined to cover the injection. It was unclear why, as they had approved the previous two injections that week, as well as the next two injections that week: "For some reason, Wednesday was not the day they were feeling it." Sharon was stuck with paying the $300 for the injection, unable to afford to forgo treatment, but also unable to afford accumulated medical expenses on a teacher's salary. This would not be the last of Sharon's struggles with Cigna. While driving on the way to her first infusion after switching to Cigna, Sharon received a phone call from her doctor's office informing her that that day's treatment was not approved. Her husband subsequently spent four hours on the phone with Cigna to secure approval, but not before the infusion clinic had closed for the day. In the meantime, her B-cells were proliferating, which the infusion medication was designed to prevent.

Would the ensuing ten-day delay be enough to pose problems for her recovery? She didn't know, but she wondered.

Sharon isn't just worried about getting reimbursed the $300 for her Neupogen shot – though, to be sure, it is a concern. She is also worried about the future, with an upcoming PET scan to check for recurrence, which a patient advocate for Cigna advised might not be covered absent new recurrence of symptoms. While she and her family consistently have a low pulse rate and low blood pressure, her blood pressure has now risen to 145/90, a reflection of the heightened anxiety that she now feels when pursuing coverage for the treatments designed to keep her in remission. And this experience had caused in her a loss of faith in this system on which she relies for her survival.

Sharon's story of repeated adverse interactions with the health insurance system is all too familiar for many patients. As discussed in Chapter 2, in addition to 36 percent of survey respondents experiencing at least one health coverage denial, 59 percent of those experiencing coverage denials experienced not one, but *multiple* such denials. Resulting in more costly medications and tests, and often rendering treatment prohibitively expensive, these denials of coverage can have a profound impact on the scope of care that is ultimately out of reach despite being insured and can thus have destabilizing effects on the affected patients' health and financial security.

Figure 3.2 displays a bar graph of the percentage of respondents across the previous categories who, conditional upon having experienced a denial, reported that they had experienced not just one, but multiple coverage denials. The horizontal dashed line indicates the sample-wide share of respondents with multiple denials (59 percent), such that bars extending beyond the horizontal line indicate that that characteristic is associated with more repeated denials.

There continues to be support for the *LGBTQ hypothesis*: performance of a difference-in-means test shows that such individuals are 20 percentage points more likely than their counterparts to experience multiple denials ($p = 0.00$). Although the effects of *college graduate, English first language, fair or poor health, income below $50,000,* and *see doctor four or more times annually* all go in the expected directions, they do not reach conventional levels of statistical significance.

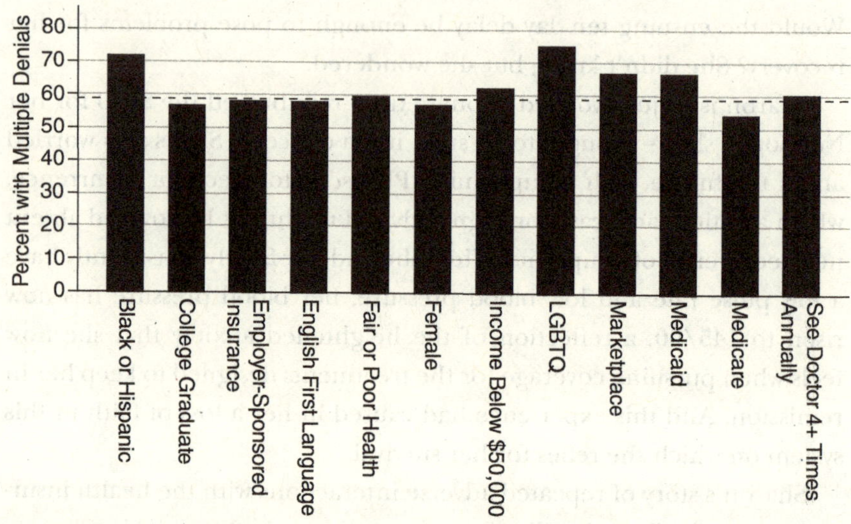

3.2 Characteristics associated with multiple denials.
Source: Survey of the 482 respondents who were denied at least once, among the 1,340 total surveyed.

While Black or Hispanic respondents are not more likely to experience an initial coverage denial, once they face health insurance barriers, such individuals appear to be 16 percentage points more likely to have repeated adverse interactions with their insurers ($p = 0.00$). And, as future chapters highlight, these denials cause even more disruption to their health and financial security, making these multiple denials even more significant. This finding is supported by the multivariate analysis laid out in the Appendix.

This survey cannot disentangle whether the overall high rates of repeated coverage denials are driven by limited understanding of health plan benefits or by greater reliance on health services that insurers have resisted covering. That the services denied include a broad spectrum of prescribed care beyond potentially low-value, high-cost scans – extending to prescription drugs, specialist office visits, surgeries, and emergency care – suggests that the answer is ultimately a combination of these factors. However, this raises important findings about how, *even within the insured population*, this practice of coverage denials can deepen the divides between those who have health plan benefits simply on paper and those who meaningfully have such benefits in practice.

CONCLUSION

Through survey and interview evidence, this chapter contributes to our understanding of the prevalence of, and susceptibility to, coverage denials in the American health care system. While Daniel spoke to the advantages he had when he navigated the American health care system, he nevertheless had the health vulnerabilities experienced by many I surveyed and interviewed. With six in ten American adults having a chronic disease, and four in ten American adults having two or more chronic diseases,[27] it is vital to understand what this means for those seeking to access their prescribed care.

While prior scholarship examined coverage denials drawing on claims-based analysis within narrower segments of the health care system, the survey- and interview-based approach I take allows me to not only look across public and private insurance, but also assess an individual patient's demographic vulnerabilities to denials. An analysis at the patient level allows us to understand better who is experiencing this practice to a greater or lesser extent, given demographic factors and insurance status, which is essential to answering broader health policy questions about effects on health and economic inequality in the United States. And while many of the expected demographic variables did not prove to be significant, Black and Hispanic individuals appear to have more repeated coverage denials, and what remains to be seen is the extent to which, *once denied*, those from marginalized groups have greater difficulty weathering the storms of administrative burden – a subject that I explore in the chapters that follow.

The effect of socioeconomic status on vulnerability to coverage denial is less clear from these survey data. While, at first blush, it might be intuitive to suspect that those more adept at understanding one's schedule of health benefits would be more likely to avoid coverage denials, what I actually find is that less affluent survey respondents were less likely to experience a denial. To the extent that this reflects economic considerations in the likelihood of medical malpractice litigation – with less affluent patients less likely to sue – prior authorization may operate as an *appropriate* guardrail on prescribing, with the caveat that comprehensive patient histories are not always taken into consideration by insurers, as

Chapter 2 laid bare. While this survey cannot disentangle higher- from lower-value care denials, what can be gleaned is that perverse incentives to prescribe certain care may backfire for patients, leaving them to navigate complex and administratively burdensome health insurance appeal processes in a manner that, as Chapters 2 and 7 highlight, can be financially and psychologically destabilizing.

Ariana's experience of being denied coverage for treatment for her high-risk pregnancy was, sadly, not an outlier. With an overall denial rate of 38 percent (compared with 33 percent among men), I find that the women in my survey were more vulnerable to denial than were their male counterparts. What's more, those identifying as LGBTQ were *significantly* and consistently more vulnerable to this insurance practice.

One of the reasons that may account for these higher rates of denials in these populations may be disparities in reliance on prescription drugs that require prior authorizations that may result in delay and denial. After all, not only is there high reliance on PrEP among the gay and bisexual male community, but also women are significantly more likely than their male counterparts to take prescription drugs. In fact, eighteen-to-thirty-four-year-old women are 26 percentage points more likely than their male counterparts to take prescriptions, though this gender gap narrows with age.[28] It is thus instructive to examine in depth the scope of coverage denials within the specific realm of prescription drugs.

CHAPTER 4

Prescriptions Are a Headache

Having my insulin get denied colored the way I interacted with insurance for the rest of my life.

Patient

"It's like a steak knife is going through the side of my face," Becky explained of her rare headache disorder. Becky, a thirty-one-year-old elementary school teacher in Houston, Texas, and her wife enrolled in Becky's employer's Blue Cross Blue Shield (BCBS) HMO health plan. She considers herself an informed consumer of health care and had been reasonably satisfied with her plan benefits until she began to need treatment for a rare headache disorder that would lead her down the path of trying multiple medications for off-label uses, yielding only mixed success securing insurance coverage.

Though she has been generally healthy, Becky suffers from short-lasting unilateral neuralgiform headache attacks with conjunctival injection and tearing (SUNCT), a rare condition that results in severe, debilitating headaches largely in the ocular or periocular area. The pain from the headache was so significant that she was unable to work for a couple of months, so she sought treatment with a neurologist whose research focuses on the class of headaches from which she suffers, who was initially able to secure for her a combination of seizure and migraine medications.

But, at some point, her body seemed to acclimate to the medication, necessitating a higher dose of Emgality in order to be optimally effective. The problem was that, due to a utilization management tool of a quantity limit – that is, a limit on the amount of medication permissible

within a time frame (e.g., thirty pills or one injectable pen per month) –
BCBS would only approve coverage of the lower dose that no longer
offered adequate relief from her "excruciating" symptoms, making sleep
the only respite that she has from pain. When BCBS denied her neurologist's request for prior authorization for the higher dose, she realized the
medication would cost over $600 per month out of pocket, something
she could not afford on a teacher's salary. "It's been a real nightmare."

Becky has now cycled through other medications in the hope of finding one that will work for her, though so far she has had no luck with
the alternatives. She anticipates having to enlist her neurologist to write
a letter to her insurance company, asking to reverse the previous denial
of the Emgality dosage increase.

Becky's condition is not the only headache disorder that insurers
have resisted treating. Patients suffering from migraines likewise experience significant insurance barriers in accessing prescribed treatments.

The American Migraine Foundation estimates that at least 39 million Americans live with migraines,[1] which constitute the second leading
cause of disability in the United States.[2] For many, migraines are not just
unpleasant, but *incapacitating*, with significant light and sound sensitivity
among the possible symptoms.

Despite the debilitating nature of migraines, securing insurance coverage for their treatment has proved to be no easy feat. According to
Dr. Courtney White,[3] a Thomas Jefferson University Hospital neurologist with additional training in headache medicine, one of the barriers
to coverage stems from the fact that many migraine-specific treatments
are newer, developed beginning in 2018,[4] and are quite expensive,
whereas migraines were previously treated off-label with older and less
expensive medications typically used to treat such conditions as hypertension, seizures, or depression. In light of this added cost of on-label
treatments, utilization management tools such as prior authorization
figure prominently.

Insurance barriers can in some cases stem from limited understanding of the debilitating impact of migraines. Dr. White reflected, "I've
had one insurer go, 'You have bad headaches, so we're not approving
your medication.' People still think it's just a bad headache, even though
we've found it's a neurological disease that works in a pathway similar

to epilepsy." This disconnect between coverage guidelines and medical research can result in people with a debilitating condition having prescribed care kept out of reach – not to mention leaving them in a compromised state amid subsequent burdensome health insurance hurdles associated with appealing.

Some of these denials may be short-sighted. Despite the costliness of migraine-specific treatments, coverage denials can be costly not only to the patient, but also to the insurer if the patient seeks emergency department treatment for intravenous versions of medication that they have been unable to obtain on an outpatient basis. In fact, severe headaches account for 3.5 million emergency department visits annually in the United States.[5] These emergency department visits for migraine treatment come with a hefty price tag of an estimated $700 million annually.[6]

With two-thirds of Americans taking prescription drugs, about 9 percent of which are brand drugs and thus more expensive and subject to more prior authorization,[7] it is useful to explore the unique barriers that people face in getting coverage for their prescriptions.

Notably, the drug classes that most commonly require prior authorization are anticholesterol drugs (22 percent), narcotic analgesics (13 percent), sleep medications (12 percent), antidiabetic medications (10 percent), and antidepressants (9 percent), which is to say, drugs used to treat very common medical conditions.[8] For example, between 2015 and 2018, just over 13 percent of American adults were taking an antidepressant,[9] 11.6 percent of Americans are diabetic,[10] and an estimated 47 million Americans take a cholesterol-lowering medication such as a statin,[11] thus constituting a large swath of patients vulnerable to the insurance practices at the heart of this book. What's more, for many of these drug classes, coverage barriers are highly and potentially immediately consequential, whether constituting unmanaged glucose levels or unmanaged depression symptoms, or else exorbitant out-of-pocket medical costs.

That prior authorization now extends to even lower-cost medications is especially significant because a 2011 American Medical Association white paper finds that prior authorization results in 20 percent of first-time requests being denied by insurers. To be sure, this does not equate to a *final* denial: the analysis also finds that 39 percent of physicians appeal the vast majority (80 percent or more) of rejections of prior authorization requests for prescription drugs,[12] though doing so is burdensome both for patients and for their physicians. Despite the high rate of appeal and reversal of denials, Dr. Jack Resneck finds that prior authorization leads to 37 percent of prescriptions initially rejected at the pharmacy being abandoned by patients, leading to suboptimal care and the potential for worsened patient conditions.[13] Thus, while denials may result in initial cost savings, they can also be quite destabilizing, whether exacerbating burden or leading to exacerbation of one's medical condition.

Several scholars have examined the impact of prescription drug prior authorization on access to care for particular medical conditions. In fact, there was observed a 32.3 percent reduction in the rate of initiating bipolar treatments in the aftermath of implementing Maine's prior authorization policy for Medicare and Medicaid coverage, with untreated bipolar depression potentially associated with challenges such as substance use disorder, lost work and increased financial stability, and suicidal thoughts and actions.[14] What's more, a 2018 survey of children with epilepsy found that prior authorization was required in 38 percent of the cases and proceeded smoothly only 49 percent of the time, with 37 percent experiencing a delay of seven or more days in starting a new drug and 38 percent experiencing a lapse in coverage of their current drug. And examination of oral anticancer drugs revealed that introduction of a new prior authorization not only increased the likelihood of treatment discontinuation within 120 days but also increased the time until the next refill by nearly 10 days relative to patients whose plans did not institute such a policy change.[15] Thus, this practice appears to have an acute effect within the large population of Americans taking prescription drugs – including populations that may not be well-positioned to endure long delays in treatment.

That treatment delay or abandonment can in fact come with a higher price tag for insurers is borne out by the data: in the context of treatment for type 2 diabetes, health services researchers have found there to be higher plan-paid health care costs among those whose type 2 diabetes medication had prior authorization requirements that kept the medication out of reach than among those who qualified for and received the prescribed medication.[16] Moreover, among schizophrenia and bipolar patients on Medicaid, patients on plans whose formularies (the insurer's list of approved drugs) were more restrictive and prevented access to the prescribed drugs were more likely to be hospitalized rather than treated on an outpatient basis.[17] Given that inpatient care is substantially more expensive than outpatient treatment, these findings raise questions about the effectiveness of prior authorization in achieving insurers' overarching cost containment objectives. Indeed, Wendell Potter reflected, "I would argue that the jury is still out whether it is an effective deterrent, and that prior authorization probably adds as much cost as it saves."[18]

To be sure, as in the case of the MRI scans discussed earlier, there is some degree of overprescribing across many of these categories, and prior authorization seeks in part to guard against that overtreatment. It is worth noting, however, that among the drug classes most commonly assigned prior authorization requirements, just one class – antidepressants – is among the four categories of drugs singled out by physician researcher Daniel Safer as a common locus of overprescribing.[19]

This chapter seeks to highlight the tensions and administrative burdens that can arise when patients are caught in the middle between their physicians (who may prescribe in good faith or may have incentives to overprescribe, whether due to outdated practices, concerns about medical malpractice, or the influence of the powerful pharmaceutical industry) and their health insurers. These barriers become even more pronounced when there is inadequate individualized review before coverage denials are issued. So, while there is marked variation in prior authorization reliance across drug categories and across insurance types and plans, this chapter highlights the risk of coverage denial and, in turn, care and financial disruption that so many of these patients face, especially given the notably high cost of prescription drugs in the United States.

I turn now to explore the broader drug formulary context in which these coverage denials are rendered, as well as the key players in this process – namely, pharmacy benefit managers (PBMs). I then highlight how prior authorization is administered in the context of prescription drugs, drawing on both data and interview evidence from patients and physicians.

DRUG FORMULARIES

To understand the decisions underlying prescription drug coverage and denials, it is instructive to consider the origins of the adoption and implementation of drug formularies, or continually updated lists of prescription drug products that are designated "tiers" that identify whether a drug is preferred or non-preferred, the latter of which translates to higher cost-sharing (or patient financial responsibility). While tiering is not wholly consistent across insurance plans, the general pattern is as follows: Tier 1 consists of generic drugs, Tier 2 consists of preferred brand-name drugs, Tier 3 consists of non-preferred brand-name drugs, Tier 4 consists of preferred specialty drugs, and Tier 5 consists of non-preferred specialty drugs, which are the most expensive. When higher-tier drugs are prescribed by physicians, patients experience more prior authorization and risk coverage denials, finding themselves caught in the health insurance bureaucracy.

The rationale for these tiers is simple. They are meant to encourage the use of generic drugs and to help patients and physicians to select between therapeutically similar brands because cost-effective substitutes are often available.[20] For example, over twenty brands of statin drugs can work to lower one's cholesterol level, and health plans make calculations about which subset of these drugs to cover – that is, which ones to include on their formularies. Though coverage denials for prescription drugs may be due to medical necessity determinations, some barriers to care arise when patients change plans or insurers update their formularies, resulting in patients' prescribed drugs no longer being covered even though they were previously judged medically necessary.

HISTORICAL BACKGROUND. The first drug formulary for a private civilian hospital was developed in 1816 with the publication of the *Pharmacopoeia of the New York Hospital,* listing the drugs available in its hospital pharmacy. Just four years later, America saw the publication of the *United States Pharmacopeia,* which offered guidelines on medicinal substances in response to concerns about the danger of poor-quality medicines.[21] By 1967, 26 states had some form of drug formulary, ranging from 100 to 900 items.[22]

Alongside the development of formularies, insurers in the increasingly managed care-focused health care setting also sought to control the utilization of pharmaceutical benefits. Thus, America saw the development of prior authorization requirements, generic drug substitution, copayments, spending limits, and audits aimed at guarding against both fraud and costly prescription drug overutilization.

Prescription drug benefits are managed by each individual health plan. Congress addressed the importance of drug formularies in the Medicare context in its 2003 passage of the Medicare Modernization Act, which created a prescription drug benefit for seniors and for younger individuals with disabilities who are covered by Medicare. This health policy development was especially important because, while seniors represented about 13 percent of the population, they consumed approximately 30 percent of all prescription medications.[23] This privatized Medicare Part D, which could be administered through Medicare Advantage or through a stand-alone prescription drug plan, operated under the assumption that low prices could be negotiated in exchange for preferred placement on drug formularies.[24] The expectation was that the adoption of this formulary system would increase reliance on generic drugs because of their comparable efficacy and lower costs to patients.

In 2006, CMS developed rules to manage how private plans under Medicare Part D create and manage drug formularies. Pharmacy and Therapeutics (P&T) Committees comprised of clinicians, pharmacists, nurses, legal experts, and administrators were developed to recommend formulary placement for individual drugs.[25] Drawing on the medical and clinical literature, FDA-approved prescribing information, relevant information on the use and experience of medications, current therapeutic use and access guidelines, economic data such as drug costs and related health care costs, and health care provider recommendations, fifty-seven major therapeutic categories were identified by the P&T Committee, and each formulary was required to have at least two products in each drug category. Separately, CMS identified six protected classes of drugs (anticonvulsants, antidepressants, antineoplastics, antipsychotics, antiretrovirals, and immunosuppressants) for which insurance plans were required to cover all or nearly all medications, in order to safeguard broad access to these treatments.

Table 4.1 Formulary designations

Insurer	Aimovig	Humira	NovoLog	Latuda (Lurasidone)
Aetna	Non-form.	Preferred specialty	Preferred brand	Non-form.
Elevance	Tier 3, PA, QL	Tier 4, PA, QL, Specialty	Non-form., QL, ST	Non-form.
Centene	Non-form.	PA, Specialty	Tier 5, QL	Tier 3, PA
Cigna	Tier 3, PA, QL	Tier 5, PA, QL	Non-form.	Tier 4, QL
Health Net	Tier 3, PA, QL	Tier 5, PA	Non-form.	Tier 4, QL
Humana	Tier 2, PA, QL	PA, QL	Tier 2, PA	Tier 2, QL
Kaiser Permanente	Non-form.	QL	Non-form.	Non-form.
Tufts Health Plan	Tier 2, PA, QL	Tier 4, PA, QL, Specialty	Non-form.	Non-form.
UnitedHealthcare	QL, ST	QL	Tier 3, QL	Tier 3, QL
UPMC	PA, QL	Specialty, PA, QL	Non-form.	PA, QL

Navigating access to prescription drug coverage is made only more complex by the marked variation across insurers' formularies, which can lead to frustration among patients who do not know what will be covered. What's more, many physician interviewees characterize this prescribing environment as a "black box."

VARIED FORMULARIES. Having a medication approved as medically necessary under one insurance plan is no guarantee that it will be covered if a patient changes health insurers, such as due to a change in employment or selecting a different plan on the ACA marketplace.

To illustrate the marked variation across insurers, I consider here the subcutaneous injectable migraine medication Aimovig at the dose of 140 mg/ml, the list price of which is $768 per month; the subcutaneous immunosuppressive drug Humira at the dose of 40 mg/0.8 ml, the list price of which is over $7,000; the NovoLog Flexpen, the list price of which is around $150 for a supply of 15 ml of insulin for the treatment of diabetes; and Latuda (lurasidone) at the dose of 40 mg, a month's supply of which can cost $1,500, for treatment of bipolar depression and schizophrenia. These brand-name drugs thus span wide-ranging medical conditions frequently reviewed for coverage by insurers, and outside of the sphere of generic substitutes, there may also be widely divergent levels of coverage. In Table 4.1, I provide the designations (Non-form., non-formulary; PA, prior authorization; QL, quantity limit) for these four brand drugs across ten commercial health insurers, whose formularies I searched online to identify levels of coverage.

One can immediately observe significant variation in whether the drug is covered at all – for example, Aimovig is not in the Aetna and Cigna formularies, but it is in the Elevance and UnitedHealthcare formularies – as well as variation in the tier at which the medication is designated, which affects the out-of-pocket cost for the patient. There are generally quantity limits, meaning that one might be able to obtain only one or two injectable pens per month, even if the patient is prescribed a higher dosage due to their specific condition (e.g., because the lower dose ceased to be adequately effective, as was the case for headache patient Becky). Similarly, a patient on Latuda might get a rude awakening if they switched from UnitedHealthcare (Tier 3 and with a quantity limit) to Aetna (non-formulary), especially if other depression treatments had proved less effective through trial and error. This variation in coverage status and cost-sharing can create information barriers both for patients and for physicians as they work to identify the best *and most sustainable* treatment options for patients' conditions.

What accounts for the wide variation in formulary designations across insurers? According to former Cigna Vice President Wendell Potter, the answer is simple: "kickbacks, and I use that word very deliberately."[26]

To be sure, he noted, PBMs – or private companies that work with health insurers and large employers to manage prescription drug benefits – do play a significant role in shaping pharmacy benefits for the American public. However, "in this industry, it's perfectly legal for insurance companies to cut deals with pharmaceutical companies. If you put a certain drug on a formulary that's expensive, the insurance company will get a kickback from the pharmaceutical company. They will use other terms. They won't use *that word*. A common term that they will use in the industry is 'consideration.' But it's a kickback. It's all about the money. It's not about what is best for the patient." That these relationships between insurers and drug companies could lead to more expensive drugs being prioritized on formularies offers just one glimpse of how entrenchment of multiple for-profit health care institutions can actually drive costs *up* in the American health care system, while also risking leaving patients behind when these costly drugs require prior authorization and thus their administration perhaps gets delayed if not denied.

The constraints of formularies can cause consternation both among physicians and among their patients. "We don't just prescribe drugs for the fun of it. There are criteria for most of these medications," UCLA pulmonologist and critical care physician Dr. Russell Buhr reflected. Despite established clinical guidelines, Dr. Buhr noted that his patients might be denied coverage for soft mist inhalers when the insurer prefers a dry powder-based inhaler, even though a frail older patient might have difficulty with that formulation.[27] "But this is a multi-billion-dollar industry that wants to keep its medical loss ratio as low as it can," which is to say that there is an incentive to constrain the amount that insurers spend on medical claims.

These strains on physicians are exacerbated by insurers' evolving reliance on prior authorization from year to year, which can compromise the ability to accurately calibrate expectations about what will be easy for the patient to access and what may require more back-and-forth with the insurer. In a December 2024 American Medical Association survey of 1,000 practicing physicians, 75 percent of physician respondents noted that the number of prior authorizations required for prescription medications has increased in the last 5 years.[28] Similarly, a 2019 survey of 1,602 specialist physicians by the Regulatory Relief Coalition found that 80 percent of respondents said that insurers have increased the requirements of prior authorization over the past years.[29]

Further variability within hospital and health system formularies can lead to onerous prior authorizations, coverage denials, and care disruptions. The Associate Director of Ambulatory Pharmacy at a New York City hospital observed very little consistency between the health system formulary (i.e., drugs administered on inpatient units or through outpatient infusion centers) and those drugs purchased through the insurers when patients seek to obtain outpatient prescriptions at the pharmacy. The alternative would involve evaluating the payer mix of the hospital's patients and identifying the extent to which drug A tends to be preferred over drug B and adapting the hospital formulary accordingly. However, it was observed, "That doesn't happen most of the time."

The result might be a rude awakening for the patient because hospitals may start patients on drugs on the inpatient unit without accounting for whether their insurer will cover it on an outpatient basis, or whether it will be in a prohibitively expensive tier. This can lead to a coverage denial when the patient seeks to fill outpatient prescriptions upon discharge. These denials are, in turn, particularly challenging to appeal because the prescription was filled by an inpatient unit physician rather than one of the patient's regular providers, making follow-up communication and coordination of care far more difficult.

This dynamic can often be at play in insulin prescribing. When patients are admitted and become newly diagnosed with diabetes, they are discharged with an insulin prescription but may face complications when seeking to obtain it if their insurer prefers Humalog to Novolog, or vice versa. While they are comparably effective drugs, they are not interchangeable, and patients may be more responsive to one than the other, making coverage denials in this context problematic for diabetic patients.

Compounding the challenge of varied formularies is the fact that insurers update their formularies on an annual basis – sometimes adding drugs, but sometimes subtracting them. While insurers will sometimes provide a letter informing the patient and prescriber of the formulary change a few months ahead of time, it is not guaranteed that such notifications will be provided in advance of the prior authorization's expiration, with such renewals often being required annually. Dr. Buhr reflected of this, "If you got a patient stable who's been very tenuous for a long time, formulary changes are very frustrating because you *finally* got this person under control and then they can't get the treatment."[30] Thus, coverage denials driven by limited formularies can not only induce delays in access to prescribed treatments but also disrupt physicians' longer-standing treatment approaches, especially with patients who are more precarious or for whom fewer treatment options are available.

Having evaluated how varied and changing formularies can lead to uncertainties in prescribing and level of coverage, it is instructive now to consider the role of PBMs in the management of these formularies, and their acceleration of reliance on higher-cost drugs, which tend to have accompanying prior authorization burdens.

THE ROLE OF PHARMACY BENEFIT MANAGERS

Political choices of privatization of the American health system extend to how Congress has provided for prescription drug benefits, maintaining a profit-motivated setting that is vulnerable to the practice of coverage denials. When insurance companies began to offer prescription drug benefits within their health plans in the 1960s, PBMs were created to help health insurers contain drug spending. These PBMs manage prescription drug benefits on behalf of private health insurers, as well as Medicare Part D prescription drug plans, state Medicaid departments, self-insured large employers, and other health insurance payers.[31] Working on behalf of these entities, PBMs develop the formularies of covered medications, negotiate discounts from drug manufacturers, and contract directly with pharmacies to reimburse for drugs dispensed to beneficiaries. The negotiation of prescription drug pricing is especially important because pharmaceutical expenditures have risen more quickly than other health care costs,[32] rendering cost containment goals even more important. However, the plain reality of PBMs is that, quite apart from cost containment goals motivating their development, they can and have contributed to America's rising health care costs.

PBMs are a site of significant consolidation, with the most prominent PBMs being CVS Caremark (which holds 34 percent of the PBM market), Express Scripts (24 percent of the market), and the UnitedHealthcare affiliate Optum Rx (21 percent of the market).[33] Thus, these three PBMs control 79 percent of the market and serve approximately 200 million Americans.[34]

Drug rebates are paid to PBMs by the drug manufacturers and can comprise 40 percent or more of the drug's list price.[35] One frustration that can arise is that the drug-specific rebates are kept confidential in contracts between PBMs and the manufacturers, thus limiting plans' ability to assess the extent to which PBMs are actually facilitating cost savings for their members. These actions have certainly paid off for PBMs, with gross profit increasing by 438 percent in ten years – from $6.3 billion in 2012 to $27.6 billion in 2022.[36] The question, of course, is what this means for consumers.

Because reimbursements to PBMs are driven in part by the rebates obtained (calculated on the basis of drugs' list prices), some have raised the possibility that PBMs are incentivized to prioritize more expensive drugs over more cost-effective alternatives. This has a few core implications. It leaves patients with more significant cost-sharing for prescriptions, which can be financially disruptive, especially for more marginalized patients. Reliance on higher-cost drugs can lead patients to face greater utilization management such as prior authorization, which can lead both to coverage denials and to administrative burdens of appealing those denials. Finally, it highlights yet another way in which privatized American health care aims at cost containment but, in reality, performs quite poorly at it.

This acceleration of reliance on prior authorization often manifests itself, in the context of prescription drugs, in the form of step therapy, which can cause insurer delays in accessing preferred treatments.

STEP THERAPY

Aimovig, a migraine-specific biologic treatment approved by the FDA in 2018, provides relief to many who are able to access it, but that is a significant caveat. Not only is it typically designated at a high tier, indicating more patient financial responsibility, but also one must first typically go through a series of previous drug trials. For example, under UnitedHealthcare coverage guidelines, Aimovig is approved once the patient has failed to achieve pain relief with, or had a contraindication to or intolerance of, two prophylactic therapies such as beta blockers (used to treat arrhythmia), Amitriptyline (an antidepressant), Topiramate (an epilepsy drug), or Venlafaxine (an antidepressant).

This process, which falls under the broader umbrella of prior authorization, is referred to as step therapy (also known as the *fail first policy*), or the policy according to which patients must try less expensive medication options before "stepping up" to more costly medications. Thus, one may need to try and fail Step 1 (usually generic, Tier 1 medications) and Step 2 (usually preferred brand drugs) before moving up to Step 3 (usually non-preferred brand drugs). Consistent with America's reliance on a for-profit health insurance system, insurers' goal in requiring this step therapy is to ensure that treatment is less costly yet equally or comparably effective. If a physician prescribes a more costly medication early in treatment, it is vulnerable to coverage denial by the insurer.

Health services researcher Kelly Lenahan and her colleagues analyze seventeen large commercial health plans' medication protocols with respect to ten diseases that are often subject to step therapy requirements. They find that plans applied step therapy in 38.9 percent of drug coverage policies, ranging from 20.6 percent to 57.5 percent across insurance plans, suggesting significant opportunities for delay in obtaining approval for the preferred drug.[37] What's more, among these step therapy protocols, just 34 percent were consistent with clinical guidelines, while 55.6 percent were more stringent than were the clinical guidelines.[38]

While step therapy certainly has the potential to appropriately steer patients toward more cost-effective alternatives that may be similarly effective for their condition, this added stringency raises serious concerns that this utilization management tool keeps appropriate care out of reach to a degree that is inconsistent with current medical protocols. And, while a majority of physicians agree that step therapy requirements can promote affordability and clinical appropriateness of care, they likewise stated that these requirements are implemented inefficiently and inflexibly, failing to account for relevant patient-specific information that might inform prescribing behavior.[39]

In light of this, it is perhaps unsurprising that health law professor Rachel Sachs and health services researcher Michael Anne Kyle observe that step therapy's "contribution to improved quality appears to be limited: a recent study examining commercial insurers' use of step therapy for specialty drugs found that only about one third of protocols aligned with clinical guidelines."[40] Thus, they argue, while administrative burdens may be appropriate when steering patients away from low-value care, burdens driven by step therapy "may hinder access to necessary care."

These step therapy requirements can not only be burdensome, but also, for some, can lead to treatment discontinuation. Maine Medicaid and Medicare patients initiating atypical antipsychotic therapy during

Maine's prior authorization policy implementation experienced a 29 percent greater risk of treatment discontinuity than did patients initiating atypical antipsychotic therapy before the step therapy policy took effect.[41] Thus, step therapy through prior authorization not only imposes rules that are more stringent than clinical guidelines dictate, but also can result in outright abandonment of physician-recommended treatments that might have been clinically appropriate care.

Apart from the frustration of being unable to prescribe the Step 2 or Step 3 drug that the physician believes to be most appropriate for the patient's condition, there is the added barrier that it can take weeks to reach the therapeutic dose necessary to demonstrate failure of a lower-step drug. Dr. White reflected on migraine treatment,

> I want to start a patient on a migraine-specific medication. For one insurance, I have to try three different medications on their formulary, *three steps*, before they'll cover any of the newer medications. And the medications they're requiring are dirt cheap, but we've known they're not as effective because they're blood pressure medications. They're seizure medications. *That's not what we're treating.* Some of these medications take a month to get up to the therapeutic dose, then you wait three months *at the therapeutic dose* for it to work. So, with three medications, it can take up to a year for the insurance to cover the migraine drug.[42]

In the meantime, the patient may be struggling with poorly managed migraines, risking lost workdays and income, and in some instances may go on disability benefits through Social Security Disability Insurance (SSDI) or Supplemental Security Income (SSI), though there are documented challenges in successfully demonstrating disability from this condition.

Imposing step therapy requirements might at first blush appear to impose effective guardrails on physician prescribing and runaway health costs, especially amid concerns about overreliance on high-cost drugs when lower-cost alternatives are available. However, as with Aimovig, step therapy requirements might not be for similar (cheaper) drugs within the same class, but rather may require that the patient try entirely different types of drugs that lead to an "apples and oranges" comparison.

Duke University neurologist Dr. Andrew Spector observed that, unlike the context of multiple similar beta blockers being on the market to treat a similar constellation of health concerns,

> in the narcolepsy world, they're taking the drug Pitolisant, which is an orphan drug – there are no other drugs like it on the market – and they'll say you can't take that drug until you've failed Ritalin, which is a totally different drug. But there's a reason I want *this* drug class. So, when there's a step therapy protocol that requires different *classes* of medications such as histamine drugs versus dopamine drugs versus norepinephrine drugs, I have a much bigger objection than when they say, "These are all in the same pharmacological family, but this one is cheaper so start there."[43]

Though laws limiting step therapy requirements have been passed in thirty-one states, the laws enacted have been "nearly impossible to enforce," are rife with loopholes, and leave over 90 percent of the United States population unable to access coverage for their prescribed treatments.[44] This results in patients experiencing coverage denials for prescribed medications and being told by their insurer to first try alternative treatments that their provider has deemed suboptimal care. What's more, their impact is further hindered by ERISA's preemption of state policymaking related to the majority of employer-sponsored insurance plans.

It is perhaps ironic that step therapy requirements can push patients toward off-label prescriptions (e.g., taking the anti-epileptic Topamax for treatment of episodic migraine). It is within the realm of such off-label prescribing that we can see not only policy complexity, but also greater vulnerability to coverage denial, to the frustration of patients and physicians alike.

OFF-LABEL PRESCRIBING AND RARE DISEASES

Coverage denials for prescription drugs vary in prevalence across different classes of drugs (which have different costs and thus different degrees of reliance on prior authorization), but one area of prescription drug prescribing in which denials are common is off-label prescribing. When a drug is administered for off-label reasons, it is being used for a disease or condition that the FDA has not approved it to treat, but when the health care provider nevertheless judges that it may be medically appropriate for the patient. Off-label uses may include a chemotherapy approved for one type of cancer but being used to treat a different type of cancer instead; the prescription of the hypertension drug Prazosin to treat nightmares related to post-traumatic stress disorder; the hypertension drug Clonodine to treat ADHD as well as nicotine withdrawal; the beta blocker Propranolol to treat tremors; and the antipsychotic drug Seroquel to treat insomnia, to name just a few such uses.

Off-label prescribing occurs in every area of medicine, though it may be more prevalent in medical fields where the patient population is less likely to be included in clinical trials – for example, people who are pregnant, children, or psychiatric patients.[45] It is estimated that 21 percent of prescriptions by office-based physicians were for off-label use, accounting for a total of 150 million such prescriptions.[46] Off-label prescribing was found to be most common (46 percent) in the treatment of cardiac conditions.[47]

There are several reasons why such off-label prescribing may be the appropriate course of action by the provider, whether because a medication was not studied for a specific population, a life-threatening or terminal medical condition may motivate the pursuit of a broader range of logical and available options, another drug in the same class may have been approved, or the conditions may be similar (e.g., anxiety and post-traumatic stress disorder) and thus indicate potentially overlapping treatments even absent FDA approval for that indication.[48] Although these treatments are by definition not FDA-approved for these uses, they can be highly effective, with a 2018 meta-analysis of twenty-five treatment comparisons finding the off-label treatment to be "clearly superior" to approved treatments a quarter of the time, while just one of the treatment comparisons indicated that the off-label treatment was "clearly inferior," such that, overall, off-label treatments were viewed favorably.[49]

Not only can these off-label prescriptions be prevalent in both inpatient and outpatient settings, but also they can become widely entrenched as standard treatments for many clinical conditions.[50] Thus, while some off-label prescribing can be experimental, it can include standard, state-of-the-art treatments, with many off-label uses even recommended by medical textbooks, research institutes, professional organizations, and pharmaceutical reference works.[51]

Off-label prescribing has been taken up by the judiciary. In the case of *United States v. Evers* (1981), the federal government had charged a physician (Evers) with misbranding a drug by using it for an off-label purpose in the treatment of arteriosclerosis, or a hardening of the arteries. The Fifth Circuit Court of Appeals determined that the off-label use was not illegal because the FDA stated that a physician may "as part of the practice of medicine, lawfully prescribe a different dosage for his patient, or may otherwise vary the conditions of use from those approved," without seeking FDA approval. However, challenges nevertheless arise not from law, but rather from what insurers will deem medically necessary and appropriate as opposed to experimental or investigational.

In the experience of Dr. Spector, the on-label drugs approved by the insurer do not always align with health insurers' cost containment goals motivating prior authorization. One of Dr. Spector's patients is on the stimulant ADHD drug Vyvanse, which is not FDA-approved for the treatment of narcolepsy, and the cost of which is approximately $350 per month. An alternative medication is Xywave, which is FDA-approved for treatment of narcolepsy, but the cost of which is approximately $5,800 per month:

> They actually force me to take the patient off the off-label drug that was working, in order to start an on-label drug that is markedly more expensive. *I was doing the cheaper route.* They were so focused on on-label versus off-label that they couldn't see the forest through the trees. This prior auth was actually *harming* their bottom line. And even though Vyvanse *is* more expensive than Adderall, they didn't factor in that it was the cheap drug *in my class.*[52]

A realm in which off-label prescribing is not only common, but the *norm,* is in the treatment of rare diseases.[53] Despite Congress's 1983 passage of the Orphan Drug Act, which incentivizes drug development to treat rare diseases (those which affect fewer than 200,000 Americans), an estimated 95 percent of the 7,000 identified rare diseases do not yet have a single FDA-approved treatment.[54] What's more, orphan drugs can be considerably more expensive and thus subject to prior authorization and vulnerable to coverage denial. Thus, the one in ten Americans with a rare disease[55] disproportionately rely on off-label therapies, which can be subject to greater insurance coverage barriers.

Given the varied and changing formularies, ever-evolving prior authorization policies, especially in the setting of higher-cost drugs, and restrictions on the prescribing of off-label treatments, one of the profound challenges faced by physicians – and by extension, their patients – is the uncertainty in the prescribing environment, which can lead to more coverage barriers and, in turn, administrative burdens. These problems are compounded by the opacity of the policies of a given patient's plan.

LACK OF TRANSPARENCY

Not only have prior authorization requirements become more onerous, but also there is a lack of transparency as to what plans' requirements are. In fact, the December 2020 American Medical Association survey revealed that 65 percent of physicians found that it was difficult to determine whether a prescription medication required a prior authorization (with 13 percent finding it "extremely difficult").

This problem is exacerbated because prior authorization requirements don't only vary across insurers; they also vary across plans *within insurers*. This compounds the complexity of the system in which providers prescribe and patients seek access to treatment. Changing and increasing prior authorization requirements place significant informational burdens on those who seek to deliver or access care.

Electronic medical record (EMR) systems such as Epic may contain this information through the additional purchase of the compatible package Real-Time Pharmacy Benefits, which is serviced by the third-party vendor Surescripts, which acts as a liaison between the EMR and the PBMs. A prescription corresponding to the patient's plan is put into the system, which does a real-time query of the patient's plan to ascertain whether the drug is preferred or non-preferred, what tier it is, and whether it requires prior authorization. The goal is to promote information dissemination at the time of prescribing, thus mitigating delays associated with coverage denials or inadequate coverage when the patient goes to the pharmacy.

But, while this wealth of information can greatly benefit patients and their physicians, not all health care providers have access to these tools. For example, while 94 percent of hospitals utilize electronic health record (EHR) data, this rate is lower among small, rural, and non-teaching hospitals,[56] and the main disparity between these categories of hospitals is in the development of comprehensive (as opposed to basic) EHR systems.[57] Thus, while physician and researcher Matthew Klebanoff and his coauthors find that 68 percent of acute care hospitals use Real-Time Pharmacy Benefits,[58] this still leaves many hospital systems (especially smaller, rural, and non-teaching hospitals) without this resource, leaving their physicians and patients more vulnerable to burdensome coverage barriers. In fact, in a 2020 survey by the non-profit organization Workgroup for Electronic Data Interchange (WEDI), 62 percent of health care providers reported that they lacked the technology to evaluate whether prior authorization was required for a prescribed medical service, diagnostic test, or medication.[59]

Even when they do have these tools at their disposal, there can still be informational barriers because, for example, there may be confusion about plan structure, given the different tiering structures of different insurers. That is, while Cigna has four tiers in its formulary, the UPMC health plan has just two, such that being told that a sought-after drug is designated as tier 2 is not necessarily actionable when it comes to reducing patient cost-sharing. Thus, while these tools can offer some insights into the extent of prior authorization burden and cost-sharing, their use does not entirely eliminate guesswork, and less resourced practices may be unable to reap these benefits.

This opacity is hardly isolated to the treatment of rare medical conditions, for which there may be particular uncertainty. To highlight this, I draw on interview evidence of barriers in accessing care for the management of chronic medical conditions including diabetes and depression.

COVERAGE BARRIERS FOR PRESCRIPTION DRUGS
FOR COMMON MEDICAL CONDITIONS

Over 131 million Americans take at least one prescription drug,[60] with particularly high prescription drug usage among those with common chronic conditions (e.g., diabetes, heart disease) and, relatedly, the elderly. It is thus instructive to examine in depth the experiences of patients facing barriers to coverage for prescription drugs for the treatment of some common medical conditions, which may ensnare patients in the delays in care and administrative burdens at the heart of this book.

BIRTH CONTROL, REALLY? "I have a J.D. and an M.P.P. If anyone can navigate bureaucracy, I can."

Ariel, a thirty-two-year-old policy counsel at a non-profit organization in Washington, D.C., couldn't believe it: she was being denied coverage for *birth control pills*. Though prior authorization is typically directed at higher-cost drugs, these pills cost $75 a month and her insurance company, UnitedHealthcare, was fighting her over it.

Ariel had switched from a Kaiser Permanente plan purchased through the ACA marketplace exchange to an employer-sponsored UnitedHealthcare plan when beginning her job. She is a fairly healthy individual and is not a heavy utilizer of the health care system, with one exception: she would get "hellish" periods with heavy bleeding for eight days a month, and that caused her pain, severe fatigue, and lost days at school or work.

Ariel is one of the many women of reproductive age who has menorrhagia, or abnormally heavy or prolonged bleeding with one's menstrual cycle, which interferes with daily activities.[61]

The treatment for this condition is simple: birth control pills, which can limit how much one bleeds, and which she began to take at the age of seventeen. Ariel has switched birth control prescriptions a couple of times, but for the most part stayed on the generic version of one particular pill because, when her insurer encouraged her to change, she experienced painful stomach cramps for two months, after which she was switched back to her previous prescription.

When Ariel switched health insurance companies to UnitedHealthcare, she was informed that, under its tiering system, not only would her birth control not be free of charge despite the ACA's elimination of cost-sharing for contraception, but it would cost $75 a month out-of-pocket because they claimed that there was not a medically necessary reason for her to be on that specific pill as opposed to one on their formulary. Ariel is not alone in this. In fact, in 2024 the Department of Labor reported that health insurers denied roughly 40 percent of exception requests related to contraceptive coverage, with one insurer denying as much as 80 percent of such requests.[62]

Ariel said,

> I just went through this experience two years ago and I'm not willing to go through it again. *This is what my doctor prescribed.* I've been on birth control for over a decade. This is not a new drug for me. This is not a particularly restricted drug. It is not an experimental drug. I'm not asking for pain pills here. *It's just birth control.*

Ariel knew how to navigate the insurance system and dutifully stayed on hold with her insurer for over an hour during her workday, though she was frustrated that it was made necessary. "I explained to them that I know my body and I don't want to mess with it. It's not worth two months of pain. I've been regulating hormones in this way for years and you want me to go off of it, not because a doctor has expressed any concern like indications of blood clots, but literally because of it not being on a list?"

To appeal, UnitedHealthcare provided her the address of a PO Box in Arkansas, and there had to be a physical letter signed by her physician. Amid the delays, Ariel was running out of birth control pills, such that she had to return to Kaiser and pay out-of-pocket for another month's supply of pills (her prescription remained active), despite it not being their conventional practice to allow this for former patients.

She wondered whether it would be easier to simply pay out-of-pocket for the birth control rather than continue to fight the appeal. She knew she needed to be able to function at her fast-paced job rather than taking the time off amid eight "horrendous" days of bleeding.

Ariel's appeal for birth control coverage was ultimately approved a month and a half later, but

> it was very clear that the system was set up to make things difficult for me. You're making me feel like I'm doing something wrong. And I never thought of my birth control as anything special until I had UnitedHealthcare. Relative to other people, I should be good at navigating bureaucracy. I am educated. I have the computer. I have job flexibility.

It should be a cakewalk for me, and it was really frustrating that it wasn't. And over birth control? Really?

DIABETES. "It colored the way I interacted with insurance for the rest of my life," Laura reflected of her experience being denied her prescribed form of insulin for treatment of her type 1 diabetes, a condition with which 1.6 million Americans live.[63] In fact, this denial helped inspire her to pursue a career in health-related research.

At the time of her diabetes diagnosis at age sixteen, she was started on a now "antiquated N and R" insulin regimen that involves a mixture of two types of insulin (NPH insulin and regular insulin) in a single shot administered twice a day, "and you have to eat exactly the same amount at exactly the same time every day based on when your two injections are." This strictly regimented routine was not an ideal option for a teenager who had a varying schedule over the school year and did not want a tightly regimented lifestyle because it affected her schooling and participation in extra-curricular activities.

Laura reflected of this time,

I distinctly remember my mom packing my lunch every day with the exact amount that I needed to eat, and you can imagine that a sixteen-year-old doesn't want to deal with that, especially as a teen girl who doesn't want to essentially be force-fed a little bit to function throughout the day. I was constantly having these lows in the afternoon in class. I was a competitive swimmer, and I was worried about going to swim practice with low blood sugar. It was quite disruptive to my life.

After a few months, Laura told her endocrinologist she would prefer to switch to a different regimen that might better suit her lifestyle. They informed her that, moving forward, she would have insulin in pens, and would take one long-acting insulin shot per day and inject short-acting insulin every time she ate or if needed to make a correction to address fluctuating glucose levels (a combination of Lantus and NovoLog insulins). However, her insurer denied coverage for the new regimen on the grounds that her current, less expensive regimen was working to control her glucose levels, and thus the adjustment was not medically necessary.

In a nation where the cost of insulin is notably high, paying out-of-pocket was not an option. Thus, Laura's parents underwent the insurance appeal process and Laura counted herself fortunate that her mother knew how to navigate the insurance system, having done "insurance-adjacent work" previously. But, even with ample knowledge of the appeal process, Laura's mom had to go through not one, but *three* rounds of appeals (to an external level of review) to secure this coverage.

This was especially striking because

> it was pretty well known at the time that the regimen they started you on was not intended to be a long-term solution for type 1. It was more of, "This is what we start you on until you get used to how this works, and then we'll eventually transition you to a regimen with more flexibility once you get comfortable with dosing, which becomes more complicated." It was known that what I was trying to switch to was better, more effective, and in general what most providers would prefer.

Being denied not for experimental treatment, but rather for the *optimal* treatment, gave Laura a "crash course in how crazy the system is."

The new insulin regimen eventually got approved by her insurer a few months later, and she would remain on this new regimen for over a decade. She couldn't imagine being on the old regimen and having "anything remotely close to the life I've had."

But this experience came at a price. This denial didn't just delay Laura's access to the preferred insulin regimen. It reshaped the way she saw the health care system in which she was participating. When she needed to replace her insulin pump years later, she reflected,

> Having that experience freaked me out a little and I really needed to understand what the insurance was going to be covering and *which* pump would they cover. So, I was anxious about the whole process, and I think it kept me from going back on a pump sooner than I potentially would have if I didn't have that experience looming over me.

Laura is one of the multiple type 1 diabetes patients I interviewed about challenges securing coverage for their prescribed insulin, and all followed a similar pattern. For some, the challenges stemmed from being unable to access their preferred form of insulin, such as denials of Humalog in favor of Novolog. Others faced barriers to accessing insulin pumps that were essential to their use of the drug. Still others were denied continuous glucose monitors on the grounds that their hemoglobin A1C was not sufficiently high as to require this additional monitoring of glucose levels. What puts this setting of insulin apart from other conditions is its importance not simply for quality of life, but for life itself.

Some patients prevailed in accessing their prescribed medications to manage their diabetes. For others, depletion of savings accounts was preferred to navigating the labyrinthian system before them.

INFLAMMATORY BOWEL DISEASE. A few months after receiving an appendectomy, Liz, a first-year law student, began to feel significant, concentrated pain in the same region where she had had surgery months earlier. However, she delayed seeking in-person medical attention amid the COVID-19 pandemic. Eventually, she went to urgent care, which ordered a CT scan that revealed small intestinal inflammation, on the basis of which they recommended that she pursue additional testing with a specialist. By the end of that summer, she had been preliminarily diagnosed with Crohn disease, a form of inflammatory bowel disease (IBD) affecting approximately 1 in 250 people.[64]

After making the Crohn's diagnosis, Liz's gastroenterologist, who specialized in identifying which biologics are most appropriate for which clinical presentation of IBD, initially prescribed a mild oral medication which required a prior authorization request. This was eventually denied by her university's Health Net plan, so Liz instead went on a gastrointestinal-specific steroid that proved to be entirely ineffective.

Rather than appeal the initial denial, they pursued a prior authorization for the immunosuppressive drug Stelara, the cost of which is over $12,000 per month.[65]

Despite the step therapy protocol for Stelara, Liz's doctor conveyed that there was research showing that it was a good first-line drug, with fewer adverse effects than many alternatives. They submitted the prior authorization, which was denied in a letter with incorrect as well as misspelled information about Liz's medications.

This time, her gastroenterologist appealed on Liz's behalf to try to secure her Stelara coverage, providing Health Net with ample information about her case and research studies demonstrating that it was the best option. Months later, this appeal was denied. Along with the denial letter, Health Net sent Liz a "150-page packet, a lot of which were blank pages. It seemingly was just an intimidation tactic. It was nonsense."

In the meantime, Liz was on a steroid that was working inadequately. "I was thankful that we were doing Zoom school because I needed to just keep my camera off and sometimes be horizontal during class." It turned out that Liz was intolerant to high doses of steroids: she was initially placed on what is an average dose and it prevented her from sleeping for four days straight. On the lower dose, it wasn't managing her symptoms well. It seemed there was no path forward on this drug.

"I called everyone I could think of. I talked with the university's insurance coordinators. I talked to my Dean of Students. I got free legal advice through the law school. I talked to my professor. I talked to so many people. Not one of them directed me to the independent medical review process." Eventually, her doctor's office said that they had done all that they could with the appeal, and that she could try filing a grievance with Health Net.

"I told Health Net, 'I do believe I'm going to get this eventually. Let's not make it harder on either of us.'" One insurance staffer with whom Liz spoke said, "Honestly, we don't read appeals unless the Department of Managed Health Care makes us."

Liz filed a grievance over the phone, having drafted a letter in which she outlined how the clinical policy does not match FDA indications and called on her to do step therapy on medications that were either generally out of favor or even contraindicated for her disease profile. Health Net said that they lost the grievance, so she resubmitted it via certified mail, along with a list of the reference numbers for each of her many phone calls over the months.

After doing independent research and reading the large packet that Health Net had sent her with the initial denial of her appeal, she decided to pursue the independent medical review through the California Department of Insurance. Less than a month later, and just two days before she was set to go on Humira instead because the appeal had taken six months, she received the approval and was able to obtain

Stelara. She received her first infusion in March 2021 after having "beaten the system."

BEHAVIORAL HEALTH. "I've done the prior authorization process enough times to know that I have to be the one to call everybody and coordinate it. But this *shouldn't* be my job," Jamie reflected.

Jamie (whom we saw briefly in Chapter 3) is a twenty-six-year-old chef on Washington State's Medicaid (Apple Health) in the greater Seattle area. In addition to struggling to obtain coverage for their testosterone, they have experienced prior authorization barriers to obtain their Attention-Deficit/Hyperactivity Disorder (ADHD) medication. Having tried multiple different ADHD medications previously, they have learned that the brand drug Vyvanse, a stimulant that costs between $300 and $400 per month, is by far the most effective for their condition. Vyvanse not only has the advantage of being less susceptible to abuse than is Adderall, but also caused Jamie the fewest side effects, whereas other drugs through which they previously cycled left them foggy or even suicidal.

The additional challenge that Jamie faces is that, because of the effects that Vyvanse does have, they need to split the dose and take two pills a day, raising challenges related to the quantity limit. "When an insurance doesn't want to cover a name brand medication, they *really* don't want to cover twice as many pills of that medication." Having this split dose helped Jamie to have an effective dose of the medication in their system for a longer period of the day, facilitating better functioning, and when the dose isn't split up, the side effects of anxiety and "fuzziness" hit them harder. Even when they were on their parents' private health insurance plan previously, they would simply get a denial at the beginning of *every* year when the prior authorization expired. "I shouldn't have to fight for my medication every twelve months."

In February 2020, Jamie sent a text message to a friend of theirs, saying, "I'm pissed that I had to be unmedicated for so long." At the time, they were "just straight-up, barely a person for three weeks."

They had just moved back into their mom's house. They had been in a difficult place emotionally but felt motivated and goal-oriented. But suddenly, unmedicated amid this coverage denial, Jamie couldn't do laundry, the dishes, or other household chores. They sometimes felt unable to simply wake up, get dressed, and eat breakfast.

"To have so much agency taken away from you because your insurance company decides that you're cured of your disease or illness on December 31, it's inhumane. How are you supposed to advocate for yourself when you're unmedicated? You're not going to feel well." Sometimes, Jamie would have enough medication on hand to tide them over amid a prior authorization battle, because they will sometimes take a lower dose if they have fewer responsibilities on a given day. But, in early 2020, they lacked such a stockpile and ran out of medication when the prior authorization expired. For three weeks, they were entirely unmedicated, which felt unmanageable, leaving Jamie "struggling to exist," let alone navigate the complexities of the health insurance system during business hours when all they wanted to do was sleep.

The approval ultimately came through after weeks of delay. But now that they are on state health insurance, they no longer take the split dose even though that's what works best for them. "I didn't have it in me to fight state health insurance. I straight-up changed my dosage because I didn't want to deal with it."

Jamie is not the only patient with whom I spoke who struggled to access prescription drugs for the management of behavioral health conditions. Far from it. Jordan's behavioral health coverage challenges stemmed not from trying to obtain ADHD medication, but rather his antidepressant Trintellix, a name brand drug used to treat major depressive disorder. A thirty-one-year-old psychiatric physician assistant in Minneapolis, Jordan gets "*extra* pissed off when as a patient I have to deal with prior authorizations because I know firsthand how needlessly prohibitive they are."

Up until being denied coverage for Trintellix (the list price of which is $444.14), Jordan was "as happy as he could be with the insurance company that I had," not having run into previous major challenges. He could access his treatments and providers. Everything was going smoothly … until the medication was denied amid a formulary change.

In addition to major depression, Jordan has a history of an eating disorder, and given many antidepressants' risks of modest weight gain, it was difficult for him to find a medication that was both effective and weight-neutral. When prescribed the selective serotonin reuptake inhibitor (SSRI) Zoloft, he gained a couple of pounds, which brought on a re-emergence of his eating disorder-related thoughts. He next tried the serotonin and norepinephrine reuptake inhibitor (SNRI) Cymbalta, which made him feel constantly tired and "foggy." He was no longer gaining weight, but he was no longer functioning fully. So, he was back to the drawing board *again*, and it was during this time that Jordan needed to return to his eating disorder treatment, during which the program's psychiatrist proposed trying the drug Trintellix.

It was weight-neutral. It had unique properties that might be suitable for his condition. Jordan agreed to try it, and the prior authorization was approved. And, as luck would have it, its effects felt like "magic. It has done wonders for me." The only side effect was a *slight* amount of nausea that was easily managed, and which went away relatively quickly.

But then he had to renew his prior authorization. He hadn't been concerned about it, because "why would it take long to approve a medication I'm already on and doing well on? And it shouldn't have been that much of a question because I've been on a *lot* of other things." Running low on medication, he called the pharmacy multiple times to follow up on whether the prior authorization had gone through. It *still* hadn't, and the cost was prohibitively expensive for long-term payment out-of-pocket, especially given his other out-of-pocket medical costs. Now, Jordan was officially out of medication.

The insurance company had dropped Trintellix from its formulary. He wasn't entirely clear on what was happening to his prescription drug coverage because it was "so convoluted," involving no notice of the coverage change, or else the notification was "buried in other things" sent to him, and it was made even more challenging because he was so depressed at the time due to his running out of medication.

Jordan thought to himself, "If I got approved for this medication, there's no reason why I should be off of this medication." His psychiatrist then did a peer-to-peer with his insurance company, which resulted in yet another denial. At one point, severely depressed, Jordan gave in and paid out-of-pocket for a one-month supply of Trintellix to avoid a further decline in his mood. "There were days when I realized the only reason why I was doing *anything* was I needed to take care of my cat. I was starting to have passive suicidal thoughts of 'What's the point in living?' If my cat weren't here, I just wouldn't see the point in continuing. It was getting really bad really quickly."

It frustrated Jordan to be having these thoughts *because he worked in mental health*. On the one hand, he was worried about himself, knowing that these were bad signs that needed to be addressed. On the other hand, he felt defeated by his insurance company. He was trying his best to keep up at work, but that drained him of what little energy he had. When he returned home, he would be overwhelmed by who to call and where to look for prescription drug coupons. While unable to afford to routinely pay for the drug out-of-pocket, he earned too high a salary to qualify for financial assistance through the drug manufacturer.

Despite his documented adverse reaction to multiple SSRIs, Jordan's insurance wanted him to go on the SSRI Lexapro, which is related to the drug that had previously made him suicidal. He knew that he would *never* place a patient on that medication given the history of suicidality when on citalopram. "It's a huge liability." In fact, Lexapro was designated as an allergy.

Jordan even explored ACA marketplace options with another insurer that would cover his Trintellix, but he found that the cost of switching insurers would exceed the cost of paying for the drug with the pharmacy-provided coupon.

In the meantime, Jordan was relying on Trintellix samples offered by his psychiatric nurse practitioner, allowing him to space out the frequency with which he had to pay out-of-pocket for the medication. Jordan began to take half of his prescribed dose to further stretch the prescription and manage its associated cost. "I was doing some pretty desperate things," Jordan reflected of this time. He was better than when he was off the medication and was no longer passively suicidal, but he was still "lower energy than I needed be. There was a lot of apathy about life, and my anxiety was still bad for a while." But when his apartment was burglarized and he experienced related trauma, he *had* to go back on the full dose, which came with a hefty price tag absent insurance coverage.

Months later, the formulary determination appeared to have changed again such that his insurer began to pay part of the cost of the drug, though he learned this not from a notification by the insurer, but simply by observing the reduced price at the pharmacy.

"I'm *very* lucky that I had the economic means to get through this time. I couldn't have imagined going on something else that seemed likely to cause all sorts of trouble. But if they were going to pay for part of this eventually, why did they make me go through all this suffering?"

CONCLUSION

For many Americans every year, a trip to the pharmacy entails not an easy picking up of a prescribed medication, but a notification of a pending prior authorization that prevents their obtaining the drug. In a time when the average American spends over $1,400 on prescription medications each year[66] and with prescription drugs accounting for 10 percent of all health care spending in the United States,[67] it is vital to understand the scope and impact of coverage denials within the realm of prescription drugs – whether because of medical necessity determinations or because of new formulary designations that exclude that which had been prescribed and was working well for the patient.

This chapter has laid bare the immense impact that the health insurance and pharmaceutical industry complexities have wrought for American patients and their prescribers. Given how much private corporations dominate the American health care system, it is perhaps unsurprising that coverage denials play such a significant role in the realm of prescription drugs. This chapter has worked to illuminate the challenges of denials through prior authorization and varied, ever-changing formularies that restrict access to approved treatments. Though prior authorization and step therapy are aimed at promoting cost containment for insurers, they can undercut those very monetary goals if patients' conditions worsen and necessitate more costly care, especially when those step therapy requirements are out of alignment with clinical guidelines – and restricting off-label treatments can even push patients toward higher-cost prescription drugs.

The highly varied nature of formularies becomes even more challenging for patients when switching insurers, which about half of Americans do every three years. This results in patients risking every few years losing access to coverage for the medications that they have long been prescribed to manage their conditions – regimens that may have required months or years of trial and error to establish. And while electronic systems are in place to streamline prior authorizations as well as to identify formulary statuses for prescription drugs, such systems are not universally adopted, leaving gaps in care and persistent information barriers within this complex and highly varied health care system. In fact, given that rural and less resourced hospitals are less likely than urban hospitals to use EHRs (not to mention Real-Time Pharmacy Benefits), the complexity that prior authorization imposes on physicians and the tools on which they come to rely (e.g., through Epic) can ultimately deepen inequities not just across patients, but across medical practices.

For some, medication denials through prior authorization led to hours or days spent on the phone with doctor's offices and insurance companies, but ultimately an approval and only a few missed doses. For others (such as Liz and Jordan), coverage denial resulted in weeks or months of suffering while appealing to access the prescribed medication. Both physicians and patients denied coverage felt a sense of loss of autonomy as well as of trust in the system in which they were operating – a loss of trust that their medical recommendations would be given due consideration, and a loss of trust in insurers' willingness to help them access their prescribed care. And, in both sets of cases, this chapter highlights that patients as well as their physicians navigated considerable administrative burdens that I discuss in depth in the chapters that follow.

CHAPTER 5

Coverage Denials and Cost Shifting to Patients

It is in moments of illness that we are compelled to recognize that we live not alone but chained to a creature of a different kingdom, whole worlds apart, who has no knowledge of us and by whom it is impossible to make ourselves understood: our body.

Marcel Proust

"CAN I AFFORD TO PAY THIS, and if not, should I just not go to the doctor at all? There were times when I was scheduled to go in, but I just skipped it and maybe two months later, I'd go, 'You've *got* to go now, because you're having symptoms.' But it's financially painful. I'm constantly asking myself, 'Should I abandon treatment?'"

Gary, a fifty-one-year-old Black man in New York City, is no stranger to delaying medical care, having gone uninsured altogether for a couple of years. After repeated denials by his marketplace plan through Cigna amid his deteriorating health, he is always waiting for the other shoe to drop.

Sometimes, it's pushing back an appointment so that he can address a medical bill. Sometimes, it's waiting until his symptoms worsen.

Gary has been in treatment for a benign tumor on his prostate, a condition that required multiple diagnostic tests billed as surgical procedures, a surgery and one-day hospitalization, repeated follow-up tests including an MRI scan, and medication to slow the growth of the tumor:

About two and a half years ago, I started to notice that the insurer would deny claims because they were expensive procedures. There's one test that he does every single time and it's $2,000 even though it takes all of four minutes. Then I had surgery where I was hailing a cab less than 24 hours later, and then the bill came, and the hospital room alone was $18,500. The insurance company started to deny the claims and force me to publicly shame them and to get my surgeon's nurse practitioner to battle it out with the insurance company to get them to change their position. They kept saying it was not medically necessary. And I work 60 hours a week. I don't have time to plead with the hospital or the doctor to reduce my bill.

While the tumor remains benign, its ongoing monitoring is important, especially because Black men are 1.7 times more likely to be diagnosed with prostate cancer than white men, and more than twice as likely to die from it.[1]

Even when his surgeon's office was successful in getting the medical necessity denial reversed, there was never relief. Gary always felt that another denial would follow for subsequent care; his trust in the health care system was veritably broken.

Sometimes, he would simply forgo care, but delaying his medical care comes at a price. Left untreated, with a benign tumor continuing to grow, he would have to urinate every forty-five minutes. Leaving the privacy of his home was an ordeal, and his work-related travel felt unmanageable at times. He could sometimes persuade a client that the work could be done virtually rather than in person, but it had an adverse impact on his quality of life. "The stress and anxiety of it can make you *more* ill when you're just trying to get better."

Gary is not alone. Of the dozens of patients interviewed, many reported spacing out treatments to avoid incurring more medical costs. For Michelle, a woman in her fifties with a particularly high risk of breast cancer, moving her breast MRI back a week to accommodate a family emergency meant being placed on an "experimental schedule," resulting in being denied coverage. While she still receives her mammograms, Michelle no longer receives the breast MRIs that her physician recommended, out of fear of encountering future denials and the burdens of appeal, and she crosses her fingers that it does not lead to cancer going undiagnosed. But forgoing the test was simply easier than fighting with her insurance company. These patients' experiences lay bare not only the risk that patients run when postponing care following a coverage denial, but also the broader distrust in the health care system that emerges from this practice, reshaping their health care utilization.

Thus, while these utilization management tools can have the effect of rationing care not due to final denial, but rather through accumulations of inconveniences, the experience of the denial is far from being merely inconvenient: as this chapter will illustrate, it is both medically and financially destabilizing.

THE SCOPE OF DELAYED CARE

Gaps in care can pose problems both for patients and for the physicians who are responsible for their care. Pennsylvania psychiatrist Dr. Daniel Block said that his patients' medications are often denied when they have little extra on hand amid the battle to resolve the denial. This, in turn, can yield liability concerns (especially given the high stakes of mental health care), such that "If someone runs out of meds because of the insurance issue, I'll document that insurance interfered with patient care."[2]

This observation of disrupted patient care is not anomalous. In a 2024 American Medical Association survey of 1,000 physicians on prior authorizations, 93 percent reported that the insurer practice of seeking prior authorization was associated with delays in access to necessary care, and 82 percent reported that prior authorization "can at least sometimes lead to treatment abandonment" by the patient.[3] It is for these reasons that 94 percent of physician respondents expressed that, for patients whose treatment required prior authorization, prior authorization had a negative effect on clinical outcomes.

In a world in which 56 percent of Americans would struggle to accommodate an unexpected $1,000 expense with their savings,[4] the average medical service denied in my survey had a cost of approximately $1,600, and 14.3 percent of denials were for care with cost exceeding $5,000, an amount that would be financially destabilizing for many. This raises significant possibilities that, absent an initial approval of coverage, delays in care will ensue. And with many patients, such as Catherine or Sharon from Chapter 2, expressing apprehensiveness not only about the initial coverage denial, but also about *future* denials, care postponement by patients may extend to other health services to avoid accumulation of health coverage disputes in a system that, in their experience, has betrayed them.

Each of the 482 survey respondents who experienced a coverage denial was asked, "Did you delay any medical treatment due to cost or uncertainty of coverage?" Overall, 50.4 percent of respondents postponed at least some form of medical care in the aftermath of their denial. What's more, half of those respondents postponed what they deemed to be "significant" amounts of medical care. Care postponement was observed across all insurance statuses, though it was lowest among those enrolled in Medicare (38 percent), compared with those enrolled in Medicaid (50 percent), employer-provided coverage (51 percent), and ACA marketplace plans (61 percent).

Respondents were then asked in an open-ended question to describe the sorts of health care they postponed in the aftermath of the denial. Responses varied widely, including delaying physical therapy, lab work, use of prescription medication, mental health counseling, treatment for bone fractures, scans, heart procedures, surgery, cancer treatment, treatment for a pulmonary embolus, and "all elective tests and procedures." Thus, coverage denials have a sweeping impact across diverse areas of medicine, with the most common form of delayed treatment being prescription medication, followed by surgery.

While care postponement is clearly prevalent, the aggregate data do not shed light on inequities. I will now discuss the theories I put forward concerning why some patients will be particularly likely to postpone their medical care.

THEORIES ABOUT CARE POSTPONEMENT

There are many reasons why one might postpone medical care following a health insurance coverage denial, but the *economic security theory* suggests that those who are on less solid financial footing will be more risk averse in pursuing further medical care, lest they accrue more medical bills. One might reasonably expect that those with lower household incomes would be more likely to postpone care in the face of denials, while denials may be less disruptive to the health care utilization of more affluent individuals, who may be better equipped to weather the storm. This is exactly

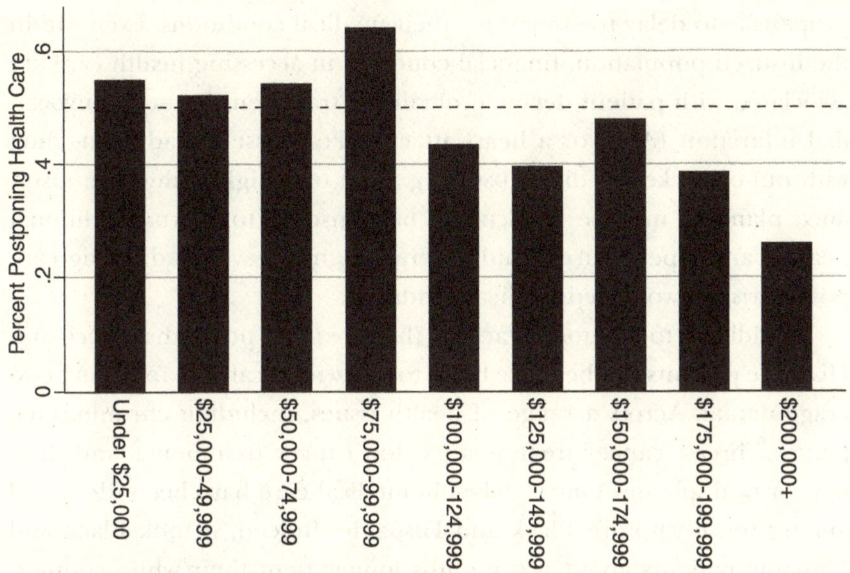

5.1 Health care postponement by income level.
Source: Survey of the 482 patients experiencing a denial, among the 1,340 patients surveyed.

what I find in Figure 5.1, which plots the rate of care postponement across income levels, with the horizontal dashed line indicating the sample-wide average rate of care postponement. Those income groups for which the bar is above the horizontal line have an above-average rate of care postponement; income groups for which the bar is below the line have a below-average rate of care postponement following a coverage denial.

Consistent with expectations, those with household incomes below $100,000 per year (that is, lower- and middle-income respondents) are significantly more likely to postpone care than are those with household incomes at or above $100,000 (that is, upper middle- and upper-income respondents). Moreover, a difference-in-means test reveals that those working multiple jobs to make ends meet are 15 percentage points more likely than their counterparts to postpone medical care in the face of a denial ($p = 0.02$). Cumulatively, this suggests that coverage denials – which previous chapters have shown are pervasive and burdensome – particularly destabilize the health care utilization of less economically secure patients.

Related to the patient's income, I expect that patients' overall concerns about affording health care costs will be associated with their propensity to delay treatment for their medical conditions. Even within the insured population, financial concerns in accessing health care are associated with patient delays in obtaining treatment for acute myocardial infarction (AMI, or a heart attack).[5] For those already struggling with out-of-pocket medical costs (e.g., due to a high deductible insurance plan), it may be particularly burdensome to accrue additional health care expenditures amid coverage denials, even if delaying care poses a risk of worsened medical condition.

In addition to economic factors, the *race theory* posits that Black and Hispanic patients will be more likely to delay medical care following coverage denial. Across a range of health issues, including chronic renal failure,[6] breast cancer treatment,[7] colon cancer treatment,[8] and therapy for multiple myeloma,[9] delays in medical care have been identified among those who are Black and Hispanic. Indeed, it took Black and Hispanic patients about two months longer than their white counterparts to begin treatment for multiple myeloma, a rare and serious cancer.[10] While delays were not studied in the context of coverage denials, I expect this population to be more likely to face delays in health care when confronted with insurance challenges.

Another demographic group in which delays in care have been documented is the LGBTQ community, giving rise to the *LGBTQ health theory*. Scholars at the University of California's Los Angeles Center for Health Policy Research identified that, even when they were covered by health insurance, gay, lesbian, and bisexual adults in California were more likely to delay seeking medical attention.[11] While one of the cited reasons for this delay is discrimination in health care, researchers at UCLA also found that bisexual men and women were the least likely of all groups to have a usual source of health care (27 percent and 24 percent respectively).[12] This is especially significant in evaluating the impact of coverage denials, because I find through survey and interview evidence that physician offices often play a key role in navigating appeals – whether engaging in a peer-to-peer phone call or crafting appeal letters supported by clinical research about the patient's condition.

What's more, within the transgender population, health policy researchers William Padula and Kellen Baker highlight access to care issues resulting from underinsurance, with many insurers declining to cover medically necessary, gender-affirming care despite non-discrimination legislation being in place.[13] Thus, with patterns of delay associated with discrimination, lower overall access to a usual source of care, and higher vulnerability to coverage denials (as illustrated in Chapter 3), I expect that those identifying as LGBTQ will be more likely to postpone health care following coverage denials.

Finally, the *Medicaid expansion hypothesis* posits that care postponement will be less prevalent in states that expanded Medicaid through the Affordable Care Act. The Center on Budget and Policy Priorities identifies that Medicaid expansion improves access to care, as well as producing better health outcomes for patients across non-behavioral and behavioral health care.[14] Thus, Medicaid expansion is not only associated with lower uninsured rates, but also increases health care utilization to manage ongoing medical conditions. In turn, I expect that this will likewise translate to reduced delays in care even in the face of insurance barriers.

I turn now to the descriptive findings.

DESCRIPTIVE FINDINGS. Figure 5.2 plots the average rate of survey respondents' health care postponement across the relevant variables.

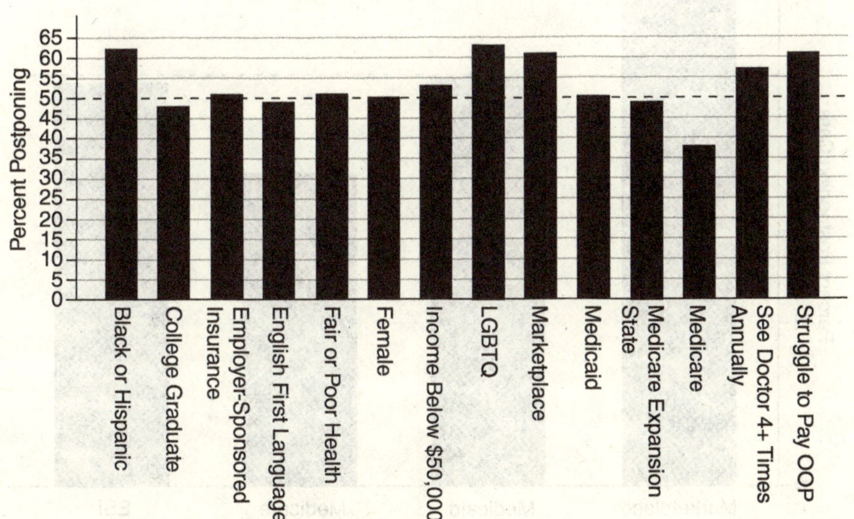

5.2 Characteristics affecting care postponement.
Source: Survey of the 482 patients experiencing a denial, among the 1,340 patients surveyed.

What is clear from the bivariate analysis – and is consistent with the multivariate logit regression findings discussed in the Appendix – is that Black and Hispanic respondents were nearly 15 percentage points more likely than their counterparts to postpone medical care following a coverage denial ($p = 0.01$). Thus, not only are coverage denials and care postponement prevalent aspects of the American patient experience, but also they appear to exacerbate health care inequities along racial lines. What's more, LGBTQ patients are more likely than their heterosexual cisgender counterparts not only to be denied coverage (see Chapter 3 findings), but also to have their health care disrupted – with a 15 percentage point difference ($p = 0.01$) – thus reinforcing health care disparities along sexual orientation and gender identity lines.

While the effect of Medicaid expansion is in the expected direction, it does not rise to conventional levels of statistical significance at the bivariate level (though, turning to the multivariate level in the Appendix, the evidence appears more compelling). What's more, while the effect of *income below $50,000* does not appear to be statistically significant, lower-income individuals appear more likely to postpone medical care

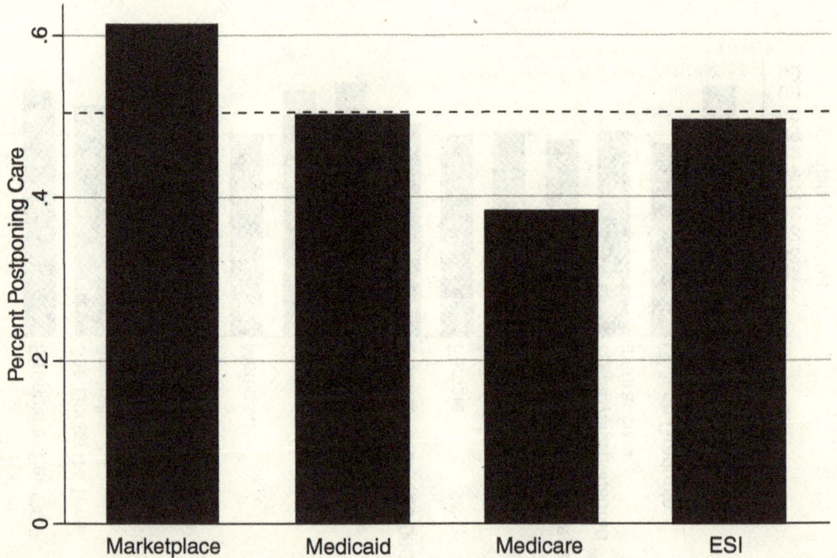

5.3 Care postponement by insurance.
Source: Survey of the 482 patients experiencing a denial, among the 1,340 patients surveyed.

when turning to the multivariate setting with the linear *income* variable ranging from 1 to 9. And, in fact, consistent with Figure 5.1, I find that those earning less than $100,000 annually are 16 percentage points less likely than their upper-middle- and upper-income counterparts ($p = 0.00$) to receive timely treatment. Further, and unsurprisingly, this care postponement is significantly more prevalent among those who are struggling with out-of-pocket medical costs – a 34 percentage point difference relative to those who do not have these financial anxieties, which understandably may lead to avoidance of new medical debts. Health care postponement also varies across health insurance sources, with those on marketplace plans most likely to delay care following a coverage denial (see Figure 5.3). Perhaps surprisingly, health status does not appear to be associated with survey respondents' care postponement.

Given that a nontrivial share of health care prescribed in the United States is of low or questionable value, to understand the impact of this care postponement, it is important to also examine whether this had an adverse effect on respondents' health status.

THE IMPACT OF HEALTH CARE POSTPONEMENT

When Jessica (from Chapter 2) was denied coverage for her SCIg to treat her severe immunodeficiency, she went untreated. She experienced constant (though not life-threatening) infections because her body lacked the antibodies to fight common infections.

"You name it, I had it," Jessica recounted, noting that in the year leading up to starting the infusion drug, she underwent fifteen or sixteen separate courses of antibiotics, putting her at risk of dangerous antibiotic resistance and requiring extensive time off from work. "Without the infusion medication, I don't have the antibodies to fight off things like strep and pneumococcal disease, any respiratory infection." She considered it a matter of luck that she was not hospitalized as she waited to secure coverage for the infusion medication, especially amid the ongoing COVID-19 pandemic.

Jessica's experience is not anomalous. In the 2024 American Medical Association survey on prior authorizations, 29 percent of physician respondents reported that prior authorization led to a "serious adverse event" for their patient. Indeed, 23 percent of physician respondents indicated that prior authorization had led to a patient's hospitalization, 18 percent of physician respondents reported that it led to a "life-threatening event or required intervention to prevent permanent impairment or damage," and 8 percent of physicians reported that it led to the patient's disability or permanent bodily damage. However, this does not disentangle the myriad reasons why prior authorizations might induce delays and denials, such as care being deemed "not medically necessary," "experimental," or "cosmetic."

Prior authorization-induced medical complications are indicated in surveys of patients as well. An American Medical Association survey of patients with diabetes revealed that not only did nearly one in five diabetic patients have to ration or skip doses of insulin because of prior authorization challenges, but 13 percent experienced a hospitalization. Thus, there is some suggestive evidence that these delays in care are associated with adverse, sometimes *seriously* adverse, effects for patients.

To evaluate the extent to which patients' health (or perceptions of their health) changed following their coverage denial, each of the 243 survey respondents who postponed medical care after a coverage denial was asked, "Did your health status change when you postponed treatment?" Respondents were given the options of "Yes, my health worsened," "No, my health stayed the same," or "No, my health improved."

Of the 243 respondents postponing care, 109, or 45 percent, reported that their health status worsened amid their delay in medical treatment. Those reporting worsened health were broadly distributed across age and educational groups. Those with household incomes below $50,000 per year were 15 percentage points more likely than their more affluent counterparts to report that their health status worsened due to care postponement ($p = 0.02$). In combination with the economic findings presented elsewhere – that less affluent individuals are less likely to appeal denials and are more likely to postpone care – this suggests that the insurer practice of coverage denials can not only impose greater administrative burdens on patients from marginalized groups, but also exacerbate health inequities along class lines.

Each respondent postponing care was then asked in an open-ended question to describe the impact that health care postponement had on their physical and/or mental health. Individuals spoke to the physical toll of delayed health care, with one respondent reporting that "unmanaged symptoms affected every part of my life," and another noting that their cancer progressed while they awaited access to care. Some respondents expressed that they were "in more pain," were "unsure at the time if my knee would ever get back to 100 percent," "unable to get my prescribed medication," and that it "got to the point where I can barely walk because they wouldn't do the knee surgery." Thus, while some respondents spoke to unmanaged pain and quality of life concerns, others spoke to serious disease progression with unknown consequences.

What was also clear from responses was not just the physical, but also the psychological toll that these experiences wrought, with respondents emphasizing – as with Gary's experience – "increased stress," having a "harder time sleeping," "increased anxiety," "mental health declined substantially," and "my depression worsened for a while, and I withdrew from my family and friends." Thus, when evaluating the impact of coverage denials, one must consider both the physical health costs associated with patients' possible deterioration and the broader psychological costs associated with seeking care in the setting of increased privatization. Moreover, 50 percent of those postponing at least some form of health care reported being "very concerned" or "somewhat concerned" about facing subsequent denials, an experience echoed in Catherine's reluctance to pursue care even once her jaw surgery was eventually determined not to be simply cosmetic.

For Ilona, a nineteen-year-old college student in Ohio, these findings of health care postponement hit close to home. Ilona experienced a severe flu and pneumonia that resulted in complications including weight loss, rendering her only eighty-two pounds despite her height of 5'3", leaving her with a body mass index (BMI) of just 14.5 rather than the normal 18.5–24.9. Her gastroenterologist referred her to nutritional services, which Ilona and her provider's office confirmed were within her schedule of insurance benefits. Despite this due diligence, after receiving four treatments with an in-network nutritionist, a superbill for $800 was submitted to her insurer, and she was promptly denied coverage on the grounds that it was not a covered service. What's more, the appeal was unsuccessful.

As a work-study student on financial aid, Ilona does not have the financial resources to cover the full cost of these services. Combining work-study earnings and support from her family, Ilona was able to pay the medical bill, but not before accumulating months of letters from her insurer and the provider seeking payment for services rendered. And Ilona has not been back to her nutritionist, despite more appointments being deemed appropriate for her condition due to her continued weight loss: "I just assume that it will be denied again." She will wait until she gets sicker, until it becomes *absolutely necessary*.

These delays in care can come at not just a health price, but a monetary one as well. A central goal underlying prior authorization is the containment of rising health care costs, yet delays in care can lead to exacerbations that necessitate more costly medical treatment.

"There's no doubt that people experience delays in care," Wendell Potter reflected on the effects of prior authorization, adding that "delays caused by prior authorization can be detrimental to a person's health and result in a hospitalization or procedure that would not have been necessary. And there are people who *die* because of prior authorization denials and delays. It's one reason why I left my job at Cigna. There is no doubt that people *die every day*."

This observation is borne out by clinical research across a range of conditions, with costs associated with cholecystectomy treatment increasing by 22 percent when delayed by just one day and by 37 percent when delayed an additional day,[15] and a 14 percent increase in cost associated with COVID-19 treatment when delayed by just one day.[16] Thus, whether due to complications or lengthened hospital stays, even modest delays in care can significantly increase costs.

Interviews with physicians supported the possibility that delay or denial of medical coverage through the prior authorization process can necessitate more costly treatment. For example, Dr. Andrew Spector noted that, when a patient was unable to secure insurance coverage for the narcolepsy medication Sunosi (the cost of which is around $1,000 without insurance), they self-medicated with five caffeine pills to stay awake and subsequently were hospitalized with cardiac arrhythmia.

These patient behaviors ultimately reflect not cost containment, but rather a *shifting* of costs from payers to patients and their physicians, who are left to navigate the labyrinthian health insurance system to access coverage for appropriate care.

For North Carolina patient Kathleen Valentini, delay induced by a denied prior authorization not only led to more costly treatment: it actually cost her life. Amid excruciating and worsening hip pain, and after receiving several weeks of physical therapy, Valentini sought the assistance of an orthopedic surgeon, who, after an inconclusive X-ray, ordered an MRI, which was denied as not medically necessary.[17] Over a month later, the insurer reversed its initial denial upon appeal, and the MRI revealed a sarcoma in Valentini's hip. Valentini was informed that, had she "come to them a month sooner, oncologists could have proceeded with chemo alone, but physicians would now have to amputate [her] leg, hip, and pelvis."[18] Thus, the approximately forty-day delay necessitated extensive, life-altering surgery.

Losing half of her lower body was bad enough, but further testing revealed that the cancer had metastasized to her right lung. Valentini died two years later, and her family brought a lawsuit contending that the delays driven by the denied prior authorization contributed to the fatal delay in her cancer diagnosis.

Valentini is not alone among cancer patients. In a 2022 survey commissioned by Cardinal Health, not only did nearly 90 percent of oncologist respondents say that prior authorization poses a significant barrier when initiating treatments for their patients, but 80 percent reported that prior authorization has negative effects on patient outcomes, with just 6 percent saying that such delays occur "rarely."[19] In fact, only 1 percent of oncologists characterized this utilization management control as having a positive impact on patient care.[20]

This offers important new context for discussion about the value of prior authorization in guarding against overutilization. To be sure, this is far from an inappropriate goal when evaluating not only the high rate of overall spending but also the extent of low-value care that is prescribed, some of which is risky to the patient. However, this survey and interview evidence combine to offer reason for more measured intervention to mitigate delays in *appropriate* care.

Having examined the adverse health impact of this insurance practice – potentially leading to worse health outcomes and even more costly treatment – I turn now to the broader economic precarity that coverage denials induce in American patients, focusing on the postponement of planned non-medical purchasing in the face of denials.

PURCHASING POSTPONEMENT

The financially destabilizing impact of health insurance denials is all too common an American experience. For Heather, the denial of her abdominal CT scan "wasn't the *worst* time in my life, but it was second," noting the $4,500 bill with which she was left. Heather had already gone bankrupt once due to exorbitant medical bills associated with the connective tissue disorder Ehlers–Danlos Syndrome (EDS) when she was working four separate jobs to try to make ends meet. She had seen the worst of it. But nevertheless, this was so devastating that she considered obtaining a Medicaid divorce, or the transfer of assets and dissolution of marriage so as to qualify for Medicaid.

Heather is one of over 500,000 Americans who file bankruptcy each year at least in part due to medical bills. In fact, it is estimated that medical debt accounts for as much as 40 percent of personal bankruptcies.[21]

What was particularly exasperating for Heather was that, after years of working as a nurse, *she knew the system.* But she counted her blessings that her husband was employed and, because both of them had been raised in or near poverty, they "knew how to thrift," even if home repairs were still sorely needed due to water damage and a "floor that's fixing to collapse."

On May 25, 2021, Heather had an emergency c-section due to an infected placenta, which led to a fever and fetal distress. Over three months later, on September 8, 2021, Heather received a transvaginal ultrasound scan because she was having significant vaginal bleeding as well as stabbing pelvic and abdominal pain since the c-section. Heather's OB-GYN prescribed a CT scan to further investigate the cause of her ongoing pain, as well as the hormonal medication estradiol to address the bleeding.

The estradiol eventually resolved most of the bleeding, but the stabbing pelvic and abdominal pain persisted. Despite this, on September 16, Blue Cross Blue Shield of Alabama denied the prior authorization for the CT scan. After calling her insurer, she was told to send additional paperwork to justify the scan and re-request prior authorization.

Three days later, the insurer told Heather to be more elaborate in yet another prior authorization resubmission. Applying her skills as a nurse, Heather wrote to her OB-GYN an elaborate description of the pain, in the hope that it would finally facilitate an approval of the CT scan. Heather wrote,

> Patient has pain rated seven out of ten on right and left sides of the incision scar, approximately one inch below scar on abdomen. A third location of pain is localized to the left lower quadrant, one inch to the left of incision scar. Pain is stabbing and cramping. Pain began on 5/25/21. Pain lessened from nine out of ten once it healed. Breathing in increases pain. Tylenol, Aleve, and Aspirin do not relieve pain. Heating pad to abdomen decreases pain to six out of ten. Cold packs exacerbate pain.

As the weeks went on, the pelvic pain continued, so she contacted her local hospital, which claimed that the prior authorization had been secured. Heather completed the long-awaited CT scan. The next day, Heather was told the prior authorization had actually been *denied* because it was not medically necessary. Heather then got two different bills: one for about $300 and another a little over $4,000. Now, Heather needed to petition her insurance company for authorization for a CT scan that had already been performed.

Heather's CT scan bill eventually got resolved (as did her pelvic pain), but not before she accrued debt and accompanying interest, feared debt collectors and bankruptcy, and contemplated divorce from her loving husband to facilitate accessing public insurance.

Heather's story of bankruptcy and desperation to forestall debt collections is all too common and aligns with the devastation that Carol and Jason's denial would have wrought had it not gotten resolved when Jason took to social media. "We're a low-income family with four children. We don't have savings, and you have so much to lose. I can't imagine how much it would have set us behind to have to pay that. We can't get yearbooks for our kids, and this year for clothes we're going to Goodwill instead of WalMart."

The KFF analysis of data from the 2020 Survey of Income and Program Participation finds that 9 percent of US adults, or roughly 23 million people, owe medical debt.[22] This collective medical debt totaled at least $195 billion in 2019, with larger shares of that debt owed by those identifying as being in poor health or disabled. Further, while 9 percent of white individuals have medical debt, 16 percent of Black individuals do, suggesting a policy problem that is not only pervasive, but also inequitable.

The Consumer Financial Protection Bureau (CFPB) estimates that $88 billion in medical debt is reflected on Americans' credit reports as of June 2021, and that 58 percent of debt on credit reports is for medical care.[23] The CFPB notes that medical debt is often unexpected, with two-thirds of such debts resulting from an acute medical need (e.g., an emergency department visit) that allows little if any time to "shop around" for an optimal price. While the prudent layperson standard is meant to offer protection to emergency department patients unable to accurately distinguish between emergent and non-emergent conditions, the evidence presented thus far suggests imperfect compliance by insurers. The burdens of medical debt are lessened in the setting of Medicaid expansion through the Affordable Care Act,[24] though, as of June 2025, ten states have declined to expand.

In January 2025, the CFPB finalized a rule removing medical debt from credit reports, thus offering significant relief to more than 15 million Americans. However, the second Trump Administration obstructed implementation of the CFPB rule, even going so far as to join forces with those filing a lawsuit to block the rule.[25] Given that this policy is in flux, coupled with the reality that many individuals may accrue non-medical debts in order to pay medical bills, it is worth exploring the broader economic impact of coverage barriers.

EVIDENCE OF PURCHASING POSTPONEMENT. I asked each of the 482 respondents who experienced a coverage denial, "Following the denial of coverage, did you delay any non-medical purchases?" The postponement of purchases is one of the measures of financial fragility employed by public policy professor Daniel Schneider and his coauthors in their 2020 analysis of the effect of the COVID-19 pandemic on household financial fragility.[26] In fact, a 2022 report in *Yahoo News* chronicled Americans forced to choose between paying utility bills and paying for their prescriptions, at times rationing medication or reducing food intake.[27] Estimating this in the specific context of coverage denials helps me to gauge the extent to which this insurer practice has a financially destabilizing effect on American patients, such as by forcing them to choose between accessing care and paying for a car or home repair.

Respondents were given the options "No, it did not affect my spending," "Yes, I delayed major purchases," "Yes, I delayed even more modest purchases," or "Unsure." This question thus helps to capture health care consumers' broader spending patterns as risk is shifted from payers to patients.

Among respondents who experienced coverage denials, 48 percent reported that they delayed non-medical purchases in the aftermath of such denials, with approximately an even distribution between the postponement of larger versus more modest purchases. Just 40 percent of respondents indicated that the denial did not affect their spending. Because what constitutes "modest" versus "major" purchases likely varies across respondents, I collapse this finding *postponed purchases* into the dichotomous variable taking the value of 1 if the respondent postponed purchases and 0 otherwise. I consider this to be a measure of the financial fragility that this insurance practice imposes on patient populations. Unsurprisingly, purchasing postponement is especially prominent (57 percent) among respondents experiencing multiple coverage denials, for whom the accumulation of medical debt is more likely.

I expect that the postponement of non-medical purchasing will be most prevalent among those already in a more precarious financial position. To be sure, even more otherwise economically secure individuals can struggle to afford their medical expenses too, given the exorbitant costs of some medical treatments – whether a costly drug or the denial of residential care for behavioral health, which I discuss in Chapter 8. Such was the case for Kevin, a Texas journalist whose son's behavioral health care faced numerous insurance denials. "We lived frugally in general. We postponed retirement plan contributions. I withdrew 401(k) money

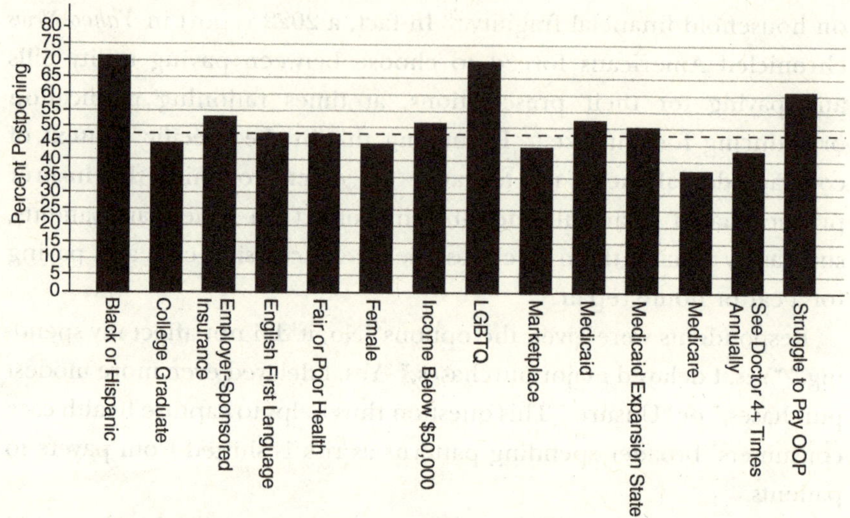

5.4 Characteristics associated with purchasing postponement.
Source: Survey of the 482 respondents who experienced a coverage denial, among the 1,340 total respondents.

early just to pay the bills. Now my wife and I are approaching retirement age with little savings."

Figure 5.4 plots the average rate of survey respondents' purchasing postponement across multiple demographic categories. Looking at the bivariate level, I find that respondents identifying as Black or Hispanic are 28 percentage points more likely than their counterparts to postpone non-medical purchasing following a coverage denial ($p = 0.00$), a finding that is consistent with the regression model displayed in the Appendix. The effect of economic status is less clear: those with lower incomes are not significantly more likely to postpone purchasing, though this financial disruption does appear to be more significantly concentrated among those already struggling to afford out-of-pocket medical costs. What's more, those who identify as LGBTQ – whom Chapter 3 highlights appear to be more vulnerable to coverage denial in the first place – also appear to have their financial lives more financially disrupted by this insurance practice. These findings highlight just one way that this insurer practice exacerbates existing vulnerabilities not just on class lines, but on race and sexual orientation lines as well. While those in Medicaid expansion states do not appear to enjoy this type of financial protection, Black and Hispanic respondents in non-expansion states are 23 percentage points more likely to postpone purchasing following a denial ($p = 0.08$).

CONCLUSION

When Heather got denied for the CT scan to diagnose her pelvic pain and bleeding, she feared the worst because she *knew* the worst. She had already experienced medical bankruptcy, and she was thankful that she and her husband could adjust their meager spending to manage a small payment to defer collections. Heather is not alone; instead, she stands with the hundreds of thousands of Americans every year for whom medical bills contribute to bankruptcy, and the many more still whose health and financial wellbeing are disrupted in less acute ways.

In this chapter, I have described the prevalence with which health insurers' denials of coverage are associated with patients' health care and non-medical purchasing postponement, and the fact that this postponement is distributed unevenly according to socioeconomic status, race, and sexual orientation. While individuals of a lower socioeconomic status are not more likely than their counterparts to be denied coverage in the first place, they are significantly more likely than their more affluent counterparts to delay medical care (whether for the denied service or other medical care). I find that those already struggling to afford out-of-pocket medical expenses, those respondents identifying as Black or Hispanic, and those identifying as LGBTQ are significantly more likely to demonstrate signs of financial fragility in the aftermath of denial of medical coverage. Thus, the insurance practice of denying medical coverage is noteworthy not only insofar as it affects millions of Americans every year, but also in the ways in which it deepens health and economic inequality, with those from marginalized backgrounds too often having health coverage on paper more so than meaningfully in practice and, relatedly, having other necessary expenses out of reach. While the effect of Medicaid expansion is not clear at the bivariate level, in the Appendix I find evidence that those in Medicaid expansion states appear to be less likely to postpone medical care, though this effect is not observed in the context of purchasing postponement.

As both the survey and interview evidence highlight, patients draw on a number of advantages to navigate the American health insurance system, though, as Heather demonstrates in her fight to obtain her CT scan, sometimes even that is not enough, and it can take a physical and psychological toll even when coverage is ultimately resolved. That is, the compliance costs and psychological costs accumulate.

Though prior authorization and utilization management more broadly have been hailed as vital to containing the costs of health care, their effect ultimately is the shifting of costs from payers to patients (as well as their physicians), imposing burdens that can keep health care and other important expenditures out of reach for patients, especially those from marginalized backgrounds. Thus, even if the practice of denials is cost containing – and in light of the high reversal rates upon appeal and the potential for exacerbations of patients' medical conditions, that is an open question – the result is that Black, Hispanic, LGBTQ, and less economically secure individuals have key expenses out of reach, meaning that they are struggling with financial insecurity and unable to access what they believe to be their health plan benefits.

Just as patients experience this shifting of risk – driving care and purchasing postponement at high rates – their physicians likewise experience a shifting of burden, which I examine next.

CHAPTER 6

Navigating Red Tape in Modern Medicine

It is not necessary to accept everything as true, one must only accept it as
necessary.

Franz Kafka, *The Trial*

THERE ARE SOME THINGS I know are going to be universally difficult – I know I can't order an MRI on anyone
without a prior authorization, no matter what your insurance is and no
matter what the condition is, because from the outpatient perspective
where I work, nothing is urgent or emergent so it usually takes about a
week," reflected Dr. Molly Weber.[1] "MRIs are universally annoying."

Dr. Weber is a family medicine physician in semi-rural Washington,
where she sees a broad range of patients. Treating the full spectrum
of medical conditions (outside of childbirth), Dr. Weber has frequent
prior authorization demands in the prescription of medications as well
as imaging. The delay in her patients' accessing prescribed care informs
prescribing decisionmaking. "When ordering brain MRIs, it's usually
something neurologic going on that I can't explain. The person is not
obviously sick enough to be in the emergency room or the hospital –
they're not obviously having a stroke – but the problem with neurologic
stuff is it has the potential to progress in an unpredictable way," and
if the approval for the MRI is delayed or inaccessible, the emergency
department might become the new, more expensive source of care.

Within the realm of prescriptions, while it is common knowledge that
health insurance plans devise their own formularies, frustrations arise
because "I as a physician have no way of knowing what's on that list. So,
if I prescribe an inhaler, I'm going to pick from a broad category and

I always pick a generic one, and at least 50 percent of the time, it'll come back and say I need to do prior auth or you can pick something else off the formulary, but the alternatives may or may not be appropriate. It's frustrating because I know this decision happened through some sort of algorithm" that patient appointments become dedicated to explaining. And while Dr. Weber does not always have strong preferences for one medication versus another in its class, the patient might experience a better response to one that the insurer does not prefer, which can in turn cause both paperwork burden and delays in care. "There are times like with diabetes medications where I know it's clinically appropriate but they're creating these obstacles."

Not all of this paperwork burden falls squarely on Dr. Weber's shoulders, as her office has a staffer dedicated to prior authorization administration, "but at the end of the day, I'm the one who has to look over whether or not I want to make a change, whether or not I want to appeal this, what are we going to say if we do appeal this. It's a huge amount of time and resources."

For Dr. Weber and other physicians interviewed, prescribing in this environment felt at times like a black box in addition to causing layers of bureaucracy apart from direct patient care. What's more, this time spent navigating the health insurance bureaucracy is non-billable hours. It is these administrative burdens on the health care system on which I focus, before returning to the patient experience.

With researchers at KFF finding in 2025 that just 0.2 percent of denied claims were appealed to plans through ACA marketplace exchanges in the 2023 plan year[2] and still just finding an appeal rate of 11.7 percent in the setting of Medicare Advantage plans' prior authorization denials (despite a nearly 82 percent reversal rate),[3] it is vital to understand better what accounts for this low rate of appeal.[4] Is it the administrative burden to the patients? Is it the information asymmetry between patients and their insurers? Is it the administrative burden to the physicians who are too overextended to navigate the hurdles of prior authorization approval?

This chapter works to highlight how, rather than containing costs in the health care system, payers' reliance on utilization management practices *shifts* burden to physicians and, in turn, to their patients. These demands broadly fall under the umbrella of what some public administration scholars have termed "administrative capital" – or the understanding of the bureaucratic rules, processes, and behaviors.[5]

One of the many layers of complexity in this system stems from the lack of uniformity of the relevant laws. Rather, as this chapter highlights, there is pronounced variation across the states, in ways that can significantly impact physicians' experience of the prior authorization "peer to peer" review process, the outcomes of which may drive additional, administratively burdensome appeal processes.

PRIOR AUTHORIZATION LAWS BY STATE

The American health care system is notoriously fragmented, with some of the health care sector regulated by the Department of Labor through ERISA (which preempts state laws that "relate to" self-insured, or self-funded health plans); Medicare, Medicaid, and ACA marketplace plans regulated by the Centers for Medicare and Medicaid Services; and some health insurance plans regulated at the state level. Consequently, the state in which one pursues medical care might have a significant effect both on the physician's and on the patient's experience of health insurance procedures and, consequently, access to benefits.

When a coverage denial is issued, the prescribing physician may engage in a "peer to peer" review with a physician employed by the patient's insurer in the hope of reversing the decision. While the medical community has hardly been a passive actor over decades of health insurance reform efforts, a source of considerable consternation among physicians is that not only are their prescribing decisions being reviewed by insurers who have not treated the patient, but also those reviewing and denying prior authorizations for insurers are generally not required to be in the appropriate specialty for the condition being treated.

Table 6.1 lays out the state-by-state requirements governing prior authorization review by insurers as of 2024, as identified by the American Medical Association (AMA).[6] Strikingly, there are numerous states currently without *any* statutes regulating the specialties of providers engaged in this practice – indeed, only twenty-eight states have

Table 6.1 State laws on prior authorization

State	Reviewer qualification
Alabama	Same or similar specialty as typically manages the medical condition, procedure, or treatment
Alaska	Licensed health care provider
Arkansas	Current and unrestricted AR medical license; physician may request same specialty
California	Competent to evaluate the specific clinical issues
Colorado	Familiar with standards of care
D.C.	Licensed physician in D.C./MD/VA in same or similar specialty
Georgia	Current and non-restricted license and in active practice in same or similar specialty as typically manages the medical condition
Illinois	Current and non-restricted license, in same or similar specialty as typically manages the medical condition
Kentucky	Licensed in same or similar specialty and subspecialty
Louisiana	Licensed and similar in education and background or same or similar specialist
Michigan	Licensed physician in same specialty as typically manages the condition
Minnesota	Same or similar specialty as typically manages the medical condition, procedure, or treatment
Missouri	Qualified health care professional licensed in the state
Montana	Physician whose specialty focuses on the diagnosis and treatment of the condition
Nebraska	Plans must ensure that a majority of those reviewing grievances have appropriate expertise
New Jersey	Denial made by physician under clinical direction of medical director licensed in NJ, appeal reviewed by board-certified physician in same or similar specialty
New Mexico	Has knowledge or consults with a specialist who has knowledge of the condition or disease
New York	Clinical peer
North Carolina	Qualified health care professional
Ohio	Clinical peer
Oregon	OR-licensed physician
Pennsylvania	Licensed provider with appropriate training, knowledge, expertise in same/similar specialty
Rhode Island	Same licensure status as ordering practitioner
Tennessee	Same or similar specialty as typically manages the condition
Texas	Licensed to practice medicine in the state
Utah	Licensed physician in the same state/district/territory as prescriber
Washington	In the same or related field
West Virginia	Similar specialty, education, and background

Source: American Medical Association

such statutes – such that a family physician might be in the position of reviewing a rare neurology case in which there is limited familiarity with the appropriate standards of care or the newly available drugs on the market. Such was the case for Nancy (from Chapter 2), whose treatment for sudden-onset hearing loss was denied not by an ENT, but rather by a gynecologist.

Among the twenty-eight states that have addressed this subject, there is marked variation in the requirements imposed. While those reviewing cases in Alabama must be in the "same or similar specialty as typically manages the medical condition, procedure, or treatment," in Texas one need only be licensed to practice medicine within the state, which is in effect an absence of regulation of reviewer qualification. In Missouri, similarly, one need only be a "qualified health care professional." But what makes one qualified *in a particular case*? In Colorado, that qualification is grounded in familiarity with standards of care in the state, while in Minnesota they must be in the "same or similar specialty as typically manages the medical condition, procedure, or treatment."

Absent requirements that one be within the same specialty or sub-specialty as the prescribing physician, one runs the risk of lack of familiarity with the relevant standards of care. After all, the US Food and Drug Administration approved fifty new drugs in 2024 and fifty-five new drugs in 2023. Ongoing pharmaceutical and other medical developments may place informational demands on physicians, especially those not engaged in the treatment of the relevant conditions. For example, among the 2024 drug approvals is Ensacove, intended for the treatment of non-small cell lung cancer. While oncologists may be acquainted with this new treatment option, as Table 6.1 indicates, in many states, such a physician is anything but guaranteed in review of such a case. This can potentially lead to erroneous denial of coverage for treatment deemed not medically necessary – which in turn generates burdens of appeal. What's more, it raises questions as to the extent to which these reviewers can fairly be characterized as a "peer."

In addition to frustration concerning reviewing physician qualifications, the AMA has characterized peer-to-peer requirements as "too often just another barrier to care," ostensibly aimed at collaboration and transparency, but in practice simply representing another "time-consuming and potentially detrimental use of UM [utilization management] by insurance companies."[7]

This has not always been the case. In the 2024 physician survey by the AMA, just 16 percent of physicians reported that the physician-appointed "peer" often or always has the appropriate qualifications, while 39 percent reported that they rarely or never do. This is consistent with the experience of Dr. Andrew Spector, who noted that, whereas peer-to-peer review once served as a valuable resource through which to explain treatment decisions that may have required clarity given a particular clinical presentation, "now, peer-to-peer is getting on the phone with someone who tells you why they denied it. They're not there to listen to an argument, and they have no power to overrule the decision. It serves no value anymore. I haven't done a peer-to-peer in ages because they became worthless. I write out my appeals on paper now and I just fax them."[8]

Similarly, while Dr. Weber is sometimes successful in peer-to-peer reviews, it typically involves giving them information that they should have already had related to the patient's case to "check their boxes." However, in one instance, Dr. Weber recounted the review of a prior authorization request for a computed tomography (CT) scan of the chest and abdomen as part of a workup for night sweats of unclear origin, for which "there's a pretty clear indication for a CT scan here because it could be indicative of malignancy." However, the insurer approved the abdominal CT but denied the chest CT despite their having been ordered for the same reason. In the peer-to-peer, it was advised that she instead pursue an X-ray, despite the record reflecting that she *had* ordered an X-ray, which was unremarkable, but less informative than a CT scan.

The prevailing sentiment among physicians interviewed was, "Is it just another barrel that we have to jump over?"

Dr. Russell Buhr similarly reflected that, in the last five years, this process had never resulted in him discussing a case with a fellow pulmonologist, despite his high level of expertise, with three board certifications and dual MD and PhD degrees. "It's not really fair to say I'm talking to my peer when I get a retired nephrologist who's just reading down a checklist, which is just an administrative process."[9] And these peer-to-peer reviews – which 56 percent of physician respondents in the 2024 AMA survey indicated have been on the rise in the last five years – are not just frustrating in principle, but administratively burdensome in practice, requiring time commitment and coordination with other responsibilities.

Dr. Courtney White sees headache patients in her clinic four days per week, leaving only one day per week during which she has the flexibility to do peer-to-peers and other administration. In a recent encounter, the insurer denied coverage for her patient's Botox injections for chronic migraines (or migraines occurring at least fifteen days per month), seeking additional medical necessity documentation to ensure that the Botox was not being administered for cosmetic purposes. She provided the additional information requested. The insurer then requested still more information, which she again supplied in a third letter to them. She was then directed to do a peer-to-peer review of the case, which she sought to schedule. She was informed that she would be contacted within seventy-two hours, but over a week had passed before they reached out to her. In the meantime, her patient's migraines were left untreated over the course of what would be a six-week-long insurance dispute about the medical necessity of the only FDA-approved treatment for chronic migraine.

A consistent characterization of peer-to-peers was the frustration that, although extensive information was provided with the initial request for prior authorization, it did not appear to be reviewed. Dr. Tom Wallach noted that, while his prior authorizations are almost always ultimately approved, "it's even more frustrating because I submitted all the information on the front end – the letter of medical necessity and the citations. They're making me go through month-and-a-half delays, hoping I'll bail. Some people do. I'm stubborn."[10] Such bureaucratic hoops, on which I elaborate in the section that follows, are easier for more well-resourced medical facilities to jump through than for facilities with more limited resources (which in turn tend to serve patients of lower socioeconomic status). This is consistent with the Table 6.2 findings from the ModernMedicine report that substantial physician staff time must be allocated toward the processing of prior authorizations, including the peer-to-peers that they can elicit – support staff that not all practices can spare for this purpose.

This widespread variation in prior authorization management across the states is important because the practice of prior authorization is sweeping across the health care sector, with KFF finding that 99 percent of Medicare Advantage plans now require prior authorization for some services and 83 percent of Medicare Advantage enrollees are in plans that apply prior authorization to mental health

Table 6.2 Time spent on prior authorizations per week

Time spent	Physician	Physician staff
>20 hours	1%	17%
16–20 hours	1%	12%
11–15 hours	7%	30%
1–10 hours	67%	32%
0 hours	24%	9%

Source: ModernMedicine

coverage.[11] The extent of reliance on prior authorization in mental health is particularly problematic because mental illness is notably underdiagnosed and undertreated in older populations.[12] Furthermore, a December 2024 survey by the AMA found that only 10 percent of physicians reported contracting with health plans offering exemption from prior authorization.[13]

To be sure, the state variation in prior authorization requirements applies only to certain segments of the health care market. Any reform to the peer-to-peer process that happens at the state level will have a limited effect because the majority of employer-sponsored insurance is governed by ERISA, which preempts state policymaking related to self-insured health plans. Absent policy intervention, the accumulated inconveniences impose significant administrative burdens on physicians seeking to provide treatments to their patients, rationing health care not through final denial, but rather through hassles that are difficult to overcome (especially in the context of resource constraints) and thus cause care to be kept out of reach, for at least some period of time.

Having discussed the variable but generally burdensome experience of peer-to-peer reviews, I now evaluate through interview evidence the broader administrative burdens that prior authorization and coverage denials impose on physicians.

ACCUMULATED BURDENS: RATIONING BY INCONVENIENCE

Though much of the focus of this book is on the patient experience of prior authorization and the broader swath of coverage denials, it is abundantly clear that physicians pay a hefty price for insurers' decisions not to cover the care that they prescribe – and that this, in turn, affects patients' ability to access their prescribed treatments in a timely manner. In fact, economist Abe Dunn and his coauthors observe that physicians' costs of fighting health insurers to collect payment, combined with revenue never collected, lead "physicians [to] lose 18 percent of Medicaid revenue to billing problems, compared with 4.7 percent for Medicare and 2.4 percent for commercial insurers" – and this does not even account for administrative barriers preceding care delivery (e.g., prior authorization).[14]

Apart from physicians' hassle arising from the principle of prior authorization, especially as it is often implemented (such as with inefficient peer-to-peers and limited individualized review of patient histories), there are substantial time and documentation burdens associated with this practice. "Much more often than not, we can get the drugs we need, but only *after* we jump through all the hoops, thereby delaying the care," Dr. Spector reflected of this. "It's frustrating because you're going to win in the end. You know the criteria. You know the patient qualifies for it. Yet you're battling *week after week, delay after delay* for what you know they qualify for because you know the policy."[15]

A sleep specialist, Dr. Spector cares for many patients with narcolepsy, for which they can be prescribed the drug Pitolisant. When completing the prior authorization paperwork for the drug, Dr. Spector specifies the narcolepsy diagnosis and the fact that the patient has failed to respond to other drugs, "but eventually they come back with a Part B of the prior auth, where they ask, 'Did you screen the patient for drug abuse?' First, that has *nothing* to do with whether I'm going to put them on Pitolisant, which is not even a controlled substance. Second, if they wanted to know that, they could have asked it on Part A. But they created this Part B, which has now created extra weeks' worth of delay." There was, from his perspective, no rhyme or reason for it: he never knew what he would have to face on a given day. "It feels like there are people sitting around a room conspiring to figure out how to delay care further. And every day that they can delay your care is money kept in their pocket longer."

Moreover, as Dr. Wallach alluded to, there is no guarantee that people will endure these hurdles, especially in practices with more limited staffing to shoulder the added administrative burdens. It is for this reason that I characterize this process as health care rationing by inconvenience, or accumulation of inconveniences. While treatments may *eventually* be approved, they will be obtained only if the patient and physician withstand the necessary endurance test to reach it.

So, what is the extent of this so-called rationing? It is helpful first to consider how often physicians process prior authorizations.

FREQUENCY OF PRIOR AUTHORIZATIONS. It is clear that prior authorization processes have drawn the ire of physicians and physician organizations, but how often do physicians have to complete these processes? The 2023 Council for Affordable Quality Healthcare (CAQH) index estimated that there were 280 million prior authorizations processed in 2023 alone, looking across manual, partially electronic, and electronic prior authorizations.[16] What's more, a 2024 survey by the AMA found that physicians complete an average of thirty-nine prior authorization requests per week, which required an average of thirteen hours per week of non-billable time away from direct patient care.[17]

Though estimating somewhat fewer hours spent on prior authorizations, the ninetieth Annual Physicians Report by Medical Economics highlights the wide range of resources devoted to prior authorization processing (a source of uncompensated care), with physician staff time being especially substantial (see Table 6.2).[18] What's more, the average number of hours spent on prior authorizations is only an incomplete picture of its impact on physicians' practices because a high percentage of physicians' time gets absorbed with not only pursuing the prior authorizations but also explaining the process (along with potential anticipation of delays) to their patients.

This heavy frequency of prior authorizations comes with a cost: 89 percent of AMA physician respondents described prior authorization as contributing to physician burnout.[19] It is for this reason that physician and researcher Neil Busis and his coauthors emphasize, when writing on the need to streamline prior authorization, that "[c]linician well-being is essential to high-quality patient care" and that these burdensome insurance processes can thus pose harms to physicians and patients alike.[20] Despite the need for burden reduction, while most prior authorizations must be renewed annually, some prescription drugs even require renewal every six months – even when being prescribed for the management of a lifelong condition (e.g., narcolepsy).

Reliance on private insurance contributes to the widespread frustration with prior authorization and denials issued through this mechanism. Though prior authorization is applied to a narrow subset of health services under Medicare (e.g., durable medical equipment, prosthetics), Dr. Spector observed that commercial insurance is

> markedly worse than traditional Medicare. I've never gotten a Medicare denial that wasn't a basic form of step therapy. It was never the Prior Auth Part Bs or the short windows to respond or your patient gets denied, all the little tricks that commercial insurances are throwing our way. If Medicare isn't going to cover it, they just say they're not covering it and at least you can move on. It's not all of the hoops and waiting and paperwork.[21]

Though prior authorization was initially aimed at cost containment with respect to expensive care, these barriers are no longer isolated to costly treatments. One of Dr. Spector's patients is on a 15-mg dose of escitalopram (the generic version of the antidepressant Lexapro) and, because a 15-mg pill is not manufactured, she is prescribed one and a half 10-mg pills. The patient was then notified by her insurance company that only thirty pills per month would be covered, and she had to choose between 10- and 20-mg doses, even though Costco sells the prescribed pills for $6. "They're fighting her on $6 worth of pills, and she wants me to write a letter. And every year, we'll have to do these prior auths, as if I don't have enough to do, to save her the $6. She didn't know it was $6, so I'm not blaming her, but this is extra work we now have to do, and I guarantee it's going to cost more than $6 worth of my time to write the letter."

Not only did Dr. Buhr likewise speak to the frustration that denials might be overturned on the basis of information that had been submitted with the initial prior authorization, but he observed that these denials – which oftentimes are really *delays* – can lead to hospitalization "because there is good data that some of these biologics can reduce hospitalizations by decreasing severe exacerbations."[22] Thus, these frequent prior authorization-induced delays can lead insurers to save money on prescription drugs while *losing* money on hospital care. However, patient churn through health insurers can contribute to myopic decisionmaking when reviewing, and often disputing, the necessity of prescribed care.

While it would seem at first blush that a system at risk of *losing* insurers' money would underline a need for reform, fragmentation of responsibility for payment can impede progress. After all, the pharmacy benefit manager pursuing cost savings on a drug may not be attuned to the possibility of losing money on inpatient care that becomes necessary if the patient goes untreated.

A teenage girl in Montana knows this risk all too well. Given a new diagnosis of severe Crohn disease, she was hospitalized with a body mass index (BMI) of only twelve and given nutritional therapy and a recommendation that she begin to take the biologic drug Humira (the list price of which is around $7,000 per month), which was denied due to step therapy requirements that Dr. Lauren Wilson felt were incompatible with the severity of this case. In fact, she noted, it was one of the two most glaring errors she had seen in her career. Dr. Wilson waited on the phone, getting connected to three different staffers, and ultimately left a voicemail and pursued an alternative, less preferred treatment to manage the disease for which the patient was just hospitalized.[23]

Not only are these burdens on physicians pervasive, but also they appear to be increasing, a subject that I now explore.

RECENT INCREASES IN ADMINISTRATIVE BURDEN. Administrative burdens in health care have significantly increased in recent years. The 2023 annual CAQH report indicated that the time per manual prior authorization increased from sixteen minutes in 2018, to twenty-one minutes in 2019, to twenty-two minutes in 2022, a 38 percent increase in just four years.[24] What's more, the upper bound of what physicians might spend on prior authorization increased from forty-five minutes in 2019 to forty-eight minutes in 2022. Although these changes may in isolation appear modest, with the high volume of prior authorizations, the time taken adds up.

Even within the context of the COVID-19 pandemic, when a 2021 Medical Group Management Association poll asked medical groups, "How did payer prior authorization requirements change since 2020?" 81 percent of medical group respondents indicated that prior authorization requirements had increased, while 17 percent indicated that they had stayed the same, and just 2 percent stated that they had decreased.[25]

Those who reported that prior authorization requirements had increased in the past year said that they had had to add full-time staff to handle prior authorization work for several reasons, including

> [t]raining for several variations/inconsistencies across payers on PA requirements; [f]requent updates in payer requirements (e.g. site of service updates); [u]nderstanding vague or opaque requirements, especially regarding step therapy; [i]ncreasing rates of claim denials and requirements for peer-to-peer reviews; [s]low responses from payers for approvals, including lengthy holds for phone calls. These increased prior authorization requirements and staffing needs come at a time when 88 percent of health care workers report difficulty recruiting medical assistants.[26]

Thus, in addition to the philosophical frustrations with the practice, there is a significant "time tax" associated with securing prior authorizations, and the complexity of inconsistent requirements across insurers places significant learning and compliance costs on physicians and their staffs. And, while some physicians will work tirelessly to ensure that their patient gets the preferred treatment, with greater burden, there is greater risk that the prescribed care is abandoned in favor of an alternative treatment that might not be optimal, but which is preferred instead of the patient being left untreated. This dynamic highlights an unintended consequence of prior authorization implementation: while a central goal is to mitigate overprescribing, it can actually drive *underprescribing* to avoid this burdensome process. After all, prior authorization burdens place significant demands on medical practices, which must develop the organizational capacity to manage this administration. This often requires hiring staff specifically dedicated not to direct patient care, but to prior authorization administration.

STAFFING FOR PRIOR AUTHORIZATION MANAGEMENT. The administration of prior authorizations and pursuing the reversal of denials take time and money that some health care facilities are better able to manage than are others.

Dr. Buhr reflected on his good fortune that, in his academic practice, he has office staff who take care of prior authorizations for him, such that he needs to intervene only to provide additional supplementary information, do a peer-to-peer, or appeal a resulting denial. But this requires ample resources; his academic medical practice has five staff members who are dedicated to managing prior authorizations. "If they're making somewhere around $60,000 a year to be a mid-level administrative professional, we're talking $300,000 a year in salary alone to deal just with prior authorization, and it *still* takes two days, and the patient has to go to pharmacy twice. It's a huge number of resources. And we're just *one* department spending this."[27]

This experience is consistent with a Cardinal Health Specialty Solutions survey of oncologists, which revealed that 70 percent of participating oncologists have full-time staff dedicated to managing prior authorizations and benefits issues.[28] Similarly, Dr. Spector observed that his office at Duke University has two registered nurses and four medical assistants, all of whom handle a lot of the prior authorization challenges, "but it means that they're not doing the actual nursing job of triaging phone calls and helping with refills. A *very* large percentage is time spent filling out PA forms. We clearly spend more money on staff than we would have to if that were not a job requirement."

Some physicians are not so lucky. Prior authorization burdens fall more squarely on Dr. White's shoulders during her one day off from clinical work. The two exceptions are prior authorizations for imaging and for Botox injections: "We literally hired someone whose job is just to get those authorizations for a single medication because it's so much work and so much of a barrier."

For Dr. White, frustration emanated not only from the individual experience of burden, but also from the reality that extensive administration was taking away from patient care at a time when patients may wait several months to be able to see a neurologist. Thus, physician administrative burden can intersect with access issues for patients not only because burnout can drive physician workforce shortages, but also because administrative time can reduce appointment availability. And compounding all of this is the reality that this is uncompensated work.

Having elaborated on the many administrative and financial hurdles that physicians face with prior authorization management, I turn now to highlight how physician administrative burden intersects with patient administrative burden.

ADMINISTRATIVE BURDENS TRICKLING
DOWN TO PATIENTS

Not surprisingly, physicians are not the only ones to bear the brunt of administrative burden stemming from prior authorization and its associated delays and denials of coverage. Patients not only are the ones who have their care delayed, but also often find themselves as go-betweens with overextended physicians and their health insurers in an effort to obtain their prescribed care.

One patient, Ben, reflected of his insurance battles, "I wouldn't say that it's dehumanizing because it exposes all of the frailties of the human condition." Ben is a type 1 diabetic who was denied coverage for a continuous glucose monitor (CGM) – demonstrated to be clinically valuable in regulating blood sugar and improving the quality of life for a broad range of diabetic patients[29] – because his hemoglobin A1C (a blood test reflecting blood sugar levels over the previous couple of months, and a key tool for diagnosing prediabetes and diabetes) was, though qualifying as diabetic, deemed inadequately high for him to be eligible for this continuous monitoring.

To obtain his first CGM under his Ohio-based insurer Medical Mutual, Ben went to his endocrinologist, who pursued the prior authorization. First, Medical Mutual informed them that he hadn't supplied enough measurements of his glucose levels. Then, he was denied because his numbers weren't sufficiently abnormal – ironically, due to Ben's effective management of his condition.

Ben appealed the decision through a system that was "byzantine, getting passed around to a few people, who referred me to do more paperwork and documentation." He then joined forces with his endocrinologist's office, which was tasked with putting together medical research and documentation to support the appeal. A few weeks later, Medical Mutual again denied the CGM, leaving him to pay the heavy (and seemingly unnecessary) financial burden of paying out of pocket for it, which he felt fortunate to be able to do.

Upon switching to UnitedHealthcare, Ben was faced with yet another burden of appeal: when petitioning for the prior authorization for a new CGM, UnitedHealthcare requested additional information to assess medical necessity, but gave Ben's endocrinologist a mere twenty-four hours to provide that information. Ben immediately contacted his endocrinologist's office, informing them of the narrow window within which to respond. The endocrinologist immediately talked with UnitedHealthcare's claim processing company, which subsequently informed Ben of the denial on the grounds that they "had not received a timely response" – which this chapter has highlighted is difficult for physicians to offer when balancing clinic duties and insurers' stringent constraints.

His endocrinologist offered to help with the appeal of UnitedHealthcare's adverse determination, and it took another three weeks for it to be reversed, though it was frustrating because "knowing what an emergency or urgent care visit costs, they still put so many roadblocks in front of something that reduces these visits." Even having won the appeal, the psychological cost of the appeal process was significant for Ben. When he would hit the roadblocks in effort to secure coverage, he would wonder to himself, "Is there something wrong with me? Do I not deserve this? Do I think my need is more important than it really is? The process makes you feel *so small*."

CONCLUSION

This chapter has, through both public data and interview evidence, laid out physician administrative burdens to navigate in the setting of prior authorizations and coverage denials, which drive additional hurdles of appeals. It is because of these burdens that I characterize insurers' denials of prescribed care as *rationing by inconvenience*, with many patients and physicians highlighting the opportunities and temptations to abandon the effort to secure coverage for the prescribed course of treatment, despite the initial denial not constituting a *final* denial of coverage. Rather, denials (often, though not exclusively, through prior authorization) operate as substantial deterrents from pursuing care that appears to be within one's scope of health benefits because they impose accumulated inconveniences associated with appealing. In fact, quite apart from narrowly targeting overprescribing in the American health care system, these inconveniences can combine to drive underprescribing of certain medical care.

Moreover, I have highlighted how imposing these denials can undercut prior authorization's goal of cost containment, with substantial monetary cost associated with the mere *processing* of prior authorizations (as opposed to patient care), and burdens distributed throughout the medical industry. What's more, these processes of utilization management and resulting denials shift many costs from insurers to physicians and their patients, creating a new health and economic insecurity, as well as strain on patients' and physicians' administrative capital. And with this insecurity and confusion about insurance processes comes a loss of trust in the system into which patients pay or contribute monthly premiums, leading some to question the system itself and even to forego additional care.

Many physicians spoke to the frustration that they must do the "song and dance" of prior authorization (and relatedly, peer-to-peer review), with psychiatrist Daniel Block observing a seeming arbitrariness to denials attributable to the insurer taking the attitude, "Because I feel like it."[30] And this is not a mere administrative problem, Dr. Block added: "Whatever the medication is treating is going to get worse. My ADHD patients may have unproductive days at work. Someone may get in a car accident because they're not focusing well that day. Someone could have a precipitous increase in their depressive symptoms." While some of these coverage disputes are over disagreements about appropriate courses of treatment, one of Dr. Block's patients was denied coverage for a drug they had taken for years, simply because the prior authorization did not use the specific language "could not tolerate" in relation to other medications in their step therapy – an error that would prove burdensome to rectify. Keeping care out of reach not only creates headaches for physicians who might have identified a workable regimen before their patient changed insurers or the insurer changed formularies, but also can in some cases lead to worsening conditions that disrupt treatment protocols and even undercut cost containment objectives.

Medical cases are reviewed by providers outside of the relevant specialty, despite standards of care varying across specialties, with physicians noting that there may be a lack of familiarity with the breadth of available drugs and their appropriateness to particular patients. While some states have sought to address the implementation of prior authorization, such as by requiring that the reviewing provider be in the appropriate specialty, such reforms address only a small part of the picture due to the fragmentation of oversight over the American health insurance apparatus.

That prior authorization imposes burdens on physicians and their practices was a consistent theme across interviews, and it is supported by data on the rising number of prior authorizations required in recent years, even with respect to *generic* medications for which there are not cheaper alternatives. This physician administrative burden can come at the cost of physician burnout in a setting of a physician workforce shortage. In fact, former CMS Administrator Seema Verma stated in 2020 that "[p]rior authorization requirements are a primary driver of physician burnout,"[31] which was deemed a public health crisis.[32] Former AMA President Gerald Harmon similarly hailed in a 2022 speech the AMA's efforts to remove administrative barriers such as prior authorization that can lead to burnout.[33]

Integral to all of this is concern about physician autonomy. According to Dr. Block, "this is such a critical issue of medicine, and there's so much interference with patient care because of greed. I understand that there must be cost containment, but there's got to be some kind of reform of how much control insurance companies have over our patient care. It's egregious. There are so many draconian policies."

The mitigation of these administrative burdens is no easy task and strikes at the heart of conversations about privatization of the American health care system. Though the traditional Medicare appeal process proves onerous, it is necessitated with far less frequency than in managed care settings, given Medicare's much more tightly circumscribed reliance on utilization management. American health care policy has largely been placed in the hands of private actors over which public officials exercise limited control despite documented barriers to enrollees' access to prescribed care. As the scope of coverage denials (including the frequency of their overturning) continues to come to light, there should be renewed conversations about the extent to which private insurance should remain a fixture in the American health care delivery.

CHAPTER 7

Who Wins and Loses Appeals

> We have productivity metrics. It's not like we have unlimited time to do these reviews. We probably have ten or fifteen minutes or so and, depending on how easy it is to find the information we need, that may not be adequate. And we're told denying things is okay because people can appeal.
>
> Anonymous physician working for Elevance

PHYSICIANS ARE HARDLY the only actors who experience administrative burdens resulting from coverage denials – far from it – and the patient experience of burden often translates into feelings of frustration and dismay that dissuade them from appealing denials, not to mention, as Catherine's story in Chapter 2 and Ben's story from Chapter 6 highlight, a feeling of dread and waiting for the other shoe to drop.

Researchers at KFF find in 2025 that fewer than 1 percent of denied claims are appealed internally, ranging from 0 percent (CareSource Indiana, Inc.) to 31 percent (PacificSource Health Plans of Oregon).[1] What's more, just 5,000 external appeals – that is, appeals to independent reviewers external from the plan – were filed by marketplace enrollees in 2023. Though this claim-level analysis highlights the apparent infrequency with which patients challenge these denials, what remains unknown is *which* patients (who may have accrued many denials) are pursuing this process.

Among internal appeals, the appeal outcomes vary widely, with reversal rates ranging from 10 percent (CHRISTUS Health Plan Louisiana) to 89 percent (Blue Care Network of Michigan), but with an overall reversal rate close to 50 percent. This raises questions about the frequency with which patients experience protracted appeals and the accompanying administrative burdens of pursuing this process. Such was the case for Samantha, a twenty-nine-year-old treatment-resistant adult-onset Still's disease patient who reflected, "I feel like there's a price tag on my life and I'm not worth their bottom line." Her battle for a bone marrow transplant would send her down the road of repeated appeals – both internal and external – and their associated administrative burdens.

Still's disease is a rare inflammatory disorder that can affect the entire body, featuring fevers, rashes, and joint pain, with additional risks including inflammation of the heart and excess fluid around the lungs. Having been born with multiple genetic illnesses, Samantha learned from an early age the importance of becoming an expert both in her medical condition and in the health care bureaucratic maze.

Samantha is allergic to the one available drug to treat her condition and would go into anaphylactic shock with it, requiring admission to the intensive care unit. Sometimes she could take extensive pre-medication and use post-treatment epi-pens to help preserve this as a stop-gap measure, but, in April 2019, she ceased to respond to it. Then, her team of physicians concluded that she needed a bone marrow transplant.

Getting it approved seemed straightforward enough: there was consensus among the medical team, she had pursued other less aggressive medical avenues, and she was out of other options. However, Cigna deemed the bone marrow transplant "investigational" and thus outside of her plan benefits. So began what would turn out to be months of repeated appeals, along with accompanying overwhelm and decline in morale.

Her physicians initially assumed that the importance of this treatment simply had not been made sufficiently clear to Cigna, especially because the reviewing physician was in family medicine and thus likely unfamiliar with the nuances of this rare disease, with which fewer than 1 in 200,000 adults are diagnosed.[2] They submitted additional documentation to support her case, while Samantha spent hours on the phone with Cigna while lying in bed at home or in the hospital. It drained her energy, but it was life or death and "the clock was ticking," and Samantha wasn't ready to die. The pages of her notebook filled as she continued discussions with insurance staffers, physicians, and social workers, each exchange diligently documented.

Even though a bone marrow transplant was not just the best option but the *only* option available, the appeal was likewise denied. As Samantha's medical team braced for another round of appeal, they raised concerns that, given how rare Still's disease is, the Cigna doctors might not have been equipped to make an appropriate determination. This concern was borne out: the appeal was denied *again*, and, along with the decision, Samantha was provided with a pamphlet specifying that investigational treatments for rare diseases were not covered. The National Institutes of Health estimates that 30 million Americans, or 10 percent of the population, have one of the approximately 7,000 known rare (or orphan) diseases, but, as Chapter 4 illustrated, within this setting there is significant off-label prescribing.[3] The challenge is securing coverage – especially when treatment comes with a hefty price tag, and when reviewing physicians may be in any number of specialties other than that typically managing the given medical condition.

To aid these appeals, her physicians in hematology–oncology, rheumatology, immunology, and genetics, and the hospital's transplant coordinator, were all navigating the health care bureaucracy with phone calls and letters to Cigna. In the meantime, Samantha was in and out of the hospital as her health was continuing to decline and leading her to develop cyclical fevers of 104 °F or higher. Though taking periodic breaks, she would continue to be on the phone in pursuit of coverage and "a fighting chance."

"These denials really hurt my feeling of self-worth," Samantha recounted. "There was an increasing sense of desperation. At this point, I'm twenty-three. I'm not ready to die. I want to get to see my godson go to preschool. I want to see my little brother graduate from nursing school. And there's a treatment option that could be curative, but I'm being told monetarily, 'You are not worth trying to save.'"

At one point, Cigna's transplant coordinator informed Samantha that Cigna *would* be willing to cover repeated ICU admissions every time that she went into anaphylaxis from the $60,000 drug (which at this time was happening nearly bi-weekly). It puzzled Samantha, because ICU admissions at that frequency over the course of the remainder of her life would accumulate to more than the cost of the transplant. Something didn't add up.

Samantha's doctors then filed for an external appeal, which involved extensive paperwork, an interview with the social worker, and a compilation of the prior denials, testing, letters from all four medical departments, and letters from oncologists at other specialized children's hospitals who had done successful transplants in her category of disease. This information was then sent out for review to the independent medical reviewer, without knowing when a decision would be reached. Her doctors sought to expedite the external appeal, but Samantha didn't qualify: "Basically, I wasn't dying fast enough."

Feeling like she was "running against the clock," she got married that August so that her partner would have power of attorney should she become incapacitated. And, just days before their wedding, Cigna denied the external appeal on the grounds that *though it was medically necessary*, from a legal standpoint, Cigna was not obligated to cover the cost of treatment because it was investigational.

The only remaining hope was to find a clinical trial with enough funding to cover the cost of her transplant. Luckily, they found a clinical trial at the University of Pittsburgh Children's Hospital, which was studying rare auto-inflammatory diseases. A couple of days after Samantha's wedding, she was accepted into the trial, and the hospital's Board of Directors agreed to cover her transplant through its charity foundation.

Samantha cried. "It felt like I was being told, 'You're worth a chance.' It felt like the world went from black and white to, suddenly, there were colors again."

Samantha would ultimately (about a year after discovering her drug allergy) secure the necessary grant from the Be a Match Foundation. She recounted a day a couple of months after her transplant when she woke up and, for the first time she could recall, she wasn't in pain.

Samantha is now back in Iowa and in full remission, but that was not the end of her insurance struggles. Post-treatment, she developed an aggressive lymphoma for which her doctor recommended CAR-T therapy, a cancer therapy that uses the patient's T-cells to fight cancer. However, this was also denied. Unable to receive the traditional radiation therapy because of her bone marrow transplant, she instead received high doses of the one chemotherapy that her doctors thought would work and that her insurance would approve. "The denials and appeals never end. The mistake that Cigna made was in not killing me sooner."

Yet, through all this turmoil, Samantha spoke to her advantages in navigating the system: her education, her language skills, and the health literacy that she knew from a young age that she would need to acquire. Even with this skillset, she recounted having to be her own lawyer multiple times a day, and she would ask, "How is someone's grandmother supposed to do this? How is someone with four children supposed to navigate this? The deck is stacked against you at *every* single turn."

Samantha's is just one of the stories of protracted efforts of patients appealing to access their covered benefits and, in Samantha's case, life-saving treatment. Many spoke to the resources on which they drew – education, language fluency, knowledge of the health care system – yet described nevertheless getting ensnared in their insurer's red tape, sometimes demanding creative solutions. Indeed, for Jessica, whose SCIg we saw denied in Chapter 2, appeals with Blue Cross Blue Shield felt so fruitless, despite the assistance of her physician's office and specialty pharmacy, that, in an effort at "grasping at straws," she resorted to contacting her United States Senator, Bill Cassidy, a physician himself.

To her surprise, Sen. Cassidy's office contacted the Louisiana Department of Insurance and, within just three days, a peer-to-peer review of her case was scheduled with Blue Cross Blue Shield and the approval came a couple of days later. After four total months of appealing, the coverage issue for her SCIg had been resolved in a matter of days. "It seemed like they didn't want to get in trouble once his office got involved." However, the experience led her to wonder, *Why did it come to that? And who has the wherewithal to endure the repeated inconveniences of appeal?*

For both Samantha and Jessica, eventual success – after accumulating significant health and psychological costs – reflected a dimension of administrative capital, or "bureaucratic know-how," which can range from objective knowledge of legal rights and bureaucratic procedures (thus reducing learning and compliance costs) to acquired firsthand experience of navigating bureaucracies (e.g., health insurers).[4]

Chapter 6 highlighted how utilization management tools resulting in coverage denials might, rather than contain costs, instead *shift* costs to

American physicians and, by extension, their patients. Here, I examine administrative burdens directly experienced by the patients themselves, in addition to examining the extent to which these burdens may be unevenly distributed across populations, deepening patients' health and economic insecurities as they seek to access prescribed care.

That is, given business professor Jeffrey Pfeffer and his coauthors' observation of a host of interactions that employees have with their insurers[5] – whether taking time to obtain prior authorizations, understand the scope of their health benefits, fill out claim forms, or appeal denials – American health insurance utilization is rife with "sludge." This not only requires up-front investments to learn to navigate, but can constitute barriers to accessing care, especially for those less adept at learning these processes.[6]

Before turning to my nationwide survey analysis of insurance appeals and reversals, I discuss the broader administrative burdens of appeal, as well as the informational barriers that patients face when navigating these processes. I then discuss publicly reported data on rates of appeal and independent medical review in California, New York, and New Jersey, which make data publicly available over multiple years. I use these data to analyze patient administrative burden as well as success navigating these health care bureaucracies.

THE APPEAL PROCESS: FRAGMENTED AND BURDENSOME

Much to the consternation both of patients and of their physicians, the American health care system is notoriously fragmented. This can yield a health care setting in which not only do patients have limited knowledge, but, moreover, economist and law professor Einer Elhauge observes that "[i]ndividual decision makers responsible for only one fragment of a relevant set of health care decisions may fail to understand the full picture, [and] may lack the power to take all the appropriate actions given what they know."[7] This fragmentation is not inevitable: health law professor David Hyman observes in the United States a high level of fragmentation in health care delivery in comparison with other complex industries.[8] Consequently, health care consumers may face additional administrative burdens – whether the learning costs of understanding one's options once coverage has been denied, the compliance costs of grasping the various rules and procedures, or the psychological costs of emotional overwhelm amid this navigation anxiety, especially when health care is kept out of reach (at least for the time being). With the National Association for Adult Literacy estimating that just 12 percent of Americans have proficient health literacy skills[9] – and with particularly low levels of health literacy observed among those from marginalized groups – this fragmentation can be both consequential overall as well as inequitable in its imposition of barriers to accessing prescribed care when coverage denials arise.

That administrative burdens can impede access to benefits is a familiar insight. Pamela Herd and Donald Moynihan detail numerous costs that constitute administrative burden: the target population's lack of knowledge about a program (learning costs), the difficulty of knowing what is required in order to comply with the terms of a program (compliance costs), and the lack of individuals' autonomy over themselves (psychological costs).[10] And individuals' "human capital" – education, money, social networks, intelligence, psychological resources, and health – can influence how people cope with administrative burdens, with some better able than others to weather these storms. The imposition of burden thus shifts risk from payers to individuals, with greater risk shouldered especially by marginalized populations.

Administrative burdens in the American health care setting can take a variety of forms, as health services researchers Michael Anne Kyle and Austin Frakt observe in the prevalence of common patient administrative tasks of scheduling, obtaining information, prior authorizations, resolving billing issues, and resolving premium problems, any of which can potentially lead to delayed or foregone care.[11] While 73 percent of their survey respondents engaged in at least one administrative task and 24.4 percent reported administrative burden, I argue that the burdens are in fact more expansive than just care disruption, extending to the absorption of patient time and energy that might be in short supply.

While health insurance bureaucracies vary in structure, the basic process of appealing is the same. There is a petition for reconsideration of the denial through the peer-to-peer process, followed by a formal appeal, followed by an external review that entails an independent review of the patient's medical records.

The documentation for such appeals can be quite intimidating to the average health care consumer, with some insurers (e.g., UnitedHealthcare of Arizona) going so far as to compile a sixteen-page single-spaced document outlining each of the Level 1, Level 2, and Level 3 processes applicable to both standard and expedited review of denials. And, within the realm of traditional Medicare, whose target population is older and consequently may have more limited health literacy amid cognitive decline, the appeal process is particularly draconian, with no fewer than *five* stages: (1) reconsideration from the health plan; (2) review by an Independent Review Entity (IRE); (3) decision by the Office of Medicare Hearings and Appeals (OMHA); (4) review by the Medicare Appeals Council; and (5) judicial review by a federal district court. These Medicare beneficiaries may fare particularly poorly in the setting of Medicare Advantage, which imposes costs on this older population when drawing on the utilization management tools of managed care.

The significant learning costs of Medicare enrollment were brought to light in economist Jason Abaluck and Jonathan Gruber's analysis highlighting that, with the 2006 rollout of Medicare Part D prescription drug coverage under the Medicare Modernization Act of 2003, the wide range of available prescription drug plans led to choice overload, or so much complexity that seniors made suboptimal plan choices, leading to more out-of-pocket medical expenses or, potentially, forgoing medical care.[12]

While this speaks to Medicare *enrollment* features as opposed to the appeal process in the aftermath of a denial, the same concept applies: having navigated the health care system to enroll in health coverage, they must then navigate yet another system to access prescribed care, in some cases becoming overwhelmed to the point of not acting in their own best interest.

The extensive administrative burden of challenging coverage denials makes all the more troubling what one physician interviewed reflected of his work reviewing claims for the prominent health insurer Elevance (formerly known as Anthem): "We're told denying things is okay because people can appeal."[13] The problem is that many people do not appeal. In fact, as Carol and Jason (from Chapter 1) reflected of their own experience, "I think they hope people will just pay and not complain." In light of Jason Abaluck and Jonathan Gruber's analysis of informational barriers impeding patients' sound health insurance decisionmaking,[14] I turn now to the informational barriers that patients face in going about appealing coverage denials.

COVERAGE DENIALS AND INFORMATION ASYMMETRIES

To understand the impact of these bureaucratic appeal processes, it is helpful to know patients' level of understanding that these processes are in place. Moreover, given the low rate of appeal documented by researchers at KFF, there are open questions as to whether patients have a reasonably accurate understanding of the odds of prevailing when appealing decisions by health insurance giants. Do the learning costs examined in the setting of insurance enrollment extend to the health insurance appeal process?

Each of the 187 survey respondents who was denied coverage but did *not* appeal was asked, "Were you aware that appealing the insurance company's decision was an option available to you?" Of these respondents, 39 percent reported that, at the time, they were unaware of their ability to appeal their health insurer's denial of coverage, while just 28 percent reported that they were aware of their ability to do so. The remaining third of respondents were unable to recall whether they knew of this option at the time of the denial. In fact, when asked to cite the main reason for not appealing, the most common reason cited was lack of knowledge that there was an appeal process available. This adds some needed clarity as to the few appeals of denied claims identified by KFF within the realm of ACA marketplace plans: for many patients, it was unclear that appealing was an option in the first place.

This is perhaps surprising, given that by law, under the ACA, insurers must not only provide the rationale for why coverage was denied but also inform the enrollee of their ability to appeal. The challenge is that many interviewees emphasized the lack of clarity with which this information was conveyed, sometimes in fine print on the denial letter, on a separate page that they might have easily thrown out, or in language that was opaque, leaving them unclear on how to proceed. Thus, even when the law compels providing the necessary information, the health literacy demands can interfere with patients' comprehension, leading them to accept the denial as a final answer rather than pursuing the issue further.

Health insurance is notoriously complicated, made even more so by the reading level at which related materials are written. While the average American reads at around an eighth-grade level and 20 percent of Americans read at or below the fifth-grade level, most health insurance documents are written at a tenth-grade level or higher.[15] The result is that many American adults cannot accurately decipher printed health care materials that outline their rights. This opaque communication from insurers reinforces Pamela Herd and her coauthors' observation that "street-level bureaucrats can alter ... costs. They can choose to engage in active outreach or withhold information in ways that adjust learning costs."[16]

Knowing one's right to appeal in the first place is an important precursor to the decision whether to accept the decision (forgoing care, choosing an alternative treatment, or paying out-of-pocket) or else to seek reversal. Each respondent who did not appeal their denied claim and cited lack of awareness of the appeal process as their main reason for not appealing was asked, "Knowing that insurance appeals are an option available to you, how much more likely are you to appeal a future coverage denial?" Fifty-four percent responded that this information would make them more likely to appeal their own denials, should they arise again. This not only indicates significant missed opportunities to challenge past denials, but also highlights opportunities for information-disseminating policy interventions to increase insurer accountability through appeals.

Patients might not appeal because they don't know they are able to, or because they might think they have little chance of success when confronting a large health insurer. In fact, "Didn't think I would win" was the second most common reason survey respondents cited for opting out of the appeal process.

Within my survey sample, spanning public and private insurance, 52 percent of those who appealed at least one denial experienced a reversal – that is, they won their appeal. This is consistent with Capital Public Radio's finding that California patients win appeals about half the time[17] and a 2011 Government Accountability Office (GAO) report on four states (Connecticut, Maryland, New York, and Ohio) finding that patients were successful 39 percent (New York) to 59 percent (Connecticut) of the time when appealing directly to their health insurer in the 2009 plan year (see Table 7.1).[18] Further, a 2006 study by America's Health Insurance Plans (AHIP) over the years 2003 and 2004 revealed that appeals filed for external review were also reversed about 40 percent of the time,[19] while KFF analyses of marketplace claim data reveal reversal rates close to 50 percent.

But how aware are patients of these decent odds in patients' favor?

Each of the 1,340 respondents in my survey was asked, "Approximately what percent of the time would you guess that people win appeals against their health insurance companies?" Respondents were given options ranging from 1–10 percent to 91–100 percent. Figure 7.1 displays the results.

What one can see plainly is that respondents tend to underestimate the odds of success in an insurance appeal, with 51 percent of respondents believing that one wins between 1 and 20 percent of the time, and just 23 percent of respondents estimating a reversal rate exceeding 40 percent, the lower bound of the estimate of reversals in the 2011 GAO report.

What's more, this underestimation is not evenly distributed: Those who are not college-educated are 8 percentage points more likely than their college-educated counterparts to underestimate the frequency with which people prevail in health insurance appeals, and those whose

Table 7.1 Appeal success in challenging health insurance coverage denials

State	Type of insurer	Data year	Percentage prevailing in internal appeals
Connecticut	HMOs	2009	53
	Indemnity managed care organizations	2009	59
Maryland	HMOs, non-profit health service plans, and commercial insurers	2009	50
New York	HMOs	2009	39
	Commercial insurers	2009	47
	Non-profit indemnity insurers	2009	48
Ohio	All insurers	2009	48

Source: Government Accountability Office (2011).

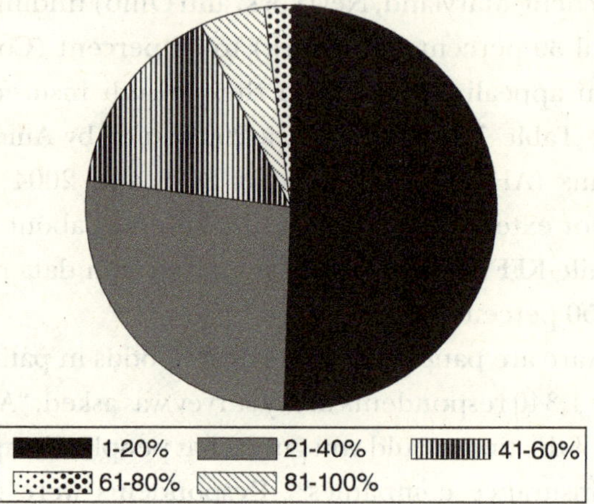

7.1 Estimated odds of prevailing in insurance appeals.
Source: Survey of 1,340 US adults.

annual household income is below $50,000 are 10 percentage points more likely than their more affluent counterparts to underestimate this frequency of success. Thus, informational barriers in health insurance appear to disproportionately affect those of lower socioeconomic status, potentially driving these populations to opt out of appealing their own denials.

These learning costs are but one critical aspect of administrative burden that can impede patients' pursuit of remedy and successful navigation of the American health care system.

APPEAL PROCESSES AND ADMINISTRATIVE BURDENS ON PATIENTS

That administrative burdens prevent patients from pursuing relief about health insurance barriers is a matter that has attracted growing scholarly attention. Examining data on Medicaid beneficiaries' administrative fair hearings (or administrative processes to appeal decisions by the Medicaid agency, whether concerning eligibility, benefits, or services), political scientist Jamila Michener finds astonishingly low appeal rates of 86 out of every 100,000 beneficiaries in New York and 26 out of every 100,000 beneficiaries in Florida.[20] The decision not to take informal, let alone formal, action against the Medicaid program is not distributed evenly, with socioeconomic status, race, and perceived institutional responsiveness (that is, the degree to which beneficiaries believed that the health care bureaucracy was responsive to their needs) all influencing patient behavior. However, across patients there appeared to be a pronounced feeling of disempowerment in navigating these processes. Moreover, Michener finds a significant relationship between time taken to resolve cases and the rate at which beneficiaries appealed,[21] suggesting that inefficiencies (or perhaps even *perceived* inefficiencies) in appeal processes can lead patients to opt out of appealing coverage denials.

Consistent with this, many of the patients interviewed had appeals that lasted months or even years, an endurance contest on which they contemplated giving up (and, in some cases, *did* give up). Depending on whether these abandoned appeals were for denied prior authorizations or denied claims, this can lead to forgone care or patients being left with significant, even destabilizing medical bills (as was the case for Heather in Chapter 5).

I now examine my survey findings on the frequency and experience of health insurance appeals.

FREQUENCY OF APPEALS. Each of the 482 survey respondents who experienced at least one coverage denial was asked whether they appealed. Overall, 61 percent of those denied at least once answered "yes." While this proportion is considerably higher than the low appeal rates observed by researchers at KFF in the context of ACA marketplace and Medicare Advantage plans, this is a different unit of analysis, examining at the self-reported patient rather than the claim level, which also excludes prior authorizations. Thus, while the proportion of denied claims that are appealed *in a given year* is low, we do not know from publicly available data how many denied claims an individual had or how patients might respond differently to care being kept out of reach by prior authorization. Within my patient-level data, a patient might have experienced multiple coverage denials over the course of a lifetime and submitted one appeal, which would then enter this sample. And, in fact, the proportion reporting having appealed declines from 61 percent to 53 percent among those experiencing only a single denial.

Another inconsistency in the data can be attributed to the broad definition of "appeal," which could perhaps be better characterized as "challenges of denials." That is, while the publicly available data reflect only the submission of formal internal appeals, 13 percent of those in my sample who experienced denials sought to resolve the dispute through a phone call to the insurer, with another 2 percent challenging their denial through social media outreach to their insurer. In fact, while many were unable to recall their method of appeal, just 86 of the 482 denied patients (18 percent) could recall specifically mailing a letter, faxing an appeal, or sending a secure email, a share that is closer to prior estimates such as in the Medicare Advantage context, where 11.7 percent of denied prior authorizations are appealed. Thus, while this broader definition is perhaps a more complete picture of ways that health care consumers seek to reverse coverage denials rather than taking the initial denial as a final answer, its different unit of analysis and more sweeping reach contribute to a somewhat different picture. Of course, as the chapter will later emphasize, given the centrality of completed internal appeals in advancing to the level of independent external appeals, this higher reported rate of survey respondents appealing demands this further context.

THE EXPERIENCE OF APPEALING. Each of the survey's 295 respondents who challenged a denial was asked how long it took for the insurer to render the decision. No distinction was made in the survey between internal and external appeals. While 32 percent of respondents indicated that the appeal took "less than one month," 13 percent indicated that it took three to six months, 13 percent indicated that it took six months to a year, and 4 percent indicated that the appeal took over a year (see Table 7.2). Thus, for 30 percent of respondents, the appeal took three months or more,[22] which, depending on the nature of the medical issue, could have significant ramifications for patient health outcomes. These longer-lasting appeals did not appear to be more prevalent among the 29 percent of respondents who were denied coverage in the amount of $5,000 or more. While the implications of this delay depend on whether the treatment had already been received, it is notable that, for most patients, the time spent resolving a denial is measured in months,

Table 7.2 Duration of appeals

Time to appeal	Count	Percentage
Less than one month	33	32.4%
One to two months	29	28.4%
Three to six months	13	12.8%
Six months to a year	13	12.8%
More than a year	4	3.9%
Still pending	4	3.9%

Source: Survey of 295 respondents appealing following denial, from among 1,340 total respondents surveyed.

Table 7.3 Experienced and perceived burdens of appealing

Type of burden	Administrative burden cost	Experienced	Perceived
Time spent on process	Compliance	20.0%	18.7%
Money seeking legal advice	Compliance	8.5%	18.7%
Language barriers	Learning	2.0%	2.7%
Lack of medical knowledge	Learning	11.9%	16.6%
Confusion about denial rationale	Learning	14.6%	11.8%
Confusion about appeal process	Learning, compliance	12.6%	13.4%
None	N/A	2.4%	24.1%

Source: Survey of the 482 patients experiencing a coverage denial, among the 1,340 total respondents surveyed.

not days or weeks, amplifying both the health insecurity and the financial insecurity of American patients.

Each of the 482 respondents who experienced a denial was also asked about the challenges they faced in pursuing their appeal if they did appeal ($n = 295$), and the challenges they perceived in the appeal process if they did not ($n = 187$). They were given the following options and could check as many as they wished: time spent on the process, money seeking legal advice, language barriers, lack of medical knowledge, confusion about the denial rationale, confusion about the appeal process, or none. Table 7.3 reports the results.

When looking to those who did appeal their denials, while 20 percent of respondents expressed concerns about the time that an appeal would take and 15 percent were unclear on why the coverage was denied in the first place, just 2 percent of respondents indicated that there were no burdens associated with the appeal process. Twenty-eight percent of respondents cited sources of confusion, whether about the rationale for the denial (15 percent) or about the bureaucracy of the appeal process (13 percent). Eight percent cited money for legal representation as a barrier to appealing, though very few respondents ultimately pursued litigation, likely attributable in part to the lack of legal liability that health insurers face in most employer-sponsored plans.[23]

Among those opting out of appealing, 19 percent were deterred by the perceived barrier of time spent pursuing the appeal, while an equal proportion were concerned that a significant amount of money would be required to litigate an appeal (despite the actual infrequency of litigation), and a similar proportion of respondents (17 percent) were deterred by confusion as to the denial rationale and the appeal process itself.

It is hardly surprising that the burden of time could keep care out of patients' reach, hearkening back to Annie Lowrey's characterization of Americans left to be their own social workers and disability law experts in a system that imposes on American patients and others a "time tax."[24]

In the context of prior authorization, the increased burden of time needed to resolve health insurance disputes can constitute such an inconvenience as to deny health benefits because patients cannot pay that "tax." The frequency with which respondents identified struggles with understanding their denial or the appeal process likewise speaks to Pamela Herd and Donald Moynihan's characterization of both learning and compliance costs.

The main reasons why people did not appeal were lack of awareness that they could (28 percent) and skepticism about their ability to win (18 percent), reinforcing the challenges wrought by patients' information barriers and the perceived obstacles of bringing a case against, to use law professor Marc Galanter's vocabulary, the "repeat players" of health insurance giants.[25]

That patients can be impeded by administrative burdens can be particularly problematic because burdens reinforce inequality by undermining the reach and effectiveness of public programs, because some patients may be more targeted than others, and because of the resources required to overcome those burdens.[26] As this research shows, this burden can extend from the setting of public programs to private insurance as well, rife as it is with cost containment tools that come with accompanying administrative hassle. What's more, these hassles can feel particularly pronounced for those from more marginalized groups, further deepening existing health and economic inequities.

Despite the administrative burdens to which these survey respondents pointed, the Medicare Advantage setting to which I now turn highlights precisely why it can be so valuable to endure these barriers, because, conditional upon patients appealing (which just under 12 percent do, according to KFF), most patients fare well and are able to access their prescribed care.

REVERSALS IN MEDICARE ADVANTAGE. That reversal rates can actually be quite high has been brought to light within the context of Medicare Advantage. In a September 2018 report by the US Department of Health and Human Services Office of the Inspector General (OIG), it was revealed that Medicare Advantage Organizations (MAOs) overturned 75 percent of their own denials (approximately 216,000) between 2014 and 2016.[27] Eighty-two percent of the overturned denials were for payment to providers for services already rendered to the beneficiaries, while 18 percent were reversals of denied prior authorizations.[28] Inspector General Daniel Levinson found during the same period that independent medical reviewers overturned additional denials by MAOs, ruling in favor of beneficiaries and providers and raising the concern that "some Medicare Advantage beneficiaries and providers were initially denied services and payments that should have been provided."[29] In fact, independent medical reviewers overturned an additional 27,000 denials per year, and the Centers for Medicare and Medicaid Services cited 56 percent of the 140 audited MAO contracts for violations related to inappropriately denying requests for prior authorization of services and/ or payment.[30]

Researchers at KFF similarly found that while just 11.7 percent of denials by Medicare Advantage organizations were appealed, nearly 82 percent of those appeals resulted in reversal in 2023,[31] highlighting the value of appealing, costly though it is to patients' time, energy, and other resources. This seeming necessity of appealing is even more important in this setting because prior authorization denials are on the rise in Medicare Advantage plans, with 7.4 percent of prior authorizations denied in 2022, compared with 5.8 percent in 2021.

The OIG report raises serious concerns about the high rate of reversal because so few beneficiaries and providers appealed denials in light of appeals' confusing and overwhelming nature. This is especially true for those beneficiaries who are older and/or critically ill, with those opting not to appeal potentially going without the prescribed health care service when it is most needed. Thus, the accumulated inconvenience for patients and their physicians drives gaps in care.

While we have good aggregate data on internal appeals within segments of the health insurance market, we still have limited information about *who* is appealing denied medical coverage, and, conditional upon appealing, the factors that lead one to be successful in doing so. To answer such questions, within my nationwide survey of 1,340 US adults, I asked those who reported that they had experienced at least one denial a set of questions about their experience appealing (or declining to do so), and I use these data to analyze the factors associated with one's likelihood of appealing a denial and being successful in doing so.

I now lay out my core theories that I explore in understanding who appeals denials.

THEORIES ABOUT WHO APPEALS

Many of the patients interviewed highlighted the advantages with which they navigated their insurance appeals. They spoke about their education, their work experience, their accumulated understanding of the health care system, and their knowledge of their right to appeal at all. This raises the question of the extent to which limited information drives many people to opt out of appealing.

This chapter has illuminated the information barriers that patients face in health insurance appeals: 39 percent of those not appealing reported that, at the time, they were unaware of their ability to appeal their insurer's denial of coverage. Moreover, while multiple studies have estimated the rate of prevailing in an insurance appeal to be between 39 percent and 59 percent, 51 percent of respondents estimated the likelihood of success to be 20 percent or lower. Consistent with Pamela Herd and Donald Moynihan's characterization of learning costs that many Americans face when navigating public programs, the *limited information theory* posits that those who estimate a lower probability of success in a health insurance appeal will be less likely to appeal their own denial.[32] That is, they will not place high value on incurring the costs of appealing.

After all, patients whom I interviewed pointed to the numerous administrative burdens that they experienced when seeking to access their health plan benefits, whether long wait times on the phone, lack of knowledge about the process, or difficulty coordinating between their insurer and their physician's office. What's more, patients whom I interviewed likewise reflected on the intimidation of challenging their large health insurer, especially one that was dominant in their region – sometimes even being fearful of naming their insurer in the anonymized interview. It would be only natural to be disinclined to take the necessary time away from work and family obligations – especially in the setting of a health challenge – to navigate an appeal that one believes is unlikely to be successful. That is, even once patients have overcome the learning costs associated with health insurance, they make a choice whether to try to overcome the compliance costs, and many opt out.

While health literacy did not appear to be a significant determinant of patients' ability to avoid experiencing denials (with the caveat that members of the most health-literate demographic groups are also most likely to sue), once thrust into the position of navigating a complex health insurance appeal process, I expect health literacy to be a far more significant factor. That is, patients must be aware of their right to appeal. They must be effective in communicating health information between their physician and their health insurer. They must be able to navigate a complex bureaucracy. What's more, more affluent individuals may be more likely to obtain favorable outcomes, because they are potentially better able to draw on administrative and economic capital to work the system to their benefit.[33]

Considering the demonstrable administrative burdens of appealing, the *health literacy theory* posits that greater health literacy may aid patients appealing to access their prescribed care, while those who are less health-literate will be less inclined to appeal their denials. This results in their being among the many Americans each year who opt out of appealing. While Jamila Michener finds mixed support for the effect of county-level education on Medicaid appeal frequency, within the state of Florida she finds that, as the percentage of the county with a high school education or higher increases by one unit over time, there is a 3 percent increase in the number of Medicaid appeals.[34] And Pamela Herd and Donald Moynihan assert that the stresses of poverty can reduce cognitive capacity, "making people who feel threatened or exhausted more likely to make poor long-term choices," which in this case may include opting out of fighting to access health plan benefits.[35]

What's more, white and Asian/Pacific Islander adults have higher levels of average health literacy than do Black and Hispanic adults, who tend to have considerably lower levels of health literacy.[36] Thus, I expect that those identifying as Black or Hispanic will be less likely than their counterparts to pursue appeals.

Related to the difficulty of deciphering health insurance materials, several scholars have identified that language barriers pose significant challenges in access to health care. Language barriers impede high levels of satisfaction among patients, and such barriers are associated with fewer clinic visits, less understanding of physicians' explanations, more reliance on the emergency department, less follow-up, and less satisfaction with health services.[37] And, in analyzing emergency department patients, physician and researcher Jane Brice and her coauthors find that there are dramatically lower levels of functional health literacy among Spanish speakers than among native English speakers.[38]

While health insurance information can be made available in multiple languages, the *language theory* raises the possibility that, given the extensive administrative burdens associated with the American insurance appeal process, there will be particular burdens on non-native speakers of English. Moreover, language minority status may serve as a proxy for being less well acquainted with the unique complexity of the American health insurance system.

Health insurance appeals arise in the setting of a health concern, whether chronic (such as Jessica's treatment for immunodeficiency) or acute (such as Jim's hernia that needed surgical repair). Several of the patients whom I interviewed spoke about the physical and emotional burden of appealing, made even more difficult when they were ill. They spoke to several hours spent on the phone, getting rerouted from person to person at their insurer, getting disconnected by phone, and having to track down fax machines that neither they nor their work offices had, all while feeling unwell. Turning to academic analysis of this policy problem, Pamela Herd and Donald Moynihan not only document psychological costs associated with verifying program eligibility, but also find that certain life factors, including health problems, can simultaneously increase the need to access assistance while also undermining the ability to navigate the burdens that arise while seeking that assistance.[39] That is, mental and physical health conditions can impede patients' levels of executive functioning, making bureaucratic interactions even more difficult. The *health status hypothesis* thus argues that those who are in worse physical health will be less likely to pursue administrative appeals.

The Appendix for this chapter lays out in a multivariate regression framework the findings on who appeals, indicating that those estimating low rates of reversal are 11 percentage points less likely than their counterparts to appeal their own denial, and that lower-income people are significantly less likely than their counterparts to appeal, such that someone earning $25,000 annually is 9 percentage points less likely than someone earning $100,000 annually to appeal to access health benefits. I focus here on the broader descriptive findings.

DESCRIPTIVE FINDINGS. Figure 7.2 plots the average appeal rate across the relevant demographic categories.

I find support for the *limited information theory*, with Figure 7.3 highlighting the progressively increasing appeals across expected value of appealing, with the horizontal line indicating the sample-side average share of respondents appealing. While just under 57 percent of those estimating that denials are reversed less than 20 percent of the time appeal their own denial, 70 percent of those estimating reversal rates of 40 percent or higher do so. What's more, performance of a difference-in-means test reveals a statistically significant 11-percentage-point-lower rate of appealing among those estimating a reversal rate of less than 20 percent ($p = 0.02$). This pattern holds when the analysis is isolated to formal

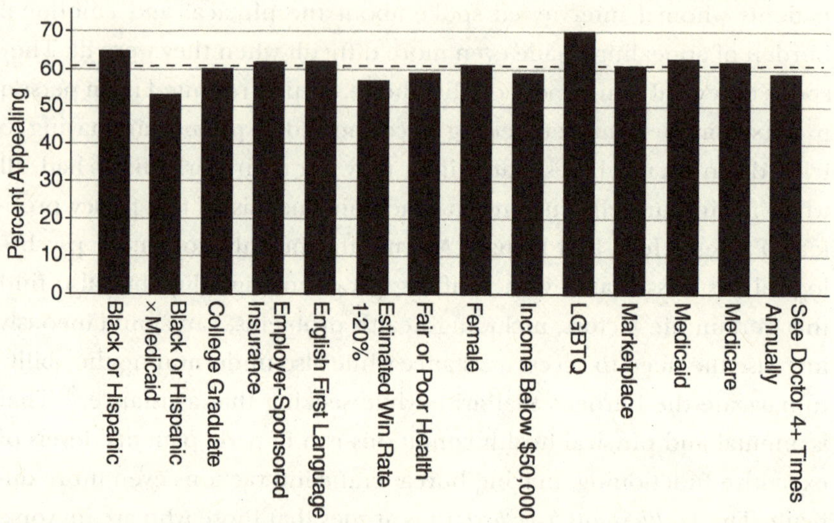

7.2 Characteristics associated with appealing.
Source: Survey of the 482 patients experiencing a denial, among the 1,340 patients surveyed.

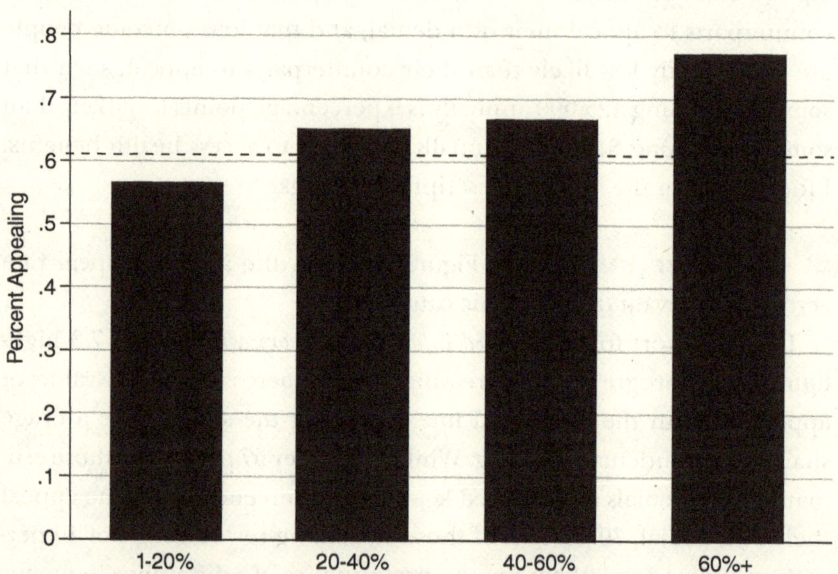

7.3 Percentage appealing denials, by estimated win rate.
Source: Survey of 482 respondents denied, from among the 1,340 total respondents surveyed.

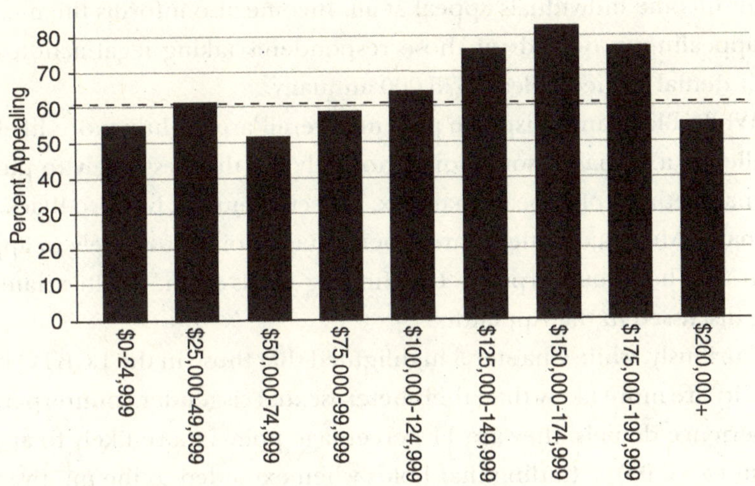

7.4 Appeal rates by household income level.
Source: Survey of 482 respondents denied, from among the 1,340 total respondents surveyed.

appeal methods of mail, fax, and a secure email. To be sure, aggregate rates of reversal do not mean that one is likely to prevail in one's own case, which may have distinctive features that make it more or less likely to yield a reversal by the health insurer. However, this finding highlights the value of improving accessibility of information about appealing so as to at least reduce the inequities in knowledge about these processes and their potential value.

I find mixed support for the *health literacy theory*: while college graduates are no more or less likely to appeal coverage denials, lower-income patients appear to be significantly less likely to challenge denials than are more affluent patients (see Figure 7.4). In fact, while just under 55 percent of patients earning less than $25,000 annually submit some form of challenge to a denial, that rate jumps to over 72 percent among those earning at least $125,000 annually. In fact, on turning to the multivariate regression setting in the Appendix, I find that each $25,000 decrease in annual household income is associated with a 3 percentage point decline in one's likelihood of appealing. Given that the stresses of poverty can exacerbate the experience of administrative burdens, it is understandable that the more affluent individuals navigate these processes to obtain coverage, and it is perhaps surprising that so many lower-income individuals appeal at all. Income also informs the method of appealing: two-thirds of those respondents taking legal action over their denial earned at least $75,000 annually.

While Black and Hispanic patients overall are slightly more likely to challenge a denial in some form, not only are they less likely to pursue formal methods of appeal (mail, fax, or secure email), but also Black and Hispanic Medicaid patients are 8 percentage points less likely to appeal than are their counterparts. This finding holds in the multivariate setting discussed in the Appendix.

Curiously, while Chapter 3 highlighted that those in the LGBTQ community are more likely than their heterosexual cisgender counterparts to experience denials, they are 11 percentage points more likely to appeal them ($p = 0.03$), a finding that holds when extended to the multivariate setting, which can be found in the Appendix to this chapter.

I do not find support for the *language barrier theory*: while those who are native English speakers appear to appeal at higher rates, the difference is not statistically significant. I find mixed support for the *health status theory*: those identifying as being in fair or poor health appear to be 7 percentage points less likely than their healthier counterparts to pursue formal avenues of appeal, though this effect disappears when the analysis is broadened to the full range of challenges identified.

Of course, initiating the appeal is just the first step toward securing health insurance coverage following a denial. One must be able to successfully navigate these processes, likely coordinating with a physician's office and compiling the appropriate records with which to make a compelling case for coverage being appropriate for one's condition. I now examine descriptively the result of these appeals, with the multivariate regression analysis provided in the Appendix.

OUTCOMES OF APPEALS

Of the 295 sample respondents who appealed their denials, just over 52 percent prevailed in their appeal, a finding consistent with the GAO's 2011 report on 39 to 59 percent of appeals being successful across the states examined. In fact, on isolating the analysis to those who pursued more formal processes of mail, fax, or secure email, I find an even higher

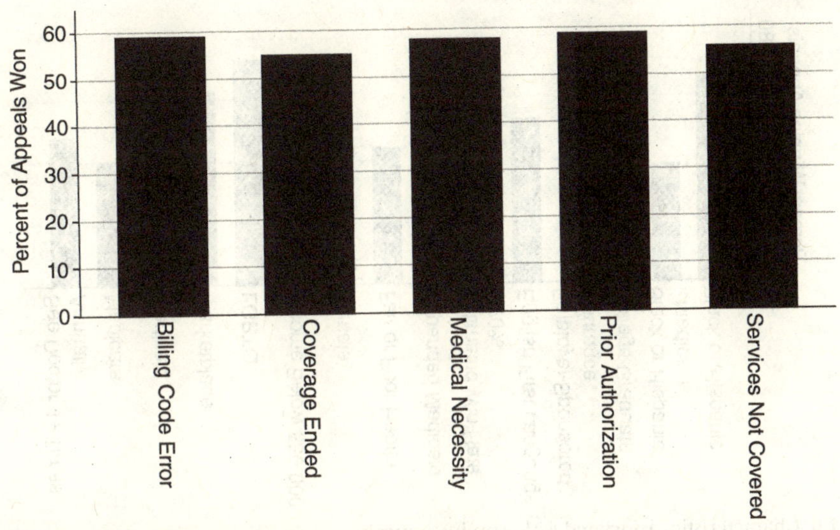

7.5 Percentage of appeals won, by denial rationale.
Source: Survey of 295 respondents appealing denials, from among the 1,340 total respondents surveyed.

reversal rate of 66 percent, highlighting the value of pursuing these processes, administratively burdensome though they can be.

It does not appear to be the case that some types of denials (e.g., medical necessity, services not covered) are more likely to be reversed than are others. As Figure 7.5 highlights, the rates of reversal are remarkably similar across self-reported denial rationales. Though this variable relies on respondents' ability to recall complexities about health insurance and thus is imperfect, this consistency nevertheless bolsters my confidence in collapsing these different categories into the single variable of *denials*.

Figure 7.6 displays the average proportion of survey respondents prevailing in appeals across different categories.

Curiously, whether looking at the bivariate level in difference-in-means tests or at the multivariate level (see the Appendix), few of the demographic factors associated with appealing appear to be predictive of successful appeal, with a couple of exceptions. As Figure 7.7 highlights, survey respondents in excellent health ($n = 197$) were quite successful in their appeals (72 percent of denials were reversed), whereas the success rate declines steadily when the analysis is extended to those in fair, poor, or very poor health (44 percent of denials reversed). This is

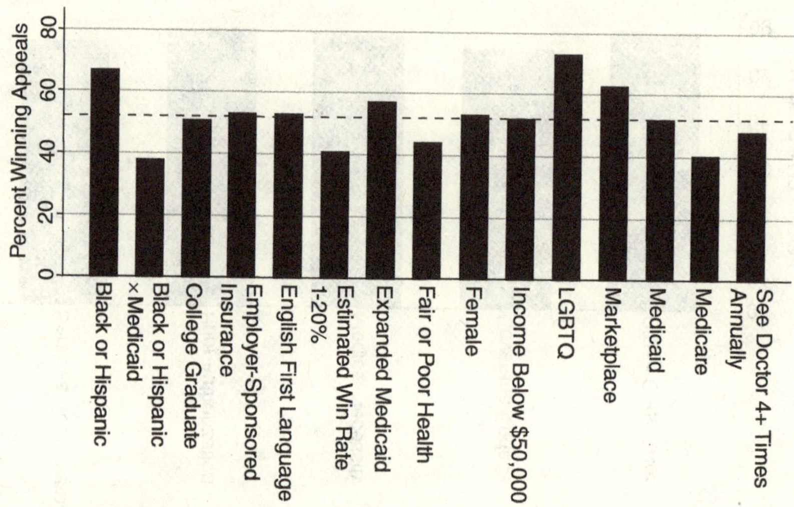

7.6 Characteristics associated with winning appeals.
Source: Survey of 295 respondents appealing denials, from among the 1,340 total respondents surveyed.

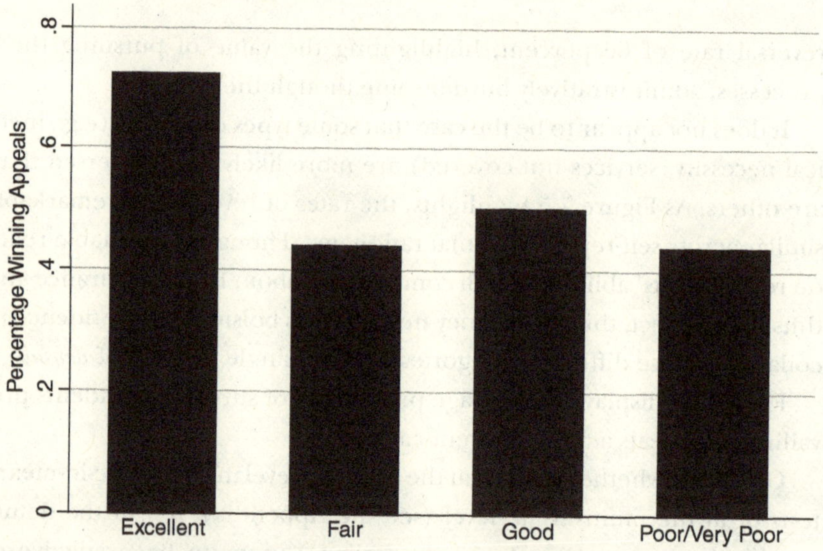

7.7 Proportion winning appeals, by health status.
Source: Survey of 295 respondents appealing denials, from among the 1,340 total respondents surveyed.

consistent with the experience of Samantha, who, though able to find a clinical trial, was placed in the difficult position of navigating conversations with health insurance staff, social workers, and physicians while in the hospital and battling high fevers and even adverse reactions necessitating ICU admission, and still got denied. That is, the administrative burdens of appeal – from the navigation challenges to the psychological costs – were particularly pronounced in the setting of worse health such as (in the case of Samantha) being left to wade through this insurance bureaucracy from a hospital bed. To be sure, denials do not always arise in the context of illness – they might arise in the setting of an injury for which a physician believes a costly scan is medically indicated – but, when they do, they can be particularly costly and impose barriers to getting ultimate coverage approval.

What's more, as I note in the Appendix when discussing the multivariate results, members of the particularly marginalized group of Black or Hispanic Medicaid patients are significantly less likely than their counterparts to prevail upon appeal. In fact, I find that, within this population, just under 38 percent of respondents prevailed in their appeals. This is especially notable because, while some survey respondents indicated that they did not appeal because it was easier to pay the claim, this is a population particularly unlikely to be able to afford to pay out-of-pocket for denied care. This highlights the troubling ways that health insurance coverage denials can reinforce along both race and class lines the existing, pronounced inequities in Americans' access to health care.

State health policy may also be a relevant factor, with those in Medicaid expansion states 17 percentage points more likely to prevail in appeals than are those in non-expansion states ($p = 0.01$). Medicaid expansion through the ACA is associated with patients being more likely to have a usual source of care, which may aid in the coordination of successful insurance appeals.

The loss of an appeal, especially for sicker or marginalized populations, can have far-reaching effects, not only dissuading further appeal (e.g., through the external appeals to which I turn next), but also potentially discouraging the appeal of future denials. For Angela, who sought coverage for her son's enteral formula on which he relied to survive, the repeated denials and days spent on hold with her health insurer wore her down so much that, despite the high cost of the prescribed formula, she reflected, "Can I say this time fighting through this process was worth it? No. I got nothing. It would have been more time efficient if I had just accepted the denial. The paperwork adds up and is overwhelming when you just want to focus on your kid doing well."

Thus far, the focus of this chapter has been on patients' knowledge and pursuit of internal appeals – that is, appeals within the health insurance company. But that is not the final determination of coverage. I now consider the processes through which patients may go if they extend their challenge to external appeals.

EXTERNAL APPEALS

Not only can the for-profit nature of most of the American health insurance system require appealing coverage denials, but also health reform choices have changed the range of appeal options. The ACA required that all non-grandfathered plans provide patients with the ability to internally appeal all denials and, if they lose an appeal within the insurance company, to appeal the case again to an external reviewer (or independent review organization [IRO]). However, a rule promulgated in 2011 under the ACA determined that not all denials are eligible for external review. Rather, the denials must be grounded in "medical necessity" or a similar clinical judgment.[40]

This limitation is quite consequential. In fact, KFF researchers find in their analysis that medical necessity determinations account for only 2 percent of claim denials within marketplace plans in the 2023 plan year, accounting for just over 4.3 million of the 73 million in-network denied claims across behavioral and non-behavioral health. Rather, the insurance industry uses hundreds of different codes for claim denials and adjustments – from "The diagnosis is inconsistent with the patient's age," to "Charges do not meet qualifications for emergent/urgent care," to "Procedure/treatment has not been deemed 'proven to be effective' by the payer."[41] Moreover, despite a 2022 OIG report finding that 13 percent of prior authorization denials by Medicare Advantage were wrongful (that is, the denial did not align with Medicare coverage guidelines),[42] physician and health services researcher Aaron Schwartz and his coauthors find that just 1.4 percent of Medicare Advantage claims were denied on medical necessity grounds.[43]

My analysis includes denials through prior authorization, when medical necessity is a central consideration, and thus there is a higher proportion of medical necessity denials in my survey sample. However, the rule promulgated under the ACA nevertheless leaves a large swath of denials without a source of review external to the health insurer when an internal appeal is unsuccessful. But, within this slice of health insurance appeals, what is the outcome, and how do these outcomes vary across denied health care services? To answer this, I compare administrative burdens associated with external appeals across states and then provide closer examination of select states' administrative data.

COMPARATIVE ADMINISTRATIVE BURDEN IN STATES' EXTERNAL REVIEW PROCESSES. All states allow for some process according to which patients can pursue external appeals following a denial of coverage, but some states take greater steps to exacerbate or mitigate the associated administrative burden of this level of appeal. Table 7.4 identifies each state's process: the prerequisites for external appeal, the ways these appeals may be submitted, and any direct financial cost to the patient.

What is perhaps striking is the marked variation in the experience of pursuing an external appeal in different states. For example, in California, one must file an internal appeal and wait for thirty days from its filing (but need not have received a decision) and may submit the appropriate information online or by mail or fax. In contrast, in Kentucky, one must first exhaust administrative remedies, physically mail the appeal documentation, and pay $25 if the denial is upheld by the external reviewer. In fact, Kentucky is one of ten states in which one may be compelled to pay a small fee to receive an external review. While exceptions may be made if the $15–25 fee is beyond one's ability to pay, this not only requires knowledge of the exception, but also imposes an additional documentation burden for the patient. What's more, twelve states have the sole submission method of physically mailing the documentation, which can come at a potentially significant postage cost, depending on the volume of medical records. These two factors can combine to leave less affluent patients more risk averse, and thus less

Table 7.4 State external review processes

State	Requirement to obtain external review	Emergency bypass of internal review	Method of external review	Fee for external review
Alabama	Internal appeal	Yes	Phone, fax, mail	$0
Alaska	Internal appeal	Yes	Mail, email, fax	$0
Arizona	Internal appeal	Yes	Mail	$0
Arkansas	Internal appeal	Yes	Phone, mail	$0
California	Thirty days from initiation of appeal or complaint	Simultaneous expedited submission	Mail, fax, online	$0
Colorado	Second-level internal appeal	Yes	Mail, fax, online portal	$0
Connecticut	Internal appeal	Yes	Mail, email	$0
Delaware	Internal appeal	Yes	Phone, email	$0
D.C.	Internal appeal	Yes	Mail	$0
Florida	Internal appeal	Yes	Phone, fax, mail	$0
Georgia	Internal appeal	Yes	Mail, online	$0
Hawaii	Internal appeal	Yes	Phone, mail	$15
Idaho	Internal appeal	Yes	Mail, fax	$0
Illinois	Internal appeal	Yes	Mail, email, fax, online	$0
Indiana	Internal appeal	No	Mail, fax, online	$0
Iowa	Internal appeal	Yes	Mail, email	$0
Kansas	Internal appeal	Yes	Mail, email	$0
Kentucky	Internal appeal	Yes	Mail	$25 if insurer upheld in expedited review
Louisiana	Internal appeal	Yes	Online	$0
Maine	Second-level internal appeal	No	Mail, online	$0
Maryland	Internal appeal	Yes	Mail, email	$0
Massachusetts	Internal appeal	Yes	Mail, fax, online	$25
Michigan	Internal appeal	Yes	Mail, online	$0
Minnesota	Internal appeal	Yes	Email, fax, mail	$0
Mississippi	Internal appeal	No	Mail	$0
Missouri	Internal appeal exhaustion suggested	N/A	Mail	$0
Montana	Internal appeal	No	Mail	$0
Nebraska	Internal appeal	Yes	Mail, online	$0
Nevada	Internal appeal	Yes	Mail	$0
New Hampshire	Internal appeal	Yes	Mail	$0
New Jersey	Internal appeal	Yes	Mail, email	$25
New Mexico	Internal appeal	Yes	Mail, email, fax	$0
New York	Internal appeal	Yes	Mail, email, fax, online	$25
North Carolina	Internal appeal	Simultaneous expedited submission	Mail, fax, online	$0
North Dakota	Internal appeal	Yes	Mail	$25

Table 7.4 (cont.)

State	Requirement to obtain external review	Emergency bypass of internal review	Method of external review	Fee for external review
Ohio	Internal appeal	Simultaneous expedited submission	Mail, email, fax	$0
Oklahoma	Internal appeal (most cases)	Yes	Mail	$0
Oregon	Internal appeal, avoiding care disruption, disputing appropriate level of care, or coverage rescinded	Yes	Online	$0
Pennsylvania	Internal appeal	Simultaneous expedited submission	Mail, email, fax	$0
Rhode Island	Internal appeal	Yes	Mail, fax, online	$25
South Carolina	Internal appeal, amount of care must be $500 or more	Simultaneous expedited submission	Mail, email	$0
South Dakota	Internal appeal	Simultaneous expedited submission	Mail, email, fax	$25
Tennessee	Internal appeal	Simultaneous expedited submission	Mail, email	$0
Texas	Internal appeal	Yes	Mail, fax	$0
Utah	Internal appeal	Yes	Mail, email, fax	$0
Vermont	Internal appeal	Yes	Mail, email, fax	$25
Virginia	Internal appeal, unless related to cancer care	Simultaneous expedited submission	Mail, email, fax	$0
Washington	Internal appeal	Yes	Mail, fax	$0
West Virginia	Internal appeal	Simultaneous expedited submission	Mail	$0
Wisconsin	Grievance	Yes	Mail, email	$0
Wyoming	Internal appeal	Simultaneous expedited submission	Mail	$15

likely to pursue every available avenue to access prescribed health care, while those with more comfortable financial standing may have this care more within reach.

Unsurprisingly, the ease with which patients can file these external appeals has a significant effect on the volume of such appeals filed. In 2024, Pennsylvania's Department of Insurance instituted an Independent

External Review process, the results of which it released in January 2025, hailing the 50.1 percent reversal rate for patients. However, in the state with a population of approximately 13 million people, just 517 cases had been brought to their doorstep. To be sure, it is a new program and thus has limited visibility, with patients and their physicians less likely to be familiar with the potential benefits of pursuing this avenue. But, even with multiple modes of submission of appeal materials – thus promoting equity across financial standing and different levels of technological literacy – one must first exhaust the internal review process, with the only exception of simultaneously submitting for expedited review if appropriate to the case.

California offers a study in contrast here, with a lower barrier to entry, given that anyone injured by a health insurance company in California may file if they have waited thirty days from having filed an internal appeal, even if the case is still being reviewed by the insurer. Thus, while one must file an appeal (which the survey and publicly available data indicate that many people do not do), one need not exhaust all remedies if the insurer is not operating in a timely manner. And while just 170 independent medical reviews were pursued through the California Department of Insurance, 111, or 65 percent of them, were overturned, resolving in favor of the patient. What's more, an additional 2,838 independent medical reviews were pursued through the California Department of Managed Health Care, which resulted in the plan's decision being overturned in 46 percent of cases where the prescribed care was deemed "experimental or investigational" and in 52 percent of medical necessity cases.

Some other states have taken measures to reduce the administrative burden associated with navigating insurance appeal processes. For example, Washington's Office of the Insurance Commissioner not only offers written tips for how to file an appeal, but also provides a searchable database of independent reviews by diagnosis and insurer and a video that reduces the learning and compliance costs associated with this process that many patients find challenging and overwhelming. Washington even provides template letters for patients to send to their insurers to demonstrate how to request additional information about their case, and the relevant documentation that may be needed for internal and external

Letter template to request documents used by your health plan to make their decision
[Personalize this letter as needed, especially the information in brackets]

[Your name]
[Your address]

[Date]
[Address of your health plan's appeal department]

Re: [Name of the insured]
Plan ID number: [Your plan ID number]
Claim number: [Your claim number]

To whom it may concern:

I'd like to request you send all of the following to me:

1. A detailed description of why my claim was denied
2. A written statement of the clinical rationale for the decision
3. Instructions for how to obtain the clinical review criteria used to make the determination
4. All notes your company made in my file
5. A description of what you need to overturn the denial

My provider and I will need these as we prepare to appeal your determination on the claim referenced above.

I look forward to your direct response as soon as possible.

Sincerely,

[Your name]
[Your address and phone number]

7.8 Template letter provided by the state of Washington.
Source: Washington State Office of the Insurance Commissioner.

appeals (see Figure 7.8), as well as offering guidance on maintaining call logs of contacts with insurers and physician offices. These factors combine to reduce greatly for the patient the administrative burdens of appeal, in addition to helping patients to make better informed decisions about *whether* to expend time and energy toward this higher-level appeal.

Thus, while some states have imposed onerous administrative barriers to appealing – not only requiring the exhaustion of internal remedies, but also imposing limited modes through which to transmit external appeals, which may come with a direct financial burden – others serve as models in burden reduction and thus promote better access to health care, especially for marginalized groups less able to overcome administrative burdens.

I now examine in greater depth the independent medical review process within the states of California, New York, and New Jersey.

THE SCOPE AND TRENDS OF INDEPENDENT MEDICAL REVIEWS. When California patients face coverage denials, they have the option to submit complaints or independent medical reviews to the California Department of Managed Health Care, an agency that works to protect consumers' health care rights and ensure a stable health care delivery system, and which regulates 96 percent of commercial and government health plan enrollment in health plans regulated by the State of California.[44] One may also pursue independent medical reviews through the California Department of Insurance, which regulates companies selling health insurance in California, but which does not regulate self-insured health plans, Medicare, or Medi-Cal (the state's Medicaid program).

I identified from the California Department of Managed Health Care the complete list of the 109 insurance plans (whether comprehensive, psychological, or pharmacy), the number of complaints against each of these insurance plans, the number of independent medical reviews (IMRs) of these plans' decisions, and the outcomes of these IMRs. While this does not capture IMRs pursued through the California Department of Insurance or Covered California (through which ACA marketplace plans may be purchased), and there are still other plans not regulated by this agency (for example, self-insured employer-sponsored health plans governed by ERISA), it nevertheless captures a wide enough swath of the health care market that I can make meaningful inferences about the resolution of coverage denials.

Table 7.5 displays key information related to each of the twenty insurance plans with the highest California enrollment for the 2020 plan year. In 2020, IMRs were pursued in just eleven of these twenty health insurers (with one of these plans having only two IMRs over the course of the year), and there was marked variation in the extent to which such reviews resulted in the plan's position being upheld. For example, while 50 percent of Kaiser Foundation Health Plan, Inc. IMRs resulted in Kaiser's position being upheld, this was the case in just 21 percent of IMRs of Blue Cross of California Partnership Plan, Inc. While the rate of reversal

Table 7.5 Complaints and IMRs in California health plans

Insurer	Enrollment	Complaints	IMRs	Upheld
Kaiser Foundation Health Plan, Inc.	9,092,069	2,317	251	50%
Blue Shield of California	3,377,076	1,922	969	29%
Blue Cross of California	2,801,967	1,104	534	31%
Human Affairs International of California	2,746,002	0	0	NA
Local Initiative Health Authority for Los Angeles County	2,514,995	520	93	35%
Health and Human Resource Center, Inc.	2,082,668	0	0	NA
Health Net Community Solutions, Inc.	1,966,701	333	80	35%
US Behavioral Health Plan, California	1,811,933	9	2	0%
Inland Empire Health Plan	1,483,747	142	75	61%
Blue Cross of California Partnership Plan, Inc.	904,985	100	56	21%
Orange County Health Authority	886,067	0	0	NA
Magellan Health Services of California	838,529	0	0	NA
UnitedHealthcare of California	730,721	337	64	31%
Heritage Provider Network, Inc.	703,026	0	0	NA
ACN Group of California, Inc.	702,067	1	0	NA
Molina Healthcare of California	665,456	62	15	40%
Partnership HealthPlan of California	637,424	1	0	NA
Beacon Health Options of California	622,240	0	0	NA
Managed Health Network	579,099	0	0	NA
Health Net of California	538,017	358	88	27%

of denials is not synonymous with an "error rate" – there may have been complexity in a patient's individual case, new facts came to light, or it was easier to simply pay for the service – a reversal rate of 79 percent is striking and raises important questions about the accuracy with which medical necessity is judged, with errors being highly consequential to the patient's experience of administrative burden as well as their health outcomes.

I then identified from the California Health and Human Services Open Data Portal the universe of independent medical reviews by the California Department of Managed Health Care between January 2001 and May 2022. This dataset comprises 33,238 observations, 52 percent of which resulted in the plan position being upheld and 48 percent of which resulted in the plan position being overturned,[45] a figure consistent with KFF and Government Accountability Office analyses, as well as with my survey.

The overall median time to render a decision was nineteen days across the sample, and twenty-one days among standard (as opposed to expedited) reviews. Whether this means an expected three weeks *without treatment* depends on whether the denial was pre-service (e.g., via prior authorization) or a claim denial (e.g., denying an emergency department visit as medically unnecessary). The IMR notes indicate that there is variation in whether the patient was seeking authorization or reimbursement, with over 16 percent of patients seeking reimbursement for health services already rendered and many reports not indicating one way or another.

These observations span 27 diagnosis categories (plus "Other" and "Not applicable"), with the most common diagnoses yielding IMRs being "Orthopedic/musculoskeletal" (5,900), "Mental disorder" (4,864), "Cancer" (3,014), "Central nervous system/neuromuscular dystrophy" (2,576), and "Cardiac/circulatory problem" (1,721). The IMRs also spanned 32 treatment categories (plus "Other" and "Not applicable"), with the most common treatments yielding IMRs being "Pharmacy" (8,240), "Diagnostic imaging and screening" (5,020), "Mental health" (3,717), "Durable medical equipment" (2,171), and "Orthopedic procedure" (1,404). That pharmacy benefits would account for such a high share of these cases is hardly surprising, given that they were the second-most-prominent denial category in my survey.

In Figure 7.9, I plot the rate at which IMRs result in the overturning of the plan's original decision, across treatment categories for which there were at least 100 observations, yielding 26 treatment categories displayed. One can observe marked variation in the frequency with which IMRs result in reversal, with 72 percent of IMRs related to autism treatment resulting in reversal, while just 29 percent of IMRs related to chiropractic care result in reversal, with emergency/urgent care, mental health, and pharmacy falling at 43 percent, 52 percent, and 53 percent respectively. Interestingly, despite the concerns about excessive ordering of diagnostic scans (as discussed in Chapter 2), here I find that in California, 48 percent of denied diagnostic imaging and screening is eventually covered through the IMR process rather than being abandoned.

For each of the 33,238 observations, there is an accompanying explanation of the patient's clinical history and the assessment of the IMR. For example, in the 2022 central nervous system case of a female between ages forty-one and fifty, the IMR overturned the insurer's assessment of whether to cover an MRI of her arm, deeming the MRI to be medically necessary:

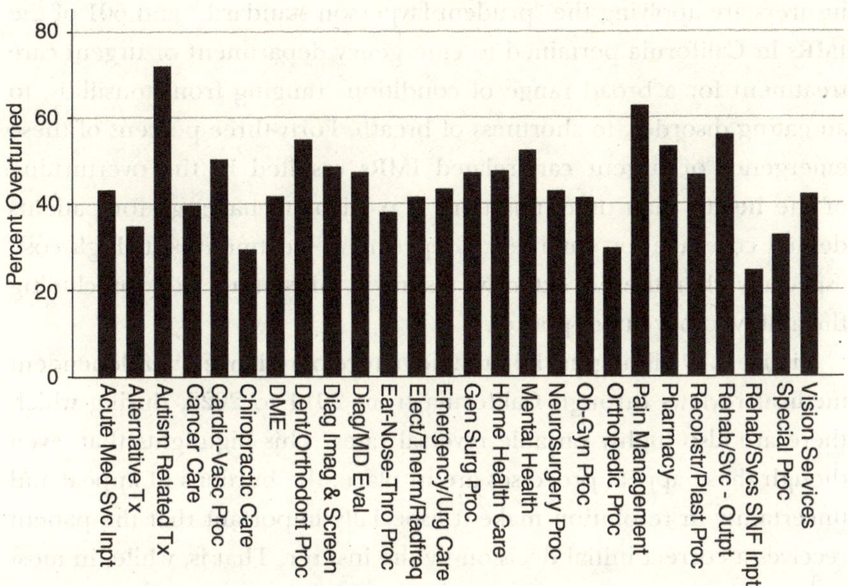

7.9 California IMR reversals by treatment category.
Source: California Department of Managed Health Care.

Given that anatomical abnormalities or defects, such as prominent cervical ribs, fracture calluses, or compressive tumors are commonly demonstrated on imaging and may support a history and physical examination consistent with thoracic outlet syndrome, the service at issue was medically indicated. Therefore, MRI of the left arm was medically necessary for the evaluation of this patient. Final Result: The reviewer determined that the service at issue was medically necessary for treatment of the patient's medical condition. Therefore, the Health Plan's denial should be overturned. Credentials/ Qualifications: The reviewer is board certified in neurology with sub-specialty certification in vascular neurology and is actively practicing.

Thus, the IMR is by a physician not only within the appropriate specialty, but within the relevant subspecialty, a feature noticeably absent from the peer-to-peer process based on interviews with physicians and the limited state legislation governing prior authorization within certain segments of the health care market. And, in this case, the IMR resulted in the patient gaining coverage.

As discussed in Chapter 2, a non-trivial number of coverage denials were for emergency department care, raising questions about how insurers are applying the "prudent layperson standard," and 601 of the IMRs in California pertained to emergency department or urgent care treatment for a broad range of conditions ranging from tonsillitis, to an eating disorder, to shortness of breath. Forty-three percent of these emergency or urgent care-related IMRs resulted in the overturning of the health plan determination. A particular challenge for patients denied coverage for emergency department treatment is its high cost, especially when there is extensive testing in this setting, likely precluding the ability to pay out-of-pocket.

Figure 7.10 highlights the variable nature of reliance on independent medical reviews through California from 2014 to 2023, during which there are also highly variable reversal rates. This highlights that, even though these appeal processes are in place, the burdens of appeal and uncertainty in resolution make it especially important that the patient receives a correct initial decision by the insurer. That is, while, in most years, patients pursuing this avenue of appeal have a decent chance at success (a "coin flip" or a bit better), the administrative burdens of internal appeal and the learning costs of advancing to an external appeal compound to reduce access to this valuable tool to obtain health insurance coverage.

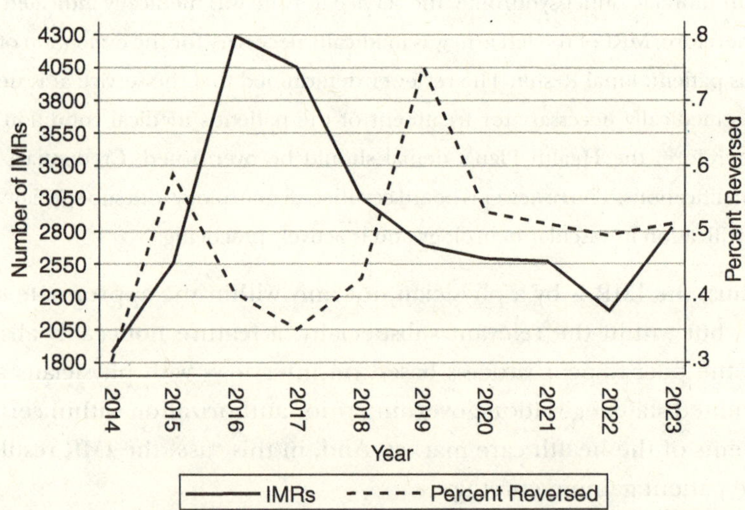

7.10 IMR volume and reversals in California Department of Managed Health Care. Source: California Department of Managed Health Care.

Of course, patients are ill-equipped to judge for themselves what is medically necessary, and too often find themselves facing several rounds of appeal to access prescribed care. Adjudicating between necessary and unnecessary care is beyond the scope of this study. What is of interest is how patients – especially marginalized patients – manage these denials, whether by paying out-of-pocket, appealing, or forgoing care, and the administrative burdens that they face in the process.

California's IMR results are similar to those observed through data from the New York Department of Financial Services, which catalogues closed external appeals with information on the underlying diagnosis, treatment, denial reason, health plan, sex, age, and decision year. This database comprises 17,925 total external appeals within the state of New York that were resolved between 2019 and May 2022 across a broad swath of diagnosis categories, with 41 percent of external reviews of medical necessity cases resulting in a complete overturning of the decision from the lower level of review, though with wide variation across diagnoses (see Figure 7.11). That mental health care is denied with considerable

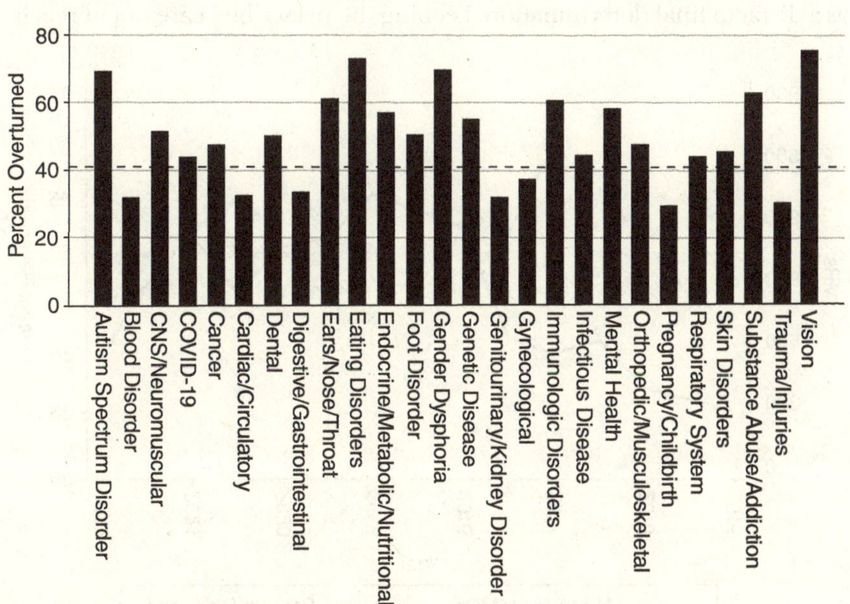

7.11 Percentage of external appeals overturned in New York State, 2019–2022.
Source: New York Department of Financial Services.

frequency is not only important context for the chapter that follows, but also highlights a setting in which overcoming the learning, compliance, and psychological costs of appeal may prove particularly grueling due to the very nature of the illness.

Drawing on semi-annual reports to the legislature on the independent health care appeals program created under the Health Care Quality Act, I find that New Jersey likewise exhibits marked variation over time in the filing of IMRs, and in terms of their success (see Figure 7.12). The figure displayed reflects only a subset of those filed – for example, in the first half of 2022, 1,310 external appeals were filed with the New Jersey Department's vendor, but 665 were accepted for review and 520 appeals were completed – which perhaps reflects not only the desire for the additional review of case files, but also the need for greater patient knowledge about the cases appropriate to such review given the associated learning costs. What's more, as the 2022 report to the New Jersey legislature notes, even with an overall increase in volume of external reviews since 2015, considering the number of residents who are enrolled in managed care plans, the numbers still remain quite low, such that the plan's denial may operate as a de facto final determination, keeping the prescribed care out of reach.

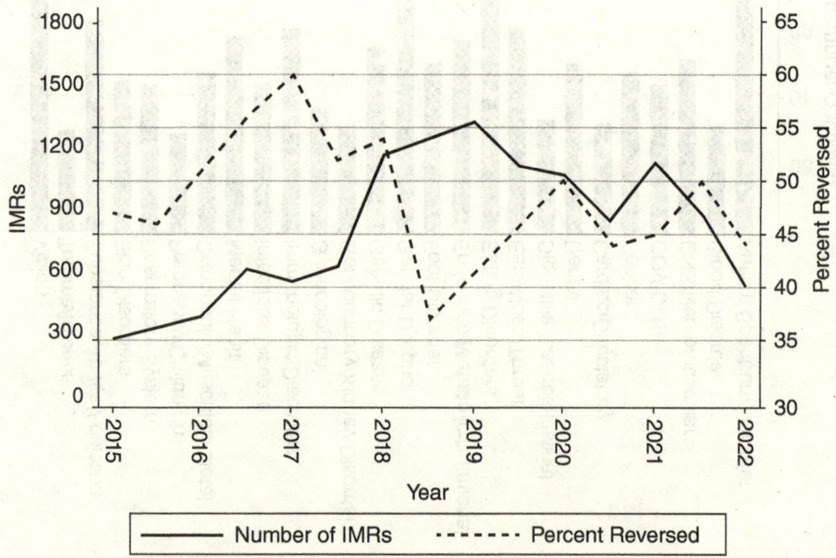

7.12 IMRs and reversals in New Jersey, 2015–2022.
Source: New Jersey Department of Banking and Insurance.

When independent medical reviews are capitalized upon, they can be of great benefit to the patient, but what is clear from this cross-state analysis is that few patients pursue this avenue, whether due to limited knowledge or limited time and energy, especially given the frequent requirement of exhaustion of internal remedies.

This analysis offers new insights into the value of these external appeals, but also the hurdles (informational and otherwise) associated with navigating them. While independent (or external) reviews are an essential mechanism through which to have cases assessed by entities separate from health insurers and often yield favorable results for patients, these processes can be burdensome and thus reinforce inequities in who pursues this route, especially because internal appeals and their associated inequities are a vital precursor to this.

And even with the proliferation of different levels of appeal processes, one must not lose sight of the psychological toll of these denials and their leading to cumbersome navigation of health insurance bureaucracy. Reflecting on her long battle to secure IVIg treatment for her son, Susan reflected, "I wouldn't say the appeal process made me an alcoholic, but it definitely pushed me over the edge. When you're going through it, you don't always realize the toll it's taking on you. It's *afterwards* that you look around and see the tornado damage. But when you're in the middle of it, you're just trying to keep your head on straight and not scream at people."

CONCLUSION

Having discussed in previous chapters the scope of coverage denials and the administrative and emotional burdens that this insurance practice places on physicians, here I discussed through survey, interview, and public data the administrative burdens placed specifically on patients, both through internal review processes and through independent, external review processes. While public data shed light on the breadth of health concerns that lead patients to pursue this higher level of appeal (e.g., with the state Department of Managed Health Care or its equivalent) and the frequency with which denials are reversed, they do not shed light on the demographic vulnerabilities to opting out of appeal and thus being unable to access health plan benefits kept out of reach by health insurers. To assess that, I drew on interviews and my original nationwide survey data, in which all respondents who experienced denials were asked whether they appealed their denial and, if so, whether the insurer reversed its initial decision.

In part because of the high frequency with which respondents experienced not one denial, but *multiple* denials, I observe here a high rate of appeal of at least one denial experienced (61 percent, though with the caveat that this includes broader efforts to challenge denials, such as by phone), of which 52 percent were successful, suggesting a potentially higher value of appealing than many suspect. While education and language status are, surprisingly, not associated with one's propensity to appeal or to win in doing so, each $25,000 increase in one's household income is associated with a corresponding 3 percentage point increase in likelihood of appealing a denial. What's more, it is clear not only that there are significant information barriers, but also that this limited information about one's potential to win a health insurance appeal (which is to say, significant underestimation of reversal rates) can significantly deter patients from appealing their own denial of coverage. This is important because one's likelihood of winning an appeal amounts to what is essentially a coin flip. That is, despite being administratively burdensome, it appears that there often are significant payoffs to expending this effort – whether that means gaining access to a costly medication, obtaining a long-awaited scan, or being able to avoid charges for a costly emergency department visit. The challenge is that not only is there significant overall burden, but also that burden is distributed unevenly, particularly harming patients who are sicker, less affluent, or Black or Hispanic patients reliant on Medicaid, which has largely fallen within the sweep of managed health care and employs extensive utilization management such as prior authorization.

The inequitable nature of this health insurer practice is reflected in the fact that, even once the administrative burdens of initiating an appeal have been overcome, sicker and Black and Hispanic Medicaid patients are the least likely to win appeals. Thus, denials can not only exacerbate health challenges, but also reinforce along race and class lines America's already pronounced disparities in health care access and raise concerns about insurers' apparent perception that denying coverage is acceptable because appeal processes are in place.

After all, these denials and appeals often arise in the setting of a health concern, which makes the "time tax" potentially even more overwhelming and, as Annie Lowrey puts it, a "public policy cancer." And, while Samantha knew to document every relevant conversation and could withstand the endurance contest of making numerous calls to her insurer from her hospital room, many patients would not. What's more, while states have in place processes to allow for independent review, the common requirement that patients first exhaust internal appeal processes – and sometimes even pay a small fee – limits the reach of these policies.

Even in states such as California, which takes steps to reduce the administrative barriers associated with independent medical reviews, of the 170 such appeals made to the California Department of Insurance in 2024, just 9 (5 percent) were filed by patients identifying as Hispanic (despite nearly 40 percent of the state being Hispanic) and zero were filed by patients identifying as Black. Thus, the compounding administrative burdens appear to keep care out of reach for marginalized populations in ways that the literature did not previously appreciate. However, state health policies that help patients to have a usual source of care can mitigate some of this administrative burden, promoting better coordination of appeals between patients and their physicians rather than patients being left to fend for themselves.

CHAPTER 8

The Special Difficulties of Mental Health

JOANNE, A MOTHER OF TWO IN NEW YORK CITY, is no stranger to navigating mental health coverage for her daughter. She has been doing so for years. In addition to the challenge that psychiatrists are far less likely than are other medical specialists to accept insurance benefits,[1] her teenage transgender daughter Eli has required high-level treatment that their insurer has resisted covering. "Medical denials are frustrating to start with, and appealing denied mental health claims is even more mind-boggling," she reflected.

Eli does not only experience gender dysphoria. She has been diagnosed with attention deficit hyperactivity disorder (ADHD), anxiety, depression, and obsessive-compulsive disorder (OCD). Though weekly outpatient therapy had initially sufficed, by the time Eli was in eighth grade, she was having increased difficulty regulating her emotions and, despite her good team of mental health providers, was experiencing worsening depression. It became clear that Eli needed more care than a once-a-week forty-five-minute session, which her outpatient psychiatrist could not accommodate. As time progressed, they came to the mutual conclusion that Eli needed more support, and, in May 2020, Eli agreed to go to a short-term (up to ninety-day) residential treatment facility.

As Joanne described,

> We got approved for ten days the first time, then *three* days the next time, then seven days, then four days. You're on a string because if the insurance doesn't approve you that time, you've got about twenty-four hours to go and get your kid. It was horrible. You can't make any plans because we need to be able to get her if she's not approved for more

224

care. And they also know they can be yanked the next day. How does that help them recover?

Joanne was lucky, being only a two-hour drive away from the facility, but this facility served patients from across the country, who would be at a greater disadvantage amid a coverage barrier.

Eli came home after having shown some improvement and did a partial hospitalization program (PHP), but its short length and Zoom setting amid the COVID-19 pandemic limited Eli's engagement with the program. In April 2021, she broke down and said that she needed to go to Bellevue Hospital because she was self-harming and having escalating suicidal ideation.

The psychiatric team agreed that Eli needed more intensive, longer-term care, and Joanne identified a thirty-to-seventy-five-day program in California. However, she would have to obtain new prior authorizations every few days. It was eventually denied because she was responding to treatment. Given Eli's extensive history of suicidality and emotion dysregulation, the facility nevertheless advised, "If aftercare plan [long-term residential treatment facility] is not followed, client's prognosis is poor. Parents are unable to contain client, and it is likely that client will regress into old behaviors, which pose a serious risk to client and family safety. Client's emotional dysregulation remains intense and creates severe disruption in client's ability to function in daily life." In other words, the higher-level care was viewed as medically necessary.

Joanne splurged on an education consultant to help her find the next appropriate, gender-affirming treatment facility for Eli's needs. They ultimately selected a program in Utah, and they called UnitedHealthcare to secure prior authorization, which was denied despite Eli's previous discharge summary advising this level of care. Instead, they were advised to arrive at the program for evaluation – requiring an expensive cross-country flight for an uncertain outcome – and a coverage decision would then be rendered.

The prior authorization was denied upon Eli's arrival at the facility, with the explanation, "You are motivated for recovery and participating in your treatment. You are medically stable. You are taking your medications as prescribed and doing better." This frustrated Joanne because not only had she received consistent guidance from Eli's treatment team, but also she had seen firsthand Eli's rapid deterioration when not in higher-level care. This did not appear to be overtreatment of her child.

The cost of the treatment facility is $14,000 per week, an enormous financial strain to avoid Eli being sent home while actively suicidal. As part of the first level of appeal, Joanne included a letter from the shorter-term residential facility, which stated, "While in treatment, Eli was able to stabilize on medications and learn more effective coping skills to regulate emotions. However, at discharge, Eli continued to have difficulties implementing coping mechanisms," including with respect to maintaining medication adherence and remaining physically safe.

The appeal was again denied because her condition was improving and she was medication-compliant in that setting. Further, UnitedHealthcare gave Eli's therapist only a two-hour window within which to return the call and provide greater detail about Eli's case. Because the therapist had multiple appointments that day, the call was not returned at the end of the day, which UnitedHealthcare asserted was not in a sufficiently timely manner. Joanne was in tears.

To assist with the second-level appeal, they hired a lawyer. Together, they spent over twenty-five hours crafting the appeal, and Joanne recognized her advantages in being able to do so. Their lawyer sent UnitedHealthcare over 200 pages of documents, including Eli's medical records. To front the necessary costs while the appeal proceeded, she liquidated her inheritance from her parents and drew on additional family financial support. "This is what you do when it's your kid. You have no choice. We're fortunate in that my parents have the means to do this. We would have cashed in my 401(k). We had no choice. It was an untenable situation for everyone, including Eli, to continue living the way we were living and walking on eggshells."

UnitedHealthcare has thirty to sixty days to respond to the appeal, and Joanne is waiting with bated breath. "This is all a game, and you need to understand the different pieces. You have to fight *tooth and nail* to make sure your child has a semblance of a future. It shouldn't be this difficult to help our children."

Joanne and Eli are two of the many people with whom I spoke who struggled to navigate insurance coverage – including repeated prior authorization battles – within the realm of mental health care, bringing together many themes of this book, including the need for a high degree of health literacy, the burdens of appeal both for patients and for their providers (including the psychological costs), and the difficult choice between care postponement and financial instability.

In 2023, approximately 59 million US adults experienced mental illness and nearly half did not receive treatment.[2] While this inadequate access stems from a range of issues including insurance coverage and provider shortages (especially amid growing demand), barriers to obtaining covered treatments constitute one facet of this health policy problem.

Like with medical and surgical benefits, when seeking care for mental health conditions, one must demonstrate medical necessity, which can be more difficult when the mental health symptoms are not related to a physical illness with accompanying tests (e.g., scans or blood tests).[3] However, despite the severity of some mental health cases, prior authorizations for intensive treatment might need to be renewed every couple of days by insurers, which, as this book has highlighted, have substantial discretion in making coverage decisions. And, given the opacity of medical necessity guidelines (coupled with the reality that the practice of medicine is both art and science), it can be difficult to glean whether a denial is appropriate.[4] What's more, in the setting of a mental health crisis, not only can the psychological costs of this insurance navigation be even more pronounced for the patient and their family, but also denials can be particularly consequential.

In the 2023 plan year, researchers at KFF evaluated claim denials (as distinct from denials issued through prior authorization) by Affordable Care Act (ACA) marketplace plans and found that 11 percent of medical necessity-based denials of coverage were for the receipt of behavioral health benefits. In my survey sample, 11 percent of those denied coverage were seeking either outpatient or residential behavioral health care.

Denials in this realm of health care can affect a large swath of Americans. It has been estimated that about one in four adults experiences a diagnosable mental health disorder each year, with many individuals such as Eli suffering from more than one such disorder at a time.[5] Drawing on interview evidence as well as reporting by the organization ParityTrack, I show that patients seeking behavioral health treatment can face pushback from insurers in multiple ways, whether outright denial of coverage or denial of *adequate* coverage, and the laws in place safeguarding behavioral health coverage prove inadequate for far too many. And these denials of prescribed care are burdensome both for patients and for their physicians, who are less likely than other physicians to be equipped to overcome these constraints.

PRIOR AUTHORIZATION IN MENTAL HEALTH CARE

Prior authorization challenges abound not only in the realm of longer-term care facilities, but also in outpatient care (as discussed in Chapter 4), with which child, adolescent, and adult psychiatrist Dr. Mark Wilson is all too familiar.

"It's gotten worse every single year," Dr. Wilson assessed of prior authorization within psychiatric medications. "It was bad for a while, and it hurts me so much to criticize it, but the ACA was based on private insurance, and it feels like private insurance went, 'We're going to take on all these new people, so we're going to nickel and dime everyone to death.'"[6] This sentiment was echoed in Chapter 1 by former Cigna executive Wendell Potter. It was a marked expansion of the number of covered individuals, including sicker individuals, without relaxation of obligations to shareholders, rendering the tools of managed care – namely, prior authorization – especially attractive.

Historically, the two classes of drugs in which prior authorization primarily arose in the behavioral health setting were brand drugs and stimulant drugs. Now, Dr. Wilson observed,

> more and more, every med is at risk of demanding a prior authorization, *even if I am prescribing it as generic.* There are times when I have to submit information for a prior authorization for generic Prozac, fluoxetine, which is absurd. A certain generic drug, Venlafaxine extended-release tablet, exists and is technically generic, but it might as well be a brand-new medicine that's brand-name because they almost never cover it.

Consistent with the neurology setting discussed in Chapter 4, step therapy requirements in behavioral health drugs can extend to entirely different classes of drugs that may be inappropriate for the patient's condition. For example, while Abilify is classified as an atypical antipsychotic, it can be used as an adjunctive therapy in combination with an antidepressant for the treatment of major depressive disorder. However, Dr. Wilson explained,

> There might be a prior auth saying that's denied because they need to fail [the other antipsychotic drugs] risperidone and olanzapine first, which sometimes are fine options but some of them aren't FDA-approved for adding on to antidepressants so I might not want them. I can't prove beyond the shadow of a doubt that my patient *must* be on that med until they've been on it, but they want my patient to potentially suffer on another medication first and save some bucks.

As prior authorization barriers arise, the patient may be forced to either pay out of pocket for a month's supply or forgo medication for a few days, which, depending on the medication's half-life, can be deleterious to the patient's mental health condition and broader functioning. While tools such as GoodRx can help patients to reduce their cost-sharing, in the setting of rising costs of many antidepressants,[7] this may be inadequate protection.

This prior authorization administration can be particularly burdensome in the mental health setting not only for patients, but also for physicians. After all, psychiatry is the medical specialty in which practitioners are most likely to operate out of a solo practice,[8] rather than having the resources of, for example, an academic medical practice equipped with the enhanced staffing discussed in Chapter 6. Thus, while providers across specialties experience administrative burden, health services researchers Jane Zhu and Matthew Eisenberg have asserted that mental health professionals "lack the significant financial, operational, and administrative support needed for claims processing, revenue cycle management, and health information technology," including the electronic medical record tools discussed in Chapter 4.[9] Given this context, it is also more likely that the prior authorization administration may fall more squarely on the shoulders of physicians themselves rather than support staff, leading to "administrative friction" and disinclination to participate in insurance networks, which in turn perpetuates difficulties accessing covered treatment.[10]

Though this book has emphasized patient and physician administrative burden, these burdens extend even farther. Sean Erreger, a licensed clinical social worker in Saratoga Springs, New York, has worked on inpatient psychiatric units, in the emergency department, and at an adolescent treatment program. He has seen it all, from the risks posed by inappropriate denials to the seeming "black box" of prescribing when there is extensive variation in policy across health insurers. Some denials that emerged from this setting were, to Sean, galling. He recalled treating a patient who had jumped off a bridge into freezing cold water, survived the fall, and was admitted to the medical floor for three days, at which point he denied current suicidality. Because of this, the insurer determined that the patient did not meet the coverage criteria for admission for inpatient psychiatric care.

> As a social worker, I'm not putting my name to this, and I'm going to do everything I can to document that I said that this is not right. But depending on the insurance, there's a lot of variability in how long it takes to resolve. I used to work weekends and sometimes insurance companies wouldn't have their mental health prior auth person available on the weekend. *Are you kidding me?* You have to jump through so many hoops. It's absurd, as though psychiatric emergencies don't happen on the weekend.[11]

This is not to say that there aren't workarounds, especially through drug manufacturers' provision of coupons for brand-name drugs to substantially reduce cost-sharing. Los Angeles psychiatrist Dr. Kyle Smith observed that, once patients are able to pay the reduced price for three months while determining whether the medication is effective,

> I can then contact the insurance company and say, "This patient is doing really great on this drug. She has failed four other drugs. Please approve this," and they pretty much always approve it. If I had to do the prior auth first, it would be a total waste of time because it would take me a week to do it and they might not even accept it, and in the meantime the patient doesn't have the right medication in that interval.[12]

While this can be a valuable way to mitigate delays in care and administrative burden, it requires physician knowledge of the system. What's more, not only is use of drug companies' coupons restricted to patients with commercial insurance, but also they are not available for all drugs and they tend to steer patients toward costlier drugs, exacerbating the high prescription drug costs observed in the United States. In fact, the number of drugs with coupons increased from 200 in 2008 to over 800 in 2018, and the introduction of coupons increased the number of drugs sold without generic substitutes sold by 23–25 percent in the commercial segment of health insurance, thus illustrating this practice's contribution toward higher spending, including when used as a workaround in the setting of prior authorization.[13] What's more, while the availability of manufacturer coupons is associated with patients initiating treatment, coupons are used for a median of three refills and many patients discontinue treatment when coupons are no longer available. Given the longer-term nature of many behavioral health conditions, physicians must thus become familiar not only with which drugs have coupons available, but also with the duration of that availability so as to mitigate disruptions in care.[14]

Cumulatively, these provider reflections highlight that, while there are avenues to promote patients' access to needed treatments, they can demand significant knowledge of the behavioral insurance benefits system. This system is made even more complex for patients and their prescribers due to American health insurance's fragmentation between behavioral health and physical health benefits through "carve-outs."

BEHAVIORAL HEALTH CARE FRAGMENTATION

The American health care system is notoriously fragmented, and this is no less true in the setting of behavioral health. Health insurers increasingly contract with specialized managed care entities to manage behavioral health claims. This dynamic is referred to as a carve-out. For example, while UnitedHealthcare processes medical and surgical benefits, United Behavioral Health manages its behavioral health benefits. Similarly, Aetna's behavioral health benefits are processed through

Aetna Behavioral Health, and Cigna behavioral health benefits are administered through Cigna Behavioral Health. Though advocates have hailed their greater efficiency, these carve-outs can create added administrative burden for physicians, in addition to raising the compliance costs for patients, who must know the phone or fax number and mailing address with which to communicate about matters of coverage.

Examining this fragmented landscape of mental health coverage, law professor Barak Richman and his coauthors observe that "carved-out mental health benefits might contribute to the many harms of fragmentation, including poorly coordinated care" as well as overprovision and duplication of certain services.[15] These carve-outs allow mental health benefits administrators to establish specialty provider networks, negotiate competitive service fees, institute treatment protocols, and monitor consumption of mental health services. Behavioral health carve-outs expanded in the 1990s with the growth in reliance on managed care, which coincided with the growth in reliance on prior authorization. A primary motivation for these carve-outs is cost containment, with the separate administration of behavioral health and medical claims associated with a reduction in the costs of mental health care, especially in the context of hospitalizations.[16]

These managed care arrangements are on the rise. In 2004, twenty states had carve-out arrangements, typically through contracts with organizations that had expertise in behavioral health; by 2019, that number had risen to forty-three states within the managed Medicaid setting.[17]

Part of the reason for their reduction in overall health costs is because nearly 25 percent of mental health services provided are not supported by clinical evidence and carve-outs may promote closer monitoring of mental health care consumption.[18] That is, even as some mental health cases can be life-threatening, this is a setting of overutilization – though health economists Rena Conti, Alisa Busch, and David Cutler find that antidepressant overprescribing is less prevalent (less than 20 percent) than had previously been estimated.[19] This finding notwithstanding, the push for more evidence-based treatment is consistent with Eric Patashnik, Alan Gerber, and Conor Dowling's observation that "[p]rofessional self-regulation should ensure that doctors recommend the best treatments for patients, but it sometimes disappoints."[20] That is, as we have seen in the context of the overuse of high-tech imaging (e.g., for low back pain), physicians are imperfect at policing each other's prescribing.

One critical caveat to Barak Richman and his coauthors' findings is that if mental health carve-outs do expand mental health insurance, those benefits are disproportionately channeled to white and high-income individuals, thus raising equity concerns.[21] This fragmentation has led economist Deborah Haas-Wilson to conclude that care coordination is difficult when balancing separate financing services for medical services and behavioral services, leading to potentially lower quality of care and even *higher* spending.[22]

A key challenge with this health insurance complexity is that patients have limited understanding of their health benefits. Psychiatrist Dr. John S. Smolowe noted, "The patient is unaware of these subcontractors … Yet if we send the claim to the wrong entity, they disregard it," and if it takes longer than ninety days to resolve, the bills may denied for lack of timely filing.[23] Thus, failure to understand the division of insurer responsibility amid mental health carve-outs can impose not only learning costs about insurance design but also compliance costs of more complex claim processing, creating far too many opportunities for patients to fall through the cracks. This dynamic is consistent with Pamela Herd and Donald Moynihan's observation that when patients are unaware of a program's intricacies, they may be unable to access even programs for which they are eligible. What's more, Pamela Herd and her coauthors observe in a separate analysis that "[t]he presence of multiple actors and conflicting incentives in service delivery also contribute to burden" and inequities. While their analysis focuses on public–private partnerships in social policy, it is no less true when extending the logic to behavioral health carve-outs of one's insurance benefits.[24] Thus, the American health insurance system can impose informational barriers and administrative burdens, and, as the previous chapters have shown, this insurance complexity can impede patients' ability to successfully appeal to access their prescribed care in a timely manner.

While the discussion thus far has considered the administration of mental health benefits within managed care, it is helpful now to evaluate the legal protections of health insurance coverage, as well as where the law falls short.

MENTAL HEALTH PARITY AND SHORTCOMINGS IN COVERAGE

Though Congress has passed mental health parity legislation, America has not yet realized its promise. The Paul Wellstone and Pete Domenici Mental Health Parity and Addiction Equity Act of 2008 (MHPAEA) (PL 110-343) amends ERISA to prevent group health plans from providing less favorable benefit limitations on mental health/substance use disorder (MH/SUD) benefits than on medical/surgical benefits. The enactment of this legislation marked a critical expansion on the legal protections offered by the Mental Health Parity Act of 1996, in which Congress prohibited large group health plans from imposing more restrictive annual or lifetime dollar limits on mental health benefits than those observed for medical/surgical care. Though originally aimed at group health plans, the ACA extended the MHPAEA's provisions to individual health coverage.

According to the MHPAEA, if a health plan includes medical/surgical benefits as well as MH/SUD benefits, the financial requirements (e.g., deductibles and copayments) and quantitative treatment limitations (QTLs; e.g., the number of visits or days of coverage permitted) that apply to MH/SUD benefits may not be more restrictive than other requirements. Thus, for example, there may not be quantitative limits for psychotherapy when limitations do not exist for physical therapy. Moreover, if out-of-network medical/surgical benefits are provided, out-of-network MH/SUD benefits must be provided as well.

The MHPAEA further imposed parity requirements with respect to non-quantitative treatment limitations (NQTLs), such that a plan may not have more stringent standards in coverage guidelines and prior authorization requirements than is applied to medical/surgical care. These NQTLs include determinations of medical necessity or medical appropriateness, whether the treatment is experimental or investigational, formulary design for prescription drugs and the types of drugs that require prior authorization and step therapy, standards for provider admission to participate in a network (including reimbursement rates), plan methods for determining "usual, customary, and reasonable" charges to the insurer, and exclusions based on one's failure to complete a course of treatment.[25] Thus, for example, step therapy requirements may not be imposed more stringently in the context of behavioral health prescriptions than for other prescription drugs. Like with medical/surgical benefits, the MHPAEA requires that "the reason for any denial under the plan … be made available on request or as otherwise required by the plan administrator."[26]

While the MHPAEA holds sweeping promise in promoting access to mental health coverage, laws are only as good as their enforcement, which in this case has proved challenging. The provisions of the MHPAEA pertaining to private sector employer-sponsored health plans are enforced by the Department of Labor's Employee Benefits Service Administration and the Department of the Treasury, while the Department of Health and Human Services has primary enforcement over non-federal governmental plans, such as those sponsored by state and local employers.[27] The division of responsibility for ensuring mental health parity across federal agencies and state regulators can make it difficult for any one agency to take ownership of the policy problem, potentially undercutting accountability when it comes to enforcement.

What's more, the 2022 Department of Labor Report to Congress highlighted the additional challenge of obtaining adequate information from plans and health insurers so as to assess compliance or lack thereof with the law's demands.[28] Health policy researcher Rachel Presskreischer and her coauthors analyzed state insurance departments' oversight of mental health parity and found not only that enforcement of parity was driven by a range of factors including interpretation of legal vagueness and state political priorities, but also that the assessment of NQTLs across behavioral health versus medical/surgical benefits felt akin to comparing apples to oranges. Compounding this challenge, accurate analysis of the extent of parity compliance demands a level of clinical knowledge that may go beyond the capacity of insurance departments.[29] It is because of this complexity – coupled with regulators' reliance in part on complaint data, the existence of which depends on patients understanding their rights to protection and choosing to complain – that researchers at the Commonwealth Fund assessed in 2024 that many health insurers have not fully complied with the law's requirements.[30]

Thus, in addition to outright denials of coverage for prescribed care, the uneven enforcement of the MHPAEA means that patients across the country also find themselves inadequately protected. Following the Department of Labor's 2022 Report to Congress on the limitations in delivering on the promise of the MHPAEA, members of Congress introduced the Parity Enforcement Act of 2023 (to provide for civil monetary penalties for parity violations), the Mental Health Matters Act (to support mental health services for youth), and the Behavioral Health Coverage Transparency Act of 2022 (to increase oversight of parity requirements including by auditing insurance providers), though none of these legislative efforts came to fruition.

STATE-LEVEL ENFORCEMENT OF MENTAL HEALTH PARITY. The number of mental health parity enforcement actions varies widely across the states, some of which rely on "market conduct exams," which help regulators to identify how health insurers are processing and paying claims. I examined states' market conduct reports compiled by ParityTrack, a national leadership coalition founded and led by former Representative Patrick Kennedy, which are documented in Table 8.1. Surprisingly, state challenges of health insurers' coverage shortcomings are few and far between: only twelve states engaged in enforcement actions as of July 2025. Among these enforcement efforts, penalties ranged from corrective action (California) to an $18 million settlement (New York), with most of the penalties assessed being more modest (e.g., around $1 million).

Reported violations of parity, often resulting in wrongful coverage denials, included instances of the following natures: disproportionate imposition of prior authorization requirements for MH/SUD treatment and the utilization of medical necessity criteria that resulted in higher claim denial rates for such care (Connecticut); greater restrictions on the approval of medications for serious mental illness and alcohol dependency than for other health conditions, and lack of timely notification of denied claims (Delaware); failure to use appropriate medical necessity guidelines and the denial of claims as out-of-network when they were in-network (Illinois); wrongful denial or wrongfully low reimbursement for behavioral health services (New York); and categorical denial of behavioral health treatments such as applied behavior analysis (Oregon).

Table 8.1 Mental health parity enforcement actions by state

State	Parity enforcement actions
California	July 2017 requirement of Kaiser Permanente to enter into corrective action plan to ensure parity compliance, potential fines
Connecticut	July 2020 and January 2021 stipulation and consent order against four health plan subsidiaries, over $1 million in fines and education payments
Delaware	Health plans fined $1.33 million for mental health parity violations in 2020/2021, second round of market conduct mental health parity exams including $735,000 for parity violations (2021)
Illinois	State levies $2 million in fines against five health plans due to parity violations in July 2020
Massachusetts	Assurance of discontinuance agreements executed with five health plans and two behavioral health organizations (February 2020) along with over $900,000 in fines
Minnesota	Department of Commerce alleged Medica violated mental health parity laws, required company to make systematic improvements to coverage, imposed $300,000 fine (July 2023)
New Hampshire	Market conduct examinations identify deficiencies with Anthem and Harvard Pilgrim Parity compliance (February 2020)
New York	United to pay over $18 million to settle disputes regarding alleged parity violations (August 2021)
Oregon	State assesses over $550,000 in fines against four health plans for parity violations (March 2017)
Pennsylvania	State fines UMPC health plans $250,000 for parity and ACA violations (December 2021)
Rhode Island	State requires BCBS of Rhode Island to pay $5 million in mental health care (September 2018)
Washington	UHIC failed to show how it administers MH/SUD benefits in accordance with parity law, given higher rates of medical necessity denials for MH/SUD treatment. Fined $500,000 (October 2023).

Source: Parity Track

Indeed, the Connecticut Insurance Department's July 30, 2020 market conduct report on Oxford Health Insurance and UnitedHealthcare revealed a number of erroneous claim denials for MH/SUD treatment, including using a denial code when requesting additional information, incorrectly denying claims as not authorized when authorizations were on file, providing incorrect denial codes, and incorrectly denying claims as out-of-network. Although these errors may be rectified upon appeal, as previous chapters highlight, many denials are not appealed, those that are may be from more economically advantaged individuals, and the experience of denial can disrupt patients' health and economic wellbeing – in this case, in an area of health that can also be life-endangering.

While these twelve states have taken significant enforcement actions to ensure parity in the face of denials of coverage for behavioral health treatment, most states have taken no such actions. Moreover, with so many health plans being enforced not by the states but by the Department of Labor due to ERISA's preemption of state policymaking that relates to self-insured health plans, this only scratches the surface of violations. For some enrolled in ERISA-governed health plans, class action litigation has proven to be an avenue to challenge wrongful denials within the mental health sphere, though ERISA bars plaintiffs from recovering damages.

In April 2022, the class action case *M. C. W. v. Blue Cross and Blue Shield of Texas, Inc.* was filed, holding that Blue Cross and Blue Shield (BCBS) of Texas unlawfully denied coverage for services rendered at licensed residential treatment facilities on the grounds that the services were not medically necessary. According to the lawsuit, when making coverage determinations, BCBS relied on medical necessity criteria that are not disclosed to patients and are more restrictive than those applied to comparable medical services rendered at skilled nursing facilities (which fall under the umbrella of medical/surgical benefits). Thus, it was argued, the plan was in violation of the MHPAEA.

The complaint argues that through "reli[ance] on extra-contractual protocols and guidelines in assessing the medical necessity of behavioral health services," the guidelines "narrow[ed] the certificate's definition of medical necessity," and resulted in an abuse of discretion and, in turn, wrongful coverage denial. BCBS indicated upon appeal,

> Based on the information provided, you did not meet MCG care guidelines for Partial Hospital Behavioral Health Level of Care …. Your mood and anxiety symptoms have improved. You were medically stable. You had social support. You were able to care for yourself well enough. You could have continued to get better and work on communication skills and coping skills in a lower level of care. You had access to a lower level of care. From the information provided, you could have been treated in a less intensive setting such as Mental Health Intensive Outpatient.

Thus, not only was the patient denied coverage for residential treatment on the basis of reasoning that would sound quite familiar to Joanne and Eli, but also coverage for the step-down level of care was denied. This would ultimately emerge as a class action lawsuit concerning wrongful coverage denial of MH/SUD benefits.

To be sure, litigation is far from a costless endeavor, and the inequities Chapter 7 highlighted in appeal processes are replicated within the pursuit of justice through the American legal system. But this case points the way toward greater understanding of the role of courts in accessing denied mental health benefits, and another case has emerged in prominence: *Wit v. United Behavioral Health.*

WIT V. UNITED BEHAVIORAL HEALTH. Through its behavioral health carve-out, United Behavioral Health (UBH) administers behavioral health benefits for those enrolled in UnitedHealthcare's plans, serving over 45 million patients. The claims of thousands of UBH class members across the country were denied under thousands of health plans that contained language describing covered services and exclusions.

Though addressing behavioral health coverage, it was brought not as a parity case, but rather as an ERISA case because, according to lead attorney D. Brian Hufford, rather than comparing behavioral health benefits with medical benefits, the counsel are identifying instances in which behavioral health coverage decisions are violating the terms of the insurance plans.[31]

According to the lawsuit, the internal guidelines were not only very limited, but also had an acute-based focus, precluding continued coverage for severe depression when the patient was no longer in an acute state but continued to have chronic symptoms. But, as Hufford observed, "Just because you're not acute doesn't mean you're cured. This acute care model makes no sense. The insurers are imposing their judgments, and those judgments are influenced by their own financial interests." This class action lawsuit involves over 50,000 plaintiffs who are "similarly situated" (a requirement for class certification), and who argue that UBH had breached its fiduciary duty under ERISA, and that it had arbitrarily and capriciously denied benefits to enrollees because of its reliance on overly restrictive guidelines.

The *Wit* litigation has been protracted, to say the least. On November 3, 2020, Northern District of California district judge Joseph Spero ruled that, because of the denial of benefits, the plaintiffs should be allowed not only to recover benefits owed, but also to enforce participants' rights under the terms of the insurance plan. Thus, the plaintiffs were entitled to bring legal action against UBH. The plaintiffs' goal was for UBH to relinquish its profits resulting from illegal or wrongful conduct. Ultimately, Judge Spero denied UBH's request for summary judgment and ordered that UBH reprocess 67,000 wrongly denied behavioral health claims. The *Wit* decision constituted a groundbreaking moment in which it was revealed, for the first time and through a lengthy trial, how insurance plans can rely on substandard treatment guidelines to deny coverage for behavioral health care services.[32]

However, on March 22, 2022, the Ninth Circuit Court of Appeals reversed the lower court's ruling, which Hufford characterized as

> one of the most disappointing decisions I've seen. It came down to, United can have discretion to basically do what they want with their guidelines, without ever evaluating that United was making decisions based on their own financial interest. This case was recognized as probably the most significant decision in twenty years in this area, and to have it essentially be thrown out in such an off-handed way in a non-precedential memorandum opinion just shows you some of the problems with our health care system.

Following the Ninth Circuit reversal, the plaintiffs filed for en banc review, which occurs when all judges in the circuit (as opposed to a three-judge panel) hear the case. On January 26, 2023, the Ninth Circuit issued a new superseding opinion that affirmed part of the district court opinion, while nevertheless holding that those wrongly denied could *not* have their claims reprocessed. In August 2023, the Ninth Circuit issued yet another opinion that vacated its January 2023 ruling and opened the door to the reprocessing of wrongly denied claims upon a rehearing of the case. "I've never seen this happen before in my almost forty years of practice," Hufford observed of the ongoing litigation.

The *Wit* case concerning mental health claims highlights a few core limitations of this recourse in the face of wrongly denied coverage. The protracted nature of these lawsuits highlights that for those who may require immediate relief – such as seeking coverage of very costly residential treatment to address an acute state of depression or disordered eating – legal intervention may be slow to offer the needed respite from medical bills. What's more, in most employer-sponsored plans, one cannot recover monetary damages, but rather can only obtain the benefits owed, such as through claim reprocessing (as in the case of *Wit*). Thus, the most fruitful avenue for pursuing legal recourse is class action litigation, which is subject to numerous constraints related to class certification, and which can encounter substantial procedural delays. That is, while class action litigation can be a potent and high-profile mechanism through which to hold insurers accountable, for many people whose mental health coverage is denied, the only recourse is the administrative appeal avenue, the administrative burdens of which this book has laid bare.

CONCLUSION

This chapter has brought to light the numerous hurdles that patients face in securing coverage for prescribed care within the realm of behavioral health, treatment for which tens of millions of Americans receive every year. Most of the administrative burdens seen elsewhere in the American health insurance system are replicated here, though this population may be particularly disadvantaged due to the combination of inadequate parity protections and a condition that may amplify the experience of psychological costs.

While some of the prior authorizations are consistent with those found in non-behavioral health care (e.g., for brand or otherwise costly medications), other hurdles appear to be unique and inconsistent with existing federal parity legislation. Although there are "tricks of the trade" – whether in the choice of first-line treatment or in reliance on coupons with which to test the efficacy of brand medications prior to pursuit of a prior authorization – the administrative burdens of this insurance practice can be more pronounced in this setting both because navigating insurance bureaucracy may be especially taxing for someone experiencing unmanaged mental health symptoms and because of these clinicians' higher rate of operating in solo practices rather than having substantial staffing support.

The fragmentation of the American mental health care system contributes both to informational barriers and to enforcement challenges – all the while pertaining to a realm of health care where there may by definition be both more pronounced psychological costs as well as the need for more time-sensitive access to care. With many health insurers creating carve-outs for behavioral health care, patients must be aware of this structure and know to whom to submit which claims, lest they be discarded, causing delays in accessing benefits or payment. And, while many parity cases are under the jurisdiction of the Department of Labor through ERISA, the fragmentation of regulatory responsibility across federal agencies and state regulators imposes obstacles in effectively holding insurers accountable. This can, in turn, perpetuate barriers to accessing behavioral health benefits – and, while there are appeal processes in place (as well as the possibility of class action litigation in select cases), recurrence of severe depression or other acute conditions can render this a particularly time-sensitive setting in which to experience these obstacles.

Part of the challenge stems from the opacity of what constitutes appropriate medical necessity guidelines for behavioral health care. Absent adequate enforcement, access to mental health care may be denied to patients who carry health insurance that ostensibly includes behavioral health benefits.[33] One possible avenue for reform is empowering the Department of Labor to enforce civil monetary penalties for violations of mental health parity, to strengthen the protections of the MHPAEA.

For some, coverage denials result in overwhelming medical debts that they hope to address through litigation, slow and tedious though it may be, or the depletion of savings. For others, denials result in abandonment of treatment, which can have devastating consequences, whether exacerbating mental health symptoms, increasing the likelihood of incarceration, or even taking life-threatening actions.

This chapter brings to light the need for bolstered enforcement of parity, a subject raised in the 2022 MHPAEA Report to Congress. Both in terms of overall access issues and for equity reasons, such changes will be welcome for many, helping to reduce the disconnect between the legislative guarantees of the MHPAEA and the scope of benefits that patients enjoy in practice.

CHAPTER 9

A Path Forward

"**I** HAVE TO FIGHT FOR *EVERYTHING* I DO," Lisa reflected of her experience in the American health care system. Lisa, a fifty-eight-year-old mother of three in the outskirts of Los Angeles, was diagnosed by a neurologist with primary progressive multiple sclerosis (MS) right after her twins were born in 1997.

In the years that followed, *technically* her MS has progressed only slowly, but she lost her ability to walk in 2010. She has been entirely bedbound for years, but she finds that her greatest struggles stem from "idiot doctors and my insurance, which pulled the rug out from under me. I'll never get out of this bed because of them."

In 2021, Lisa began to get Medicare through her disability benefits, having previously relied on her husband's insurance through Independence Blue Cross. Lisa grew up in an affluent family and growing up, she didn't have to worry about expenses or her health care. She never saw the other side of the coin until her MS diagnosis, which changed her life and at times made her want to give up on life.

First, the denials were for ambulances, aggregating to $6,000 due to concerns about their medical necessity as well as a practice known as surprise billing, which Congress prohibited in the No Surprises Act in 2021. Then, there were denials for rehabilitation and physical therapy.

Lisa had a bad fall in 2013. "Instantly, everything from my chest down was affected. I couldn't move anything." Upon arrival at the hospital, her pain had subsided, and the doctors attributed her fall to her MS, but no X-rays were performed to assess the extent of her injuries. It turned out that she had fractured her spine, though this was not discovered until 2018, and by then it "was too late and nobody cared anymore."

When Lisa lost the use of her legs, she didn't remember much because it threw her into the depths of suicidal depression. Within eight months, she had to have colostomy and urostomy surgeries that "stopped my way of life." Not only that, but there were complications requiring that she go back a year later to have the surgery redone.

Rehabilitation was what Lisa mainly needed due to her MS and her fall, but she didn't realize it at the time. She asked her doctors what she should do to aid in her recovery, and they didn't help her to obtain "these boots that you're supposed to be wearing when you're bed bound. They have stirrups on them to keep your legs aligned." Over the course of the next few years, her legs "flopped to the side," and it caused problems in her hips, knees, and ankles. "When I finally realized what was happening to my body, it felt too late."

By 2018, Lisa was ready to take her life but, instead, she sought help. The doctors who helped her got her into a rehabilitation facility, where she received intensive and successful rehabilitative physical therapy treatment for thirty days, finally giving Lisa hope that her life could change for the better.

Then her insurance company said that continued rehabilitation treatment was no longer medically necessary and thus would not be covered. She was sent home, where, lacking adequate home care, her limitations reverted to their prior state. When Lisa tried to get at-home physical therapy, she was given a mere four sessions total because further treatment was deemed to be "not medically necessary."

During this time, Lisa began to blog and tweet about her experience, and Independence Blue Cross found her posts and had someone from their corporate office contact her. He said that they wouldn't authorize her additional rehabilitation because she had been diagnosed with MS. This was particularly infuriating to Lisa because her insurance benefit plan allowed additional physical therapy treatments. It simply wasn't authorized *in her case.*

Lisa's pain management doctor runs the rehab facility in which she received treatment for a month, and she pleaded with him to go to bat for her. But he replied flatly, "There's nothing more we can do." "Just four sessions are not helping me at all. It's doing nothing but causing me more pain," Lisa said, feeling defeated both by her doctors and by her insurer.

When Lisa got denied by her insurer, first she communicated with Independence Blue Cross's parent company Accolade and then she "went through every level of appeal there is." But the insurer's doctors, "had never seen my legs, had never seen *me*, but said my treatment wasn't medically necessary. They overruled my doctors. How does that work, in the United States of America? How can *their* doctors be running *my* health care?"

Now, Lisa appeals everything, out of necessity:

> They want you to think that you're stuck with these bills. They want you to think there's nothing you can do. They do it just because they know that most people don't understand the appeals process, and they hope that people who have to appeal are elderly or disabled and don't know their rights. I think they believe that we're all ignorant or incompetent.

Lisa also spoke to the financial impact of these insurer processes, especially for those who do not understand the process:

> If I didn't know how to do these appeals, I'd probably have to file for bankruptcy. You shouldn't *have* to appeal every time. We're still paying off one of our kids' college educations. Now I ask, do I worry about my health first, or do I worry about collections? Do I buy a full set of groceries this week or do I not, in case I have a medical bill? It's scary.

These concerns are even more troubling because "when you have MS, stress is not our friend *at all*." To avoid the stress and "run-around" of insurance appeals, she delays her medical care, which creates different stressors for her. "I just want a break. The stress from having to deal with this makes me want to sleep for days. I tried hurting myself four times because living in this bed is not living."

Lisa reflected wistfully on her earlier years of healthiness, and the life-altering course that her MS diagnosis and her fall had taken her on: "Now I realize that insurance is great unless you need it. If you need it, you're screwed because they don't want to pay. Nine times out of ten, I win my appeals, but just having to do it is so hard. I can't believe that this is health care."

Lisa's story reflects so much of what has formed the basis of this book: the problem of coverage denials; the particularly acute experience of denials and appeals that people in poor health experience; the learning, compliance, and psychological costs of being denied coverage and having to navigate the complexities of the American health insurance system in the setting of a health problem (whether physical or mental); the financial cost of not appealing and potentially having to choose between health care and other necessities; and, perhaps most fundamentally, the loss of trust in the American health care system on which she relies and which she too often feels is failing her.

Over the course of these pages, I have illustrated the ways coverage denials – often, though not exclusively, through prior authorization – and the related administrative burdens of appeal deepen the economic and racial divides between those who enjoy meaningful access to their health plan benefits and those whose benefits exist mainly on paper. Rationing care by inconvenience, health insurers impose administrative barriers on patients and their physicians as they pursue coverage approval. In doing so amid America's growing reliance on managed care, health insurers have bred a new health and economic insecurity, which at the current pace will only increase with greater privatization and, in turn, insurer reliance on prior authorization.

In some cases, challenges stem from the lack of an individualized review of the patient's history, especially amid a complex or otherwise unusual clinical presentation. That is, is this a healthy thirty-five-year-old with no family history of gastrointestinal cancers, or is this a thirty-five-year-old with a significant family history of colon cancer, such that earlier or more regular screening is appropriate as opposed to overtreatment? Such was the case for Sean, who was denied positron emission tomography (PET) scans to check for recurrence of his aggressive cancer. In other cases, challenges stem from the insurer's reviewing physician lacking adequate familiarity with the patient's condition, such as with Nancy's rare ear, nose, and throat (ENT) procedure being denied coverage by a gynecologist. In still others, there appeared to be either inadequate review of the patient's history, or costs that the insurer deemed to be too exorbitant for coverage to be justified (such as with Jessica from Chapter 2, whose SCIg was denied despite her near-constant infections that put her at risk of antibiotic resistance).

This is made even more difficult by patients' lack of familiarity not only with how best to navigate the health insurance system, but also with the scope of the problem itself, such that one patient, Abby, reflected,

> The biggest barrier to forcing insurers to change things is no one knowing what's going on. So many people – my friends and family – when they hear what I'm doing in fighting the insurance company, they're going, "What? I don't understand this." People aren't even aware that this is happening. They just see that something isn't covered, and they accept it and go on, not realizing that the way they're jerking you around isn't okay.

Moreover, Abby's repeated hospitalizations amid denial of enteral formula to receive adequate nutrients led her to question whether prior authorization might *compromise* a goal of cost containment in her care.

To Abby's point, what remains to be seen is the extent to which the December 2024 response to the assassination of UnitedHealthcare CEO Brian Thompson will, out of shocking and inexcusable events, raise among the broader American population awareness of these common insurance barriers and foster dialogue about solutions.

Despite patient and physician consternation with this practice, it has been entrenched across multiple periods of proposed and enacted health care reform. This seems to offer validation for political scientist Jonathan Oberlander's astute observation that "[t]he American health care system presents an intriguing paradox: it is perennially in crisis, yet seemingly impervious to comprehensive reform."[1] However, recent years have witnessed greater physician as well as politician pushback against utilization management, though largely due to its inefficiencies rather than centering on the resulting inequities. I now discuss the central challenges and potential solutions to promote equitable access to care.

LIMITED RISK ASSESSMENT AND THE GROWING RELIANCE ON AI

Amid frustrations of overprescribing in areas of medicine such as high-tech imaging and some classes of prescription drugs, it is understandable that insurers would impose guardrails on low-value care, some of which stems from defensive medicine as well as entrenchment of medical practices amid an "unhealthy politics." However, questions remain as to *which* prescriptions are indeed appropriate, and which ones can reasonably be deemed not medically necessary.

To make an accurate judgment of this, proper risk assessment is imperative, although it may in many cases be lacking, given the need to process high volumes of prior authorizations in a short span of time. In the experience of Skylar, a twenty-one-year-old college student, this lack of individualized review was all too clear when her magnetic resonance imaging (MRI) for back pain was denied despite the accompanying symptoms of leg weakness and falls ("what I could do at seventeen I couldn't do at nineteen").

"There was a loss of trust in the insurance system, and I imagine if my family financial circumstances were different, it would have had a very different impact on me," Skylar reflected. In fact, the repeated challenges in obtaining coverage led to a delayed diagnosis and treatment of their debilitating case of Ehlers–Danlos Syndrome that is so debilitating that they now use a wheelchair.

A physician reviewing claims for Elevance likewise pointed to the decontextualized review of patient files, such that, while some denials emerge from health care facilities simply submitting incorrect or incomplete information, the insurer does not take into account the range of non-clinical factors that might make continued higher-level care appropriate for the patient:

> Say we have two patients with similar medical problems and who are functionally close to baseline, and one has supports and lives in a one-story home, and the other has stairs and no support. Those patients look the same on paper. We've been told to ignore those factors when reviewing coverage, even though they're highly relevant to recovery. You can't rely on home health for everything. Sometimes they've said you can discharge the patient to a *hotel* for a bit. Seriously? That's been surprising.

The inadequate individualized review has been borne out in additional research. A March 2023 *ProPublica* investigation of Cigna practices revealed that denials were conducted through an automated system absent review of patient files, such that an average of 1.2 seconds was spent on each case.[2] A former Cigna doctor said of this system, "We literally click and submit," such that "It takes all of ten seconds to do fifty at a time." Though not all claims are processed through this system, it highlights vulnerabilities to denial absent adequate review of relevant patient history.

This dynamic is only going to be exacerbated as health insurers turn increasingly to artificial intelligence (AI) programs through which to inexpensively process large volumes of prior authorizations and claims. While there are obvious efficiency gains from harnessing this technology in managing the care of millions of subscribers, the potential for error comes with real consequences to the patient's health and experience of administrative burden. Indeed, in a class action lawsuit filed in November 2023 in Minnesota, UnitedHealth faced the allegation that it issued denials through an AI program (nH Predict) known by defendants to yield an astonishing 90 percent reversal rate upon appeal, resulting in the wrongful denial of coverage to elderly patients covered by its Medicare Advantage plans.[3] nH Predict works to predict how much care an elderly patient "should" require given a constellation of factors (patient age, diagnosis, living situation, and physical function), irrespective of the prescribing physician's individualized assessment of the patient. What's more, the lawsuit alleges that employees who deviate from the nH model's determinations face discipline or even termination.

Despite the program's high error rate, the lawsuit alleges that UnitedHealth continued to "systematically deny claims using their flawed AI model because they know that only a tiny minority of policyholders ... will appeal denied claims, and the vast majority will either pay out-of-pocket costs or forgo the remainder of their prescribed post-acute care." When errors arise, they can be devastating both for patients and for their families. While Medicare Advantage plans typically entitle enrollees to 100 days of nursing home care following a 3 (or more)-day hospitalization, the lawsuit alleges that, with the use of nH Predict, "[p]atients rarely stay in a nursing home for more than 14 days before they start receiving payment denials."

This lawsuit highlights several challenges, especially considering the proprietary nature of insurers' decisionmaking processes. Not only is there inadequate individualized review, but also the errors are assessed in the context of elderly patient populations, for whom the stakes are particularly high because this population tends to have both greater health needs and lower health literacy. And in the context of high-cost treatment (e.g., nursing home care), paying out-of-pocket for care is rarely an option.

UnitedHealthcare is not the only health insurer engaged in this practice – far from it. Not only does Humana face a similar lawsuit involving nH Predict, but in July 2023 Cigna likewise faced a class action lawsuit in California's eastern district, concerning its use of the AI program PxDx (an abbreviation of procedure-to-diagnosis) in claim processing and, in turn, denials. The lawsuit alleges that a single medical director used this AI program to deny 60,000 claims in a single month, which is said to violate California law compelling medical professionals to engage in "thorough, fair, and objective" reviews of insurance claims. And, in a case similar to the UnitedHealthcare lawsuit concerning nH Predict, Rep. Cathy McMorris Rodgers (Republican, Washington) wrote to Cigna in May 2023 that the high rate of successful appeals of PxDx determinations may indicate that patients were being left to pay out-of-pocket for medical care that actually ought to have been covered under their insurance contracts.[4]

This is not to say that technology cannot be useful in claim management at the scale of large health insurers such as these, and it is likely unrealistic to expect the wholesale abandonment of tools geared toward promoting efficiency and curbing overhead. However, these lawsuits point to the real vulnerabilities to which patients are exposed in the context of errors that inevitably arise (seemingly at alarmingly high rates).

After all, what this book has highlighted is that when denials are rendered – whether by individuals or AI programs – patients (especially patients from marginalized groups) face administrative burdens that disrupt their health and economic lives, *even if they eventually prevail upon appeal.*

Though federal oversight of this has not been implemented, in January 2025, California's Physicians Make Decisions Act (SB 1120, introduced by State Senator Josh Becker) went into effect, ensuring that denial recommendations assessed through AI tools are first reviewed by a physician in the appropriate specialty. Such an approach may strike an optimal balance between harnessing technological tools to streamline approvals in prior authorization and claim processing while ensuring appropriate review of cases before barriers are imposed. Time will tell whether California's regulation of AI in health care ultimately proves to be a "laboratory of democracy" and a model for other states.

FRAGMENTATION

Strategic choices of health care design in the United States have exacerbated the effects of coverage denials. The fragmented nature of the American health insurance system not only creates information barriers for patients, but also makes more difficult the task of holding health insurers accountable amid wrongful denials.

The division of plans among private and public insurance, some of which limit legal recourse, is just the start. What's more, there are mandatory arbitration provisions to which one must agree when enrolling in the health insurance plan, such that health insurance lawyer Scott Glovsky observed,

> Most insurance companies require you to agree that if there's ever a dispute, you waive your right to go to court and you have your case decided by a private arbitrator, who is either a retired judge or a retired lawyer or a lawyer who does arbitrations. Basically, it's a system designed to minimize liability for insurance companies. And there's a reason why insurance companies are always trying to compel arbitration and policyholders are always opposed to it.[5]

These factors combine to offer private insurers significant insulation from accountability.

Arbitration, a form of alternative dispute resolution (ADR), originally sought to facilitate swift and informal adjudication of business disputes, though since the 1970s its application has proliferated amid efforts toward immunity against bad faith claims. But while mandatory binding arbitration arrangements are hardly unique to health care – with 55 percent of workers subject to mandatory arbitration with respect to such issues as Title VII of the Civil Rights Act of 1964, the Americans with Disabilities Act, the Family and Medical Leave Act, and the Fair Labor Standards Act[6] – their effects are felt acutely in the context of life-or-death decisions such as health coverage. Such arbitration cases increased amid the COVID-19 pandemic, and to the detriment of workers, with an American Association for Justice report finding that workers were awarded money in just 1.6 percent of cases.[7] This is but one aspect of the difficulty of holding large corporations, including health insurers, accountable.

Moreover, outside of the American legal system, fragmentation can be seen between pharmacy and other medical benefits and, as Chapter 8 highlighted, between behavioral health and medical/surgical benefits through carve-outs. This fragmentation undercuts insurer accountability and responsiveness amid delays or denials of health coverage and imposes high informational costs on enrollees, who may have difficulty deciphering who to contact for assistance or a claim payment. These informational barriers are not evenly distributed, but place particular burdens on those from marginalized backgrounds, who may struggle amid this added complexity of accessing health coverage.

For professor of law and medicine David Hyman, the fragmented nature of the American health care system contributes to higher costs but lower quality, with inefficient coordination among physicians, hospitals, insurers, and others.[8] These features led economist and law professor Einer Elhauge to characterize the American health care system as "coupl[ing] the mother of all team production problems with the mother of all refusals to use centralized ownership structures to solve them."[9] With so many inefficiencies built into the American health care system, it is little wonder why so many Americans opt out of appealing coverage denials, and why the burdens of appeal would deepen inequities among patients.

CHURN

One speculated rationale for insurers' denial of coverage is that patients change health insurers over time (this dynamic is referred to as *patient churn*) and thus may no longer be enrolled with their current insurer at the time that disease progression is observed. About a fifth of health insurance policyholders cancel their health policy each year,[10] and a 2021 ValuePenguin survey of 1,795 insured Americans found that 45 percent were considering switching their plan or coverage to a provider that better meets their needs and/or price point.[11] There is additional turnover stemming from employer groups canceling their existing policies and selecting different health insurers, for reasons such as saving money on premiums, as well as patients aging into the Medicare population.

Shortened relationships between insurers and patients can undercut the incentive to invest in preventive care, such as a continuous glucose monitor for a diabetic like Ben from Chapter 6. These up-front investments in chronic disease management are rewarded with payoffs at a later point in time (e.g., less need for aggressive treatments due to well-managed A1C). However, shortening the relationship between the insurer and the policyholder may lead to fewer investments in future health, despite the adage that an ounce of prevention is worth a pound of cure.[12]

What's more, the dynamic of coverage denials can *exacerbate* issues of churn in American health insurance, with 56 percent of my survey respondents indicating that they considered switching health insurers because of their denial, and 24 percent of survey respondents actually doing so. This dynamic is amplified among older patients due to the near-universal movement of patients from commercial insurance to Medicare at age sixty-five. Thus, patient churn may contribute both to frequent coverage denials – which this book has demonstrated are associated with administrative burden, delays in care, and financial fragility – and to the rising health care costs that practices such as prior authorization are ostensibly aimed at curbing.

PROFIT MOTIVES AND ACCOUNTABILITY

One cannot confront the challenges of coverage denials without considering the largely and increasingly privatized health care system in which they exist. Generally low trust in government tends to contribute to a system in which, as of 2023, a Gallup poll found that just a third of Americans trust the American health care system. Surprisingly, however, even with this diminished trust, a majority of respondents (54 percent) expressed a preference for private rather than government-run insurance.

Some of this preference lies in Americans' perceptions about government inefficiency and, consequently, a perceived comparative advantage of reliance on private enterprise. In fact, 56 percent of Americans described government as "almost always wasteful and inefficient" in an April 2024 survey by Pew Research Center, though there are partisan gaps in this perception.[13]

But, despite this common narrative over recent decades, the data tell us something quite different, at least in the health insurance setting: while traditional Medicare spends approximately 2 percent of its funds on administrative costs, private insurers tend to spend approximately 15 percent of their funds toward overhead.[14]

Though America has witnessed the historic, collective will to expand the number of covered individuals through the Affordable Care Act (ACA), bringing the uninsured rate to a historic low, attempts at reform since the enactment of Medicare and Medicaid have operated within the confines of the managed care system. And while government intervention has proven immensely effective in bringing people into the insured pool, it has proven comparatively ineffective at ensuring that those individuals can meaningfully access the care they are prescribed. As long as the public preference for privatization endures, it is difficult to foresee an impetus for Congress to rein it in.

Some of the care denied is undoubtedly driven by a combination of physicians' defensive medicine practices and an "unhealthy politics" that undermines evidence-based medicine, as illuminated by the work of political scientists Eric Patashnik, Alan Gerber, and Conor Dowling.[15] While Congress has pursued tools to rein in unnecessary prescribing, such as the ACA's establishment of the Patient-Centered Outcomes Research Institute (PCORI) to promote comparative effectiveness research, it has ultimately proven ineffective in changing America's relationship to medical evidence.[16]

Yet, as the accounts in this book highlight, the extension of denials to tests and treatments that are the standard of care highlights the dangerous possibility that denials reflect not just guardrails on overprescribing but also profit motivations overtaking attention to evidence. Indeed, it was estimated that the automated claim processing system PxDx saved

Cigna billions of dollars,[17] though at the price of denying claims without individualized review of patient files.

HEALTH CARE INDUSTRY CONSOLIDATION

Health insurer consolidation poses challenges in reconciling health insurers' profit motives and quality health care. After all, just five health insurers (UnitedHealthcare, Elevance, Aetna, Cigna, and Kaiser) account for 55 percent of the national health care market,[18] and there is even more pronounced market concentration within particular regions of the country. KFF researchers find that, within states, the market share of the largest three health insurers ranged from 16 percent (New York) to 94 percent (Alabama and Alaska), with a median of 64 percent (Oklahoma) and Kaiser Permanente alone occupying 52 percent of the market share in California in 2021. Moreover, seven national health insurance companies (UnitedHealthcare, Humana, Aetna, Anthem, Centene, Cigna, and Molina) had nearly 70 percent of the Medicare Advantage market in 2022.[19] Health care consolidation can also be seen among pharmacy benefits managers, as illustrated in Chapter 4, with CVS/Caremark, Express Scripts, and Optum Rx accounting for the vast majority of the market.

This consolidation can not only lead to high barriers to entry into health insurance markets, but also affect patients, such as in the form of higher premiums absent robust competition.[20] Moreover, it has been speculated that the significant financial challenges that the COVID-19 pandemic posed to the health care industry only exacerbated this trend of consolidation.[21]

This trend puts pressures on health insurers, potentially placing them in a bind in prior authorization and claim processing. Dr. Mario Molina, former CEO of Molina Healthcare, reflected,

> I worry about consolidation. If you look at health care now, there are a handful of health plans that just dominate. That limits competition. I worry about pressures on profitability in publicly traded health plans. Your duty as a publicly traded health plan is to maximize your share price, which usually translates into maximizing earnings. It's hard for

people to know what the quality of care is. It's hard for *providers* to know what the quality of care is. I think that the purpose of health care is to take care of patients: restoring them to health and keeping them healthy. There's this tension between serving the patient or serving the investor. It's really difficult. I thought for a long time that as a public company, we could do both, but I think the forces of consolidation make that more and more difficult.

The American College of Emergency Physicians (ACEP) shares this concern, observing "egregious insurer behavior related to emergency care" in the Medicare managed care market in the name of cost containment.[22] Antitrust authority over the health care industry is divided between the Department of Justice (DOJ) and the Federal Trade Commission (FTC), but efforts toward meaningful oversight have proved anemic. In fact, in 2017, the DOJ approved *all* insurance mergers.[23] Although the FTC blocked four hospital mergers (which drive up medical costs) under the Biden Administration,[24] there has been less attention by the agency to insurer mergers.

THE NEED FOR EVIDENCE-BASED MEDICINE

This book has sought to illuminate the challenges that insurer discretion has wrought on American patients, not to mention their physicians. This discretion is driven in part by the variation in the evidence basis of different forms of health care for which patients might seek coverage. For example, while prescription drugs undergo double-blind clinical trials prior to receiving FDA approval – thus indicating a substantial degree of evidence basis – high-tech imaging (e.g., MRIs) may be considered to fall within the sphere of lower-value care, despite approximately 40 million such scans being prescribed annually in the United States.[25] This is not to say that such tests should not be prescribed, but rather that there may be greater uncertainty in clinical guidelines. This uncertainty can, in turn, amplify insurers' discretion when determining, for example, the frequency with which scans should be ordered to check for cancer remission, which requires balancing the potential benefit of the information gleaned from the scan against the potential for patient harm.

For example, EviCore's guidelines on the medical necessity of scans for recurrence of head and neck cancer state that, if the post-treatment PET/computed tomography (CT) scan is negative, "further surveillance imaging is not *routinely* indicated" (emphasis added), with discretion existing within the word "routinely" as applied to individual cases. When this discretion results in coverage denials, this can lead to delays in prescribed care, the exacerbation of underlying health conditions and financial fragility, and administrative headaches for the patient and their physician.

Political scientists Eric Patashnik, Alan Gerber, and Conor Dowling shed important light on the politics of evidence-based medicine, and the barriers to reliance on stronger evidence bases.[26] While acknowledging that diagnostic imaging is critical to identifying the correct diagnosis and course of treatment, low-value imaging (e.g., for atraumatic pain or minor head injury) has been found to be a common inappropriate use of health care resources.[27] Improving both the adherence to evidence bases and promoting clarity in coverage guidelines can help to reduce uncertainty in prescribing. The result may be that physicians can more effectively target prescribing toward what will be both appropriate and covered for their patients, thus reducing the administrative burdens with which they and their patients might otherwise be consumed.

OPPORTUNITIES FOR POLICY REFORM

"We have probably the most inefficient health care system on the planet and prior authorization is a big component of it," Wendell Potter opined.

Because of the fragmented nature of the American health insurance system – with some plans regulated by the Department of Labor through ERISA, others regulated by the Centers for Medicare and Medicaid Services (housed within the Department of Health and Human Services), and some regulated at the state level – there are multiple avenues for federal or state-level advocacy to reduce the reliance on prior authorization and the coverage denials issued through that process. Here, I offer some opportunities that may help to combat this policy problem.

INVESTING IN STATE CONSUMER ASSISTANCE PROGRAMS. "You don't hand someone a pop gun when they're going up against an AR-15," reflected Ted Doolittle. "You need someone who knows the tricks of the trade."[28]

Ted would know. The Healthcare Advocate for the State of Connecticut from 2017 to 2023, Ted and his office staff would help patients free of charge through the bureaucratic process of appealing denied medical claims. The Office of the Healthcare Advocate (OHA) is Connecticut's state agency that is dedicated to helping consumers navigate their health insurance and care. Staffed with nurses, lawyers, paralegals, and others, they assist patients with billing and enrollment issues, clarifying the scope of covered benefits, or assisting with appeals of coverage denials, including through prior authorization. Depending on the particular circumstances, they might offer advice on a case, compile appropriate documentation, assist with writing the appeal letter, and conduct the appropriate follow-up, such as appearing before Medicare administrative law judges. Though Connecticut is not the only state to have such an office, it is unusual in its level of sophistication.

While these resources are highly valuable, the OHA is somewhat limited in its visibility. Referrals to its services can come from many different sources, including the Department of Children and Families, the state marketplace (Access Health CT), and even the denial letters themselves, though many physicians and their patients are unaware of this resource.

While the most marginalized patients are not guaranteed to reap these benefits due to lack of awareness, the office's efforts often pay off, with approximately half of the patients' denials ultimately getting reversed in whole or in part – and with free professional assistance that can help to relieve the burdens on which this book has focused. Thus, Ted argued, consumer assistance programs (CAPs) should be more fully integrated into the health insurance landscape across the nation:

> If we're going to have these plans where denial is a big part of the business plan, you've *got* to level the playing field. And we know tricks of the trade that people don't know. If you blow that deadline, sometimes if you ask nicely, they will let you file a late appeal letter. They'll make a one-time exception. People don't know that, so they don't ask.

Though not addressing the bigger problem of coverage delays and denials, ensuring wider adoption of, and investment in, state consumer assistance programs to assist with health insurance disputes can help to alleviate patients' administrative burden and promote equitable health care access.

STATE-LEVEL REFORMS: LABORATORIES OF DEMOCRACY. Justice Louis Brandeis famously declared in 1932 in his *New State Ice Co. v. Liebman* dissenting opinion, "It is one of the happy accidents of the federal system that a single courageous state may, if its citizens choose, serve as a laboratory; and try novel social and economic experiments without risk to the rest of the country." In keeping with this sentiment, much of the progress and opportunity to rectify these health insurance barriers has been located at the state level.

Despite its historic recalcitrance toward sweeping health insurance reform and continued opposition to single-payer health care, prior authorization has been integral to the state legislative agenda of the American Medical Association (AMA) for at least fifteen years, with advocacy taking the form of writing model bills, as well as drafting regulations and legislative language. These efforts have been successful, with many states across the ideological spectrum being amenable to reform.

"We've had some pretty decent success. Every year there's probably a dozen forms of legislation out there – whether broad reforms that try to tackle it all, or very targeted bills that are addressing a problem that has come up," AMA Senior Attorney Emily Carroll noted.[29] These proposed (and, in some cases, enacted) reforms address, among other things, the required qualifications for insurers' reviewing physicians, aiming to ensure that they are licensed to practice in the same, or similar, specialty as typically handles the patient's condition.

Targeted policy proposals have also taken aim at such issues as streamlining and advocating for more prior authorizations to be processed electronically rather than manually, reducing the volume of prior authorizations, and regulating wait times for their resolution. Within some states' legislative bills are provisions addressing prior authorization within Medicaid, in which approximately a fifth of the nation's population is enrolled. In 2023, New Jersey, Washington, D.C., and Tennessee took action to reform prior authorization by, for example, promoting transparency and efficiency in prior authorization processing and preventing retroactive coverage denials following a prior authorization approval.

However, the 65 percent of covered workers in self-insured health plans[30] are left untouched by these advances in state-level health policy reforms because of ERISA's preemption of state laws "relate[d] to" its provisions. For these plans, federal legislation is needed.

While many of the targeted reforms take aim at distinct segments of the health insurance market, Emily Carroll raised the possibility that – to Justice Brandeis's point – health insurance reform at the state level could lead to more expansive policy adoption. After all, she observed, there is an administrative burden to separating plans and prior authorization practices, whereas uniformity may promote efficiency not only for doctors and their patients, but also for insurers themselves.

In light of the outcome of the 2024 election, in which Donald Trump secured re-election with Republican majorities in both chambers of Congress, attention will no doubt turn to state rather than federal efforts toward health policy reform. While (as with state flexibility in Medicaid expansion) this will leave America not with uniform progress but rather with a patchwork system, it is in keeping with the intent expressed in the McCarran–Ferguson Act of 1945, in which Congress limited federal regulation of the insurance industry, leaving the states as its primary regulators.

Toward that end, states have been tasked with regulatory goals ranging from the development of market conduct examinations into insurer actions (as seen in Chapter 8's examination of mental health parity violations), enforcement of consumer protection laws, and the development of standards for independent, third-party medical reviewers of claim processing, which this book has sought to highlight the importance of in guarding against wrongful denial. In fact, Pennsylvania's newly articulated independent external review process highlights the progress that can be made at the state level to help to ensure reversal of wrongful denials – though, as Chapter 7 highlighted, the administratively burdensome requirements that patients exhaust all internal remedies can stymie the potential for more sweeping change.

Thus, America's federalist system of governance may ultimately prove to be for better *and* worse, with patients left behind in many states, while other regions move the needle on this issue and potentially lay the groundwork for more systemic change amid more favorable political conditions.

FEDERAL REFORMS: CLOSE, BUT NO CIGAR. Several federal reforms to prior authorization have been proposed, targeting which physicians must submit prior authorizations, the extent to which they are electronic, and the speed with which they must be processed, at least within some segments of the health insurance market. If implemented, they would likely mitigate some of the administrative hassles highlighted over the course of this book, though they do not strike at the heart of the profit motives underlying this insurer practice.

GOLD CARDING. Targeting Medicare Advantage plans, the American Medical Association has supported the Getting over Lengthy Delays in Care as Required by Doctors ("GOLD CARD") Act of 2023 (HR 4968), introduced on July 27, 2023 and sponsored by Rep. Michael Burgess (Republican, Texas). The legislative text states that, in the context of Medicare Advantage plans that require prior authorization,

> a physician shall be exempt from the prior authorization requirements under such process for the period of such plan year with respect to a specific item, service, or group of similar services, if during the preceding plan year at least 90 percent of prior authorization requests submitted to such organization by such physician for such item, service, or group were approved by such organization (including any approval granted after an appeal).

This "gold carding" reform effort has been supported by several different health care organizations, including the AMA, American Hospital Association, American Pharmacists Association, and American Academy of Family Physicians.[31] A key limitation is that this exemption is determined not at the national level, but at the organization level (that is, UnitedHealthcare and Cigna would make separate determinations of gold card status), if not at the more granular *plan* level. Given the number of different plans offered by major insurers – for example, UnitedHealthcare offers eight Medicare Advantage plans in Pennsylvania alone – it is easy to see how complex the management of gold card status might become.

In fact, rather than operating as a burden reduction measure, it has the potential unintended consequence of simply creating *different* administrative burdens for physician practices, which become tasked with determining whether they are exempt from prior authorizations for UnitedHealthcare as opposed to Cigna or Elevance, and for which prescribed services (e.g., head CT versus CT of the abdomen). What's more, insurance plans are still given power to decide what constitutes medically necessary care, a form of oversight that many physicians have resisted. The bill, if enacted, would be implemented through rulemaking by the Secretary of Health and Human Services, which specifies prior authorization requirements for Medicare Advantage plans. The bill was referred to the House Subcommittee on Health, but no further action was taken.

While this policy has not yet been implemented at the federal level, some states have pursued this approach, with West Virginia being the first to pass a gold card exception in 2019 such that health care providers are exempt from prior authorization requirements if they have a 100 percent approval rate for a given service for six months. Texas passed a similar gold carding law according to which physicians with a 90 percent prior authorization approval rate over a six-month period for certain services are exempt from prior authorization requirements. *MedPage Today*'s editorial board member Anders Gilberg characterized the Texas law as a "fantastic first step" and a "foot in the door" toward improvement of the prior authorization process. One challenge, however, is that the Texas Department of Insurance reports that, as of December 2023, only 3 percent of Texas physicians and health care professionals met the criteria for a gold card, given the stringency of eligibility requirements, thus suggesting that additional measures are needed for the law to operate as intended.

As part of broader prior authorization reforms, Michigan similarly compelled commercial health insurers regulated by the Michigan

Department of Insurance and Financial Services to adopt a gold card program applicable to those who have a high approval rate of prior authorizations – at least a 92 percent approval rate of prior authorizations over each of the two years evaluated by the insurer. However, as with Texas, the gold card exception is applied not only at the plan level but at the *service level*, suggesting a need for extensive recordkeeping and, in turn, potentially limited impact on administrative burden reduction. Gold carding legislation has additionally been proposed in California, Colorado, Indiana, Kentucky, Louisiana, Mississippi, New York, and Oklahoma, in addition to which Vermont is piloting a gold carding program.

IMPROVING SENIORS' TIMELY ACCESS TO CARE ACT. The Improving Seniors' Timely Access to Care Act of 2021 (HR 3173), sponsored by Rep. Suzan DelBene (Democrat, Washington), was introduced on May 13, 2021 with the support of a bipartisan group of 309 cosponsors in the House of Representatives. The central goal of this legislation is to ensure that Medicare Advantage plans "(1) establish [an] electronic prior authorization program … and issue real-time decisions with respect to prior authorization requests for items and services identified by the Secretary …; (2) meet the transparency requirements …; and (3) meet the beneficiary protection standards specified." The bill was referred to the House Ways and Means Committee and the House Energy and Commerce Committee, and, on September 14, 2022, the House passed the bill by a voice vote, though it stalled in the Senate amid a suboptimal Congressional Budget Office Score.

This legislation would help to reduce the administrative burdens and heightened monetary costs for the 38 percent of prior authorizations that are not already electronic. What's more, by shortening the time to receive a coverage decision, it would help to mitigate the delays in care illuminated in Chapter 5, with many patients going without care for days or even weeks amid prior authorization-induced limbo.

Amending legislation to ensure that these electronic prior authorization policies are adopted not just in Medicare Advantage plans, but across public and private insurance will be essential to addressing not only administrative burdens writ large but also, more specifically, delays in patient care. With reduced wait times to receive coverage determinations, physicians and patients can more efficiently choose alternative courses of treatment that will receive insurance coverage, rather than being relegated to the delay and "song and dance" about which patients and physicians alike expressed frustration. An important caveat is that electronic prior authorization does not reduce the risk that one might be denied coverage and instead be redirected to inferior tests and treatments. As neurologist Dr. Andrew Spector put it, "I don't need a timelier denial. I need an *acceptance*."

The Improving Seniors' Timely Access to Care Act was reintroduced on June 13, 2024 as S. 4532 by Sen. Roger Marshall (Republican, Kansas), who is also trained as an obstetrician/gynecologist, along with then-Sen. Sherrod Brown (Democrat, Ohio), then-Sen. Kyrsten Sinema (Independent, Arizona), and Sen. John Thune (Republican, South Dakota). Then-Sen. Brown said of the proposed legislation, "Right now, too many older Americans enrolled in Medicare Advantage are forced to deal with unnecessary delays when seeking out medical treatment. We need to update the Medicare Advantage program so it works better, faster, and is more transparent for patients and providers." Though the bill received fifty-nine cosponsors, a strong signal of bipartisan support even in the hotly partisan and polarized conditions that characterize the modern political era, no Senate action was taken following its referral to the Senate Finance Committee.

Despite supporting the introduction of this and related legislation aimed at prior authorization within the sphere of Medicare Advantage plans, in the last several years, the AMA has not made a major effort to address self-funded insurance plans governed by ERISA, in part due to its complexity and primarily because of ERISA's preemption of state laws. Thus, the proposed interventions into prior authorization address only a slice of the health insurance market, leaving untouched a substantial share of employer-provided health plans. Moreover, while targeting prior authorization is likely to have a significant effect on the share of denials issued, this does *not* account for the broader scope in which denials may occur, such as through non-adherence to the "prudent layperson standard" in emergency department care or other post-treatment evaluations.

On January 17, 2024, the Centers for Medicare and Medicaid Services finalized a federal Interoperability and Prior Authorization rule to improve the prior authorization process, in particular the timeliness of processing to ease patient and health care provider burdens.[32] Then-Secretary of Health and Human Services Xavier Becerra said of this rule, "When a doctor says a patient needs a procedure, it is essential that it happens in a timely manner," observing the "limbo" in which far too many American patients find themselves while waiting for their insurer's approval. Thus, by streamlining and digitizing prior authorizations, unnecessary delays will be curtailed. Impacted payers must implement the rule's provisions by January 1, 2026.

Of course, as with previously discussed legislative efforts on this subject, it does not challenge the very institution of prior authorization and its, by design, second-guessing of physician decisionmaking through mechanisms that induce administrative burden.

ERISA REFORM. Federalism has long held a space in American health care policy, perhaps most prominently in states' decisions whether to expand Medicaid through the ACA. The Employee Retirement Income Security Act runs counter to this federalist principle by providing that the federal ERISA law would preempt state policy in areas that "relate to" the Act's core provisions.

ERISA's human impact can be observed in the story of Mr. Frank Wurzbacher, who, upon receiving the diagnosis of prostate cancer, was prescribed Lupron injections for which his self-insured health plan held that he would be largely responsible.[33] What his insurer would instead cover in full was the surgery of castration in light of the aggressiveness of the cancer. Unable to afford the cost of the injections, he was instead castrated. Shortly after the surgery was performed, his insurer notified him that he was no longer responsible for the additional $180 per monthly injection.

Because Mr. Wurzbacher was in a self-insured plan governed by ERISA, he was ineligible to sue to recover damages, because ERISA only allows patients to recover benefits (in his case, the injections) and *not* compensatory damages.

ERISA reform is critical not only because of its role in state preemption, which has significantly impeded state health policymaking, but because it is estimated that 65 percent of American workers (and 83 percent of workers in large firms) are in ERISA-governed self-insured health plans – a marked increase from the 46 percent of workers in self-insured plans in 1996. This trend toward self-insuring reflects this approach's comparative administrative ease and economic benefits, as well as such plans' ability to avoid satisfying state health insurance laws. The previously discussed legislation backed by the AMA and coalitions within Congress works to mitigate the burdens and unnecessary delays associated with prior authorization administration in plans not governed by ERISA. However, those efforts do not strike at the heart of insurer incentives to deny coverage in the first place.

A key problem with ERISA (likely unanticipated by the authors, who were substantially more focused on pension reform) is that, although it allows denied patients to recover the *benefits* owed (e.g., the treatment, minus any cost-sharing), it does not permit the recovery of damages, and it leaves the recovery of attorney's fees to the discretion of courts. This creates both equity and accountability problems that speak to the themes of this book. It creates equity challenges because less affluent patients will be unwilling and unable to risk being responsible for the costs of litigation to challenge a coverage denial that they believe to be wrongful. It creates accountability challenges because attorneys will be risk averse in taking on health insurance cases that lack a monetary value. And, aware of this vanishingly small pool of would-be plaintiffs, insurers have more latitude to deny coverage because they cannot be penalized in the event of a wrongful denial. Mobilizing denied patients to bring suit when, for example, their prescribed radiation therapy was denied and they experience an exacerbation of their condition may provide an important enhancement of accountability in this private health insurance setting, helping to overcome the perverse incentives of the status quo.

The value of an ERISA damages enhancement can be seen plainly in light of law professor Sean Farhang's litigation model, which describes the likelihood with which a plaintiff will initiate a lawsuit, based on the following calculus: $EV = EB(p) - EC$, where EV is the estimated value of the lawsuit (that is, what the patient stands to gain), EB is the expected benefit to be gained in the lawsuit (whether the cost of the treatment or damages), p is the probability of prevailing in the lawsuit, and EC is the estimated cost of pursuing the lawsuit (that is, the cost of attorney's fees).[34] In the case of ERISA, the expected benefit is quite low because no damages can be recovered, so the patient may only obtain the treatment that was initially denied. What's more, the recovery of attorney's fees is uncertain, leaving the expected value so low as to explain why so few such cases are brought. Increasing the potential for benefit and attorney's fee recovery upon successful litigation would therefore increase (potentially quite dramatically) the plaintiff's likelihood of bringing a suit, thus increasing the likelihood that lawyers would bring such cases against insurers.

The striking limitation on remedies available to patients enrolled in ERISA-governed health plans is not lost on health insurers. Indeed, former Cigna executive Wendell Potter reflected on this,

> Within an insurance company, especially the big ones like Cigna, which has a high percentage of enrollees in self-insured plans, there's a constant awareness of ERISA damages provisions. These companies know that they're shielded by ERISA. They know that a patient who is denied coverage for a transplant or any other procedure is limited in terms of what their legal remedies are. They know this, and that affects their behavior. They know that they're not going to be paying a lot of money out of revenues if someone is successful in overturning a denial or even trying to. And in many cases, the patient has died, so there's no remedy. These companies have battalions of lawyers who are intimately familiar with ERISA because it pertains to so much of their business. And they can become instantly aware if an enrollee is enrolled in a self-insured plan or a full-insured plan.[35]

Thus, not only are insurers aware of ERISA-governed patients' limited legal recourse, but also this awareness drives them to treat coverage decisions differently, potentially resulting in a higher rate of denials.

Expanding the range of possible plaintiffs in litigation over ERISA plans will be vital to ensuring health insurers' accountability. While ERISA was written primarily as a pension law, it has since evolved in ways unforeseen by the enacting Congress, given the growth of managed care.

Between 1997 and 1999, Congress contemplated ERISA reform through a Patients' Bill of Rights championed by Rep. John Dingell (Democrat, Michigan) – who characterized it as "as fine a piece of work as I've ever seen in Congress"[36] – and Sen. Ted Kennedy (Democrat, Massachusetts), who viewed the lack of accountability for health insurers as a "license to maim and kill."

Despite a favorable scoring by the non-partisan Congressional Budget Office and the backing of President Clinton, there was a substantial divide between the Democrats' strongly enforced version of the bill and Republicans' substantially weaker version. What's more, some raised concerns about cost and frivolous lawsuits, and the impeachment of President Clinton diminished any appetite for bipartisanship. Thus, the Patient's Bill of Rights never came to pass. Although substantial health reform has taken place since the failed efforts toward a Patients' Bill of Rights, it has largely emphasized expanding the number of covered individuals, rather than improving coverage for the insured population. This has been especially true in light of ever increasing polarization in Congress and, in turn, the narrower range of options for potential health reform, which political scientists Craig Volden and Alan Wiseman demonstrate is particularly gridlocked.[37]

To be sure, there are limitations to even this expansive federal reform. After all, litigation under ERISA would require of patients immense burdens that mirror in the legal setting what was observed in the insurance appeal setting, which is fraught with headaches and inequities. Indeed, litigation can be so time-consuming (typically requiring the exhaustion of administrative remedies in the first place, just as with independent medical reviews) that some denied patients may become too ill to reap the benefits of their lawsuits. Thus, while the addition of litigation incentives may promote insurer accountability and offer greater recourse to patients who were harmed by wrongful denials, it nevertheless still leaves many people behind.

It is highly unlikely that the 119th Congress would meet with greater success in pursuit of ERISA reform. Though path dependence accounts for some of ERISA's continued entrenchment, there are additional political and policy-relevant realities that impede change. For example, while the interests that gain from ERISA's provisions are increasingly entrenched (private insurers and large employers), the patients harmed by its core provisions are diffuse. What's more, with historic polarization, it is doubtful that we will soon observe a "critical juncture" within which conditions will be ripe for reform. The status quo is sticky, but this chapter nevertheless seeks to offer a roadmap for progress from which patients and their physicians alike benefit.

INDEPENDENT MEDICAL REVIEWS. Several patients reflected on the value of obtaining independent medical reviews (IMRs) amid their health insurer's intransigence, and Chapter 7 highlights how some states have carved out opportunities for this recourse. Such reviews are by independent medical experts who evaluate whether the prescribed care is medically necessary or experimental or otherwise inappropriate, and they have the power to overturn the insurer's initial determination (as was the case with Liz in her pursuit of Stelara). But, with exhaustion of internal remedies typically required, their potential has thus far been unrealized.

Continued expansion of IMR opportunities and eliminating the requirement for exhaustion of remedies would streamline the appeal process rather than requiring patients to endure the administrative burdens of insurers' multi-level appeal processes discussed in Chapters 6 and 7. The ACA determined that all self-insured health plans and health insurance issuers must contract with independent review organizations and promoted uniformity in such review efforts. As we see growth in these review processes along with improved patient awareness of them, patients may find themselves less deterred by the bureaucracy of appealing, in turn holding insurers more to account for their determinations of medical necessity.

DEFINING MEDICAL NECESSITY. Health insurer discretion in making medical necessity decisions has posed consistent challenges in guarding against inappropriate denials. Health insurers (especially private health insurers) can capitalize on this discretion to justify adverse benefit determinations. Reducing the discretion-laden nature of coverage determinations can help to reduce the perverse incentives that we observe in the name of cost containment, enhancing the extent to which patients are able to access their plan benefits. What's more, it can reduce for providers the sense of prescribing in a "black box," uncertain if or when prescribed care will be approved for their patients.

Though the issue has not been confronted at the federal level, California has addressed this discretion within the context of behavioral health care. On September 25, 2020, California Governor Gavin Newsom signed into law SB 855, which dramatically increased health insurers' coverage obligations for the diagnosis and treatment of mental health and substance use disorders. SB 855 not only expands mental health benefits to require coverage of medically necessary basic and intermediate health care services (e.g., partial hospitalization and residential treatment), but also requires that these medical necessity guidelines be based on determinations by the non-profit, clinical professional association of the relevant clinical specialty and may not be amended by health insurers.

Though SB 855 is specific to mental health and substance use disorders, such legislation is conceivable at the federal level through amendments to both ERISA and the MHPAEA. A federal definition of medical necessity, reviewed by a non-profit third party, would offer needed standardization that could help to obviate the problem of wrongful denials and broader uncertainties about what care will be accessed and when.

What is of course missed in these proposed state and federal reforms is the very underlying nature of these denials: the for-profit dynamic of the American health care system, which patients, providers, *and former actors within the insurance industry* bemoaned. It is not surprising that a for-profit health insurance corporation (health-related or otherwise) with fiduciary responsibility to shareholders will be concerned about taking on significant costs (e.g., approving high-cost treatments) that will affect the bottom line, or that an efficient way to avoid incurring these costs is to impose restrictions on access to those services.

Yet, as I have worked to illuminate over these pages, this dynamic leads to adverse consequences both for health care costs (with denials sometimes driving more costly treatment down the line) and for physicians faced with administrative burden and burnout, and of course for patients' physical, mental, and financial wellbeing. While a range of federal and state reforms can improve claim processing to reduce the extent of delay induced by denials (e.g., by mandating electronic prior authorization and more timely processing), streamline appeals, ensure that cases are reviewed by physicians of the appropriate specialty, and facilitate lawsuits in the event of denial, such policy reforms do not take aim at the denials themselves. Doing so requires no less than reimagining the structure of the American health care system itself.

One conclusion is inescapable: the privatization of American health care – through reliance on tying employment to private health insurance and shifting from traditional to managed Medicare and Medicaid – has led patients to suffer as insurers aim at not only cost containment, but also profit maximization through reliance on the tools of utilization management and the discretion of defining medical necessity. As these processes shift costs from payers to patients and their prescribers, Jacob Hacker's observation that "Medicare should be the model for health security"[38] rings true, as it is the setting in which one finds not only high levels of coverage but also limited reliance on utilization management and, consequently, the lowest incidence of coverage denials in my study. However, this comparative advantage may soon dissipate, with the second Trump Administration pursuing the imposition of new prior authorization requirements within the traditional Medicare population. On June 27, 2025, the Centers for Medicare and Medicaid Services (CMS) announced in a press release that it would be seeking to "test ways to provide an improved and expedited prior authorization process ... helping patients and providers avoid unnecessary or inappropriate care and safeguarding federal taxpayer dollars" as part of a broader effort to "root out waste in Original Medicare." While guarding against overutilization is important both for the patient and for appropriately allocating resources in the health care system, this imposition of the Wasteful and Inappropriate Service Reduction (WISeR) Model has the potential to exacerbate in the Medicare setting the challenges illuminated within the managed care setting. The policy set to go into effect is relatively narrow in scope, though its ultimate objective is to carve a path toward broader reliance on prior authorization in traditional Medicare.[39]

Efforts toward health care expansion have historically been challenging and rarely met with success in recent decades. Apart from the notoriously failed effort at health care reform under the Clinton

Administration, the passage of the ACA in 2010 met with staunch resistance from the Republican Party, barely eking out sixty Democratic votes in the Senate to avoid a filibuster. But, against all odds, the United States government coalesced around legislation that provided historic expansion of health care access despite reinforcing reliance on the private health insurance system in which coverage denials prevail.

America can again, if it so chooses, make progress on health insurance, though the 2024 election results do not suggest that the times they are a-changin' in this respect. Though Donald Trump infamously referred to his "concepts of a plan" for health care, his re-election points to the likely acceleration of seniors' reliance on Medicare Advantage, in which 99 percent of enrollees have prior authorization requirements for at least some services, along with the reintroduction of administratively burdensome work requirements to sustain Medicaid eligibility alongside the historic cuts to Medicaid funding in the "One Big Beautiful Bill." In addition to President Trump expressing positive attitudes toward Medicare Advantage, the Heritage Foundation's Project 2025 called for making Medicare Advantage the default enrollment option for seniors, and Centers for Medicare and Medicaid Administrator Mehmet Oz proposed placing all non-Medicaid patients onto Medicare Advantage plans.[40] Thus, administrative burden in health insurance will likely be exacerbated, at least within some segments of the market.

What is perhaps curious is that, despite voting for a ticket that has expressed desire to "repeal and replace" the ACA and further privatization, Americans' trust in the American health care system is quite low, and the appetite for expansion quite pronounced. A November 2023 Gallup poll found that 59 percent of Americans view it as the government's responsibility to ensure that all Americans have health coverage,[41] with just 31 percent having a favorable opinion of the health care industry as of August 2024 Gallup polling.[42] What's more, a March 2021 Morning Consult poll found that 68 percent of Americans favor a public option, with 55 percent of Americans favoring Medicare-for-All. Despite this seeming political opportunity, there have not been meaningful efforts toward that goal due to the calcification of partisanship, and issues of the economy and democratic decline have understandably occupied much of the federal government's attention in recent years.

Of course, a critical question is the form that any such reform would ultimately take when political conditions are conducive, whether operating within the constraints of a system reliant on prior authorization or confronting more sweeping change.

#FIXPRIORAUTH OR #ENDPRIORAUTH?

A familiar call from the American Medical Association and many physicians on social media has been to #FixPriorAuth, citing its increase in administrative burdens on physicians, delays and adverse health outcomes for patients, and contribution to physician burnout.[43] Former AMA President Dr. Jack Resneck expressed that prior authorization often amounts to a "guessing game" such that "We don't actually know what piece of information the health insurer is looking for, so we send a bunch of explanations. But if it doesn't exactly match what the health plan employee is looking for on their computer screen, then oftentimes it won't get approved – even if it's justified and evidence-based."[44]

For some, the high reversal rates upon appeal suggest that at least some of this administrative burden is unnecessary. According to Dr. Resneck, "The fact that health plans eventually relent and admit that the treatment is appropriate is evidence that the health plan didn't need to put up these barriers in the first place. But in the meantime, patients are not getting treated. And in some cases, we know patients just get frustrated and walk away."

The question then becomes, should prior authorization be reformed, or should it be eliminated altogether? The AMA has sought reform to "right size" prior authorization, in part because "getting rid of prior authorization is just not a realistic starting point in negotiating with a health plan. It shuts down any conversation because they're in love with their utilization management tools," observed Heather McComas, Director of Administrative Simplification Initiatives for the AMA.[45] Others have called for a more radical transformation of claim and prior authorization processing in the American health care system.

Indeed, even those who have worked within the insurance industry have their skepticism about the utility of maintaining prior authorization within the American health care system. "Some see it as inappropriate denial or delay, and sometimes it *is* inappropriate denial or delay. To the extent that I think insurance companies can do away with prior authorization, I think it would be beneficial. Nobody likes it. Even the *health plans* don't really like it," Dr. Mario Molina observed.

Part of the reason for this skepticism is the reality that administering prior authorization is administratively burdensome not only for health care providers, but also for health plans themselves. Though some of these costs could be mitigated with the assistance of artificial intelligence, there remain challenges of potential inaccuracies in case assessment.

While many physicians have joined in the call to #FixPriorAuth, others are more skeptical about the ability to meaningfully reform it, viewing the problem as more systemic than fixable through tailoring. "I get really frustrated with the efforts to reform prior auth," Dr. Andrew Spector reflected,

> We do almost all of them electronically already. It doesn't make a bit of difference. Great, we can save some trees and I'd rather do it electronically, but *that's not the point*. It's still a disaster of a system. None of the problems I've experienced have been because it's an electronic or a paper application. Electronic prior authorization won't touch the fact that I'm ordering unnecessary tests for patients who can't get CPAPs that have been denied. It's not going to do anything for these prior auth part B delays.

Dr. Spector's inherent skepticism about the use of prior authorization is borne out by the data. One study found that the removal of prior authorization requirements in a Medicare Advantage setting was associated with a decrease in opioid utilization, an increase in medication-assisted therapy use, and a 19 percent reduced incidence of relapse, thus highlighting the apparent impediments experienced by opioid users under prior authorization requirements.[46]

To some, the problem is the philosophical concept of prior authorization itself: that there is a middleman dictating the courses of treatment of patients they have not seen and may not be licensed to treat. Dr. Spector reflected,

> We need to make the case that any physician involved in this process is practicing medicine without a license, and any reviewer who is not a

licensed practitioner is not allowed to be involved in the process. They say they're not denying care, just coverage, but how is that any different when it's completely cost prohibitive to get care any other way? When they say it's not medically necessary, how is that not making a medical determination for my patient?

Ophthalmologist Dr. Will Flanary ("Dr. Glaucomflecken") has similarly characterized insurance companies as "practicing medicine without a medical license," emphasizing the untenable nature of the status quo.

The irony of prior authorization is that, although it ostensibly aims to combat overprescribing of tests and treatments, its current implementation may *overcorrect*, instead inducing *underprescribing* or *inappropriate prescribing of suboptimal treatments* by physicians seeking to avoid administrative hassles over prior authorization regarding Drug A by instead prescribing Drug B. Thus, this insurance process can not only impede quality patient care among those who are denied, but also reshape the quality of care that *is* delivered to American patients.

Of course, there are concerns that total abandonment of all utilization management methods might induce runaway health care costs. Dr. Troyen Brennan, former Chief Medical Officer of Aetna, observed that, absent prior authorization, to control costs in a cost- and profit-minded health insurance system, insurers might resort to increasing premiums and out-of-pocket medical costs for patients, an unanticipated consequence of prior authorization reform of which policymakers should be mindful.

As these pages have illuminated, insurers have an arsenal of tools with which to minimize costs – whether prior authorization broadly applied, step therapy within the realm of prescription drugs, quantity limits for costly prescriptions, or the less discussed retrospective review of emergent or non-emergent care that has been delivered but the necessity of which has not yet been determined. One way to manage the dual values of cost containment and burden reduction may be reliance on audits of physician prescribing. Auditing prescribing outliers and issuing random audits of others would make physicians aware that their clinical judgment may be reviewed for medical necessity through a larger-scale retrospective review, with prior authorization operating as a penalty for overprescribers rather than the default for all. Reliance on an audit system would not impose barriers to receipt of care across the board, meaning that the overprescribing would be addressed without impeding access and imposing burden for those prescribing higher-cost but necessary care. Dr. Lauren Wilson reflected,

> In my mind, instead of putting a hurdle a priori to getting the care they need, if you find a disturbing pattern in prescribing, just chase it down rather than delaying care for the masses. They have the data. Go after the problematic actors. Let these people do their work and use the data that you have in order to find out if you have a problem.[47]

CONCLUSION

Hundreds of millions of medical claims are denied every year, and over a third of my survey respondents had experienced at least one (often more than one) coverage denial. In light of the scope of this barrier to health care, it is perhaps surprising that this is the first comprehensive investigation into the scope of this health policy problem. The challenges are not shouldered by patients alone, but rather are shared among patients and their physicians, all of whom must harness immense administrative capital to not only learn the rules of the game but also deliver optimal results in this setting of insurance complexity. While the patients in question are insured, the findings highlight the uniquely American experience of having coverage on paper but not meaningfully in practice. Thus, this book examines through a new lens the large-scale problem of under-insurance, and the injustices that patients across the nation feel when denied the care prescribed by physicians whom they trust.

This book highlights how insurers frequently second-guess physician determinations of appropriate care (whether correctly, such as in the case of defensive medicine, or incorrectly, as in the case of inadequate review of patient histories), leaving patients caught in the middle, forced to navigate with their families the labyrinthian American health care bureaucracy that defies even medical professionals.

Though there are not pronounced disparities in who is initially denied (notwithstanding somewhat higher vulnerability to denials among women and the LGBTQ community), when examining the *effects* of these denials, the inequality implications of this practice come into clear view, with patients who are of lower socioeconomic status and Black and Hispanic patients most acutely affected by these barriers, whether opting out of appeal, delaying care, or experiencing greater financial fragility. This economic impact can come with a hefty price in a country where it is notably expensive to be poor.

How the United States will move forward is unclear. With renewed attention to the burdens of prior authorization, there may be windows of opportunity to advance reforms of its administration. But there are many competing issues on the legislative agenda, and such legislation does not confront the underlying policy problem of profit-maximizing health insurers' latitude to deny coverage for appropriate care in a health care system that is only becoming *more* heavily privatized.

Even though none of the 111 interviews conducted included a question about politics, the majority of subjects volunteered thoughts on health care reform, moving away from the for-profit context in which they experienced denials of coverage for treatment ranging from MRIs to an antidepressant, to hearing aids, to a life-saving bone marrow transplant. And, while many of those with whom I spoke eventually prevailed in their appeals, they spoke to the advantages on which they relied to secure their care, and the learning, compliance, and psychological costs that they accrued in fighting these battles.

Some knew to take diligent notes of the days, times, and names of insurer staffers with whom they spoke. Others acquiesced to suboptimal treatments. Still others harnessed their social media resources to shame their insurers and escalate their cases. Some conducted extensive medical research, becoming experts in the disease with which they or their loved ones had been diagnosed. Many became defeated and abandoned all efforts at appealing, whether paying out-of-pocket or forgoing that which had been prescribed. All spoke to the difficulty of navigating these battles while struggling with an illness or caring for those who were ill.

The stories you have read are many, but they are only some of those that inspired the pages in this book. Many more deserve mention: the man whose bone growth stimulator was denied as investigational; the woman whose pain injections were denied as not medically necessary the night before they were scheduled; the MS patient whose medication was denied, leaving her to struggle to obtain a coupon from the drug manufacturer when appeals felt fruitless.

And there are so many more. As Samantha (from Chapter 7) reflected of her long-term battle for her bone marrow transplant,

> I learned from an early age, if you want to live, you have to be able to fight these battles. You have to have a level of literacy that is master's degree or higher in public health or a legal background in order to navigate this. You have to get creative and look for back doors. But they couldn't kill me when I was that far down. At this point, I'm so much stronger and I'm going to find a way forward.

Appendices

APPENDIX TO CHAPTER 1

A snowball sample of 111 interviews was identified by means of social media recruitment and word-of-mouth advertising about the research. The purpose of the interviews was to highlight the many and varied human stories behind my patient survey data, and to provide additional perspectives of physicians and other health care workers, lawyers, patient advocates, and those within or formerly within the insurance industry. Initially tweeting and posting on Facebook that I was seeking to find patients and physicians who had experiences they would like to share regarding interactions with health insurance companies, I garnered the attention of dozens of interviewees, both patients and health care workers (whether physicians, therapists, or social workers). In many interviews, I asked whether there was anyone else whom they recommended I talk to, to broaden my pool of interviewees, and I was connected with Facebook groups of patient communities.

I then searched on Twitter for posts of people with whom I had not yet interacted, but who were expressing frustration with such issues as prior authorization, denials, and appeals, whether for public or private insurance, and I reached out to those accounts with requests for interviews. Some of those whom I interviewed introduced me to patient communities through Facebook groups dedicated to medical conditions or parents of children with those conditions, and I sought interviews through those spaces as well. Most interviews were conducted over the phone and by Zoom between May and August 2022, with a small number of interviews added later. All interviewees were provided with consent forms approved by the Institutional Review Board of Oberlin College, and they were permitted to withdraw from the study at any time.

Approximately 60 percent of patient interviewees were female, with about 35 percent of interviewees identifying as male, and 5 percent identifying as non-binary. Interviewees ranged in age from nineteen to seventy-five. Approximately 60 percent of interviewees were in employer-provided health plans, while the remainder of patient interviewees were distributed across Medicare, Medicaid, and marketplace exchange plans, though most of the Medicare and Medicaid beneficiaries were in managed care plans.

Interviews were semi-structured, lasted an average of forty minutes (though they ranged from twenty to ninety minutes), and were recorded for transcription purposes. Patients were asked about their demographic background, where they get their health insurance and their general level of satisfaction with it, and their health status and the sorts of health problems which had brought them into the health care system. They were then asked to walk me through their experience of coverage delay or denial in as much detail as they could recall, including the stated reason for the denial and the impact that it had on their physical and financial wellbeing. They were asked the cost of their pursued treatment and whether they could access it without insurance coverage. They were then asked about their experience with appealing the denial (if they did so), including what their physician's role was in the process, what administrative burdens they encountered, what the outcome of the appeal was, and the time it took to obtain a decision. They were asked about any health care that they had postponed due to the coverage denial, and its impact on their health status, as well as any non-medical purchasing that they had postponed due to the denial, and medical debts taken on. They were asked what they thought helped make them successful in their appeal. They were asked about the emotional toll of navigating the health insurance bureaucracy, and their level of concern that they will experience more coverage denials in the future. Finally, they were asked about aspects of their experience that we hadn't yet touched on, that they were comfortable sharing.

Physicians were asked questions focused on the following core subjects: the area of medicine in which they practice and the patient population they serve; the services that they prescribe that are typically subject to prior authorization; to what extent (if at all) they had observed changes in prior authorization's implementation over the course of their practice; the impact of prior authorization and related delays on their patients' care; and the extent and impact of administrative burden within their practices.

They were asked to walk through the process of fulfilling a request for prior authorization, including how long it takes them to submit it, what kind of support staff they require in order to keep up with it, and how long it can take to receive a determination. They were asked to reflect on any delays that their patients experience with prior authorization, and on potential health impacts (drawing on examples when available). They were asked how often their office experiences denials, whether that varies by public or private insurance, and to walk me through the process of appealing denials. They were asked how often they do peer-to-peer reviews with physicians in their specialty, and the implications of reviews by out-of-specialty physicians. They were asked how often their appeals were successful, and whether reversals are typically because they have provided new information on the patient's case. Finally, they were asked about aspects of their experience that had not yet been addressed.

APPENDIX TO CHAPTER 3

I measure whether each respondent identifies as *female*, which takes the value of 1 if they do so, and 0 otherwise. I asked each respondent to specify their highest level of education completed and categorized *education* as a variable ranging from 1 (less than high school) to 5 (postgraduate studies). Each respondent was asked whether English is their first language, and *English first language* takes the value of 1 if English is the respondent's native language, and 0 otherwise. *How often see doctor* is a continuous variable ranging from 1 (less than once every two years) to 7 (four or more times year). That 21 percent of respondents reported seeing their physician "less than once every two years" is consistent with an OnlineDoctor.com survey finding that 18 percent of Americans have not seen a doctor in the last five years.[1] Further, each respondent was asked whether they identify as *LGBTQ.*

I control for several other factors as well: the individual's self-reported *fair or poor health* status, the respondent's *age* (given values ranging from 1 for age eighteen to twenty-four to 6 if aged over sixty-five), their household income (ranging from 1 if under $25,000 to 9 if over $200,000), and whether they identify as *Black or Hispanic*. Lastly, I include health insurance indicator variables, including *marketplace*, *Medicare*, *Medicaid*, and *employer-provided* insurance.

The dependent variable, *denied coverage*, takes the value of 1 if the respondent indicated that they had ever experienced a coverage denial, and 0 otherwise. Because the dependent variable is dichotomous, a logit model is appropriate. Because the logit specification is nonlinear, its effects cannot be interpreted directly; thus, I present in model 1 of Table A3.1 the marginal effects with standard errors in parentheses.

Consistent with expectations, I find that women are 6 percentage points more likely to be denied coverage than are their male counterparts, and LGBTQ respondents are 13 percentage points more likely to be denied. Respondents who are in worse health are 6 percentage points more likely to experience a denial. The effects of *education*, *race*, and *income* do not appear to support the *health literacy hypothesis*, though may offer limited evidence in support of the *defensive medicine alternative hypothesis*.

SurveyMonkey performs balancing across several demographic categories as well as region. Weighting should be used with caution and does not consistently produce findings different from the unweighted data and can even introduce bias. Indeed, Chedia Haddad and coauthors write, "one cannot simply assume that using the weighted method will always result in a more accurate estimate of the population."[2] Further, statistician Luke Miratrix and his coauthors assert that weighted and unweighted data from simulations did not produce substantially different sample average treatment effect (SATE) estimates, and the unweighted estimates "avoided the substantial loss of statistical power that accompanies weighting."[3]

However, because there were still some imbalances between the sample and nationwide population, in an alternative specification, I additionally performed raking, or iterative proportional fitting, which assigns a weight value to each of the 1,340 survey respondents such that those

Table A3.1 Predicting coverage denials

	Model 1	Model 2	Model 3
Female	0.06*	−0.06	−0.12*
	(0.03)	(0.05)	(0.06)
Education	0.03**	0.01	0.03
	(0.01)	(0.01)	(0.03)
English first language	0.09*	−0.06	−0.01
	(0.04)	(0.09)	(0.11)
How often see doctor	0.04***	−0.00	−0.01
	(0.01)	(0.01)	(0.02)
LGBTQ	0.13***	0.16**	0.20***
	(0.04)	(0.06)	(0.06)
Fair or poor health	0.06+	0.03	−0.03
	(0.03)	(0.05)	(0.07)
Age	−0.01	−0.03+	−0.02
	(0.01)	(0.01)	(0.02)
Income	0.02*	0.02	−0.00
	(0.01	(0.01)	(0.01)
Black or Hispanic	−0.02	0.12*	0.21**
	(0.03)	(0.06)	(0.07)
Insurance: Medicare	0.09	0.04	0.03
	(0.06)	(0.11)	(0.13)
Insurance: Medicaid	0.22***	0.08	0.25***
	(0.07)	(0.11)	(0.10)
Insurance: Marketplace	0.19**	0.10	0.13
	(0.07)	(0.10)	(0.13)
Insurance: Employer	0.18***	0.05	0.04
	(0.05)	(0.10)	(0.12)
Number of respondents	1,340	1,340	482

$***p < 0.001, **p < 0.01, *p < 0.05, +p < 0.10$

who are overrepresented are downweighted, while greater weight value is given to those who are underrepresented on the basis of population values. Results are presented in the model 2 column of Table A3.1.

To estimate the vulnerabilities to repeated denials, I estimate the same covariates discussed above, but instead with the dependent variable of *multiple denials*, which takes the value of 1 if the respondent experienced multiple coverage denials, and 0 if they experienced only one such denial (that is, I run this analysis *within the denied population*). Because the dependent variable *multiple denials* is dichotomous, I again use a logit model specification, and present in the model 3 column of Table A3.1 the marginal effects with standard errors in parentheses. Interestingly, here I find that, while LGBTQ respondents are still significantly more likely to experience both an initial denial and subsequent denials, women are *less* likely to have this *repeated* adverse interaction with insurers. However, Black and Hispanic respondents are significantly more likely to experience ongoing insurance barriers.

APPENDIX TO CHAPTER 5

To measure the effect of *income* on care postponement, I again measured *income* ranging from 1 to 9, and I asked each respondent whether they struggle to afford out-of-pocket medical costs, with 19.4 percent responding that they experience such struggles "most of the time" and 34.6 percent responding that they experience such struggles "some of the time," while the remaining 46.0 percent responded with "rarely" or "never." *Struggle to pay out-of-pocket* is a dichotomous variable taking the value of 1 if respondents answered that they struggle to afford out-of-pocket medical costs "most of the time" or "some of the time," and 0 otherwise.[4] I estimate these economic indicators in separate models because of their correlated nature.

I account for the previously discussed demographic characteristics of survey respondents: *Black or Hispanic, LGBTQ, female, age, fair or poor health, education,* and *insurance source.* Lastly, I asked each respondent the state in which they reside, and if that state *expanded Medicaid,* it was coded as 1, and 0 otherwise.[5]

Because the dependent variable is dichotomous, a logit specification is appropriate. Results are displayed in Table A5.1. Results were consistent when restricting the regression analysis to the core variables of the hypotheses discussed above, without the additional controls.

Consistent with expectations, each $25,000 increase in one's household income is associated with a 3 percentage point decline in one's likelihood of postponing medical care. What's more, when controlling for *income,* Black and Hispanic respondents are 11–12 percentage points more likely to postpone medical care, and LGBTQ respondents are likewise more likely to do so. Also in alignment with expectations, I find that those in Medicaid expansion states are less likely to postpone medical care following a denial of coverage. Being in worse health does not appear to be associated with postponing care.

Table A5.1 Predicting care postponement

	Model 1	Model 2	Model 3
Income	−0.03*	−0.03**	
	(0.01)	(0.01)	
Struggle to pay out-of-pocket			0.32***
			(0.05)
Black or Hispanic	0.12*	0.11+	0.09
	(0.06)	(0.06)	(0.06)
LGBTQ	0.13*	0.10+	0.09
	(0.05)	(0.06)	(0.06)
Female		−0.03	−0.01
		(0.05)	(0.05)
Education		0.00	−0.01
		(0.02)	(0.02)
Age		−0.03	−0.02
		(0.05)	(0.02)
Fair or poor health	−0.02	0.01	−0.01
	(0.05)	(0.05)	(0.05)
Expanded Medicaid	−0.09+	−0.11+	−0.12*
	(0.05)	(0.06)	(0.06)
Insurance: Medicare		−0.21*	−0.19+
		(0.10)	(0.11)
Insurance: Medicaid		−0.20+	−0.17
		(0.11)	(0.11)
Insurance: Marketplace		−0.02	−0.07
		(0.12)	(0.13)
Insurance: Employer		−0.07	−0.08
		(0.10)	(0.10)
Number of respondents	482	482	482

***$p < 0.001$, **$p < 0.01$, *$p < 0.05$, +$p < 0.10$

To estimate the factors associated with purchasing postponement, I replicated the models above, with the alternative dichotomous dependent variable of *postponed purchasing* (see Table A5.2). I specify a logit regression model based on the same economic, race, sexual orientation, and Medicaid expansion hypotheses as discussed with respect to health care postponement. After all, Black and Hispanic individuals are more likely than their counterparts to have medical debts, and because of the Chapter 3 finding that Black and Hispanic individuals are more likely than their counterparts to experience not one denial, but *multiple* denials, I expect that this population will be most likely to experience the further financial destabilization of purchasing postponement.

Table A5.2 Predicting purchasing postponement

	Model 1	Model 2	Model 3
Income	−0.00	−0.01	
	(0.01)	(0.01)	
Struggle to pay out-of-pocket			0.39***
			(0.05)
Black or Hispanic	0.25***	0.25***	0.23***
	(0.06)	(0.06)	(0.07)
LGBTQ	0.26***	0.23***	0.23***
	(0.05)	(0.06)	(0.06)
Female		−0.11*	−0.12*
		(0.05)	(0.05)
Education		−0.02	−0.01
		(0.02)	(0.02)
Age		−0.05**	−0.04+
		(0.02)	(0.02)
Fair or poor health	−0.03	0.01	−0.03
	(0.05)	(0.05)	(0.06)
Expanded Medicaid	0.03	0.01	−0.00
	(0.06)	(0.06)	(0.06)
Insurance: Medicare		0.13	0.17
		(0.12)	(0.12)
Insurance: Medicaid		0.12	0.15
		(0.12)	(0.13)
Insurance: Marketplace		0.10	0.07
		(0.13)	(0.14)
Insurance: Employer		0.26**	0.30**
		(0.10)	(0.10)
Number of respondents	482	482	482

***$p < 0.001$, **$p < 0.01$, *$p < 0.05$, +$p < 0.10$

Though *income*, surprisingly, is not predictive of non-medical purchasing postponement, Black and Hispanic respondents are 23–25 percentage points more likely to postpone purchasing, and LGBTQ respondents are 23–26 percentage points more likely to do so. Unlike in the case of *postponed care*, being in a Medicaid expansion state does not appear to be associated with less purchasing postponement. Health status does not appear to be associated with purchasing postponement either.

APPENDIX TO CHAPTER 7

I control for whether one indicates an *estimated win rate of 1–20%*, which takes the value of 1 if the respondent estimated that people win health insurance appeals between 1 and 20 percent of the time, and 0 if they estimate a win percentage over 20 percent.

Annual household *income* ranges from 1 (less than \$25,000) to 9 (over \$200,000), with a mean of 3.7 (around \$70,000). *Education* ranges from 1 (less than high school education) to 5 (postgraduate education), with a mean of 3.5. I control for whether the respondent's first language is *English*, taking the value of 1 if their first language is English, and 0 otherwise. *Black or Hispanic* takes the value of 1 if the respondent identifies their race as Black or Hispanic, and 0 otherwise. *Fair or poor health* takes the value of 1 if the respondent self-reported as being in fair or poor health, and 0 if they identified as being in good or excellent health.

Table A7.1 Predicting appeals of denials

	Model 1	Model 2
Income	0.03*	0.03*
	(0.01)	(0.01)
Education	−0.03	−0.03
	(0.02)	(0.02)
Estimated win rate of 1–20%	−0.11*	−0.11*
	(0.05)	(0.05)
English first language	0.11	0.07
	(0.09)	(0.09)
Fair or poor health	−0.01	−0.02
	(0.05)	(0.05)
Black or Hispanic	0.06	0.06
	(0.06)	(0.06)
Age		0.02
		(0.02)
Female		0.01
		(0.05)
LGBTQ		0.14**
		(0.05)
Insurance: Medicare		0.15+
		(0.09)
Insurance: Medicaid		0.15
		(0.09)
Insurance: Marketplace		0.14
		(0.10)
Insurance: Employer		0.16
		(0.09)
Number of respondents	482	482

***$p < 0.001$, **$p < 0.01$, *$p < 0.05$, +$p < 0.10$

In model 2, I control for additional demographic factors: *age, female, LGBTQ,* and *insurance.*

The dependent variable is *appealed,* which takes the value of 1 if the respondent appealed their insurer's denial of a medical claim, and 0 otherwise. Because the dependent variable *appealed* is dichotomous, a logit specification is appropriate. Results are displayed in Table A7.1. Consistent with expectations, I find that each \$25,000 increase in annual household income is associated with a 3 percentage point increase in the likelihood of appealing a coverage denial, while estimating a low reversal rate makes one 11 percentage points less likely to appeal one's own denial.

To identify the factors associated with prevailing in insurance appeals, I ran a multivariate logit model using the same variables as previously,

Table A7.2 Predicting reversals of denials

	Model 1	Model 2	Model 3
Income	0.00	0.01	0.01
	(0.02)	(0.02)	(0.02)
Education	−0.08	−0.06	−0.06
	(0.05)	(0.05)	(0.05)
English first language	0.16	0.18	0.22
	(0.15)	(0.16)	(0.16)
Fair or poor health	−0.30*	−0.32*	−0.34*
	(0.14)	(0.15)	(0.15)
Black or Hispanic	0.15**	0.12*	0.17*
	(0.06)	(0.06)	(0.07)
Age		−0.01	−0.01
		(0.02)	(0.02)
Female		0.04	0.04
		(0.07)	(0.07)
LGBTQ		0.28***	0.27***
		(0.07)	(0.07)
Black or Hispanic × Medicaid			−0.30+
			(0.17)
Insurance: Medicare		−0.24+	−0.25+
		(0.15)	(0.15)
Insurance: Medicaid		−0.23	−0.13
		(0.15)	(0.18)
Insurance: Marketplace		−0.12	−0.13
		(0.18)	(0.18)
Insurance: Employer		−0.17	−0.17
		(0.14)	(0.14)
Number of respondents	295	295	295

***$p < 0.001$, **$p < 0.01$, *$p < 0.05$, +$p < 0.10$

with the exception of *estimated win rate 1–20%*, which I dropped from the specification because there is not a theoretical reason to expect that this limited information will inform appeal success. Results are presented in Table A7.2, with model 1 providing only the variables central to the core hypotheses, model 2 including additional controls, and model 3 including the interaction term of *Black or Hispanic × Medicaid*.

Here, I find that very few variables are predictive of success upon appeal, though people in worse health and Black and Hispanic Medicaid patients fare particularly poorly in this endeavor.

Figures

Tables

Acknowledgments

This book would not be possible without the unfailing kindness and generosity of many people I feel fortunate to have in my professional and personal lives.

In 2019, I was at a crossroads in my career. I had been teaching in visiting positions that had not left me with adequate time to sustain an active research agenda, which had made it difficult to propel myself into a tenure-track position. I was lost. I was fortunate enough to connect with Miriam Laugesen (to whom I will be forever indebted), who suggested that I pursue a postdoctoral position at UCLA's Department of Health Policy and Management, working with the incomparable Tom Rice.

It would be difficult if not impossible to overstate Tom's impact in not only hiring me to be his postdoctoral research associate, but also helping me to find my voice in health policy research and supporting my work on this project from its inception. From offering guidance on the pilot survey to offering extensive feedback on an early draft of a paper that morphed into this book, to always being available to offer feedback or a friendly ear amid the inevitably topsy-turvy nature of the writing and publication process, his support has been invaluable, and I will be forever grateful to him. My postdoctoral work under his guidance was truly a transformative experience for me both personally and professionally, without which this book would not have been possible.

Jerry Kominski and Laura Wherry were also immensely kind and generous with their time as I explored at UCLA the early findings that led to this book, and I am grateful to Laura for also allowing me to present an early iteration of this work to UCLA's Division of General Internal

Medicine, where I received helpful feedback toward the growth of this project. I am so fortunate to now call both Jerry and Laura friends.

Eric Patashnik's mentorship over many years has been invaluable and has contributed to this book's development in more ways than I can count. Not only did his scholarship on policy implementation and the politics of evidence-based medicine prove instrumental to my own thinking and research, but also his unfailing generosity toward me from graduate school to the present – from reading my work to offering wisdom over coffee – has helped to support my pursuit of a career in health policy and politics academia. For this guidance and support, I will be forever indebted.

I was fortunate enough to organize in January 2022 a book conference to receive in-depth feedback on the book manuscript. Its participants – Pamela Herd, Jamila Michener, Colleen Grogan, Carolyn Barnes, and Jacob Hacker – provided invaluable suggestions on the book's framing and theoretical development, helping me to broaden the book's connection to relevant literatures and to expand its relevance to the disciplines of political science, public policy, and health policy. The insights gleaned from this brilliant group of scholars whom I have long admired made the manuscript immeasurably better and pushed me to broaden my perspective on the subject matter, and for that I am eternally grateful.

When I was a visiting professor at Yale University, I had the honor and privilege of being Jacob Hacker's colleague. The impact of Jacob's work on the fields of American political economy and health policy simply cannot be overstated, and his immense generosity as a friend and mentor has shaped my scholarly thinking about American politics, policy, and health care. It is a true gift to have colleagues such as Jacob, to whom I can float a research idea and then emerge from the conversation with pages of notes about theories and literatures to which to connect my academic musings.

Pamela Herd, Donald Moynihan, and Jamila Michener deserve special thanks for so inspiring this specific research agenda. As I made my way from the law and courts world to the health policy world, I was a bit at a loss for subjects to study. Having experienced and challenged numerous health insurance coverage denials myself, I saw my experience in their writings on administrative burden and the challenges of navigating health care bureaucracies, and thus was inspired to write this very book, and to continue to build on this research trajectory. Not only was *Administrative Burden* at the heart of the health care concerns on which I had been reflecting, but upon teaching *Fragmented Democracy*, I realized how I wanted to frame this patient- and physician-centered analysis of these health insurance inefficiencies and resulting barriers to care.

A number of other scholars were kind enough to offer generous feedback on the book. Alex Hoagland was immensely thoughtful in giving chapter-by-chapter comments and suggestions from which the manuscript benefited greatly. Andrea Campbell was kind enough to offer very helpful thoughts on the overarching project and detailed feedback throughout the manuscript, and her wisdom immensely improved my framing and development of this project, from earlier stages to completion. I feel truly grateful for Andrea's guidance and support of my research, and our conversations always leave me inspired and wanting to write, and with greater clarity. Chris Witko offered highly valuable feedback both on my book proposal and on aspects of my findings that had left me perplexed. At least as importantly, Chris's friendship and wit kept me sane throughout the many stressors of this process.

I am grateful to Tim Callaghan for inviting me to present this research at the Qualitative Methods workshop at Boston University's Department of Health Law, Policy, and Management, where I received useful feedback on the methodological orientation of the work, as well as its theoretical development.

Numerous conversations with scholars of political science and public policy have also provided guidance and support toward the completion of this project, in addition to offering support that gave me the confidence to see this project through. William Adler, Julia Azari, David Bradford, Dan Carpenter, Richard Carpiano, Jonathan Cohn, Christian Grose, Jeff Lax, Miriam Laugesen, Seth Masket, Matt Motta, Mark Peterson, Eric Schickler, Dan Skinner, Craig Volden, and Aubrey Westfall deserve particular thanks.

The Roosevelt Institute provided invaluable support toward the completion of this work. I am indebted to this organization for the opportunity to be part of this intellectual community as its 2025 author-in-residence.

I am immensely grateful for the support of my superb editor, Rachel Blaifeder, for her support of this book's publication by Cambridge University Press. Her feedback on the direction of the project helped to ensure that I fulfilled this book's potential, and I am forever appreciative of the time that she took to offer feedback throughout the process. This collaboration was a gift in helping me to realize this project. I also greatly appreciate Steven Holt's superb assistance throughout the copyediting process.

I would be woefully remiss if I did not offer my sincerest thanks to the many patients who put their trust in me when sharing their painful stories of navigating the American health care system. It has been an honor of a lifetime bringing their stories to light through this book, and it has been a gift to be able to stay in touch with so many of them, whether in continued struggle with their insurer or thriving having won their battles. Their participation in this project was truly an act of courage that I will never take for granted.

The writing of this book would not have been possible without the love and support of my close friends Caitlin, Caroline, Steve, Ben, and Brooke, as well as my parents, Jillian and Steve, who made the mistake of asking what I was writing and consequently were subjected to reading depressing chapters on aspects of the American health care system that they knew me to revile from personal experience. And most of all, I am indebted to my better half, Chris Hagan, for his unconditional love and support through this process and beyond, offering feedback on chapters that depressed and enraged him about health insurance, and more importantly offering the consistent reassurance that I could see this through. I still cannot believe my luck in having found him, and it was a gift to have him with me on this journey.

For these people, I have a debt of gratitude.

Notes

PREFACE

1. United States Census. 2024. "Health Insurance Coverage in the United States: 2023." www.census.gov/library/publications/2024/demo/p60-284.html.

2. Pollitz, Karen, Kaye Pestaina, Lunna Lopes, Rayna Wallace, and Justin Lo. 2023. "Consumer Survey Highlights Problems with Denied Insurance Claims." KFF. https://tinyurl.com/2n6pkmxd.

3. Ibid.

4. Muoio, Dave. "Providers 'Wasted' $10.6B in Overturning Claims Denials, Survey Finds." Fierce Healthcare, March 22, 2024. https://tinyurl.com/mtzbd5uu.

5. Reed, Tina. "UnitedHealthcare Cutting Back on Prior Authorizations." Axios, August 10, 2023. www.axios.com/2023/08/10/unitedhealth-prior-authorization-roll-back.

6. Ibid.

7. Bengaluru, Bhanvi Satija. "Cigna Removes Prior Authorization Requirement for 25% of Medical Services." Reuters, August 24, 2023. https://tinyurl.com/yc4drwfr.

8. Sausser, Lauren. "Doctors and Patients Try to Shame Insurers Online to Reverse Prior Authorization Denials." Kaiser Health News, August 23, 2023. https://tinyurl.com/reyz672m.

9. Alltucker, Ken. "Doctors and Patients Are Worried This Large Health Insurer's New Policy Will Delay Care." *USA Today*, May 24, 2023. https://tinyurl.com/3arykexv.

10. Howard, Jacqueline. "UnitedHealthcare Shifts Colonoscopy Requirements from Controversial 'Prior Authorization' to 'Advance Notification.'" CNN, June 1, 2023. https://tinyurl.com/53b4h82v.

11. Office of US Senator Claire McCaskill. 2018. "Coverage Denied: Anthem Blue Cross Blue Shield's Emergency Room Initiative." Report, no longer available, summarized at https://tinyurl.com/3py5m8uh.

12. Optum. 2024. "The Optum 2024 Revenue Cycle Denials Index." https://business.optum.com/en/insights/denials-index.html.

13. California Assembly Committee on Privacy and Consumer Protection. 2024. "Report on SB 1120." https://apcp.assembly.ca.gov/system/files/2024-06/sb-1120-becker-apcp-analysis.pdf.

14. Lowrey, Annie. "The Time Tax: Why Is So Much American Bureaucracy Left to Average Citizens?" *The Atlantic*, July 27, 2021. https://tinyurl.com/2uaxf725.

CHAPTER 1: THE POLITICAL ORIGINS OF COVERAGE DENIALS

1. Lee, Anna Marie. "Most Americans Can't Afford a $1,000 Emergency Expense, Report Finds." *CBS News*, January 23, 2025. www.cbsnews.com/news/saving-money-emergency-expenses-2025.

2. US Food and Drug Administration. 2025. "Generic Drugs." www.fda.gov/drugs/buying-using-medicine-safely/generic-drugs.

3. Wernau, Julia. "Health Insurers Deny 850 Million Claims a Year. The Few Who Appeal Often Win." *Wall Street Journal*, February 12, 2025. https://tinyurl.com/2ewtkap8.

4. Martin, Anne, Micah Hartman, Benjamin Washington, and Aaron Catlin. 2024. "National Health Expenditures in 2023: Faster Growth as Insurance and Utilization Increase." *Health Affairs* 44(1), www.healthaffairs.org/doi/10.1377/hlthaff.2024.01375.

5. Gunja, Munira, Evan Gumas, and Reginald Williams. 2023. "U.S. Health Care from a Global Perspective, 2022: Accelerating Spending, Worsening Outcomes." The Commonwealth Fund, Issue Brief. https://tinyurl.com/my4shaz3.

6. Peter G. Peterson Foundation. 2024. "The Share of Americans without Health Insurance in 2023 Remained Low." Report. www.pgpf.org/article/the-share-of-americans-without-health-insurance-in-2023-remained-low.

7. The Commonwealth Fund. 2024. "The State of Health Insurance Coverage in the U.S." Issue Brief, November 21, 2024. https://tinyurl.com/48cbtwd7.

8. Peter G. Peterson Foundation. 2024. "Why Are Americans Paying More for Healthcare?" www.pgpf.org/article/why-are-americans-paying-more-for-healthcare.

9. The Commonwealth Fund. 2024. "The State of Health Insurance Coverage in the U.S." Issue Brief, November 21, 2024. https://tinyurl.com/48cbtwd7.

10. Brownlee, Shannon. 2007. *Overtreated: Why Too Much Medicine Is Making Us Sicker and Poorer*. New York, NY: Bloomsbury USA, pp. 1–2.

11. Skinner, Daniel. 2019. *Medical Necessity: Health Care Access and the Politics of Decision Making*. Minneapolis, MN: University of Minnesota Press, p. 4.

12. Hacker, Jacob. 2019. *The Great Risk Shift: The New Economic Security and the Decline of the American Dream*, 2nd ed. New York, NY: Oxford University Press, p. 9.

13. Schattschneider, E. E. 1935. *Politics, Pressures, and the Tariff*. New York, NY: Prentice-Hall, Inc., p. 288.

14. Skocpol, Theda. 1992. *Protecting Soldiers and Mothers: The Political Origins of Social Policy in the United States*. Cambridge, MA: Belknap Press of Harvard University Press, p. 58.

15. United States Census. 2024. "Health Insurance Coverage in the United States: 2023." www.census.gov/library/publications/2024/demo/p60-284.html.

16. Mettler, Suzanne. 2011. *The Submerged State: How Invisible Government Policies Undermine American Democracy*. Chicago, IL: University of Chicago Press.

17. Mettler, Suzanne. 2010. "Reconstituting the Submerged State: The Challenges of Social Policy Reform in the Obama Era." *Perspectives on Politics* 8(3): 803–824.

18. Kolb, Kristen, David Radley, and Sara Collins. 2024. "Trends in Employer Health Insurance Costs, 2014–2023: Coverage Is More Expensive for Workers in Small Businesses." The Commonwealth Fund, Report. https://tinyurl.com/bdekk8yz.

19. "Employer-Sponsored Coverage Rates for People Ages 0–64 by Age." KFF. 2023. https://tinyurl.com/4cy79pmj.

20. Health care provisions were eliminated from what would become the Social Security Act of 1935, though it laid the groundwork for further reform, and President Harry S. Truman campaigned tirelessly for a national health insurance program but faced insurmountable opposition.

21. Roosevelt, President Franklin Delano. "Speech at Meeting on Economic Security at the White House," November 14, 1934. www.ssa.gov/history/fdrstmts.html#advisec.

22. University of Virginia Miller Center. "Presidents and Health Care: Franklin Roosevelt." https://millercenter.org/health-care-policy/presidents-health-care.

23. Kooijman, Jaap. 1999. "Sooner or Later On: Franklin D. Roosevelt and National Health Insurance, 1933–1945." *Presidential Studies Quarterly* 29(2): 336–350.

24. Balat, David. "The Employer–Health Insurance Connection an 'Accident of History.'" *The Hill,* November 9, 2019. https://tinyurl.com/3uw9bftt.

25. Bartlett, Bruce. "The Question of Taxing Employer-Provided Health Insurance." *The New York Times,* July 30, 2013. https://tinyurl.com/bdcv86jm.

26. Pentecost, Michael. 2007. "The Future of Employer-Based Health Insurance." *The Permanente Journal* 11(2): 91–93.

27. Truman, President Harry S. "Special Message to the Congress Recommending a Comprehensive Health Program." November 19, 1945. https://tinyurl.com/37ptvt7k.

28. Truman, President Harry S. "Special Message to Congress on Health and Disability Insurance." May 19, 1947. https://tinyurl.com/3evs4wxc.

29. Social Security Administration. "Social Security History: The Evolution of Medicare." https://tinyurl.com/4xf6c4sj.

30. University of Virginia Miller Center. "Presidents on Health Care: Dwight Eisenhower." https://millercenter.org/health-care-policy/presidents-health-care#DDE.

31. Pentecoste. "The Future of Employer-Based Health Insurance."

32. Eisenhower, President Dwight D. "Special Message to the Congress recommending a Health Program." https://tinyurl.com/3ntbp9y9.

33. Kennedy, President John F. "Statement by the President on the Defeat of the Medical Care Bill." July 17, 1962. www.presidency.ucsb.edu/documents/statement-the-president-the-defeat-the-medical-care-bill.

34. Johnson, President Lyndon B. "Special Message to Congress: Advancing the Nation's Health." January 5, 1965. https://tinyurl.com/4tajsfrv.

35. Johnson, President Lyndon B. "Remarks with President Truman at the Signing in Independence of the Medicare Bill." July 30, 1965. https://tinyurl.com/m5ctn9r7.

36. Woolhandler, Steffie and David Himmelstein. 2017. "The Affordable Care Act: How Nixon's Health Reform Proposal Became Democrats' Albatross." *International Journal of Social Determinants of Health and Human Services* 47(4): 612–620.

37. Caress, Barbara. "The Dark History of Medicare Privatization." *The American Prospect,* January 24, 2022. https://prospect.org/health/dark-history-of-medicare-privatization.

38. Nixon, President Richard. "Special Message to the Congress Proposing a Comprehensive Health Insurance Plan." February 6, 1974. https://tinyurl.com/3vpwbruy.

39. Seervai, Shanoor and David Blumenthal. 2017. "Lessons on Universal Coverage from an Unexpected Advocate: Richard Nixon." The Commonwealth Fund Blog. https://tinyurl.com/2y7yhct8.

40. According to the Social Security Administration, prior to 1965, barely over half of the population aged sixty-five or older were insured for hospital care, and even fewer had coverage for outpatient care.

41. Gray, Virginia, David Lowery, and Erik Godwin. 2007. "The Political Management of Managed Care: Explaining Variations in State Health Maintenance Organization Regulations." *Journal of Health Politics, Policy, and Law* 32(3): 457–495.

42. Hacker, Jacob S. and Theodore R. Marmor. 1999. "How Not to Think about Managed Care." *University of Michigan Journal of Law Reform* 32(4): 661–684.

43. Peterson, Mark. 2002. "Managed Care Redux." *Journal of Health Politics, Policy, and Law* 27(3): 345–352.

44. Starr, Paul. 1995. "What Happened to Health Care Reform?" *The American Prospect* 20: 20–31.

45. Representative Charlie Norwood (Republican, GA), a champion of the Patients' Bill of Rights, expressed it thus: "Their mind is on Clinton's problems. You can't carry on a conversation up here for more than one minute before impeachment comes up. The Senate put off the health care issue, but it's not going away." See also Pear, Robert. "Bill Defining Patients' Rights Dies in Senate." *The New York Times*, October 10, 1998. www.nytimes.com/library/politics/101098congress-health.html.

46. Patel, Yash and Stuart Guterman. "The Evolution of Private Plans in Medicare." The Commonwealth Fund. Issue Brief, December 2017. https://tinyurl.com/474cz9pc.

47. McGuire, Thomas, Joseph Newhouse, and Anna Sinaiko. 2011. "An Economic History of Medicare Part C." *Milbank Quarterly* 89(2): 289–332.

48. Oberlander, Jonathan. 2003. *The Political Life of Medicare.* Chicago, IL: University of Chicago Press.

49. Xu, Lanlan, Pete Welch, Joel Ruhter et al. 2023. "Medicare Advantage Overview: A Primer on Enrollment and Spending." ASPE Office of Health Policy Issue Brief. https://tinyurl.com/5e6yujan.

50. Ibid.

51. Biles, Brian, Jonah Pozen, and Stuart Guterman. "The Continuing Cost of Privatization: Extra Payments to Medicare Advantage Plans Jump to $11.4 Billion in 2009." The Commonwealth Fund. Issue Brief, May 2009. https://tinyurl.com/3p25s5rx.

52. Morgan, Kimberly J. and Andrea Louise Campbell. 2011. *The Delegated Welfare State: Medicare, Markets, and the Governance of Social Policy.* New York, NY: Oxford University Press, p. 109.

53. Freed, Meredith, Jeannie Fuglesten Biniek, Anthony Damico, and Tricia Neuman. 2024. "Medicare Advantage in 2024: Enrollment Update and Key Trends." KFF. https://tinyurl.com/d39m5fx3.

54. MACPAC. 2022. "Medicaid Managed Care Capitation Rate Setting." www.macpac.gov/wp-content/uploads/2022/03/Managed-care-capitation-issue-brief.pdf.

55. Hinton, Elizabeth and Jada Raphael. 2025. "10 Things to Know about Medicaid Managed Care." KFF. www.kff.org/medicaid/issue-brief/10-things-to-know-about-medicaid-managed-care.

56. MACPAC. 2011. "The Evolution of Managed Care in Medicaid." June 2011 Report to Congress. https://tinyurl.com/444pt5tx.

57. Schneider, Andrew. 1997. "Overview of Medicaid Provisions in the Balanced Budget Act of 1997, P.L. 105–33." Center on Budget and Policy Priorities. www.cbpp.org/sites/default/files/archive/908mcaid.htm.

58. KFF. 2024. "Total Medicaid MCO Spending." https://tinyurl.com/2jyw24py.

59. Hinton, Elizabeth and Jada Raphael. 2023. "A Closer Look at the Five Largest Publicly Traded Companies Operating Medicaid Managed Care Plans." KFF. July 6, 2023. https://tinyurl.com/mpm996sp.

60. Hacker, Jacob. 2002. *The Divided Welfare State: The Battle over Public and Private Social Benefits in the United States.* New York, NY: Cambridge University Press.

61. Obama, Barack. 2010. "This Is What Change Looks Like." Speech delivered on March 22, 2010. https://obamawhitehouse.archives.gov/blog/2010/03/22/what-change-looks.

62. Starr, Paul. 2011. *Remedy and Reaction: The Peculiar American Struggle over Health Care Reform.* New Haven, CT: Yale University Press.

63. Herd, Pamela, Hilary Hoynes, Jamila Michener, and Donald Moynihan. 2023. "Introduction: Administrative Burden as a Mechanism of Inequality." *The Russell Sage Foundation Journal of the Social Sciences* 9(5): 1–30.

64. Biniek, Jeannie Fuglesten, Nolan Sroczynski, Meredith Freed, and Tricia Neuman. 2025. "Medicare Advantage Insurers Made Nearly 50 Million Prior Authorization Determinations in 2023." KFF. https://tinyurl.com/2mrr23nt.

65. The ACA initially withheld federal funds from states that declined to expand Medicaid. However, in *National Federation of Independent Business v. Sebelius* (2012), the Supreme Court majority led by Chief Justice John Roberts held that Medicaid expansion could be incentivized, but could not be a "gun to the head."

66. Hacker, Jacob, Alexander Hertel-Fernandez, Paul Pierson, and Kathleen Thelen, eds. 2022. *The American Political Economy: Politics, Markets, and Power.* New York, NY: Cambridge University Press.

67. Galanter, Marc. 1974. "Why the 'Haves' Come Out Ahead: Speculations on the Limits of Legal Change." *Law and Society Review* 9(1): 95–160.

68. Hacker, Hertel-Fernandez, Pierson, and Thelen, eds. *The American Political Economy*, p. 22.

69. Hacker. *The Divided Welfare State*, p. 284.

70. Ibid., p. 28.

71. Pierson, Paul. 2000. "Increasing Returns, Path Dependence, and the Study of Politics." *American Political Science Review* 94(2): 251–267.

72. Hacker. *The Great Risk Shift*.

73. Former American Medical Association President Dr. Jack Resneck characterized as "Kafkaesque" a prior authorization for treatment of severe eczema, leading him to

be "horrified." Robeznieks, Andis. 2023. "Once a Burden, Prior Authorization Has Become a Nightmare." American Medical Association. https://tinyurl.com/p84xantx.

74. Glaucomflecken. 2023. "Prior Authorization Reform Bill." https://glaucomflecken.com/take-action-prior-authorization-reform-bill.

75. Clowe, J. L., R. Scalettar, and J. S. Todd. 1993. "A New Partnership for Change." *Journal of the American Medical Association* 269: 1164–1165.

76. Starr. *Remedy and Reaction.*

77. Ibid.

78. Oberlander, Jonathan. 2003. *The Political Life of Medicare.* Chicago, IL: University of Chicago Press.

79. Kirzinger, Ashley, Marley Presiado, Isabelle Valdes, and Mollyann Brodie. 2023. "KFF Tracking Poll March 2023: Public Doesn't Want Politicians to Upend Popular Programs." KFF. https://tinyurl.com/296awhsh.

80. Hacker, Hertel-Fernandez, Pierson, and Thelen, eds. *The American Political Economy,* p. 7.

81. Rakshit, Shameek, Matthew Rae, Gary Claxton, Krutika Amin, and Cynthia Cox. 2024. "The Burden of Medical Debt in the United States." Peterson-KFF Health System Tracker. www.healthsystemtracker.org/brief/the-burden-of-medical-debt-in-the-united-states.

82. Optum. 2024. "The Optum 2024 Revenue Cycle Denials Index." https://business.optum.com/en/insights/denials-index.html.

83. Miller, Andrew, Robert Shor, Thad Waites, and B. Hadley Wilson. 2018. "Prior Authorization Reform for Better Patient Care." *Journal of the American College of Cardiology* 71(17): 1937–1939.

84. Interview with Dr. Mario Molina, May 18, 2022.

85. Peter G. Peterson Foundation. 2023. "Almost 25% of Healthcare Spending Is Considered Wasteful. Here's Why." https://tinyurl.com/4acyjnuy.

86. America's Health Insurance Plans. 2020. "Key Results of Industry Survey on Prior Authorization." www.ahip.org/resources/key-results-of-industry-survey-on-prior-authorization.

87. EviCore. 2020. "Gold Carding: An Overview of 'Gold Carding' in Prior Authorization Programs." Issue Brief. https://tinyurl.com/ycypb36a.

88. Miller, T. Christian, Patrick Rucker, and David Armstrong. "'Not Medically Necessary': Inside the Company Helping America's Biggest Health Insurers Deny Coverage for Care." *ProPublica,* October 23, 2024. https://tinyurl.com/5c4w5wa7.

89. American Hospital Association. 2020. "Addressing Commercial Health Plan Abuses to Ensure Fair Coverage for Patients and Providers." https://tinyurl.com/bddx56jv.

90. Ibid.

91. Ernst, Claire. "Prior Authorization Pains Growing for 9/10 Physician Practices." Medical Group Management Association, September 19, 2019. www.mgma.com/mgma-stats/prior-authorization-pains-growing-for-9-10-physician-practices.

92. American Medical Association. 2022. "Competition in U.S. Health Insurance: A Comprehensive Study of U.S. Markets." Report. www.ama-assn.org/system/files/competition-health-insurance-us-markets.pdf.

93. Ibid.

94. Interview with Dr. Troyen Brennan, January 30, 2023.

95. Interview with Wendell Potter, June 28, 2022.

96. Data were missing for 2020.

97. Institute of Medicine (US) Committee on Utilization Management by Third Parties. 1989. *Controlling Costs and Changing Patient Care? The Role of Utilization Management.* Washington, D.C.: National Academies Press.

98. Ibid.

99. Behrendsen, Jessica. 2017. "A Brief History of How We Got to Electronic Prior Authorization." *CoverMyMeds.* Text no longer online, but linked to via https://insights.covermymeds.com/medication-access-report/2020.

100. Social Security Administration. "History of SSA during the Johnson Administration 1963–1968." www.ssa.gov/history/ssa/lbjleg1.html.

101. Institute of Medicine (US) Committee on Utilization Management by Third Parties. *Controlling Costs and Changing Patient Care?*

102. Ibid. See text at www.ncbi.nlm.nih.gov/books/NBK234998.

103. Gruber, Lynn R., Maureen Shadle, and Cynthia L. Polich. 1988. "From Movement to Industry: The Growth of HMOs." *Health Affairs* 7(3): 197–208.

104. Zwanziger, Jack and Rebecca Auerbach. 1991. "Evaluating PPO Performance Using Prior Expenditure Data." *Medical Care* 29(2): 142–151.

105. Buck, Jeffrey and Herbert Silverman. 1996. "Use of Utilization Management Methods in State Medicaid Programs." *Health Care Financing Review* 17(4): 77–86.

106. Resneck, Jack S. 2020. "Refocusing Medication Prior Authorization on Its Intended Purpose." *Journal of the American Medical Association* 323(8): 703–704.

107. Wickizer, Thomas and Daniel Lessler. 2002. "Utilization Management: Issues, Effects, and Future Prospects." *Annual Review of Public Health* 23: 233–254.

108. Ibid.

109. Kurani, Nisha, Jared Ortaliza, Emma Wager, Lucas Fox, and Krutika Amin. 2022. "How Has U.S. Spending on Healthcare Changed over Time?" Peterson-KFF Health System Tracker. www.healthsystemtracker.org/chart-collection/u-s-spending-health care-changed-time.

110. Schwartz, Aaron, Troyen Brennan, Dorothea Verbrugge, and Joseph Newhouse. 2021. "Measuring the Scope of Prior Authorization Policies Applying Private Insurer Rules to Medicare Part B." *Journal of the American Medical Association* 2(5): e210859.

111. Bergthold, Linda A. 1995. "Medical Necessity: Do We Need It?" *Health Affairs* 14(4): 180–190.

112. Skinner, Daniel. 2019. *Medical Necessity: Health Care Access and the Politics of Decision Making.* Minneapolis, MN: University of Minnesota Press.

113. Ibid., p. 20.

114. Lipsky, Michael. 1980. *Street-Level Bureaucracy: Dilemmas of the Individual in Public Service.* New York, NY: Russell Sage Foundation, p. xv.

115. Council for Affordable Quality Healthcare. 2024. "2023 CAQH Index Report." www.caqh.org/hubfs/43908627/drupal/2024-01/2023_CAQH_Index_Report.pdf.

116. Council for Affordable Quality Healthcare. 2024. "Administrative Transaction Costs by Provider Specialty." https://tinyurl.com/5x9nzhfz.

117. Ibid.

118. America's Health Insurance Plans. 2021. "Evaluation of the Fast Prior Authorization Technology Highway Demonstration: Final Report." https://tinyurl.com/33txbkvr.

119. Pecci, Alexandra Wilson. "Electronic Prior Auths Save Time, but Don't Change Approval Rates." *Health Leaders*, April 8, 2021. https://tinyurl.com/mr4j5x9m.

120. Council for Affordable Quality Healthcare. 2020. "Conducting Electronic Business Transactions: Why Greater Harmonization across the Industry Is Needed."

121. Lee, Victoria, Todd Berland, Glenn Jacobowitz et al. 2020. "Prior Authorization as a Utilization Management Tool for Elective Superficial Venous Procedures Results in High Administrative Cost and Low Efficacy in Reducing Utilization." *Journal of Vascular Surgery: Venous and Lymphatic Disorders* 8(3): 383–389.

122. Beland, Daniel and Jacob Hacker. 2004. "Ideas, Institutions, and American Welfare State 'Exceptionalism': The Case of Health and Old-Age Insurance in the United States, 1915–1965." *International Journal of Social Welfare* 13(1): 42–54.

123. Hiltzik, Michael. "California Fines Aetna (but not Enough) for Wrongly Denying Claims for ER Visits." *Los Angeles Times*, September 3, 2020. www.latimes.com/business/story/2020-09-03/california-aetna-er-denials.

124. Lo, Justin, Michelle Long, Rayna Wallace, Meghan Salaga, and Kaye Pestaina. 2025. "Claim Denials and Appeals in ACA Marketplace Plans in 2023." KFF. https://tinyurl.com/bdzkxdd3.

125. Schwartz, Aaron, Yujun Chen, Chris Jagmin et al. 2022. "Coverage Denials: Government and Private Insurer Policies for Medical Necessity in Medicare." *Health Affairs* 41(1): 120–128.

126. Biniek, Jeannie Fuglesten, Nolan Sroczynski, and Tricia Neuman. 2024. "Use of Prior Authorization in Medicare Advantage Exceeded 46 Million Requests in 2022." KFF. https://tinyurl.com/2mrr23nt. (KFF overwrote the report on the previous plan year.)

127. Grimm, Christi A. 2022. "Some Medicare Advantage Organization Denials of Prior Authorization Requests Raise Concerns about Beneficiary Access to Medically Necessary Care." US Department of Health and Human Services Office of Inspector General Report. https://oig.hhs.gov/documents/evaluation/3150/OEI-09-18-00260-Complete%20Report.pdf.

128. Muoio, Dave. "Providers 'Wasted' $10.6B in Overturning Claims Denials, Survey Finds." Fierce Healthcare, March 22, 2024. https://tinyurl.com/4jbwrrxh.

129. Optum. 2024. "The Optum 2024 Revenue Cycle Denials Index." https://business.optum.com/en/insights/denials-index.html.

130. Change Healthcare. 2022. "The Change Healthcare 2022 Revenue Cycle Denials Index." Report. https://interactive.healthleadersmedia.com/revenue-cycle-denials-index.

131. Gottlieb, Joshua, Adam Hale Shapiro, and Abe Dunn. 2018. "The Complexity of Billing and Paying for Physician Care." *Health Affairs* 37(4): 619–626.

132. Office of the Inspector General, Department of Health and Human Services. 2018. "Medicare Advantage Appeal Outcomes and Audit Findings Raise Concerns about Service and Payment Denials." Report. https://oig.hhs.gov/documents/evaluation/3140/OEI-09-16-00410-Complete%20Report.pdf.

133. Hacker, Jacob S., Suzanne Mettler, and Diana Pinderhughes. 2007. "Inequality and Public Policy," in Lawrence Jacobs and Theda Skocpol (eds.), *Inequality and American Democracy: What We Know and What We Need to Learn.* New York, NY: Russell Sage Foundation, pp. 156–213, 172.

134. Commonwealth Fund. 2024. "Mirror Mirror: A Portrait of the Failing U.S. Health System." *Issue Brief,* September 19, 2024. https://tinyurl.com/ayvkam5n.

135. Michener, Jamila. 2018. *Fragmented Democracy: Medicaid, Federalism, and Unequal Politics.* Princeton, NJ: Princeton University Press, p. 88.

136. Herd, Pamela and Donald Moynihan. 2018. *Administrative Burden: Policymaking by Other Means.* New York, NY: Russell Sage Foundation, p. 143.

137. Masood, Ayesha and Muhammad Azfar Nisar. 2021. "Administrative Capital and Citizens' Responses to Administrative Burden." *Journal of Public Administration Research and Theory* 31(1): 56–72.

138. Herd and Moynihan. *Administrative Burden*, p. 1.

139. Ibid., p. 3.

140. Moynihan, Donald, Pamela Herd, and Hope Harvey. 2014. "Administrative Burden: Learning, Psychological, and Compliance Costs in Citizen–State Interactions." *Journal of Public Administration Research and Theory* 25(1): 43–69.

141. Herd, Pamela and Donald Moynihan. 2020. "How Administrative Burdens Can Harm Health." *Health Affairs,* October 2, 2020. www.healthaffairs.org/do/10.1377/hpb20200904.405159.

142. Sommers, Benjamin, Anna Goldman, Robert Blendon, John Orav, and Arnold Epstein. 2019. "Medicaid Work Requirements – Results from the First Year in Arkansas." *New England Journal of Medicine* 381: 1073–1082.

143. Herd and Moynihan. *Administrative Burden.*

144. Morgan, Kimberly J. and Andrea Louise Campbell. 2011. *The Delegated Welfare State: Medicare, Markets, and the Governance of Social Policy.* New York, NY: Oxford University Press.

145. Herd, Hoynes, Michener, and Moynihan. 2023. "Introduction: Administrative Burden as a Mechanism of Inequality."

146. Pfeffer, Jeffrey, Dan Witters, Sangeeta Agrawal, and James Harter. 2020. "Magnitude and Effects of 'Sludge' in Benefits Administration: How Health Insurance Hassles Burden Workers and Cost Employers." *Academy of Management Discoveries* 6(3): 325–340.

147. Through MTurk, approximately 250,000 MTurk workers agree to answer surveys or conduct other "tasks" in exchange for approximately $1.25, and yield samples that are at least as representative as college student samples. This tool has been widely used in studying a range of experimental and survey-based political science questions.

148. Huff, Connor and Dustin Tingley. 2015. "'Who Are These People?' Evaluating the Demographic Characteristics and Political Preferences of MTurk Survey Respondents." *Research & Politics* 2(3): 1–12.

149. Clifford, Scott, Ryan M. Jewell, and Philip D. Waggoner. 2015. "Are Samples Drawn from Mechanical Turk Valid for Research on Political Ideology?" *Research & Politics* 2(4): 1–9.

150. Over 2 million individuals take surveys on SurveyMonkey's platform each day. SurveyMonkey promises a demographically diverse population from the United States. A random sample of those participants were asked whether they agreed to take my optional online survey in exchange for a small payment, after which non-responses and incomplete responses were identified and filtered out. SurveyMonkey prevents duplicate or fraudulent responses to ensure that responses are by humans rather than bots. SurveyMonkey monitors respondent metadata to detect speeding and filters or deletes individual responses from analysis. SurveyMonkey runs ongoing panel calibration studies to ensure that response quality meets industry benchmarks.

151. Bentley, Frank R., Nediyana Daskalova, and Brooke White. 2017. "Comparing the Reliability of Amazon Mechanical Turk and Survey Monkey to Traditional Market Research Surveys." *Proceedings of the 2017 CHI Conference Extended Abstracts on Human Factors in Computing Systems*, pp. 1092–1099. Full text available at https://frankbentley .com/wp-content/uploads/2021/12/chi-case-surveys.pdf.

152. I conducted interviews with three patient advocates, from New York, Connecticut, and Ohio. I interviewed six people from the insurance industry. I interviewed twenty-one health care providers. I interviewed two senior staffers at the American Medical Association. I interviewed one staffer in hospital billing. I interviewed one pharmacist. I interviewed ten health insurance lawyers. The remainder of my interviews were with patients.

CHAPTER 2: CAUSES AND TYPES OF COVERAGE DENIALS

1. Harpaz, Rafael, Rebecca Dahl, and Kathleen Dooling. 2016. "Prevalence of Immunosuppression among US Adults, 2013." *Journal of the American Medical Association* 16(23): 2547–2548.

2. Vaughan, Leslie. 2019. "Managing Cost of Care and Healthcare Utilization in Patients Using Immunoglobulin Agents." *American Journal of Managed Care* 25(6): 105–111.

3. Lo, Justin, Michelle Long, Rayna Wallace, Meghan Salaga, and Kaye Pestaina. 2025. "Claim Denials and Appeals in ACA Marketplace Plans in 2023." KFF. https://tinyurl .com/yv96mhxz.

4. United States Census Bureau. 2023. "Health Insurance Coverage in the United States: 2022." www.census.gov/library/publications/2023/demo/p60-281.html.

5. Funding and institutional review board approval for the survey were secured by Oberlin College. The pilot I survey conducted in 2020 was funded through equity, diversity, and inclusion grants from the University of California at Los Angeles.

6. Bentley, Frank R., Nediyana Daskalova, and Brooke White. 2017. "Comparing the Reliability of Amazon Mechanical Turk and Survey Monkey to Traditional Market Research Surveys." *Proceedings of the 2017 CHI Conference Extended Abstracts on Human Factors in Computing Systems,* pp. 1092–1099.

7. According to the United States Census, 37.9 percent of Americans have a college degree or higher.

8. National Alliance for Mental Illness. "Mental Health by the Numbers." www.nami.org/about-mental-illness/mental-health-by-the-numbers.

9. KFF. 2023. "Health Insurance Coverage of the Total Population." https://tinyurl.com/mntyjjjt.

10. Kearney, Audrey, Liz Hamel, Mellisha Stokes, and Mollyann Brodie. 2021. "Americans' Challenges with Health Care Costs." KFF. www.kff.org/health-costs/issue-brief/americans-challenges-with-health-care-costs.

11. ValuePenguin Staff. "Insurance Claim Denials: Worst Companies and How to Appeal." December 18, 2024. www.valuepenguin.com/health-insurance-claim-denials-and-appeals.

12. It is perhaps unsurprising that relatively few of the reported denials were among patients enrolled with Kaiser Permanente, which has been noted as having both high patient satisfaction and low patient turnover (Mahar, Maggie. "Why Are Customers of This Health Insurer So Happy?" *Time,* October 18, 2011. https://business.time.com/2011/10/18/why-are-customers-of-this-health-insurer-so-happy), the latter of which I argue is associated with greater insurer investments in preventive care.

13. Alkire, Michael. "Unnecessary Insurance Claim Denials Compromise Patient Care and Provider Bottom Lines." *STATNews,* May 1, 2024. https://tinyurl.com/34f76usf.

14. Georgetown University Health Policy Institute. "Prescription Drugs." https://hpi.georgetown.edu/rxdrugs.

15. Office of Science and Data Policy. 2022. "Trends in Prescription Drug Spending, 2016–2021." https://tinyurl.com/mvsvhmb6.

16. Witters, Dan. 2019. "Millions in U.S. Lost Someone Who Couldn't Afford Treatment." Gallup. https://news.gallup.com/poll/268094/millions-lost-someone-couldn-afford-treatment.aspx.

17. Sparks, Grace, Ashley Kirzinger, Alex Montero, Isabelle Valdes, and Liz Hamel. 2024. "Public Opinion on Prescription Drugs and Their Prices." KFF. www.kff.org/health-costs/poll-finding/public-opinion-on-prescription-drugs-and-their-prices.

18. Neighmond, Patti. "When Insurance Won't Cover Drugs, Americans Make 'Tough Choices' about Their Health." NPR, January 27, 2020. https://tinyurl.com/4musnrye.

19. Sparks, Kirzinger, Montero, Valdes, and Hamel. "Public Opinion on Prescription Drugs and Their Prices."

20. Patti. "When Insurance Won't Cover Drugs, Americans Make 'Tough Choices' about Health."

21. Pfeffer, Jeffrey, Dan Witters, Sangeeta Agrawal, and James K. Harter. 2020. "Magnitude and Effects of 'Sludge' in Benefits Administration: How Health Insurance Hassles Burden Workers and Cost Employers." *Academy of Management Discoveries* 6(3): 1–16.

22. This distribution of denied medical services does not, however, inform us of the denominator – that is, the frequency with which respondents *pursued* such services in the first place. I cannot from these data decipher the extent to which respondents pursued prescription drug care (or specialist care or mental health care) and were covered versus denied.

23. Pecci, Alexandra Wilson. "UnitedHealthcare Will Deny or Limit Coverage for ED Commercial Claims It Considers Non-emergent." *Health Leaders*, June 4, 2021. https://tinyurl.com/444k2yt2.

24. Lazarus, David. "Our Top Private Health Insurer Is Rolling in Cash. And It's Reducing Coverage." *Los Angeles Times*, July 20, 2021. www.latimes.com/business/story/2021-07-20/column-healthcare-insurance-unitedhealthcare.

25. Freeman, Liz. "UnitedHealthcare's New ER Policy Called 'Dangerous.' It Says as Many as 1 in 10 Claims Could Be Rejected." *Naples News*, June 10, 2021. https://tinyurl.com/yc5yyhtb. See also Deam, Jenny. "Unneeded ER Visits Cost Nation's Healthcare $32 Billion Last Year." *The Houston Chronicle*, July 24, 2019. www.chron.com/business/article/Unneeded-ER-visits-cost-nation-s-healthcare-32-14119665.php.

26. American Hospital Association. "UnitedHealthcare Delays Emergency Department Coverage Policy." June 10, 2021. https://tinyurl.com/3rdpv6um.

27. Office of US Senator Claire McCaskill. 2018. "Coverage Denied: Anthem Blue Cross Blue Shield's Emergency Room Initiative." Report. No longer available online, but discussed in https://tinyurl.com/myy2bh5r.

28. Ibid.

29. Ibid.

30. US Food and Drug Administration. 2019. "Appropriate Use." https://tinyurl.com/34bdv6b5.

31. Shrank, William, Teresa Rogstad, and Natasha Parekh. 2019. "Waste in the U.S. Health Care System: Estimated Costs and Potential for Savings." *Journal of the American Medical Association* 322(15): 1501–1509.

32. Jacobs, Josephine, Jeffrey Jarvik, Roger Cho et al. 2020. "Observational Study of the Downstream Consequences of Inappropriate MRI of the Lumbar Spine." *Journal of General Internal Medicine* 35: 3605–3612.

33. Mukkamala, Leyka, Sabina L. Schaffer, Matthew G. Weber, Jeffrey M. Wilde, and Adam S. Rosen. 2024. "Is Magnetic Resonance Imaging Overused among Patients Undergoing Total Knee Arthroplasty?" *Journal of the American Academy of Orthopaedic Surgeons Global Research Review* 8(10): e24.00258.

34. Lee, David and Frank Levy. 2012. "The Sharp Slowdown in Growth of Medical Imaging: An Early Analysis Suggests Combination of Policies Was the Cause." *Health Affairs* 31(8): 1876–1884.

35. *Federal Register* Vol. 87, No. 09, January 13, 2022. www.govinfo.gov/content/pkg/FR-2022-01-13/pdf/2022-00572.pdf.

36. Office of the Inspector General, Department of Health and Human Services. 2022. *Some Medicare Advantage Organization Denials of Prior Authorization Requests Raise Concerns about Beneficiary Access to Medically Necessary Care.* Report. https://tinyurl.com/3jmhhr9m.

37. Interview with Dr. Gabe Charbonneau, May 30, 2022.

38. Mount Sinai Hospital. "Eustachian Tube Balloon Dilation." www.mountsinai.org/care/ent/services/nasal-sinus-allergy/eustachian-tube.

39. Office of Management and Budget. 2024. *Tackling the Time Tax: Making Important Government Benefits and Programs Easier to Access.* https://tinyurl.com/2wdwckec.

40. Saslow, Linda. "When Insurers Deem That Surgery Is Purely Cosmetic." *The New York Times,* November 23, 1997. www.nytimes.com/1997/11/23/nyregion/when-insurers-deem-that-surgery-is-purely-cosmetic.html.

41. Appleby, Julie. "Dropped from Health Insurance without Warning: Was It Legal?" Kaiser Health News, June 5, 2019. https://kffhealthnews.org/news/dropped-from-health-insurance-without-warning-was-it-legal.

42. Ollove, Michael. "Many Medicaid Recipients Could Lose Coverage as Pandemic Ends." Pew Trusts, March 14, 2022. https://tinyurl.com/362c5pma.

43. Sommers, Benjamin, Anna Goldman, Robert Blendon, John Orav, and Arnold Epstein. 2019. "Medicaid Work Requirements – Results from the First Year in Arkansas." *New England Journal of Medicine* 381: 1073–1082.

44. Herd, Pamela and Donald Moynihan. 2018. *Administrative Burden: Policymaking by Other Means.* New York, NY: Russell Sage Foundation.

45. Mayo Clinic. 2024. "Supraventricular Tachycardia." https://tinyurl.com/3ayxutxv.

46. Blue Cross Community Health Plans in Illinois denied 14 percent of physical health claims in 2023, while a whopping 47 percent of pharmaceutical prior authorizations were denied. Just 5 percent of physical health-related prior authorization denials were appealed, yielding a 44 percent reversal rate. In 2023 in Oregon, 11 percent of prior authorizations were denied, also yielding a low 5 percent appeal rate. However, in this case just 20 percent of appeals resulted in reversal of the initial denial.

47. This attention to claims is substantially higher than that reported by *ProPublica* in its investigation of Cigna, the computer program of which facilitated the bulk denial of claims in a matter of seconds. Rucker, Patrick and David Armstrong. "A Doctor at Cigna Said Her Bosses Pressured Her to Review Patients' Cases Too Quickly. Cigna Threatened to Fire Her." *ProPublica,* April 29, 2024. https://tinyurl.com/2ds45n4p.

48. Office of the Inspector General. 2023. "AmeriGroup Iowa's Prior Authorization and Appeal Processes Were Effective, but Improvements Can Be Made." Report. https://tinyurl.com/mryfvsxt.

49. Ibid.

50. First-trimester ultrasound scans are not required for all pregnancies to confirm viability. Lee W. A., G. Nelson, V. Lala, and S. P. Grogan. 2025. *Sonography 1st Trimester Assessment, Protocols, and Interpretation.* Treasure Island, FL: StatPearls.

51. Brownlee, Shannon. 2007. *Overtreated: Why Too Much Medicine Is Making Us Sicker and Poorer.* New York, NY: Bloomsbury Press.

52. Emanuel, Ezekiel and Victor Fuchs. 2020. "The Perfect Storm of Overutilization." *Journal of the American Medical Association* 299(23): 2789–2791.

53. Rosenthal, Elizabeth. 2017. *An American Sickness: How Healthcare Became Big Business and How You Can Take It Back.* New York, NY: Penguin Books, p. 149.

54. Berlin, Leonard. 2017. "Medical Errors, Malpractice, and Defensive Medicine: An Ill-Fated Triad." *Diagnosis* 4(3): 133–139.

55. Sloan, Frank and John Shadle. 2009. "Is There Empirical Evidence for 'Defensive Medicine'? A Reassessment." *Journal of Health Economics* 28(2): 481–491.

56. Studdert, David, Michelle Mello, William Sage et al. 2005. "Defensive Medicine among High-Risk Specialist Physicians in a Volatile Malpractice Environment." *Journal of the American Medical Association* 93(21): 2609–2617.

57. Rosenthal. *An American Sickness*, p. 139.

58. Ibid., p. 151.

59. Garber, Judith. "Do Rich Patients Get Better Care, or Just More Care?" Lown Institute Blog Post, July 12, 2024. https://tinyurl.com/nhekmuzm.

60. Welch, H. Gilbert and Elliott Fisher. 2017. "Income and Cancer Overdiagnosis – When Too Much Care Is Harmful." *New England Journal of Medicine* 376: 2208–2209.

61. Lyu, Heather, Tim Xu, Daniel Brotman et al. 2017. "Overtreatment in the United States." *PLOS One* 12(9): 1–11.

62. Lapook, Jon. "Too Many Unnecessary MRIs and CT Scans?" *CBS News*, September 24, 2009. www.cbsnews.com/news/too-many-unnecessary-mris-and-ct-scans.

63. Patashnik, Eric, Alan Gerber, and Conor Dowling. 2017. *Unhealthy Politics: The Battle over Evidence-Based Medicine*. Princeton, NJ: Princeton University Press, p. 2.

64. Ibid.

65. Shmerling, Robert. 2020. "Knee Arthroscopy: Should This Common Knee Surgery Be Performed Less Often?" Harvard Health Blog. https://tinyurl.com/v5d254dy.

66. Patashnik, Eric. 2020. "Comparatively Ineffective?: PCORI and the Uphill Battle to Make Evidence Count in US Medicine." *Journal of Health Politics, Policy, and Law* 45(5): 787–800.

67. Gerber, Alan, Eric Patashnik, David Doherty, and Conor Dowling. 2014. "Doctor Knows Best: Physician Endorsements, Public Opinion, and the Politics of Comparative Effectiveness Research." *Journal of Health Politics, Policy, and Law* 39(1): 171–208.

68. Patashnik, Eric, Alan Gerber, and Conor Dowling. 2017. *Unhealthy Politics: The Battle over Evidence-Based Medicine*. Princeton, NJ: Princeton University Press.

69. Interview with Wendell Potter, June 28, 2022.

70. Interview with Dr. Tauseef Ali, May 30, 2022.

71. Kotzan, Jeffrey, Matthew Perri, and Bradley Martin. 1996. "Assessment of Medicaid Prior-Approval Policies on Prescription Expenditures: Market-Share Analysis of Medicaid and Cash Prescriptions." *Journal of Managed Care Pharmacy* 2(6): 651–656.

72. Moody, Katherine. 2016. "Survey: Consumers Switch Health Plans Often." Fierce Healthcare. www.fiercehealthcare.com/payer/survey-consumers-switch-health-plans-often.

73. Finn Partners. "Finn Partners National Survey Reveals How Fragmented Health System Places Greater Burden on Patients." February 9, 2016. https://tinyurl.com/ysp7572y.

74. Short, Pamela Farley, Deborah Graefe, and Cathy Schoen. "Churn, Churn, Churn: How Instability of Health Insurance Shapes America's Uninsured Problem." The Commonwealth Fund Issue Brief, November 2003. https://tinyurl.com/4ts2dk6d.

75. Milligan, Charles. 2015. "From Coverage to Care: Addressing the Issue of Churn." *Journal of Health Politics, Policy, and Law* 40(1): 227–232.

CHAPTER 3: WHOSE COVERAGE IS DENIED?

1. National Organization for Rare Diseases. "Syringomyelia." https://rarediseases.org/rare-diseases/syringomyelia.

2. Norris, Louise. 2025. "Women, Health Insurance, and the Affordable Care Act: The ACA Delivers a Long List of Reforms to Remedy Gender Inequality in Individual Health Insurance Market." www.healthinsurance.org/obamacare/women-and-health-insurance.

3. UCSF Health. "High-Risk Pregnancy." www.ucsfhealth.org/conditions/high-risk-pregnancy.

4. Palanker, Dania and Karen Davenport. "Women's Health Coverage since the ACA: Improvements for Most, but Insurer Exclusions Put Many at Risk." The Commonwealth Fund Issue Brief, August 2, 2016. https://tinyurl.com/2hcrfz8b.

5. Lee, William, Grant Nelson, and Scott Grogan. 2021. "Sonography 1st Trimester Assessment, Protocols, and Interpretation." StatPearls. www.ncbi.nlm.nih.gov/books/NBK573070.

6. Lee, Jusung, Krista Howard, Caleb Leong, Timothy Grigsby, and Jeffrey Howard. 2023. "Beyond Being Insured: Insurance Coverage Denial as a Major Barrier to Accessing Care during Pregnancy and Postpartum." *Clinical Nursing Research* 32(8): 1092–1103.

7. Hoyert, Donna. "Maternal Mortality Rates in the United States – 2021." Centers for Disease Control and Prevention. Report, March 2023. www.cdc.gov/nchs/data/hestat/maternal-mortality/2021/maternal-mortality-rates-2021.htm.

8. Department of Health and Human Services Office of Disease Prevention and Health Promotion. "Health Literacy." https://odphp.health.gov/our-work/national-health-initiatives/health-literacy.

9. Ibid.

10. Williams, Mark, Ruth Parker, David Baker et al. 1995. "Inadequate Functional Health Literacy among Patients at Two Public Hospitals." *Journal of the American Medical Association* 274(21): 1677–1682.

11. Kutner, M, E. Greenburg, Y. Jin, and C. Paulsen. 2006. "The Health Literacy of America's Adults: Results from the 2003 National Assessment of Adult Literacy." National Center for Education Statistics; Report NCES 2006-483. https://nces.ed.gov/pubs2006/2006483.pdf.

12. Levy, Helen and Alex Janke. 2016. "Health Literacy and Access to Care." *Journal of Health Communication* 21(1): 43–50.

13. Brice, Jane, Debbie Travers, Christopher Cowden, Matthew Young, Antonio Sanhueza, and Yolanda Dunston. 2008. "Health Literacy among Spanish-Speaking Patients in the Emergency Department." *Journal of the National Medical Association* 100(11): 1326–1332.

14. Timmins, Caraway. 2002. "The Impact of Language Barriers on the Health Care of Latinos in the United States: A Review of the Literature and Guidelines for Practice." *Journal of Midwifery & Women's Health* 47(2): 80–96.

15. *Bostock v. Clayton County* (2020) held that prohibitions against sex discrimination under Title VII of the Civil Rights Act of 1964 extended to the LGBT community. This logic was subsequently extended by the Biden Administration to other policy realms including health.

16. Kates, Jennifer, Usha Ranju, Adara Beamesderfer, Alina Salganicoff, and Lindsey Dawson. 2018. "Health and Access to Care and Coverage for Lesbian, Gay, Bisexual, and Transgender (LGBT) Individuals in the U.S." KFF. https://tinyurl.com/ymsbh33p.

17. See also Dahlhamer, James, Adena Galinsky, Sarah Joestl, and Brian Ward. 2016. "Barriers to Health Care among Adults Identifying as Sexual Minorities: A US National Study." *American Journal of Public Health* 106(6): 1116–1122.

18. Gillespie, Lisa. "Transgender People Still Denied Health Services Despite Affordable Care Act." PBS, July 23, 2015. https://tinyurl.com/4v6an9e7.

19. Padula, William and Kellan Baker. 2017. "Coverage for Gender-Affirming Care: Making Health Insurance Work for Transgender Americans." *LGBT Health* 4(4): 244–247.

20. Dubov, Alex and Liana Fraenkel. 2018. "Facial Feminization Surgery: The Ethics of Gatekeeping in Transgender Health." *The American Journal of Bioethics* 18(12): 3–9.

21. Fitzsimmons, Tim. "PrEP Use Jumps to 35 Percent among Gay and Bi Men at risk of HIV." *NBC News*, March 7, 2019. www.nbcnews.com/feature/nbc-out/prep-use-jumps-35-percent-among-gay-bi-men-risk-n980516.

22. Dawson, Lindsey, Brittni Fredericksen, and Michelle Long. 2023. "Mental Health Care Needs and Experiences among LGBT+ People." KFF. https://tinyurl.com/34suds7k.

23. Jones, Laney, Ilene Ladd, Michael Gioinfriddo, Christina Gregor, Michael Evans, and Jove Graham. 2020. "Medications Requiring Prior Authorization across Health Insurance Plans." *American Journal of Health System Pharmacy* 77(8): 644–648.

24. Park, Sungchul and Rishi Wadhera. 2024. "Use of High- and Low-Value Health Care among US Adults, by Income, 2010–19." *Health Affairs* 43(7): 1021–1031.

25. Burstin, Helen, William Johnson, Stuart Lipsitz, and Troyen Brennan. 1993. "Do the Poor Sue More? A Case–Control Study of Malpractice Claims and Socioeconomic Status." *Journal of the American Medical Association* 270(14): 1697–1701.

26. Pollitz, Karen, Kaye Pestaina, Lunna Lopes, Rayna Wallace, and Justin Lo. 2023. "Consumer Survey Highlights Problems with Denied Insurance Claims." KFF. https://tinyurl.com/y6jhh4rj.

27. Centers for Disease Control and Prevention. 2024. "Chronic Disease Prevalence in the US." www.cdc.gov/pcd/issues/2024/23_0267.htm.

28. Georgetown University Health Policy Institute. Undated. "Prescription Drugs." https://hpi.georgetown.edu/rxdrugs.

CHAPTER 4: PRESCRIPTIONS ARE A HEADACHE

1. American Migraine Foundation. 2021. "What Is Migraine?" https://americanmigrainefoundation.org/resource-library/what-is-migraine.

2. American Migraine Foundation. 2020. "How to Apply for Social Security Disability Insurance with Migraine." https://americanmigrainefoundation.org/resource-library/ssdi-migraine.

3. Interview with Dr. Courtney White, June 15, 2022.

4. Lardieri, Alexa. "FDA Approves First Drug to Prevent Migraines." *US News and World Report*, May 18, 2018. https://tinyurl.com/etk4k4ba.

5. Melillo, Gianna. 2022. "Examining Trends in Headache-Related ED Visits, Treatment." AJMC. www.ajmc.com/view/examining-trends-in-headache-related-ed-visits-treatment.

6. Ling, Yu-Hsiang, Debashish Chowdhury, and Shuu-Jiun Wang. 2024. "Treatment in the Emergency Department." *Handbook of Clinical Neurology* 199: 245–256.

7. US Food and Drug Administration. 2023. "Office of Generic Drugs 2022 Annual Report." www.fda.gov/drugs/generic-drugs/office-generic-drugs-2022-annual-report.

8. Jones, Lindsey, Carol Estwing Ferrans, Blase Polite et al. 2017. "Examining Racial Disparities in Colon Cancer Clinical Delay in the Colon Cancer Patterns of Care in Chicago Study." *Annals of Epidemiology* 27(11): 731–738.

9. Centers for Disease Control and Prevention. 2020. "Antidepressant Use among Adults: United States, 2015–2018." https://tinyurl.com/594xuyw8.

10. Centers for Disease Control and Prevention. 2024. "National Diabetes Statistics Report." www.cdc.gov/diabetes/php/data-research/index.html.

11. Katella, Kathy. "Should You Take a Statin for Your High Cholesterol?" Yale Medicine, January 22, 2024. www.yalemedicine.org/news/should-you-take-a-statin-for-high-cholesterol.

12. American Medical Association. 2011. "Standardization of Prior Authorization for Medical Services White Paper." https://dl.icdst.org/pdfs/files4/2fb4f9cb072236bd21f24851ddac7e6c.pdf.

13. Resneck, Jack. 2020. "Refocusing Medication Prior Authorization on Its Intended Purpose." *Journal of the American Medical Association* 323(8): 703–704.

14. Lu, Christine, Stephen Soumerai, Dennis Ross-Degnan, Fang Zhang, and Alyce Adams. 2010. "Unintended Impacts of a Medicaid Prior Authorization Policy on Access to Medications for Bipolar Illness." *Medical Care* 48(1): 4–9.

15. Kyle, Michael Ann and Nancy L. Keating. 2023. "Prior Authorization and Association with Delayed or Discontinued Prescription Refills." *Journal of Clinical Oncology* 42(8): 951–960.

16. Bergeson, Joette Gdovin, Karen Worley, Anthony Louder, Melea Ward, and John Graham. 2013. "Retrospective Database Analysis of the Impact of Prior Authorization for Type 2 Diabetes Medications on Health Care Costs in a Medicare Advantage Prescription Drug Plan Population." *Journal of Managed Care Pharmacy* 19(5): 374–384.

17. Seabury, Seth, Dana P. Goldman, Iftekhar Kalsekar, John J. Sheehan, Kimberly Laubmeier, and Darius N. Lakdawalla. 2014. "Formulary Restrictions on Atypical

Antipsychotics: Impact on Costs for Patients with Schizophrenia and Bipolar Disorder in Medicaid." *American Journal of Managed Care* 20(2): 52–60.

18. Interview with Wendell Potter, June 28, 2022.

19. Safer, Daniel. 2019. "Overprescribed Medications for US Adults: Four Major Examples." *Journal of Clinical Medical Research* 11(9): 617–622.

20. Huskamp, Haiden, Arnold Epstein, and David Blumenthal. 2003. "The Impact of a National Prescription Drug Formulary on Prices, Market Share, and Spending: Lessons for Medicare?" *Health Affairs* 22(3): 149–158.

21. US Pharmacopeia. 2020. "Building Trust for Over 200 Years: A Timeline of USP." www .usp.org/200-anniversary/usp-timeline.

22. Gondeck, Kathleen. 1994. "Prescription Drug Payment Policy: Past, Present, and Future." *Health Care Financial Review* 15(3): 1–7.

23. AARP. 1999. *Administration on Aging: A Profile of Older Americans.* Washington, D.C.: AARP.

24. Werble, Cole. 2017. "Formularies." *Health Affairs* Health Policy Brief Series. https:// tinyurl.com/mfbmn3te.

25. Ibid.

26. Interview with Wendell Potter, June 28, 2022.

27. Interview with Dr. Russell Buhr, June 6, 2022.

28. American Medical Association. 2025. "2024 AMA Prior Authorization Physician Survey." www.ama-assn.org/system/files/prior-authorization-survey.pdf.

29. Regulatory Relief Coalition. 2019. "Prior Authorization Is Putting Patients at Risk and Increasing Physician Burden." https://tinyurl.com/knaskzx2.

30. Interview with Dr. Russell Buhr, June 6, 2022.

31. Commonwealth Fund. 2019. "Pharmacy Benefit Managers and Their Role in Drug Spending." www.commonwealthfund.org/sites/default/files/2019-04/Explainer_ PBMs_1.pdf.

32. Seeley, Elizabeth and Aaron Kesselheim. 2019. "Pharmacy Benefit Managers: Practices, Controversies, and What Lies Ahead." The Commonwealth Fund Issue Brief. https:// tinyurl.com/48y4tkjm.

33. Bean, Mackenzie. "PBMs Ranked by Market Share: CVS Caremark Is No. 1." *Becker's Hospital Review*, March 8, 2022. www.beckershospitalreview.com/pharmacy/ pbms-ranked-by-market-share-cvs-caremark-is-no-1.

34. National Association of Insurance Commissioners. 2022. "Pharmacy Benefit Managers." https://tinyurl.com/47t5jfff.

35. Seeley and Kesselheim. "Pharmacy Benefit Managers."

36. Potter, Wendell. "Big Insurance 2022: Revenues Reached $1.25 Trillion Thanks to Sucking Billions Out of the Pharmacy Supply Chain – and Taxpayers' Pockets." Substack, February 27, 2023. https://healthcareuncovered.substack.com/p/ big-insurance-2022-revenues-reached.

37. Lenahan, Kelly L., Donald E. Nichols, Rebecca M. Gertler, and James D. Chambers. 2021. "Variation in Use and Content of Prescription Drug Step Therapy Protocols, within and across Health Plans." *Health Affairs* 40(11): 1749–1757.

38. Ibid.

39. Fischer, Michael, Aaron Kesselheim, Zhigang Lu, Kathryn Ross, Frazer Tessema, and Jerry Avorn. 2019. "Physician Perceptions of Step Therapy Prescribing Requirements." *Journal of Managed Care & Specialty Pharmacy* 25(11): 1210–1224.

40. Sachs, Rachel and Michael Anne Kyle. 2022. "Step Therapy's Balancing Act – Protecting Patients While Addressing High Drug Prices." *New England Journal of Medicine* 386(10): 901–904.

41. Soumerai, Stephen B., Fang Zhang, Dennis Ross-Degnan et al. 2008. "Use of Atypical Antipsychotic Drugs for Schizophrenia in Maine Medicaid Following a Policy Change." *Health Affairs* 27(3): 185–195.

42. Interview with Dr. Courtney White, June 15, 2022.

43. Interview with Dr. Andrew Spector, June 9, 2022.

44. Tharp, Louis and Zoe Rothblatt. 2022. "Do Patients Benefit from Legislation Regulating Step Therapy?" *Health Economics, Policy, and Law* 17(3): 282–297.

45. Wittich, Christopher, Christopher Burkle, and William Lanier. 2012. "Ten Common Questions (and Their Answers) about Off-Label Drug Use." *Mayo Clinic Proceedings* 87(10): 982–990.

46. Radley, David, Stan Finkelstein, and Randall Stafford. 2006. "Off-Label Prescribing among Office-Based Physicians." *Journal of the American Medical Association Internal Medicine* 166(9): 1021–1026.

47. Ibid.

48. Wittich, Burkle, and Lanier. "Ten Common Questions (and Their Answers) about Off-Label Drug Use."

49. Ladanie, Aviv, John Ioannidis, Randall Stafford, Hannah Ewald, Heiner Bucher, and Lars Hemkens. 2018. "Off-Label Treatments Were Not Consistently Better or Worse Than Approved Drug Treatments in Randomized Trials." *Journal of Clinical Epidemiology* 94: 35–45.

50. Wittich, Burkle, and Lanier. "Ten Common Questions (and Their Answers) about Off-Label Drug Use."

51. Henry, Veronica. 1999. "Off-Label Prescribing: Legal Implications." *The Journal of Legal Medicine* 20: 365–383.

52. Interview with Dr. Andrew Spector, June 9, 2022.

53. Inserro, Allison. "How Prior Authorization Can Impact Patients with Rare Disease." *American Journal of Managed Care*, February 28, 2022. www.ajmc.com/view/how-prior-authorization-can-impact-patients-with-rare-disease.

54. Bronstein, Max, Emil Kakkis, David Fajgenbaum, and Chip Chambers. 2017. "For Rare Disease Patients, a Pathway to Hundreds of New Therapies." Health Affairs Blog. www.healthaffairs.org/content/forefront/rare-disease-patients-pathway-hundreds-new-therapies.

55. National Institutes of Health. 2025. "Rare Diseases." www.nih.gov/about-nih/nih-turning-discovery-into-health/promise-precision-medicine/rare-diseases.

56. Assistant Secretary for Technology Policy. 2019. "Hospitals Use of Electronic Health Records Data, 2015–2017." Data Brief No. 46. www.healthit.gov/sites/default/files/page/2019-04/AHAEHRUseDataBrief.pdf.

57. Jiang, John, Kangkang Qi, Ge Bai, and Kevin Schulman. 2023. "Pre-pandemic Assessment: A Decade of Progress in Electronic Health Record Adoption among U.S. Hospitals." *Health Affairs Scholar* 1(5): qxad056.

58. Klebanoff, Matthew J., Pengxiang Li, Paula Chatterjee, and Jalpa A. Doshi. 2024. "Real-Time Prescription Benefit Tool Adoption among US Hospitals." *Journal of the American Medical Association Health Forum* 5(10): e243181.

59. Finnegan, Joanne. "More Medical Services Now Require Prior Authorizations, According to Physicians." Fierce Healthcare, January 28, 2020. https://tinyurl.com/2kdm7m27.

60. Georgetown University Health Policy Institute. "Prescription Drugs." https://hpi.georgetown.edu/rxdrugs.

61. Mayo Clinic. "Menorrhagia (Heavy Menstrual Bleeding)." www.mayoclinic.org/diseases-conditions/menorrhagia/symptoms-causes/syc-20352829.

62. Department of Labor. 2024. "FAQs about Affordable Care Act Implementation Part 64." www.dol.gov/agencies/ebsa/about-ebsa/our-activities/resource-center/faqs/aca-part-64.

63. Juvenile Diabetes Research Foundation. "Type 1 Diabetes Facts." www.breakthrought1d.org/wp-content/uploads/2023/06/T1D-Facts-One-Pager_2023.pdf.

64. MedlinePlus. "Crohn disease." https://medlineplus.gov/crohnsdisease.html.

65. Stelara. 2022. "How Much Should I Expect to Pay for STELARA?" www.stelarainfo.com/crohns-disease/cost-support-and-more.

66. OECD. 2021. "Pharmaceutical Spending." www.oecd.org/en/data/indicators/pharmaceutical-spending.html.

67. "Prescription Drug Prices in the United States Are 2.56 Times Those in Other Countries." RAND Corporation, January 28, 2021. www.rand.org/news/press/2021/01/28.html.

CHAPTER 5: COVERAGE DENIALS AND COST SHIFTING TO PATIENTS

1. ZERO: The End of Prostate Cancer. "African Americans and Prostate Cancer." https://zerocancer.org/black-men.

2. Interview with Dr. Daniel Block, August 15, 2022.

3. American Medical Association. 2025. "2024 AMA Prior Authorization Physician Survey." www.ama-assn.org/system/files/prior-authorization-survey.pdf.

4. Reinicke, Carmen. "56% of Americans Can't Cover a $1,000 Emergency Expense with Savings." *CNBC*, January 19, 2022. https://tinyurl.com/muu3j9zb.

5. Smolderen, Kim, John Spertus, Brahmajee Nallamothu et al. 2010. "Health Care Insurance, Financial Concerns in Accessing Care, and Delays to Hospital Presentation in Acute Myocardial Infarction." *Journal of the American Medical Association* 303(14): 1392–1400.

6. Ifidu, Onyekachi, Mohammed Dawood, Yakov Iofel, Jean Valcourt, and Eli Friedman. 1999. *American Journal of Kidney Diseases* 33(4): 728–733.

7. Fadewa, Stacey, Stephen Edge, Andrew Stewart, Michael Halpern, Nicole Marlow, and Elizabeth Ward. 2011. *Journal of Health Care for the Poor and Underserved* 22(1): 128–141.

8. Jones, Lindsey, Carol Estwing Ferrans, Blase Polite et al. 2017. "Examining Racial Disparities in Colon Cancer Clinical Delay in the Colon Cancer Patterns of Care in Chicago Study." *Annals of Epidemiology* 27(11): 731–738.

9. Marinac, Catherine R., Irene M. Ghobrial, Brenda M. Birmann, Jenny Soiffer, and Timothy R. Rebbeck. 2020. "Dissecting Racial Disparities in Multiple Myeloma." *Blood Cancer Journal* 10(19): 1–8.

10. Ibid.

11. Wolstein, Joelle, Shana Charles, Susan Babey, and Allison L. Diamant. 2018. "Disparities in Health Care Access and Health among Lesbians, Gay Men, and Bisexuals in California." Policy Brief. https://healthpolicy.ucla.edu/sites/default/files/legacy/Documents/PDF/2018/lgb-brief-oct2018.pdf.

12. Babey, Susan, Joelle Wolstein, Jody Herman, and Bianca Wilson. 2022. "Gaps in Health Care Access and Health Insurance among LGBT Populations in California." Policy Brief. https://williamsinstitute.law.ucla.edu/publications/gaps-health-care-lgbt-ca.

13. Padula, William and Kellan Baker. 2017. "Coverage for Gender-Affirming Care: Making Health Insurance Work for Transgender Americans." *LGBT Health* 4(4): 244–247.

14. Center on Budget and Policy Priorities. 2020. "The Far-Reaching Benefits of the Affordable Care Act's Medicaid Expansion." Report. https://tinyurl.com/y7nshf9v.

15. Schwartz, Diane, Adil Shah, Cheryl Zogg et al. 2015. "Operative Delay to Laparoscopic Cholecystectomy." *Journal of Trauma and Acute Care Surgery* 79(1): 15–21.

16. Haque, Lamiah Anne. 2021. "The Effect of Delays in Acute Medical Treatment on Total Cost and Potential Ramifications Due to the Coronavirus Pandemic." *Harvard Public Health Review* 26. https://bcphr.org/26-article-haque.

17. Gallegos, Alicia. "Insurer Delays Prior Authorization, Patient Loses Leg and Pelvis, Then Dies." *Medscape Medical News,* July 1, 2022. www.medscape.com/viewarticle/976486.

18. Ibid.

19. Nelson, Roxanne. "Prior Authorization Is 'Significant Barrier' in Cancer Care." *Medscape News,* June 14, 2022. www.medscape.com/viewarticle/975560.

20. Cardinal Health Specialty Solutions. "Oncology Insights." June 2022 Report. https://tinyurl.com/2mj5f78u.

21. Gottlieb, Scott. 2000. "Medical Bills Account for 40% of Bankruptcies." *British Medical Journal* 320(7245): 1295.

22. KFF. 2022. "1 in 10 Adults Owe Medical Debt, with Millions Owing More Than $10,000." https://tinyurl.com/m26mzzwx.

23. Consumer Financial Protection Bureau. 2022. "CFPB Estimates $88 Billion in Medical Bills on Credit Reports." https://tinyurl.com/yffbp2vu.

24. Miller, Sarah, Luojia Hu, Robert Kaestner, Bhashkar Mazumder, and Ashley Wong. 2020. "The ACA Medicaid Expansion in Michigan and Financial Health." *The Journal of Policy Analysis and Management* 40(2): 348–375.

25. Romo, Vanessa. 2025. "The CFPB Wanted Medical Debt to Be Left Off Credit Reports. That's Changed under Trump." NPR Morning Edition, www.npr.org/2025/05/26/nx-s1-5406799/cfpbs-medical-debt-credit-report-lawsuit.

26. Schneider, Daniel, Peter Tufano, and Annamaria Lusardi. 2020. "Household Financial Fragility during COVID-19: Rising Inequality and Unemployment Insurance Benefit Reductions." NBER Working Paper. https://scholar.harvard.edu/files/dschneider/files/finfrag_workingpaper_103020.pdf.

27. Francis, Marquis. "Rising Costs Force Millions of Americans to Choose between Paying Health Care and Utility Bills." *Yahoo News*, August 31, 2022. https://tinyurl.com/yc89tnje.

CHAPTER 6: NAVIGATING RED TAPE IN MODERN MEDICINE

1. Interview with Dr. Molly Weber, June 9, 2022.

2. Lo, Justin, Michelle Long, Rayna Wallace, Meghan Salaga, and Kaye Pestaina. 2025. "Claim Denials and Appeals in ACA Marketplace Plans in 2023." KFF. www.kff.org/private-insurance/issue-brief/claims-denials-and-appeals-in-aca-marketplace-plans-in-2023.

3. Biniek, Jeannie Fuglesten, Nolan Srczynski, Meredith Freed, and Tricia Neuman. 2025. "Medicare Advantage Insurers Made Nearly 50 Million Prior Authorization Determinations in 2023." KFF. https://tinyurl.com/58xkhvvp.

4. Ibid.

5. Masood, Ayesha and Muhammad Azfar Nisar. 2021. "Administrative Capital and Citizens' Responses to Administrative Burden." *Journal of Public Administration Research and Theory* 31(1): 56–72.

6. American Medical Association. 2024. www.ama-assn.org/system/files/prior-authoriza tion-state-law-chart.pdf.

7. Robeznieks, Andis. 2021. "How to Make Peer-to-Peer Prior Authorization Talks More Effective." American Medical Association. https://tinyurl.com/2ph87eun.

8. Interview with Dr. Andrew Spector, June 9, 2022.

9. Interview with Dr. Russell Buhr, June 6, 2022.

10. Interview with Dr. Tom Wallach, June 13, 2022.

11. Freed, Meredith, Jeannie Fuglesten Biniek, Anthony Damico, and Tricia Neuman. 2024. "Medicare Advantage in 2024: Premiums, Out-of-Pocket Limits, Supplemental Benefits, and Prior Authorization." KFF. https://tinyurl.com/3fve3e59.

12. National Council on Aging. 2025. "Mental Illness and Older Adults: What to Know about Symptoms and Treatment." www.ncoa.org/article/mental-illness-and-older-adults-what-to-know-about-symptoms-and-treatment.

13. American Medical Association. 2025. "AMA Prior Authorization (PA) Physician Survey." www.ama-assn.org/system/files/prior-authorization-survey.pdf.

14. Dunn, Abe, Joshua Gottlieb, Adam Shapiro, Daniel Sonnenstuhl, and Pietro Tebaldi. 2021. "A Denial a Day Keeps the Doctor Away." NBER Working Paper. www.nber.org/papers/w29010.

15. Interview with Dr. Andrew Spector, June 9, 2022.

16. Council for Affordable Quality Healthcare. 2024. "2023 CAQH Index Report." www
.caqh.org/hubfs/43908627/drupal/2024-01/2023_CAQH_Index_Report.pdf.

17. American Medical Association. "AMA Prior Authorization (PA) Physician Survey."

18. Medical Economics Staff. 2019. "90th Annual Physician Report." *Medical Economics Journal* 96(8): 10–23.

19. American Medical Association. "AMA Prior Authorization (PA) Physician Survey."

20. Busis, Neil, Babar Khokhar, and Brian Callaghan. 2024. "Streamlining Prior Authorization to Improve Care." *Journal of the American Medical Association Neurology* 81(1): 5–6.

21. Interview with Dr. Andrew Spector, June 9, 2022.

22. Interview with Dr. Russell Buhr, June 6, 2022.

23. Interview with Dr. Lauren Wilson, August 2, 2022.

24. Council for Affordable Quality Healthcare. "2023 CAQH Index Report."

25. Ernst, Claire. "Prior Authorization Burdens for Healthcare Providers Still Growing during COVID-19 Pandemic." Medical Group Management Association, May 19, 2021. https://tinyurl.com/59cktns3.

26. Ibid.

27. Interview with Dr. Russell Buhr, June 6, 2022.

28. Cardinal Health Specialty Solutions. 2022. "Oncology Insights." June 2022 Report. https://tinyurl.com/2mj5f78u.

29. Rodbard, David. 2017. "Continuous Glucose Monitoring: A Review of Recent Studies Demonstrating Improved Glycemic Options." *Diabetes Technology and Therapy* 19(Suppl. 3): S-25–S-37.

30. Interview with Dr. Daniel Block, August 15, 2022.

31. Verma, Seema. 2020. "Remarks by CMS Administrator Seema Verma at the American Medical Association National Advocacy Conference." https://tinyurl.com/3yyhju7b.

32. Noseworthy, John, James Madara, Delos Cosgrove, et al. 2017. "Physician Burnout Is a Public Health Crisis: A Message to Our Fellow Health Care CEOs." Health Affairs Forefront. https://tinyurl.com/53zpk8dc.

33. Harmon, Gerald. 2022. "A Recovery Plan for America's Physicians." https://tinyurl.com/yk2m96un.

CHAPTER 7: WHO WINS AND LOSES APPEALS

1. Lo, Justin, Michelle Long, Rayna Wallace, Meghan Salaga, and Kaye Pestaina. 2025. "Claim Denials and Appeals in ACA Marketplace Plans in 2023." KFF. https://tinyurl.com/nwnfa45r.

2. Bhargava, Juhi and Sreelakshmi Panginikkod. 2024. "Still's Disease." StatPearls. www.ncbi.nlm.nih.gov/books/NBK538345.

3. Bronstein, Max, Emil Kakkis, David Fajgenbaum, and Chip Chambers. 2017. "For Rare Disease Patients, a Pathway to Hundreds of New Therapies." Health Affairs Blog. https://www.healthaffairs.org/content/forefront/rare-disease-patients-pathway-hundreds-new-therapies.

4. Masood, Ayesha and Muhammad Azfar Nisar. 2021. "Administrative Capital and Citizens' Responses to Administrative Burden." *Journal of Public Administration Research and Theory* 31(1): 56–72.

5. Pfeffer, Jeffrey, Dan Witters, Sangeeta Agrawal, and James K. Harter. 2020. "Magnitude and Effects of 'Sludge' in Benefits Administration: How Health Insurance Hassles Burden Workers and Cost Employers." *Academy of Management Discoveries* 6(3): https://doi.org/10.5465/amd.2020.0063.

6. Ibid.

7. Elhauge, Einer. 2010. "Why We Should Care about Health Care Fragmentation and How to Fix It," in Einer R. Elhauge (ed.), *The Fragmentation of U.S. Health Care: Causes and Solutions*. New York, NY: Oxford University Press, pp. 1–20, p. 1.

8. Hyman, David. 2010. "Health Care Fragmentation: We Get What We Pay For," in Einer R. Elhauge (ed.), *The Fragmentation of U.S. Health Care: Causes and Solutions*. New York, NY: Oxford University Press, pp. 21–36.

9. Proficient health literacy was defined as being able to carry out activities such as searching documents to define medical terms and other relevant health information. The majority (53 percent) were estimated to have intermediate health literacy, while 36 percent were estimated to have basic or below basic health literacy.

10. Herd, Pamela and Donald Moynihan. 2018. *Administrative Burden: Policymaking by Other Means*. New York, NY: Russell Sage Foundation.

11. Kyle, Michael Anne and Austin Frakt. 2021. "Patient Administrative Burden in the US Health Care System." *Health Services Research* 56(5): 755–765.

12. Abaluck, Jason and Jonathan Gruber. 2011. "Choice Inconsistencies among the Elderly: Evidence from Plan Choice in the Medicare Part D Program." *American Economic Review* 101(June): 1180–1210.

13. Interview, January 6, 2025.

14. Abaluck and Gruber. "Choice Inconsistencies among the Elderly."

15. Safeer, Richard and Jann Kennan. 2005. "Health Literacy: The Gap between Physicians and Patients." *American Family Physician* 72(3): 463–468.

16. Herd, Pamela, Hilary Hoynes, Jamila Michener, and Donald Moynihan. 2023. "Introduction: Administrative Burden as a Mechanism of Inequality." *The Russell Sage Foundation Journal of the Social Sciences* 9(5): 1–30.

17. Bartolone, Pauline. "Patients Win About Half the Time They Challenge Denied Health Care Services." *Capital Public Radio*, April 1, 2014. https://tinyurl.com/4xrtpk76.

18. Government Accountability Office. 2011. "Private Health Insurance: Data on Application and Coverage Denials." Report to the Secretary of Health and Human Services and the Secretary of Labor. www.gao.gov/assets/gao-11-268.pdf.

19. Ibid.

20. Michener, Jamila. 2018. *Fragmented Democracy: Medicaid, Federalism, and Unequal Politics*. Princeton, NJ: Princeton University Press.

21. Ibid.

22. Six percent of respondents were unable to recall the length of the appeal process.

23. The Employee Retirement Income Security Act (ERISA) provides that, if one is wrongly denied coverage by an employee welfare benefit plan (i.e., a self-insured health plan), one may recover the benefit owed (e.g., the treatment) but may not recover monetary damages.

24. Lowrey, Annie. "The Time Tax: Why Is So Much American Bureaucracy Left to Average Citizens?" *The Atlantic*, July 27, 2021. https://tinyurl.com/35ynsrr7. See also, for instance, Elizabeth Cohen's finding within the context of democratic theory that political procedures use quantities of time as a mechanism to confer or deny citizenship rights. Cohen, Elizabeth. 2018. *The Political Value of Time: Citizenship, Duration, and Democratic Justice.* New York, NY: Cambridge University Press.

25. Galanter, Marc. 1974. "Why the 'Haves' Come Out Ahead: Speculations on the Limits of Legal Change." *Law & Society Review* 95(1): 95–160.

26. Herd, Hoynes, Michener, and Moynihan. "Introduction: Administrative Burden as a Mechanism of Inequality."

27. Office of the Inspector General, Department of Health and Human Services. 2018. "Medicare Advantage Appeal Outcomes and Audit Findings Raise Concerns about Service and Payment Denials." Report. https://oig.hhs.gov/documents/evaluation/3140/OEI-09-16-00410-Complete%20Report.pdf.

28. Ibid.

29. Ibid.

30. Ibid.

31. Biniek, Jeannie Fuglesten, Nolan Sroczynski, Meredith Freed, and Tricia Neuman. 2025. "Medicare Advantage Insurers Made Nearly 50 Million Prior Authorization Determinations in 2023." KFF. https://tinyurl.com/58xkhvvp.

32. See also Moynihan, Donald, Pamela Herd, and Hope Harvey. 2014. "Administrative Burden: Learning, Psychological, and Compliance Costs in Citizen–State Interactions." *Journal of Public Administration Research and Theory* 25(1): 43–69.

33. Masood, Ayesha and Muhammad Azfar Nisar. 2021. "Administrative Capital and Citizens' Responses to Administrative Burden." *Journal of Public Administration Research and Theory* 31(1): 56–72.

34. Michener. *Fragmented Democracy.*

35. Herd and Moynihan. *Administrative Burden.*

36. Cutilli, Carolyn Crane and Ian M. Bennett. 2010. "Understanding the Health Literacy of America Results of the National Assessment of Adult Literacy." *Orthopedic Nursing* 28(1): 27–34.

37. Al Shamsi, Hilal, Abdullah Almutairi, Sulaiman Al Mashrafi, and Talib Al Kalbani. 2020. "Implications of Language Barriers for Healthcare: A Systematic Review." *Oman Medical Journal* 35(2): e122.

38. Brice, Jane, Debbie Travers, Christopher Cowden, Matthew Young, Antonio Sanhueza, and Yolanda Dunston. 2008. "Health Literacy among Spanish-Speaking Patients in the Emergency Department." *Journal of the National Medical Association* 100(11): 1326–1332.

39. Christensen, Julian, Lene Aaroe, Martin Baekgaard, Pamela Herd, and Donald P. Moynihan. 2019. "Human Capital and Administrative Burden: The Role of Cognitive Resources in Citizen–State Interactions." *Public Administration Review* 80(1): 127–136.

40. Pollitz, Karen. 2021. "Consumer Appeal Rights in Private Health Coverage." KFF. www.kff .org/private-insurance/issue-brief/consumer-appeal-rights-in-private-health-coverage.

41. X12. "Claim Adjustment Reason Codes." https://x12.org/codes/claim-adjustment-reason-codes.

42. Office of the Inspector General, Department of Health and Human Services. 2022. "Some Medicare Advantage Organization Denials of Prior Authorization Requests Raise Concerns about Beneficiary Access to Medically Necessary Care." Report. https:// oig.hhs.gov/documents/evaluation/3150/OEI-09-18-00260-Complete%20Report.pdf.

43. Schwartz, Aaron, Yujun Chen, Chris Jagmin et al. 2022. "Coverage Denials: Government and Private Insurer Policies for Medical Necessity in Medicare." *Health Affairs* 41(1): 120–128.

44. California Department of Managed Health Care. 2023 Annual Report. www.dmhc.ca .gov/Portals/0/Docs/DO/2023AR.pdf.

45. The overturn rate was 51 percent among expedited independent medical reviews.

CHAPTER 8: THE SPECIAL DIFFICULTIES OF MENTAL HEALTH

1. Bishop, Tara, Matthew Press, Salomeh Keyhani, and Harold Alan Pincus. 2014. "Acceptance of Insurance by Psychiatrists and the Implications for Access to Mental Health Care." *Journal of the American Medical Association Psychiatry* 71(2): 176–181.

2. Substance Abuse and Mental Health Services Administration. 2024. "2023 NSDUH Annual National Report." www.samhsa.gov/data/report/2023-nsduh-annual-national-report.

3. Sircar, Neiloy. 2017. "Your Claim Has Been Denied: Mental Health and Medical Necessity." *Health Law and Policy Brief* 11(2): article 2.

4. Ollove, Michael. "Despite Laws, Mental Health Still Getting Short Shrift." Pew Trusts Blog, May 7, 2015. https://stateline.org/2015/05/07/despite-laws-mental-health-still-getting-short-shrift. O'Reilly, Kevin. "How Medicare Advantage Plans Wrongly Deny Prior Auth Requests." American Medical Association, May 11, 2022. https://tinyurl .com/m5nf2w63.

5. Johns Hopkins Medicine. "Statistics Related to Mental Health Disorders." https:// tinyurl.com/7s4acr58.

6. Interview with Dr. Mark Wilson, June 1, 2022.

7. Wilson, Rylee. "Costs Increasing for Many Common Antidepressants in 2024." Becker's Behavioral Health, January 19, 2024. https://tinyurl.com/y84xrpan.

8. Kane, Carol. 2021. "Recent Changes in Physician Practice Arrangements: Private Practice Dropped to Less Than 50 Percent of Physicians in 2020." Report, American Medical Association. www.ama-assn.org/system/files/2021-05/2020-prp-physician-practice-arrangements.pdf.

9. Zhu, Jane and Matthew Eisenberg. 2024. "Administrative Frictions and the Mental Health Workforce." *Journal of the American Medical Association Health Forum* 5(3): e240207.

10. Ibid.

11. Interview with Sean Erreger, June 3, 2022.

12. Interview with Dr. Kyle Smith, June 2, 2022.

13. Dafny, Leemore, Kate Ho, and Edward Kong. 2024. "How Do Copayment Coupons Affect Branded Drug Prices and Quantities Purchased?" *American Economic Journal: Economic Policy* 16(3): 314–346.

14. Kang, So-Yeon, Angela Liu, Gerard Anderson, and G. Caleb Anderson. 2023. "Patterns of Manufacturer Coupon Use for Prescription Drugs in the US, 2017–2019." *Journal of the American Medical Association Network Open* 6(5): e2313578.

15. Richman, Barak D., Daniel Grossman, and Frank Sloan. 2010. "Fragmentation in Mental Health Benefits and Services: A Preliminary Examination into Consumption and Outcomes," in Einer Elhauge (ed.), *The Fragmentation of U.S. Health Care: Causes and Solutions.* New York, NY: Oxford University Press, pp. 279–300, p. 279.

16. Ibid.

17. Horvitz-Lennon, Marcela, K. John McConnell, Sherry Glied, Jonathan Levin, Nicole Eberhart, and Joshua Breslau. 2023. "Is Carve-In Financing of Medicaid Behavioral Health Services Better Than Carve-Out?" Health Affairs. https://tinyurl.com/mvw35bej.

18. Frank, Richard, T. McGuire, S. Normand, and H. Goldman. 1999. "The Value of Mental Health Care at the System Level: The Case of Treating Depression." *Health Affairs* 18(5): 71–88.

19. Conti, Rena, Alisa Busch, and David Cutler. 2011. "Overuse of Antidepressants in a Nationally Representative Adult Patient Population in 2005." *Psychiatric Services* 62(7): 720–726.

20. Patashnik, Eric, Alan Gerber, and Conor Dowling. 2017. *Unhealthy Politics: The Battle over Evidence-Based Medicine.* Princeton, NJ: Princeton University Press, p. 85.

21. Richman, Grossman, and Sloan. 2010. "Fragmentation in Mental Health Benefits and Services."

22. Haas-Wilson, Deborah. 2021. "Competitive Effects Analysis of Centene's Proposed Acquisition of Magellan Health." Report. https://tinyurl.com/2msf85t4.

23. Richmond, Linda M. 2022. "Members Report Uptick in Plans' Claim Denials, Scrutiny, and Hassles." *Psychiatric News* 57(6), https://doi.org/10.1176/appi.pn.2022.06.6.34.

24. Herd, Pamela, Hilary Hoynes, Jamila Michener, and Donald Moynihan. 2023. "Introduction: Administrative Burden as a Mechanism of Inequality." *The Russell Sage Foundation Journal of the Social Sciences* 9(5): 1–30.

25. *Federal Register* final rule, p. 68,245.

26. *Federal Register* final rule, p. 68,247.

27. Ibid.

28. Walsh, Marty, Xavier Becerra, and Janet Yellen. 2022. "Realizing Parity, Reducing Stigma, and Raising Awareness: Increasing Access to Mental Health and Substance

Use Disorder Coverage." 2022 MHPAEA Report to Congress. https://tinyurl.com/7pxfyy9w.

29. Presskreischer, Rachel, Colleen Barry, Adria Lawrence, Alexander McCourt, Ramin Mojtabai, and Emma McGinty. 2023. "Factors Affecting State-Level Enforcement of the Federal Mental Health Parity and Addiction Equity Act: A Cross-Case Analysis of Four States." *Journal of Health Politics, Policy, and Law* 48(1): 1–34.

30. Volk, JoAnn, Emma Walsh-Aker, and Christina Goe. 2024. "Enforcing Mental Health Parity: State Options to Improve Access to Care." The Commonwealth Fund. https://tinyurl.com/2tscu3c9.

31. Interview with D. Brian Hufford, June 8, 2022.

32. Bedoya, Michelle. 2023. "Mental Health Parity in the Wake of *Wit v. United Behavioral Health.*" Health Affairs. www.healthaffairs.org/content/forefront/mental-health-parity-wake-wit-v-united-behavioral-health.

33. Sircar. "Your Claim Has Been Denied."

CHAPTER 9: A PATH FORWARD

1. Oberlander, Jonathan. 2006. "The Political Economy of Unfairness in U.S. Health Policy." *Law and Contemporary Problems* 69(4): 245–264.

2. Rucker, Patrick, Maya Miller, and David Armstrong. "How Cigna Saves Millions by Having Its Doctors Reject Claims Without Reading Them." *ProPublica,* March 25, 2023. www.propublica.org/article/cigna-pxdx-medical-health-insurance-rejection-claims.

3. *The Estate of Gene B. Lokken and The Estate of Dale Henry Tetzloff, individually and on behalf of all others similarly situated v. UnitedHealth Group, Inc. UnitedHealthcare, Inc., NaviHealth, Inc., and Does 1–50, inclusive.*

4. Heath, Ryan. "AI Lawsuits Spread to Health." Axios, July 25, 2023. www.axios.com/2023/07/25/ai-lawsuits-health-cigna-algorithm-payment-denial.

5. Interview with Scott Glovsky, July 20, 2022.

6. Colvin, Alexander. "The Growing Use of Mandatory Arbitration: Access to the Courts Is Now Barred for More Than 60 Million American Workers." Economic Policy Institute. Report, April 6, 2018. https://tinyurl.com/yjv6u7k8.

7. American Association for Justice. 2021. "Forced Arbitration in a Pandemic: Corporations Double Down." Report. www.justice.org/resources/research/forced-arbitration-in-a-pandemic.

8. Hyman, David A. 2010. "Health Care Fragmentation: We Get What We Pay For," in Einer Elhauge (ed.), *The Fragmentation of U.S. Health Care.* New York, NY: Oxford University Press, pp. 21–36.

9. Elhauge, Einer. 2010. "Why We Should Care about Health Care Fragmentation and How to Fix It," in Einer Elhauge (ed.), *The Fragmentation of U.S. Health Care.* New York, NY: Oxford University Press, pp. 1–20, p. 7.

10. Cebul, Randal, James Rebitzer, Lowell Taylor, and Mark Votruba. 2009. "Unhealthy Insurance Markets: Search Frictions and the Cost and Quality of Health Insurance." NBER Working Paper No. 14555. www.aeaweb.org/articles?id=10.1257/aer.101.5.1842.

11. Hurst, Andrew. "45% of Insured Americans Considering Health Insurance Changes during Open Enrollment." ValuePenguin, November 1, 2021. www.valuepenguin.com/consumers-changing-health-insurance-during-open-enrollment.

12. Cebul, Randall, James Rebitzer, Lowell Taylor, and Mark Votruba. 2010. "Organizational Fragmentation and Care Quality in the U.S. Health Care System," in Einer Elhauge (ed.), *The Fragmentation of U.S. Health Care.* New York, NY: Oxford University Press, pp. 37–60.

13. Pew Research Center. 2024. "Americans' View of Government's Role: Persistent Divisions and Areas of Agreement." https://tinyurl.com/3rba95pk.

14. Archer, Diane. 2011. "Medicare Is More Efficient Than Private Insurance." Health Affairs Forefront. www.healthaffairs.org/do/10.1377/forefront.20110920.013390.

15. Patashnik, Eric, Alan Gerber, and Conor Dowling. 2017. *Unhealthy Politics: The Battle over Evidence-Based Medicine.* Princeton, NJ: Princeton University Press.

16. Patashnik, Eric. 2020. "Comparatively Ineffective? PCORI and the Uphill Battle to Make Evidence Count in US Medicine." *Journal of Health Politics, Policy, and Law* 45(5): 787–800.

17. Rucker, Miller, and Armstrong. "How Cigna Saves Millions by Having Its Doctors Reject Claims Without Reading Them."

18. American Medical Association. 2021. "Competition in Health Insurance: A Comprehensive Study of U.S. Markets." Report: 2021 Update. www.ama-assn.org/system/files/competition-health-insurance-us-markets.pdf.

19. Tepper, Nona. "See Who Dominates Medicare Advantage Market This Year." Modern Healthcare, January 31, 2022. https://tinyurl.com/5dj2b7jy.

20. American Medical Association. "Competition in Health Insurance."

21. Hackett, Mallory. "M&A Activity Expected to Surge as Independent Health Systems Look for Partners." Healthcare Finance, August 27, 2020. https://tinyurl.com/bdzdju5k.

22. American College of Emergency Physicians. "The Flip Side of the Coin: A Look at the Increase in Health Insurer Consolidation." Blog post, February 10, 2022. https://tinyurl.com/hsxpfcmc.

23. Molinari, Anna. 2018. "Healthcare Mergers and Acquisitions in an Era of Consolidation: A Review and a Call for Agency Collaboration in Antitrust Enforcement." *Pepperdine Law Review* 45(2): 405–453.

24. Meyer, Harris. "Biden's FTC Has Blocked 4 Hospital Mergers and Is Poised to Thwart More Consolidation Attempts." Kaiser Health News, July 18, 2022. https://kffhealthnews.org/news/article/biden-ftc-block-hospital-mergers-antitrust.

25. Shah, Aren and Shima Saran. 2023. "A Review of Magnetic Resonance (MR) Safety: The Essentials to Patient Safety." *Cureus* 15(10): e47345.

26. Patashnik, Gerber, and Dowling. *Unhealthy Politics.*

27. Kjelle, Elin, Eivind Richter Anderson, Arne Magnus Krokeide et al. "Characterizing and Quantifying Low-Value Diagnostic Imaging Internationally: A Scoping Review." *BMC Medical Imaging* 22(1): article 73.

28. Interview with Ted Doolittle, May 20, 2022.

29. Interview with Emily Carroll, July 5, 2022.

30. Fronstin, Paul. "Trends in Self-Insured Health Plans since the ACA." Employee Benefit Research Institute Issue Brief. www.ebri.org/home/content/summary/trends-in-self-insured-health-plans-since-the-aca.

31. Paavola, Alia. "Physician 'Gold Card' Exemptions for Prior Authorizations Gain Steam." *Becker's Hospital Review*, May 4, 2022. https://tinyurl.com/3prnf58z.

32. Centers for Medicare and Medicaid Services. 2024. "CMS Finalizes Rule to Expand Access to Health Information and Improve the Prior Authorization Process." https://tinyurl.com/zhz2vd5w.

33. Congressional Hearing, Patients' Bill of Rights Act. *Congressional Record* 145(100): S8550.

34. Farhang, Sean. 2010. *The Litigation State: Public Regulation and Private Lawsuits in the U.S.* Princeton, NY: Princeton University Press.

35. Interview with Wendell Potter, January 17, 2023.

36. Pear, Robert. "House Passes Measure to Expand Rights on Medical Care." *New York Times*, October 8, 1999. www.nytimes.com/library/politics/100899patients-rights.html.

37. Volden, Craig and Alan Wiseman. 2011. "Breaking Gridlock: The Determinants of Health Policy Change in Congress." *Journal of Health Politics, Policy and Law* 36(2): 227–264.

38. Hacker, Jacob. 2019. *The Great Risk Shift: The New Economic Security and the Decline of the American Dream*, 2nd ed. New York, NY: Oxford University Press.

39. Centers for Medicare and Medicaid Services. 2025. "CMS Launches New Model to Target Wasteful, Inappropriate Services in Original Medicare." Press release. https://tinyurl.com/tvhp3bp3.

40. Oz, Mehmet. "Medicare Advantage for All Can Save Our Health Care System." Forbes, June 11, 2020. https://tinyurl.com/uf5mthrt.

41. Brenan, Megan. "Majority in U.S. Still Say Gov't Should Ensure Healthcare." Gallup, January 23, 2023. https://news.gallup.com/poll/468401/majority-say-gov-ensure-healthcare.aspx.

42. Gallup. 2024. "Healthcare System." https://news.gallup.com/poll/4708/health care-system.aspx.

43. Berg, Sara. "What Doctors Wish Patients Knew about Prior Authorization." American Medical Association, July 29, 2022. https://tinyurl.com/2ef46n89.

44. Ibid.

45. Interview with Heather McComas, July 5, 2022.

46. Ferries, Erin, Patrick Racsa, Brock Bizzell, Clay Rhodes, and Brandon Suehs. "Removal of Prior Authorization for Medication-Assisted Treatment: Impact on Opioid Use and Policy Implications in a Medicare Advantage Population." *Journal of Managed Care and Specialty Pharmacy* 27(5), https://doi.org/10.18553/jmcp.2021.27.5.596.

47. Interview with Dr. Lauren Wilson, August 2, 2022.

APPENDICES

1. Fong, Mitchell. 2021. "Nearly 1 in 5 Americans Haven't Seen a Doctor in Over Five Years." www.onlinedoctor.com/nearly-1-in-5-americans-havent-seen-a-doctor-in-over-five-years.

2. Haddad, Chedia, Hala Sacre, Ronny Zeenny et al. 2022. "Should Samples Be Weighted to Decrease Selection Bias in Online Surveys during the COVID-19 Pandemic? Data from Seven Datasets." *BMC Medical Research Methodology* 22(1): article 63.

3. Miratrix, Luke, Jasjeet Sekhon, Alexander Theodoridis, and Luis Campos. 2018. "Worth Weighting? How to Think about and Use Weights in Survey Experiments." *Political Analysis* 26(3): 275–291.

4. Alternative formulations of the variable *struggle to pay out-of-pocket* ranging from 0 (rarely or never) to 3 (most of the time), as well as a dichotomous variable coded 1 only if the respondent struggled "most of the time," produced similar results.

5. A challenge with this measure is that some of those responding to the survey indicated that the denial may have happened a couple years ago or later, such that Medicaid expansion policy may have been different at the time of the denial.

Index

Printed by Integrated Books International,
United States of America